Rating Agencies and the Fallout of the 2007-2008 Financial Crisis

Petra Lieven

Rating Agencies and the Fallout of the 2007-2008 Financial Crisis

PL ACADEMIC RESEARCH

Bibliographic Information published by the Deutsche Nationalbibliothek
The Deutsche Nationalbibliothek lists this publication in the Deutsche Nationalbibliografie; detailed bibliographic data is available in the internet at http://dnb.d-nb.de.

Library of Congress Cataloging-in-Publication Data
Names: Lieven, Petra, 1962- author.
Title: Rating agencies and the fallout of the 2007-2008 financial crisis / Petra Lieven.
Description: Frankfurt am Main ; New York : Peter Lang, [2016]
Identifiers: LCCN 2016034639 | ISBN 9783631676219
Subjects: LCSH: Rating agencies (Finance) | Global Financial Crisis, 2008-2009. | Financial crises--Government policy.
Classification: LCC HG3751.5 .L54 2016 | DDC 330.9/0511--dc23 LC record available at https://lccn.loc.gov/2016034639

ISBN 978-3-631-67621-9 (Print)
E-ISBN 978-3-653-06966-2 (E-PDF)
E-ISBN 978-3-631-69636-1 (EPUB)
E-ISBN 978-3-631-69637-8 (MOBI)
DOI 10.3726/ 978-3-653-06966-2

PL Academic Research is an Imprint of Peter Lang GmbH.

Peter Lang – Frankfurt am Main · Bern · Bruxelles · New York · Oxford · Warszawa · Wien

This publication has been peer reviewed.

www.peterlang.com

Acknowledgements

I would like to express my gratitude to all those who provided me with the opportunity to complete this research. First, I would like to thank the participants who shared their time and thoughts with me; without them, this research could not have been conducted.

I am deeply grateful to my supervisor Prof. Dr. Ahmet Aker, from the Cyprus International University, for his continuous support of my research. His valuable comments, stimulating suggestions, and encouragement helped me throughout my research and writing. Without his guidance and generous support, this dissertation would not have been possible.

Finally, I would especially like to thank my family for their constant support and patient love while I was completing the work.

Abstract

Rating agencies play a key role in the globalized financial system. Their service is valuable provided it delivers sound and credible assessments of the relative default probability of financial instruments, thus enabling a reduction of information asymmetries between issuers and investors. Nevertheless, rating agencies have faced intense criticism for their role in the recent global financial crisis, a consequence of their overrating of structured finance products. First, this research focuses on explaining and discussing the criticism leveled at the rating agencies in the fallout that followed the financial crisis. Thereafter, it investigates the role rating agencies played in the crisis and provides an understanding of the implemented, proposed, and (currently underway) reforms in regulatory frameworks, and how these affect the functioning of the rating industry. This research addresses two specific research questions. First, how can rating agencies' perceived or revealed shortcomings be resolved? Second, what proposals or solutions should be advanced or implemented to achieve the desired goals?

To answer these questions, the following research provides a brief synopsis of the events that led to the crisis, analyzes the forms of criticism the rating agencies have been subjected to and the primary problems that have become evident. In so doing, the rating agencies' position is taken into account, along with the role that they and the regulatory authorities play in the price determination process of financial markets is outlined. Following this, the research addresses U.S. regulatory issues relating to rating agencies and analyses responses to rating agencies' shortcomings from Europe, Canada, India, and Asian Pacific countries. The literature on rating agencies and the effects of regulatory measurements is used to identify answers to the questions raised. The perspectives evident within the literature reviewed are examined and discussed to provide a framework for the empirical investigations integral to this research.

In a qualitative empirical study, 21 investment executives of large financial institutions in the United Kingdom, Germany, and Switzerland were interviewed with respect to their opinions about rating agencies. Despite the critical comments after the 2007–2008 crisis, this research shows that the existing rating agencies are still considered an important source of credit risk assessment. Any tightening of the liability rules for rating agencies should take economic practicability into consideration. As a further recommendation, the rating criteria should be simplified, but not standardized. The findings of this research are useful for regulators and scholars engaged in the transformation of the rating agency industry in the present landscape of the global financial marketplace.

Keywords: Financial crisis, rating agencies, ratings, rating process, price determination, conflicts of interest, regulation, terminology, methodology, competition, liability

Table of Contents

Abbreviations

10-K report	Form 10-K Annual Report Required by the SEC
ABCP	Asset-Backed Commercial Paper
ABS	Asset-Backed Security
ABX	Asset-Backed Securities Index
AFS	Australian Financial Services
AFSL	Australian Financial Services License
AIG	American International Group, Inc.
AMF	Autorité des marchés financiers
ASF	American Securitization Forum
ASIC	Australian Securities and Investments Commission
Bayern LB	Bayerische Landesbank
BBA	British Bankers Association
BET	binominal expansion technique
BIS	Bank for International Settlements
BoE	Bank of England
CBRS	Canadian Bond Rating Service
CDO	Collateralized Debt Obligation
CDS	Credit Default Swap
CEBS	Committee of European Banking Supervisors
CEIOPS	Committee of European Insurance and Occupational Pensions Supervisors
CESR	Committee of European Securities Regulators
CFR	Code of Federal Regulations
CFTC	Commodity Futures Trading Commission
CGFS	Committee on the Global Financial System
CGFS	Committee on the Global Financial System
CMBS	Commercial Mortgage-Backed Securities
CRA	Credit Rating Agency
CRA 3	Credit Rating Agencies Regulation 3
CRARA	Credit Rating Agencies Reform Act
CRD	Capital Requirements Directive
CRISIL	Credit Rating Information Services of India
CRR	Capital Requirements Regulation
CSA	Canadian Securities Administrators
DBRS	Dominion Bond Rating Service

Dodd-Frank Act	Dodd-Frank Wall Street Reform and Consumer Protection Act
DRO	Designated Rating Organizations
EBA	European Banking Authority
EBIC	European Banking Industry Committee
EC	European Union Commission
ECB	European Central Bank
ECOFIN	Economic and Financial Affairs Council
EFSF	European Financial Stability Facility
e.g.	exempli gratia (for example)
EIOPA	European Insurance and Occupational Pensions Authority
EL	expected loss
EMH	Efficient Market Hypothesis
EMT	Efficient Market Theory
EOL	Exchange of Letters
ESA	European Supervisory Authority
ESBR	European Systemic Risk Board
ESFS	European System of Financial Supervision
ESM	European Stability Mechanism
ESMA	European Securities and Markets Authority
ESME	European Securities Market Expert Group
ESRB	European Systemic Risk Board
et al.	et alia (and others)
EU	European Union
Fannie Mae	Federal National Home Mortgage Association
FCIC	Financial Crisis Inquiry Commission
FD	Fair Disclosure (Regulation FD)
Fed	Federal Reserve Bank
FFR No. 48	Financial Regulation Release No. 48
FHLMC	Federal Home Loan Mortgage Corporation
FINRA	Financial Industry Regulatory Authority
FNMA	Federal National Home Mortgage Association
Freddie Mac	Federal Home Loan Mortgage Corporation
FSA	Financial Services Authority
FSAP	Financial Sector Assessment Program
FSB	Financial Stability Board
FSF	Financial Stability Forum
FT	Financial Times
G20	Group of Twenty

GAO	Government Accountability Office
GSE	Government-Sponsored Enterprise
HBOS	Halifax Bank of Scotland
HLCCFM	High Level Coordination Committee on Financial Markets
HM Treasury	Her Majesty's Treasury
IKB	IKB Deutsche Industrie Bank AG
IMF	International Monetary Fund
IOSCO	International Organization of Securities Commissions
JPM	JPMorgan Chase & Co.
LBBW	Landesbank Baden-Württemberg
LEVELS	Loan Evaluation and Estimates of Loss System®
LIBA	London Investment Bankers Association
MAD	Market Abuse Directive
MBS	Mortgage-Backed Security
MMF	Guidelines Money Market Funds Guidelines
NBER	National Bureau of Economic Research
n.d.	no date
NI	National Instrument
NRSRO	Nationally Recognized Statistical Rating Organization
NYT	New York Times
OECD	Organization for Economic Co-operation and Development
P	Participant
PA	Primary Analyst
para.	paragraph
PSLRA	Private Securities Litigation Reform Act of 1995
RAC	Rating Action Commentary
RMBS	Residential Mortgage-Backed Security
RMI	Risk Management Institute
S&P	Standard & Poor's
SEBI	Securities and Exchange Board of India
SEC	Securities and Exchange Commission
SF	Structured Finance
SIFMA	Securities Industry and Financial Markets Association
SPC	Special Purpose Company
SPV	Special Purpose Vehicle
TARP	Troubled Asset Relief Program
TDS	Total Debt Service
TNN	Times News Network

UCRG	Universal Credit Rating Group
UK	United Kingdom
UL	unexpected loss
UN	United Nations
US	United States
USC	United States Code
USD	US Dollar
WestLB	Westdeutsche Landesbank

List of Figures and Tables

Introduction

The financial crisis of high indebtedness has affected financial institutions and investors around the globe (Moshirian, 2010). The roots of this crisis can be traced backed to the collapse of the US subprime market, and failure of deregulation policies for the financial sector enacted by political and regulatory authorities' failures with regard to the deregulation of the financial sector (Gotham, 2009). This market sector has experienced rapid development in recent years, and the new financial instruments that have emerged have reached previously unimaginable "levels of sophistication" (Shahzad, 2013, p. 1). The major rating agencies (Moody's, Standard & Poor's, and Fitch) act as financial gatekeepers in the development of the market for structured finance instruments (Partnoy, 2006), and the rapid growth of the market for such sophisticated products would not have been possible without the involvement of these rating agencies (Darbellay, 2013). Investments in such structured finance products were at the heart of the recent crisis (Chambers et al., 2011), with rating agencies being blamed for having failed the market by providing overly positive assessments regarding the quality of these structured finance products, and being too late in adjusting their ratings to worsening market conditions (Sève, 2009). As a consequence, rating agencies became a target of ongoing international criticism directed not only against errors of judgment, but also for operating in a biased manner due to their business model in an oligopolistic market structure (Fons, 2010). Indeed, regulatory authorities, governments, bond issuers, and investors across the globe lost their blind trust in the ratings supplied by these rating agencies, and thus believe that changes must be made in order to restore market confidence (SIFMA, 2013). The initiation of regulatory responses has therefore been an international process, but there is "no consensus on a single set of reforms" (Katz, Salinas, and Stephanou, 2009, p. 5). Measures announced or undertaken fall within the objectives of managing conflicts of interest, improving the quality of rating methodologies, and increasing transparency and measurements to replace self-regulation (Katz, Salinas, and Stephanou, 2009). However, as Utzig (2010, p. 3) argues, although "the scope of the selected regulatory approach is extremely narrow" and undoubtedly has the potential "to improve corporate governance of CRAs and prevent conflicts of interests," these approaches can unfortunately do nothing to address "repeated calls for greater competition or for CRAs to be made liable for their ratings."

This research focuses on explaining and discussing the criticisms that have been leveled at rating agencies during the fallout of the 2007–2008 financial crisis. In addition, it investigates the role rating agencies played in causing the recent crisis, and provides an understanding of the reforms to regulatory frameworks that affect the functioning of the rating industry that have been proposed, implemented, or are currently underway. Accordingly, the research addresses two specific questions. First, how can perceived or revealed shortcomings be resolved? Second, what proposals or solutions should be advanced or implemented to achieve the desired goals?

To tackle these questions and to obtain an overview of regulatory measures, the following research provides a brief synopsis of the factors that led to the crisis, and then analyzes the criticism to which rating agencies have been subjected, along with the concrete problems that have become increasingly evident in recent years. In so doing, the position of the rating agencies is also taken into account. Furthermore, the role played by rating agencies and regulatory authorities in the price determination process of financial markets and US regulatory issues relating to rating agencies are outlined. Thereafter, responses to rating agencies' shortcomings from Europe, Asian Pacific countries, India, and Canada are analyzed. This research applies the applicable theoretical literature on rating agencies' perceived shortcomings, their role in financial markets, and the effects of regulatory measurements in order to identify the relevant aspects required to answer the questions raised. The perspectives drawn from the literature reviewed are examined and discussed to provide a framework for an empirical investigation. In addition, the research assesses the views of financial market participants after the global financial meltdown of 2007–2008, and explores, empirically, the impact of the crisis on market participants' perceptions of the quality of ratings provided by rating agencies, together with their liabilities. The objective of this empirical evaluation is to identify a range of possible remedies to existing problems.

In terms of the context and organization of this work, the literature covers various important features of rating agencies and their relation to the spectacular growth of structured finance products (Coval, Jurek, and Stafford, 2009; Benmelech and Dlugosz, 2010). These include the phenomenon of how the behavior of markets for securities offers lessons about the factors that determine prices, and how a regulatory structure that placed rating agencies at the center of the bond/securities market virtually guaranteed that the agencies' mistakes would have severe consequences for the financial market sector, as described by White (2010) and Kerwer (2005). Whilst highly rated structured finance products were considered safe until the crisis (Coval, Jurek, and Stafford, 2009), economic and financial environments do change, and financial markets reassessed their risk perceptions following the subprime debacle (IOSCO, 2008a). With these considerations in mind, this research is divided into seven theoretical chapters and an empirical section in order to examine the influence of the crisis on market participants' perceptions, and to identify possible remedies to existent problems.

Chapter 1 outlines what happened between 2007 and 2008, and in doing so provides a brief overview of the factors that led to the collapse of the subprime mortgage sector in early 2007 in the United States, and the subsequent end of the housing boom. Financial instruments such as mortgage-backed securities (MBS) and collateralized debt obligations (CDOs) backed by subprime mortgages were at the heart of the crisis. Nevertheless, as Benmelech and Dlugosz explain, the majority of these securities had been awarded high ratings (2010). The misjudgment by rating agencies of structured products led to dramatic declines in the value of these securities, and the agencies have been exposed to criticism ever since. Understanding of this background information is necessary in order to appreciate the exceptional nature of the recent economic and financial crisis, and why rating agencies became a specific target of intense criticism. The issues and points related to this criticism are discussed and covered from different angles within this research.

Chapter 2 reviews the main concerns that arose in the light of the 2007–2008 financial market crisis. One of the important consequences here is that the major rating agencies continue to receive substantial international attention due to the loss of confidence in their assessments by market participants. The logic underlying the existence of rating agencies in financial markets is to address the problem of asymmetrical information being passed between lenders and borrowers, a role that gained greater importance with the globalization of financial markets (Elkhoury, 2008). Accordingly, loss in confidence weakens the fundamental purpose of the agencies. The significance of the rating agencies' credit risk assessments for the market is well documented in the academic literature (Altman, 1998; Baker and Mansi, 2002). Rating agencies' actions in the subprime debacle led to severe consequences for financial markets, and the role they played in the subprime mortgage securities crisis intensified calls for agency reforms (Carbone, 2010). Understanding where this criticism came from is useful in understanding why governments, regulatory authorities, and other market participants are concerned with the transparency of rating methodologies and terminology, the lack of competition among rating agencies, perceived conflicts of interest, and what these stakeholders intend to change. These topics are addressed from different perspectives in the subsequent chapters.

In its contribution to broadening existing knowledge, Chapter 3 fills an existing gap in the literature by building upon the work of Mullard (2012) and Ryan (2012), and contributes to the discussion by highlighting and discussing the main arguments given by the rating agencies in response to the criticism and allegations made against them. This chapter also examines rating agencies' opinions about suggestions for reform with regard to issues of greater competition, their methodologies, and liability issues, as well as proven or suspected conflicts of interest. A determining factor in the research presented in Chapter 3 was the ability to analyze the range of statements submitted by ratings agencies to various investigation committees, and the comment letters they submitted to the Securities and Exchange Commission (SEC). The chapter analytically synthesizes these different strands and delivers a comprehensive overview of the rating agencies' arguments.

Chapter 4 contributes to a better understanding of the process of rating structure finance by summarizing the methods followed by the major rating agencies in conducting their analyses and assigning ratings. In so doing, it also outlines the rating process generally applied by the major rating agencies. This chapter introduces the development of structured finance products, after which it provides an overview of the rating definitions used by rating agencies, and a detailed description of how structured finance products are created, as well as the basic rating processes for structured finance products. Building on the work of Carter and Watson (2006), and Forti and Iaconelli (2001), as well as the information provided by the major rating agencies, this chapter addresses the individual steps of the general analysis processes performed by the rating agencies. It also enriches the existing literature by presenting the actual developments that take place in the processes generally applied in rating structured finance in terms of new regulatory requirements.

Chapter 5 deals with the economic theory of price and its determination, and discusses the characteristics of markets and capital markets. Through considering existing theoretical literature, the chapter examines rating agencies' significance in the price determination process of financial and capital markets. These markets are an essential feature of a modern market economy, and a precondition in order for them to function is that prices are determined freely based on the relationship between the market forces of supply and demand (Mukherjee, 2005). Rating agencies and their ratings have a tremendous impact on these markets given the complex effects of rating changes (Cohen, 2014), which also exert great influence on the prices of securities, capital flows, and the attitudes of investors (Jain and Sharma, 2008). Given the importance of the infrastructure of international capital markets, and the crucial role that rating agencies play in ensuring the efficient functioning of the financial markets, this chapter contributes to an understanding of how rating agencies affect prices, and how relevant their abstraction and reduction of reality is for the appropriate representation of the value of financial instruments and their underlying assets.

Chapter 6 provides a review of the potential reasons governing the introduction of regulatory authorities in financial markets, and comments on the objectives behind implementing regulations in this sector. This chapter offers a brief overview of how regulatory authorities attempt to set controls for capital and financial markets before referring to the impact of regulators on price formation processes. Since the regulation of rating agencies is a concern widely discussed since the crisis of 2007–2008, this chapter highlights the main regulatory issues in relation to rating agencies. In addition, it discusses the impact of rating changes, and questions whether the value of their information placed them at the core of financial decision-making, or whether they took this position because ratings are used as a regulatory tool by governments. Moreover, it provides an overview of the key regulations implemented by governmental authorities relating to rating agencies, and outlines the findings of the de Larosière Report (2009) and the Turner Review (2009). The chapter concludes with a discussion of the regulatory future for rating agencies.

Chapter 7 explores responses to rating agencies' shortcomings identified by the SEC staff, among others (2008c). This chapter enriches existing discussions regarding the appropriateness of the current initiatives by not only highlighting the main regulatory initiatives, but also considering whether measures undertaken or underway in other countries might be able to deliver feasible solutions for adopting regulations that would enable optimal rating results, as well as reduced reliance on ratings in regulations.

Chapter 8 justifies the research methodology chosen by the researcher for the empirical investigation. It describes the purpose of the investigation and the selected research approach, and provides detail on the design, sampling, the tools used for data collection, as well as the method used to analyze the data.

Chapter 9 presents the main issues identified during the research and explores alternative approaches to addressing the quality issues of financial instruments and managing the liability of rating agencies. As outlined in the theoretical section of the research, the recent crisis raised questions about the accuracy of rating agencies' methodologies, the quality of their ratings, and their responsibilities. In response to these issues, stakeholders – including regulators, governmental authorities, politicians, and commentators – have considered numerous measures and proposals to improve the quality of ratings information and regulatory framework conditions. Despite the intensity of the debate, however, there is a lack of a general consensus on how to move forward in some areas. To date, few empirical studies have focused on debt market participants' perceptions of rating agencies. For instance, Duff and Einig (2007, 2009) assessed the factors influencing ratings quality based on interview data collected in 2005, and Fennel and Medvedev (2011) focused on rating agencies' compensation model. By considering these aspects, this research makes a distinctive contribution to widening existing academic knowledge by focusing on market participants' views after the 2007–2008 meltdown, which in turn allows alternative approaches to quality issues relating to financial instruments and managing the liabilities of rating agencies to be explored. To this end, the approach used in this present research collected the views of respondents from the banking sector, investment banks, and other financial institutions in Germany, Switzerland, and the United Kingdom. The aim of this research is to identity remedies to existing problems by tackling the following questions:

(1) Are there other ways to assess the quality of financial instruments and to express varying degrees of risk factors?
(2) Should rating agencies be an autonomous state agency?
(3) What could a possible civil liability for rating agencies look like?

Thereafter, Chapter 10 comments on market participants' perceptions. The principal findings from the empirical investigation are evaluated from theoretical perspectives, together with the events that have shaped the post-crisis financial markets. In this context, the work by Duff and Einig (2007) on desirable qualities of rating agencies' is discussed, and also that of Partnoy (2006), who emphasizes the importance of stakeholder perceptions with respect to quality and credibility, arguing that rating agencies' quality as gatekeepers in financial markets is difficulty to verify. The International Organization of Securities Commissions (IOSCO) Technical Committee Code of Conduct Fundamentals for Rating Agencies, published in May 2008, offers a set of practical measures to promote transparency, and the findings of the report are compared to those of this research. In addition, the comment letters to public consultations on rating agencies by different regulatory authorities' (e.g. EC, 2010) and the newly implemented rules on rating agencies' liabilities have been taken into account. For instance, Haar (2013) provides an outline of the various rules and proposals, while the discussion also considers academic arguments related to the topics. Before concluding, limitations of this present study and suggestions for further research are outlined.

1. What Caused the Economic and Financial Crisis 2007–2008?

The financial market crisis that started in the US subprime mortgage market sector has led to dramatic economic repercussions around the world. Commentators, politicians and regulators have questioned rating agencies' role in the financial market turmoil. Particularly given that the major rating agencies Standard & Poor`s (S&P), Moody's and Fitch dominate the global market for credit assessments. These major rating agencies thus have become a central point of discussions in academic and political circles, with the focus of attention on their ratings for sophisticated structured finance products. Rating agencies created "highly rated securities that were significantly riskier than warranted by the ratings" (Partnoy, 2009a, p. 442). Since the outbreak of the financial crisis, this criticism has gained even greater significance, given the key role ratings play in the structured finance market sector (Hunt, 2009). Although there are different theories of what caused the economic and financial crisis of 2007–2008, there is a widespread notion held by academics, economists, and other experts that it was a combination of various factors that contributed to the exceptional nature, duration, and severity of the crisis (Bianco, 2008). Subprime lending and the securitization of mortgage loans (which would not have been possible without rating agencies) emerged as the leading cause (Erkens, Hung, and Matos, 2012).

The centrality of rating agencies in financial markets thus gives rise to a number of questions about the accuracy of their ratings and their methodologies in the context of structured finance products (Hunt, 2009). A further important point of criticism is that rating agencies had incentives to provide misleading information and face conflicts of interest (Stiglitz, 2009). This research provides a critical assessment of the problems and concerns raised by rating agencies. The historical section outlines how rating agencies, governments, and regulatory authorities ushered in, facilitated, and aggravated the recent crisis, and in so doing discusses the relevant aspects and factors before moving to the empirical investigations. The research commences with a summary of background information relating to the crisis in order to depict how rating agencies contributed to the crisis and "the myriad ways in which ratings drive investment decisions" (IMF, 2010, p. 85). Following this, Chapter 2, moves on to a critical analysis of the role played by rating agencies in the crisis.

1.1 Background

The origin of the financial crisis can be traced back to 2000, when the US Federal Reserve (the "Fed") started drastically reducing its key interest rate targeted at 6.5% to a historically low level of 1% by mid-2003 (Nayak, 2009; Schwartz, 2009). The Fed undertook this measure to counter the recessionary and deflationary risks present at that time after the burst of the dot-com bubble. As a result, the low interest rates created a flood of liquidity from abroad into the US economy, contributing to an increase in demand for US financial assets (Chang, 2011). Governmental institutions in the United States were attempting to address potential liquidity concerns and to stimulate overall demand in the markets. The low interest rates and easy access to money policies fueled the US government's affordable housing mission (Taylor, 2009). Supported by low interest rates and the US political system, government-sponsored enterprises (GSE) such as the Federal National Home Mortgage Association (Fannie Mae) and the Federal Home Loan Mortgage Corporation (Freddie Mac) granted loans to borrowers with inferior credit standing. This policy led to a significant rise in adjustable mortgage originations (Barth, 2009), resulting in a further reduction of interest rates for these loans (Andrew, 2008). In addition to the aggressive interest rate policy pursued by the Fed between 2000–2004, this policy thus encouraged homeownership for people at the lowest end of the socioeconomic ladder (Jareño and Tolentino, 2012).

Attracted by the growing market for mortgage loans, financial institutions and independent brokers played a significant role in increasing the number of mortgage loans granted to people who could service them only with great difficulty (Jareño and Tolentino, 2012). Banks supported this practice, since they could boost their profits through the sale and ensuing securitization of the mortgage loans. The transfer of mortgage based assets to off-balance sheet vehicles and to special-purpose companies (SPCs) and the securitization of the loans fostered the emergence of a shadow banking system in important financial market segments (Goodhart, 2008). All this led to an explosive growth in the market for subprime loans with adjustable interest rates – and real estate prices rose continuously. Moreover, in order to further increase their earnings, the banks repackaged the loans into collateralized debt obligations (CDOs), which resulted in transference of risk into the financial market (Foster, 2008). The US Securities and Exchange Commission (SEC) 2004 policy of liberalizing net capital rules for investment banks made it attractive for these institutions to increase leverage and to expand the issuance of mortgage-backed securities (MBS) (Chang, 2011). The subprime-lending sector offered investment banks the opportunity to meet the market demand for new profitable ways to invest money with "lucrative, mortgage based investment alternatives" (Beachy, 2012. p 12). Investment banks bought portions of the securities they created in the form of so-called Special Purpose Vehicles (SPVs) in order to demonstrate their confidence in the innovative financial instruments being sold (Schwarcz, 2011). A large number of mortgage-related assets were held by SPVs and investment funds (including hedge funds), which witnessed large capital withdrawals in 2007. Investment banks like Bear Stearns and BNP Paribas "stopped withdrawals and disallowed redemptions of their investment funds" with the argument that there was no price for some securities and therefore the valuation of the assets held in the funds was impossible (Laux and Leuz, 2009, p. 11–12). The effect of this was that in the event of negative market fluctuations in the fund portfolio held by investment banks, or negative developments in the credit ratings of securities bought, a negative credit leverage would occur that could consume huge amounts of the capital originally invested.

At that time, the large amount of securities distributed on the market would not have been possible without rating agencies ratings. Rating agencies tended to assign high ratings (investment grade) to MBS and CDOs, thereby enabling "loans with high risk of default [...] to be originated, packaged and the risk transferred to others" (Bianco, 2008, p. 9). The rating agencies ratings labeled these securities as safe investments (Coval, Jurek, and Stafford, 2008). This has to be understood in the context that institutional investors (pension funds, banks, insurance companies, and investment funds) are prohibited by regulatory requirements from investing in speculative securities (White, 2009b). By December 2008, the structured finance securities market "accounted for over $11 trillion worth of outstanding US bond market debt", whereby the "lion's share" in the area of structured finance securities "was highly rated by rating agencies" (Benmelech and Dlugosz, 2010, p. 161). During the period of 2007–2008, the "credit standing of structured finance securities deteriorated dramatically" (Benmelech and Dlugosz, 2010, p. 161). In a market environment characterized by rating downgrades, securities portfolios had been affected by price falls. The collapse in the market of securities backed by subprime mortgages drastically accelerated the recent crisis as a result of the massive downgrades by rating agencies. Discerning how the governance and regulation of financial markets, and specifically rating agencies, contributed to this development is vital to understanding why rating agencies have been so strongly criticized, and why there are calls for changes in approaches to financial market regulation. The following chapters deal with these issues, as they constitute the foundation of the empirical analysis. The section below will thus briefly explain the activities and developments that triggered the crisis, and the consequences of downgrading subprime-backed assets by the rating agencies.

1.2 The Financial Market Turmoil 2007–2008

Housing prices in the US real estate market peaked in early 2005 and began declining in 2006 (Cohen, Coughlin, and Lopez, 2012). Real estate prices stagnated and dropped dramatically, and subprime mortgage loans began showing signs of instability (Jickling, 2009). In consequence, a large number of low-income borrowers who had acquired mortgage loans were unable to meet their payment obligations. They started defaulting on these mortgages (Wallison, 2009). Falling housing prices around the country led to further substantial loan defaults, resulting in foreclosures (Jones, 2009). The end of the housing boom required enormous adjustments by financial institutions, the housing industry, and investors (Mulligan, 2008). In turn, rating agencies began correcting their risk assessment for asset-backed securities (Marshall, 2009).

From 2007 onwards, many US subprime lenders filed for insolvency. Between February and March 2007, more than 25 mortgage lenders declared bankruptcy (Bianco, 2008). April 2007 witnessed the insolvency of New Financial Century, which until then had been the second-largest issuer of subprime mortgages in the US market (Mizen, 2008). In June 2007, two hedge funds within the large investment bank Bear Stearns were showing signs of collapse due to their substantial investment volume in subprime mortgages. Speculation in the form of credit derivatives additionally exacerbated investment risk. With an injection of 3.2 billion dollars to bail out its funds, Bear Stearns was just able to avert a collapse (Creswell and Bajaj, 2007). In March 2008, however, it became clear that the firm did not have enough liquidity to continue its operations (Goldstein, 2008). Faced with these conditions, the Fed intervened and moved Bear Stearns, together with JP Morgan Chase (JPM), into an emergency bailout program. The rationale for this was the growing fear that panic in the financial markets could spread if no buyer for the collapsing giant could be found right away (Sorkin and Thomas, 2008). A further trigger in the crisis was Merrill Lynch's failed attempt to liquidate a part of its collateral, revealing the liquidity problems of the market for such securities (Crouhy, 2010).

Through their activities in derivatives and their giant insurance business, insurers of these securities, such as American International Group, Inc. (AIG), and the mortgage agencies Fannie Mae and Freddie Mac, which owned and guaranteed such securities, were confronted with insurance payments that could probably greatly exceed their reserves (Anonymous, *The Economist*, 2009, August 13). The market for bond insurance was completely unregulated (Andrew, 2008), and no one could guarantee that there was a sufficiently large pool of capital to hedge these swaps. However, the financial market implicitly believed that these securities had state backing, as the GSE status of Fannie Mae and Freddie Mac created this perception (Brunnermeier, 2008). In light of the fact that the two GSEs also pooled loans with 'affordable mortgage risk' under government pressure in order to expand home ownership, this point of view appears justified (Congleton, 2009). During 2007, Fannie Mae and Freddie Mac began to experience potentially large losses in their portfolios containing Alt-A[1] mortgages and subprime investments. By August 2007, nearly 16% of subprime mortgages with adjustable rates were in default (Bernanke, 2007). During the course of 2008, Fannie Mae and Freddie Mac concluded that, due to the sheer size of their retained portfolios and guarantees on mortgages, they would soon become insolvent (Kopecki, 2010). In September 2008, when it was clear that the two GSEs were in deep financial trouble, the government announced the most expensive bailout of 2008 to rescue the two institutions (which was tantamount to a state guarantee) in hopes of avoiding a failure that could send out shockwaves throughout the globe (*Financial Times*, 2008, September, 8). The bailout of the two GSEs might (erroneously) have been taken as a signal that if large financial institutions were to fail, there would be most likely government bailout guarantees (Acharya and Richardson, 2009). Rescuing the GSEs, however, could not avert the spillover of the US subprime mortgage crisis to the global markets, as implicit government guarantees for the entire banking sector would not materialize (Aikins, 2009). Moreover, it was feared that doctrines of "too-big-to-fail" would create incentives for banks to gamble for survival, "which often weakens financial institutions further" (Aikins, 2009, p. 39) as outlined further below.

1.2.1 MBS Corrections and the Securitization Business

The rating for securitized mortgage loans (initially classified by the rating agencies as low risk) deteriorated during the course of the US housing crisis (Owusu-Ansah, 2012).[2] The downgrading of mortgage-backed securities by the rating

---

1 Alternative A-paper (Alt-A) is a type of US mortgage considered riskier than 'A' or 'prime' securities and less risky than 'subprime' categories (it falls in between both categories).

2 The risk classification and thus the capital adequacy requirements for MBS with AA or AAA were lower than for regular mortgages, which for regulatory capital purposes

agencies during the months of July and August 2007 created another shock to the financial markets, exacerbated by the fact that a not insignificant portion of these securities was held in the so-called shadow banking system in the form of Special Purpose Vehicles (SPVs) not recorded on normal bank balance sheets (Acharya et al., 2009). Like hedge funds, SPVs are not subject to bank regulations, but perform many bank functions. In the meantime another aspect came to light: regulatory arbitrage (Andrew, 2008). Regulatory arbitrage manifests when financial institutions find ways to circumvent regulations. Attracted by high profits, many banks could get around regulations by establishing in-house hedge funds and shifting activities to off-balance sheets (i.e. SPVs) (Martin, 2011). No action was taken by supervisory authorities against the extent of the maturity transformation and indebtedness of these SPVs, as they complied with the rules for capital adequacy and the prohibition of maturity transformation and risk concentration. The fragmentary oversight of this sector made it almost impossible to carry out effective oversight for financial institutions (Hochberg, 2010). The dimension and scope of the shadow banking system was an unexpected surprise and comprised another negative impact on the already looming collapse of the system (Omarova, 2011). Conflicts of interest, in combination with regulatory arbitrage, also had significant bearing on the crisis. Rating agencies enter into conflicts of interest because they have to assign ratings to sophisticated new financial instruments, but are paid by those who have the greatest interests in obtaining the most favorable rating – the originator/issuer (SPV). If rating agencies wanted to boost their business, they had to give their clients the higher ratings that they wanted. As a result of this conflict of interest, AA and AAA ratings became more prevalent (Pagano and Volpin, 2010).

1.2.2 Rating Agencies

The rating agencies ratings, however, play a significant role for banks and investors, given that in many cases regulations only permit investments in investment-grade securities in order to minimize exposure to credit risk. Many banks, insurers, and pensions are required by law to sell their bonds/securities if the

---

were subject to discounts (20 – 40%). The lower the risk rating, the less capital banks are allowed to hold as a cushion. This in turn led to banks preferring to invest in MBS, than giving regular mortgage loans. There is no rational explanation for the fact that the MBS were rated better than regular mortgage loans; however, the rating agencies did not review the securitized mortgage loans, but instead merely applied a model to compute the probability of default.

ratings are no longer high enough (White, 2009b). Even though it became evident that there was a rise in payment defaults in June 2007, rating agencies still assigned high ratings. The rating agencies' downgrading of these securities on a large scale in the fall of 2007 – by several notches at once – was thus a significant contributor to the crisis (Lugo, 2013). Until November 2007, rating agencies had downgraded "over $50 billion in highly-rated collateralized debt obligations" – and another increase in downgrades was still expected (Bianco, 2008, p. 9). Given that many institutional investors were only allowed to invest in high-quality assets, the rating agencies' downgrades forced these investors to sell their assets, leading to further devaluations (Bianco, 2008). This reinforced mutual distrust in structured products among financial market participants, and is one reason why rating agencies received criticized for their role in the financial crisis.

1.2.3 Global Markets Contagion

In August 2007, it became clear that the US financial market was not in a position to resolve the subprime crisis, and that the problems had already spread beyond US borders (Kamin and DeMarco, 2012). Financial institutions around the globe were affected. At first, only financial institutions directly exposed to a significant amount of US mortgage-backed securities appeared to be affected. However, banks and countries not directly exposed to the initial shocks caused by the subprime mortgage crisis were also hit hard, as the cost of money skyrocketed (OECD, 2012).

In the United Kingdom, Northern Rock (the United Kingdom's fifth largest mortgage lender), announced liquidity problems caused by the financial crisis. As a result of this, although the "UK's Financial Services Authority (FSA) and the Treasury (the UK government's finance office) had given assurances that the bank was solvent and all deposits at the bank would be guaranteed", the bank was increasingly exposed to problems (Llewellyn, 2009, p. 103). As a consequence of this, Northern Rock approached the Bank of England for an emergency loan due to its liquidity problems. In September 2007 there was a run on Northern Rock by concerned depositors, and at the beginning of October 2007, the government and Bank of England modified the terms and conditions of emergency liquidity assistance and guaranteed deposits, a step taken to avoid further damage to the British banking sector. After this, Northern Rock was taken over by the state (Goldsmith-Pinkham and Yorulmazer, 2010). At the same time, central banks and governments around the world started to come together to search for possibilities to prevent the financial catastrophe from spreading. In Europe, the Swiss-based bank UBS recorded large losses. In Germany, public or state-oriented banks, such as the IKB, WestLB, Bayern LB, LBBW, and, private banks such as the Dresdner Bank and Hypo Real Estate were among the banks whose speculative involvement in the US housing market backfired (Paul, 2012; Mizen, 2008). In France, BNP Paribas was compelled to freeze three investment funds with assets of 2 billion euros since the bank could not perform a valuation of its funds portfolio of subprime assets (Crouhy, 2010).

Against this backdrop of uncertainty as to the extent of future defaults, declining confidence in banks' capital made it very difficult for them to raise money (Feldstein, 2009). This led to widespread uncertainty in the markets. With the breakdown in the financing of SPVs, the banks had to take these 'toxic' assets onto their balance sheets or dispose of them (Wray, 2009). As a result, another aspect that shaped the crisis significantly came to light: the impact of fair value accounting, particularly the application of market values in trading books. This led to recapitalization[3] or deleveraging[4], given that fair-value accounting requires write-downs on financial assets to adjust their value to estimates that represent the fair-value or market prices (market-to-market values; Ryan, 2008). This consequently led to increasingly higher write-offs (due to the assumed permanent reduction in the value of such securities), and thus ever-growing losses. The write-offs (unrealized losses) reflected the "exposure to future capital losses for banks if they had to sell those asserts at a fire sale" (Berrospide, 2012, p. 2). In part, this helped to counter the potentially large negative impacts for the financial markets as, due to their unknown or dubious quality, these securities "might have little to no resale value, especially if they were all hit at once with delinquencies and defaults" (Acharya and Richardson, 2009, p. 208). A further trigger in the crisis was that many large institutional investors, driven by uncertainty and fear, withdrew their funds from their collective cash pools as a measure for the restructuring of their loan agreements. Concerns about counterparts' credit quality and the fact that the degree "of the exposure to subprime-related assets was unknown" induced investors to "withdrew their funds en masse" (Berrospide, 2012, p. 13).

Since the money and inter-bank markets became tighter following the outbreak of the crisis, the situation for the banks deteriorated further, and interbank interest rates rose dramatically (Acharya and Merrouche, 2013). Banks became considerably more cautious in lending to one another, and more hesitant to engage in corporate lending. Accordingly, banks' willingness and ability to provide

---

3 Recapitalization: restructuring an institution's/company's debt and equity mixture by increasing capital made by shareholders/investors.

4 Deleveraging: restructuring an institution's/company's debt by means of selling assets.

liquidity to the market declined, and risk premiums increased significantly (Angelini et al., 2011). In the end, the tightening of liquidity by the banks and general uncertainty led to a spillover into the non-financial sector (Håverstad, 2010). The global economy entered into a downward spiral and the real economy began to feel the effects of the crisis (Berg, 2011).

In the wake of the bursting of the housing and mortgage bubbles in the United States, the entire financial system collapsed like a house of cards. Although there was "improvement [in] early 2008 relative to late 2007 due to an aggressive policy response and massive liquidity injections into the banking sector", the banking and finance sectors were still under pressure (Berrospide, 2012, p. 2). Banks around the world became entangled in the web of the financial crisis, either because of their own financial engagement in these toxic assets, or as a result of the massive crisis of confidence in the inter-bank market. Consequently, many distressed banks drifted into insolvency and had to be closed. In 2008, Lehman Brothers was declared insolvent, which had with dramatic repercussions for the financial sector that were previously considered inconceivable. All rescue efforts foundered on the US government's refusal to provide guarantees. In the Lehman case, markets shared the belief, encouraged by the Bear Stearns bailout, that Lehman was 'too big to fail' (Cochrane, 2009). A few days after the collapse, large parts of Lehman's business were taken over by the British Barclays Bank, which, a few days before, had made this move dependent on the provision of a state guarantee; this, however, could have taken weeks (Fishman, 2008). After the collapse of Lehman and rumors of considerable difficulties at the largest US insurer AIG, the government organized a USD 85 billion bailout for AIG in order to rescue it and prevent further turmoil in the financial markets (Nichita, 2009). Merrill Lynch was taken over by Bank of America and British HBOS (Halifax Bank of Scotland) was rescued by the creation of a larger Lloyds TSB (Carapeto et al., 2010). Washington Mutual and Morgan Stanley encountered major difficulties, and many more large banks and financial intuitions were to follow suit (Ivashina and Scharfstein, 2010). The US government launched the Trouble Asset Relief Program (TARP) amounting to USD 700 billion to purchase assets to rescue troubled financial institutions. The first USD 250 billion were intended for immediate use, with an additional USD 100 billion that could be released upon approval by the President, and the remaining USD 350 billion could be used upon approval by Congress (Tatom, 2008). During this time, the financial markets experienced dramatic downturns. What started in 2007 could not be contained until 2008 despite massive government intervention and state guarantees in the United States and elsewhere.

1.3 Conclusion

Understanding the factors that led to the economic and financial crisis requires an awareness of how rating agencies, government measures, and regulators of financial markets contributed to the upheaval. Since the onset of the crisis, rating agencies' legitimacy in financial markets has been questioned and the accuracy of their ratings and methodologies scrutinized. A body of scientific literature identified various important features of rating agencies' relation to capital markets as setting a de facto standard for access to the financial market (Kerwer, 2001). Additionally, their ratings have a major influence on the governance of financial markets (Kerwer, 2001). In order to fully appreciate the nature of the criticism voiced by commentators, politicians, and academics (issues that are discussed in the subsequent sections of this research), the factors that lead to the recent crisis are outlined in subsequent sections to provide essential information. Securitization allowed "trillions of dollars of risky assets to be transformed into securities that were widely considered to be safe" (Coval, Jurek, and Stafford, 2009, p. 3). The crisis revealed that these securities were indeed far riskier than had been originally assumed, bringing to light the weakness of the methods and models used by rating agencies. Risk assessment was based too heavily on statistical models and the ratings assigned by the rating agencies were rarely questioned before the financial turmoil. If the underlying assumptions and methodology are wrong, then their assessments and valuations will fail to reflect the economic reality of the financial markets. The ways in which rating agencies were able to be involved in the securitization of assets raised questions about the governance of the financial system and about the responsibility of rating agencies more generally. In the next chapter, the role of rating agencies in the financial crisis will be outlined and the main points of criticism leveled at the rating agencies will be discussed.

2. The Crisis of 2007–2008

Even before the advent of the financial crisis 2007–2008, the value of securitized assets, such as mortgage-backed securities (MBS) and collateralized debt obligations (CDOs), was increasingly being called into question. As a consequence of the smoldering crisis of confidence, the market for securitized loans dried up and banks and financial institutions (which had large commitments in such assets, whether directly or through subsidiaries) experienced enormous financial strain. In the wake of these developments, the situation worsened in mid-September 2008 with the reported insolvency of large financial institutions as described in Chapter 1. With the bankruptcy of Lehman Brothers, the financial crisis entered into a phase with far-reaching consequences for the global economy (Baldwin, 2009). Policymakers and a number of financial institutions had shared the market's mistaken belief that Lehman would be 'too big to fail'. Lehman's insolvency, and the shockwaves that spread around the globe as a result of it, was not the only reason for the crisis, but it did mark the beginning of the next phase in which market burdens changed from severe to calamitous (Poole, 2010).

The fundamental weakness highlighted by the crisis is the vulnerability of the globalized financial system to complex and interconnected risks factors (Colander et al. 2009), triggering growing worldwide concerns about the safety of financial institutions (Christopoulus, Mylonakis, and Dikapandis, 2011) and global macro-financial stability. However, a combination of several factors was the dominant force in the recent crisis (Claessens, 2010); one of these factors was the significant underestimation of risks inherent in structured finance products (Utzig, 2010). As these sophisticated new financial instruments were located at the core of the recent crisis, rating agencies came under the spotlight of criticism (Demirgüç-Kunt and Servén, 2010), as many investors relied on the assessments of financial soundness made by recognized rating agencies for their investment decision-making (Crouhy, Jarrow, and Turnbull, 2008). There is shared recognition that rating agencies failed the market on issues that have arisen from rating structured finance products, although several other factors could also be taken into account (Duff and Einig, 2009a). These factors include, but are not limited to, expansive monetary policy, the collapse of trading some financial instruments (Schwartz, 2009), macroeconomic imbalances and policy failures, as well as regulatory failures (Masciandaro, Pansins and Quintin, 2011), as outlined in Chapter 1. This chapter, however, focuses primarily on the main accusations leveled at rating agencies, concentrating on the role rating agencies played in the crisis. This chapter highlights the main criticisms made against rating agencies, namely conflicts of interest (Darcy, 2009), lack of competition (Cheng and Neamtiu, 2009), liability of rating agencies (Utzig, 2010), lack of transparency (Rousseau, 2009), deficiencies in the rating methodology (Altman et al., 2011) and their quasi-regulatory role (Cinquegrana, 2009).

2.1 On the Role of Rating Agencies

Discussions on the role of rating agencies were initially triggered by blind faith in financial innovations and the credit rating of the respective security. Although the crisis was not only caused by the rating agencies assessments of the creditworthiness of these products, they are nevertheless partially responsible for the current predicament (European Parliament, 2009). Many academics and practitioners have criticized the credit rating agencies procedures, assigning them the main share of the blame (Violi, 2010). Rating agencies have been accused of having evaluated US real estate loans too favorably, which turned out to be a misjudgment and is now considered to be one of the root causes of the 2007–2008 financial crisis (de Haan and Amtenbrink, 2011). Against this background, and the volatile movements of ratings themselves, rating agencies' approach to risk in the mortgage-backed securities sector was called into question above all (SIFMA, 2013). However, the rating agencies' role in the subprime crisis cannot be reduced to a single problem (Sinclair, 2011). Policymakers and academics around the world have identified several key issues and have undertaken measures to address the acknowledged problems with credit ratings (Hunt, 2009). These issues will be addressed later in this study. In discussing the common threads in the criticism of rating agencies, the main problems are highlighted for each individual topic in the following sections.

2.2 Rating Agencies' Role in Structured Finance

By evaluating financial instruments, corporate and government bonds, and structured products, the rating agencies make these products attractive to a variety of market participants, and thus play a central role in the financial markets (IOSCO, 2008b). Few investors are in the position or have the resources to conduct their own proprietary analysis of securitized pools of receivables, and the majority of market players thus rely on these assessments. In contrast to the situation with conventional financial products such as corporate bonds, where investors usually have relatively extensive information about the issuer, investors did not have adequate information on the underlying assets of the products and were dependent on rating agencies' judgments (Bannier and Müsch, 2008). To solve the problem of access to information, rating agencies were consulted to assist investors by providing that very information to determine whether the investment would be able to be serviced by the borrower (Portes, 2008).

Considering the scarcity of information investors had at their disposal for financial instruments that proved be high-risk in 2007, investors had to base their investment decisions on the risk classifications provided by rating agencies (Crouhy, Jarrow, and Turnbull, 2008). In the second half of 2007, rating agencies launched massive downgrades on securities that had previously been highly rated, resulting in abrupt and severe market price corrections that ultimately lead to widespread mistrust of the ratings themselves. This was particularly true after it came out that the rating agencies had several errors in their valuation models for complex structured finance products (AMF, 2009). The violation of standard total debt service (TDS) safety benchmarks and imbalances in information for investors in the structured finance products sector concealed the risk of mortgage default and the rating agencies' mistakes in assessing the true risk of these securities (Orlowski, 2008). However, as Pacces asserts, "as long as rating agencies had preserved symmetry of information, investors would have made losses on securitized mortgages, but the general panic on banks' short-term funding could have been avoided." (2010, p. 84)

The further securitization of already-securitized subprime loans (MBS) increased product complexity. Financial products derived from these securitized subprime loans fall under the category of collateralized debt obligations (CDOs), which are far more complex than conventional asset-backed securities (ABS) (Baker, 2008). Further re-structuring, however, meant that such securities also carry a higher risk of default. Until as recently as June 2007, the great majority of such financial products were awarded the highest ratings: AAA, the highest possible credit standing. High ratings were assigned even though there had already been significant levels of payment defaults in the subprime loan sector (Crotty and Epstein, 2008). Given the exposure of subprime mortgage pools to risks associated with mortgage collateral, financial markets experienced a deterioration in credit quality. The growing number of mortgage defaults triggered a high number of rating adjustments, and these downgrades subsequently resulted in corrections for CDOs as well (Fender, Tarashev, and Zhu, 2008). This indicated that rating agencies clearly underestimated the major risk inherent in these kinds of financial instruments (Pezzuto, 2012).

According to a study by the International Monetary Fund (IMF, 2008), over 75% of all mortgage loans issued in the first quarter of 2007 were securitized.

Some 80% of these mortgage-backed securities (MBS) received an AAA rating from the credit rating agencies; only fewer than 5%, however, were rated BBB or lower (White, 2009b). Without the AAA rating, there would not have been such a high demand for MBS or derivatives based on them, nor would there have been such a high concentration of these products in banks' trading books or special purpose vehicles (White, 2009b; de Haan and Amtenbrink, 2011). This flooded the market with AAA products whose risks and prices were clearly very sensitive to the situation on the housing market (de Haan and Amtenbrink, 2011).

Many institutional investors have legal and regulatory provisions that constrain their choices of financial products they are allowed to invest in. This is particularly true for to institutional investors like pension funds, money market funds, and insurance companies. Strict regulations oblige these investors to invest only in financial products with a certain minimum rating (only AAA securities or investment grade)[5] (Partnoy, 2009c). This is required for the purpose of minimizing the risk exposure (Cantor and Packer, 1994). The tranching[6] of liabilities made it possible to create more than one class of securities (Fender and Mitchell, 2005). Tranche size is directly linked to the assumed credit risk and diversification of the underlying asset pool; size thus determines the performance of each tranche (Lipton and Rennie, 2013). By virtue of the methods applied by rating agencies, it was possible for senior tranches of securitized loans to be given high ratings (Bannier and Hirsch, 2010). In case of default, the more senior tranche of a transaction is the most protected and will receive payments first. In contrast, the equity piece (the most junior tranche) will only be paid after all other (senior and mezzanine) tranche liabilities have first been settled (Brunnermeier, 2008). This process of tranching is described in greater detail in section 4.2. Consequently, such structured financial products were attractive for these investor groups (Telpner, 2003). A downgrading below the prescribed threshold, however, invariably puts these investor groups under tremendous pressure to liquidate these positions, which can result in herd behavior[7] (de Haan and Amtenbrink, 2001). This was an effect that occurred after July 2007 (Hassairi and Kahn, 2011).

5 A rating is considered investment grade if it is rated BBB or higher.

6 "[Tranching allows the issuer to exploit the *risk diversification effect* of pooling to create a low-risk and highly liquid security" (DeMarzo, p. 1).

7 Herd behavior describes how individuals in a group act together without planned direction. Keynes suggests that professional managers will "follow the herd" if they are concerned about how others will assess their ability to make sound judgments (Scharfenstein and Stein, 1990, p. 465). One example is the stock market, for which the following explanation of the pre-October 1987 bull market is often repeated: the

Downgrades did not only lead to mixed feelings; investors' concerns also focused on the nature and quality of rating agencies' assessment methods for structured finance products (Dennis, 2009). This is particularly relevant, as rating agencies are considered intermediaries in financial markets that provide potential investors guidance in the assessment of borrowers' creditworthiness (Gavras, 2012). Credit ratings are a means of reducing uncertainty about the borrowers' ability to make future payments on debt (Demerjian, 2010). As the crisis has demonstrated, however, credit rating agencies were not able to resolve the information problem in the capital markets regarding the underlying collateral of structured finance products (Sinclair, 2011). Ratings reflect only the credit risk, but not the liquidity risks, of structured products. By disregarding this important factor, an incomplete and generally overly positive picture of the risks inherent in these products emerges (Reckers, 2008). The increasing issuance of new financial instruments accelerated the pace of growth of the rating agencies' business, and as a result of this, their significance in the financial markets grew. The high volume of securitized products and the misrepresented risks – and ultimately, the distorting effects of massive loan defaults – are seen as proof that rating agencies abandoned traditional valuation techniques for financial instruments (Partnoy, 2006). Instead of behaving like intermediaries between investors and borrowers, rating agencies had incentives (see section 2.2.1) to engage in fraudulent and/or negligent practices, such as submitting false statements regarding asset quality (Darcy, 2009).

Rating agencies have been accused of reacting inadequately – and belatedly – to falling house prices and credit defaults, as rating adjustments were made after a considerable time lag (de Haan and Amtenbrink, 2011). The widely held assumption that downgrades of several notches within a very short space of time were practically impossible was proven wrong by the crisis (Bannier and Müsch, 2008). It was demonstrated that structured financial products are naturally exposed to a higher risk of downgrade by several notches than is the case with classic corporate bonds (Bannier and Müsch, 2008). This was a further trigger for the

consensus among professional money managers was that price levels were too high – the market was, in their opinion, more likely to go down rather than up. However, few managers were eager to sell their equity holdings. If the market did continue to go up, they were afraid of being perceived as lone fools for missing out on the ride. On the other hand, in the more likely event of decline, there would be comfort in numbers: how bad could they look if everybody else had suffered the same fate? The same principle can apply to corporate investment, when a number of companies are investing in similar assets. (Scharfenstein and Stein, 1990) turbulence on the financial markets, and was considered to be evidence for the poor quality of the credit ratings (de Haan and Amtenbrink, 2011). Significant changes regarding the consistency of the ratings as well as the massive downgrading that came to light during the course of the crisis were indicators that the structured products did not really meet the criteria for high ratings. Thus, the role of the rating agencies as information intermediaries, and consequently that of the ratings themselves, increasingly became the focus of criticism by a number of commentators, regulators, and politicians (Duff and Einig, 2009a; Partnoy, 2009b).

2.3 Main Points of Criticism Leveled at Rating Agencies

Criticism has been leveled at the three biggest players in the rating business: Standard & Poor's (S&P), Moody's, and Fitch (Frost, 2006). Before the crisis, rating agencies were seen as valuable sources of support for market participants, operating in financial markets under regulatory provisions. Each of the main issues raised regarding rating agencies are addressed in the following sections.

2.3.1 Conflicts of Interest in Rating Agencies' Business Model

The first accusation against the rating agencies is that not only were their ratings wrong, but that they also gave no warning of impending problems due to conflicts of interest between the issuers and the rating agencies themselves (Sinclair, 2011). Because the business relationship with the issuer boosted their incomes, credit rating agencies have been accused of excessive leniency in the assessment of structured financial products (Hunt, 2009), specifically within the context of their business model (Theurl and Schaetzle, 2011). Although the credit rating agencies fulfill a quasi-regulatory role in the financial markets, they nevertheless belong to the private sector and are profit-orientated businesses (Lynch, 2010). The typical remuneration model provides rating agencies with more than two-thirds of their revenues (de Haan and Amtenbrink, 2011). In this business model, rating agencies fees are paid by the party that has an interest in obtaining the best possible rating: the issuers of the financial products themselves (Kotecha, Ryan and Weinberger, 2010). Concerns that ratings are biased, particularly when compensated by the issuer, have increased, particularly following the extensive decline in the ratings of structured finance products during 2007–2008 (Benmelech and Dlugosz, 2010). There is some evidence to suggest that there are distorting incentives with regard to credit ratings, and this may indicate questionable behavior on the part of some market participants (Coval, Jurek, and Stafford,

2009). While rating agencies are required to provide accurate, high-quality ratings, "the issuer of a security both chooses and pays the rating agency for the rating of the security" (Altman et al., 2011, p. 444).

Nevertheless, a rating is primarily a decision-making tool for investors (Gras, 2003). On the one hand, rating agencies strive to maximize profits by providing ratings, but on the other hand, they should provide investors with an independent opinion. At this point, a serious conflict of interest arises because the market, based on these multiple interests, receives less verified data or simply less information than might otherwise be usual (Sinclair, 2011). If one looks at the rating process for structured products in the context of the principal-agent theory,[8] the result is a certain degree of information asymmetry: the issuer of financial products communicates information to market participants either directly (through media like financial reports or press releases, which is largely the case for corporate bonds) or through intermediaries such as rating agencies (which is primarily the case with structured finance products).

A number of factors determine whether information intermediaries and regulations eliminate the disadvantage of information asymmetry. One of these factors concerns potential incentive problems that lie within the intermediaries' sphere (Healy and Palepu, 2001). Information intermediaries have insight into private information, and their goal of generating more business can cause incentive problems in terms of how they assess qualitative factors, resulting in an underestimation of the risk of default. In order to compensate for the deterioration associated with quantitative criteria, information intermediaries might evaluate qualitative criteria in a more favorable way (Booth and Smith, 1986). The vigorously growing securitization market represented an incentive for rating agencies to remain attractive to their clients, thus allowing them to continue to expand their position in this market segment through assigning good ratings. Orlowski (2008) argues that, the for investors unknown exposure to information asymmetry in structured products like CDOs effectively concealed the risk of mortgage defaults, thus contributing to the crisis. There are several financial market risks

8 The principal-agent problem can be considered part of agency theory. It has similarities to game theory in that the "rules" are changed to favor specific actions preferred by the principal. An example of how the principal-agent problem occurs between rating agencies and the company (the principal) that hires them to set a credit rating. Because a low rating will increase the cost of borrowing for the company, it has an incentive to structure its compensation of the rating agency in such a way that the agency gives a higher rating than may be deserved. The rating agency is thus less likely to be objective because it fears losing future business by being too strict (Investopedia, 2013).

deriving from asymmetric information, including uncertainty of quality, hold up, and moral hazard (Morkötter and Westerfeld, 2008).

Further, rating agencies advise the same clients they later rate on how to structure and compose a security in order to obtain the best rating and subsequently rate the security designed in compliance with their specifications – a lucrative ancillary service (Buiter, 2007). This is especially prevalent in repeated commissions for rating transactions (Stuwe et al. 2012). By virtue of this creative activity, the rating agencies contributed to the development and issuance of as large a volume as possible of well-rated tranches of structured products (Theurl and Schaetzle, 2011). Clients of rating agencies can, moreover, initially refrain from publishing a rating (if the rating does not suit them) and obtain another rating from another agency (so-called 'rating shopping'), thus exerting pressure on the competing rating agencies (White, 2009b). Rating shopping offers the possibility of an issuer obtaining multiple rating 'estimates' before disclosing the rating to the public. For this so-called "shadow rating," the issuer generally pays only a small fee and is therefore in a position to consult several agencies ('shop around') and to "pick" the most advantageous rating (Skreta and Veldkamp, 2009, p. 681). Rating shopping by issuers leads to an erosion of rating standards for structured products (Utzig, 2010). The combination of the increasing complexity of structured finance products and the issuers' ability to shop for ratings creates rating bias, which can lead to ratings inflation. The linkage between asset complexity and rating shopping may encourage issuers to issue even more complex securities in order to get a broader rating spectrum, adding even more value to rating shopping. This conflict of interest affects rating prices if the vast majority of investors are not aware of the bias (Skreta and Veldkamp, 2010).

It is these considerations that have led to discussion as to whether factors other than the business model and the disclosure issue contribute to the phenomenon of rating shopping. In order to determine such factors, a number of studies have dealt with the topic. In the literature on rating shopping, there is a growing focus on the economic mechanisms that influence such behavior, showing the pros and cons. Sangiorgi, Sokobin and Spatt (2009, p. 4) assume that rating agencies truthfully disclose their information to investors and demonstrate how originator/issuers are motivated by "regulatory advantages associated with high published ratings". For rating shopping to take place, it must be the case that there are investors who are susceptible to inflated ratings or regulations that induce the issuer to achieve the highest rating. Currently, regulations provide such incentives, as many institutional investors and funds are subject to regulation based on ratings (Pagano and Volpin, 2010). However, Pagano and Volpin (2010) assume that rating agencies are not exposed to such conflicts of interest, but can define their ratings more or less opaquely depending on what is desired from the issuer. Indeed, this opaqueness surrounding securitized products was a key characteristic of the recent global crisis (Pagano and Volpin, 2010). The opaque faulty risk pricing methodology, or lack of transparency, will be highlighted in subsequent parts of this chapter, as it became evident by the drastic downgrades of AAA-rated securities that ratings were already inflated before the crisis emerged (Pagano and Volpin, 2010).

Mathis, McAndrews and Rochet (2009) and Becker and Milbourn (2008) investigated the extent to which reputational concerns can discipline rating agencies, who may be compelled to inflate their ratings to maximize their fees. While rating agencies claim "that this conflict is unlikely to bias their ratings out of concern for their reputation" (Deb and Murphy, 2009, p. 3), Mathis, McAndrews and Rochet (2009) show that the argument is flawed in the case that a large portion of rating agencies' revenues comes from rating complex securities. They further suggest that reputational concerns alone are not enough to counter this problem. These explanations for potential sources of bias played some role in the inflation of ratings, resulting in potential downgrades during the course of the crisis (Skreta and Veldkamp, 2010). However, as the authors argue, securitization is much more complex than evaluating corporate bonds, and this complexity provides for possibilities that are far beyond mathematical manipulations. With the complexity inherent to credit risk securitizations, rating agencies analysts from different rating agencies, who are presented with the same facts, can still reasonably arrive at different results, and in turn, different ratings (Skreta and Veldkamp, 2009).

In contrast to such discussions, Griffin, Nickerson and Tang (2013) argue that even if rating agencies apply their standards and issue unbiased ratings, rating inflation is a natural consequence of the rating shopping process and is not necessarily instigated by rating agencies themselves. A previous study by Sangiorgi, Sokobin and Spatt (2009) led to similar results. Sangiorgi, Sokobin and Spatt (2009) show that if investors are rational, ratings inflation induced by rating shopping does not have any adverse consequences for market participants. Skreta and Veldkamp (2009) evaluated the effects of proposed reforms in a model, allowing investors to buy assets with sufficiently high ratings or at market price, but subjected a fraction of investors to investment-grade regulations in order to create a bias. They demonstrate that inflated ratings expand investor investment possibilities. However, if the source of bias is rating shopping and not the rating agencies themselves, then investor-initiated ratings are likely to be less biased (Skreta and Veldkamp, 2009).

As the turmoil unfolded in financial markets, individual conflicts of interest also came to light. The participation of senior rating agency staff in stock options of the companies to be rated is one such example of conflicts of interest. This method of compensation – by granting shares – may have contributed to encouraging rating agency employees to incur excessive risks in the rating process for the company to be evaluated (Hunt, 2009). When members of a rating agency own the very securities that they rate, they may not be entirely objective in their judgments, which constitutes a serious conflict of interest (Bai, 2010). All this led to doubts about the strict neutrality of the rating agencies in their regard for the interests of the issuers and investors.

2.3.2 Lack of Competition

The market for the credit rating business is of oligopolistic nature, concentrated on three agencies: Standard & Poor's, Moody's and Fitch. These players dominate the rating business with a combined market share of approximately 95%.[9] The remaining 5% of the market share is accounted for by a number of smaller agencies that specialize more in niche sectors and do not represent any serious competition to the 'Big Three' (Theurl and Schaetzle, 2011). These three big agencies are responsible for 98% of all ratings issued by recognized agencies (Partnoy, 2009c). Although the number of rating agencies worldwide (between 130 and 150) has increased, given the growing demand for ratings and their significance in the finance sector, the market is largely restricted particularly in the United States, where most of the rating activity is concentrated. In addition to the dominant role played by the Big Three rating agencies, the market is characterized by minimal competition among the large agencies (Frost, 2006). This situation is further characterized by the principle of the 'two-rating norm' in which the US loan capital issues must obtain two ratings. Usually these come from Moody's and Standard & Poor's (Hunt, 2009).

In addition to the structure of the rating market, the lack of competition in this market sector is maintained by the licensing regulations for credit rating agencies (Sinclair, 2011). The agencies must meet certain standards and apply to the US Securities and Exchange Commission (SEC) for an official license as a Nationally Recognized Statistical Rating Organizations (NRSROs). In Europe,

---

9 While Standard & Poor's and Moody's each account for approximately 40%, Fitch accounts for about 15% of market share (Rousseau, 2009).

the European Securities and Markets Authority (ESMA) is responsible for the licensing. Ultimately, it is this licensing that is largely responsible for the significant market dominance of the 'Big Three', since licensing regulations can be seen as barriers to market entry (Hunt, 2009). The oligopolistic market structure also leads to insufficient transparency and erroneous risk assessments that are not subject to penalties (Theurl and Schaetzle, 2011).

2.3.3 Liability of Rating Agencies

The ratings issued by the NRSROs are used to meet a series of regulatory and contractual requirements both inside and outside the United States (Frost, 2006). Ratings dictate the capital adequacy requirements of banks, investments funds, institutional investors, and pension funds (Kotecha, Ryan, and Weinberger, 2010). During the course of the crisis, it came to light that investors who had relied on the ratings issued by rating agencies were confronted with enormous losses caused by the rating agencies' downgrades, which confirmed their misjudgment (Dennis, 2009). Given their place in financial markets, and their role in the development and marketing of structured financial products, appeals to hold rating agencies liable for their ratings seem to be justified. However, the crisis demonstrated that holding rating agencies legally accountable turned out to be more difficult than anticipated (Wildmoser, Schiffer, and Langoth, 2009). Since ratings involve both objective and subjective factors, as well as retrospective-prospective assessment procedures, ratings reside in the (legal) "Grauzone" (grey area) between factual statement and the safeguarded freedom of expression (Mühl, 2010, p. 43). The legal grey area in which rating agencies operate makes it extremely difficult to demonstrate evidence of wrongdoing on their part (Wildmoser, Schiffer, and Langoth, 2009). Consequently, credit rating agencies were very effectively excluded from civil liability. Thus, rating agencies have been able, to a large extent, to avoid liability for inaccurate ratings. One of the agencies' most successful lines of defense is based on the First Amendment of the US Constitution (Nagy, 2009). Rating agencies maintain that they are issuers of financial publications and that their ratings are in the public interest. As such, they are entitled to increased protection as 'publishers' under the "actual malice"[10] standard (Dennis, 2009, p. 1141), according to which a publisher is not liable for false statements unless he himself is proven to have intentionally caused it. This means that the statement must have been made knowing that the information

10 "The actual malice standard originated in *New York times Co. v. Sullivan*" 376 U.S. 254, 279–80 (1964) (Deats, 2010, p. 1818).

was false, or with reckless disregard of whether it was false or not (Deats, 2010). The protection of the agencies was further widened by a US Supreme Court decision that ruled that opinions not containing "provably false connotations" do not constitute a basis for liability (Dennis, 2009, p. 1141). Such legal defense tactics have increasingly come under fire (Kotecha, Ryan, and Weinberger, 2010), but these criticisms have not led to any indictment of any credit rating agency.

Rating agencies' analysis of creditworthiness is future oriented, and expresses the agencies' view of the capability of the originator/issuer to fulfill their obligations (i.e. interest, repayment of principal) arising from the loan relationship with the investor on due date (Pederzoli and Torricelli, 2005). Governments, investors, investment banks, and others rely on ratings in order to get a better understanding of credit risk (Castle, 2009). Although ratings can only be interpreted as opinion, they have received a "quasi-official status" by governments, which only corroborates the widely held belief that ratings are "in some way more than just opinions" (Royce, 2009, p. 7). "This signal to the market" diminishes the perceived necessity to conduct reasonable due diligence of the financial counterpart required by "well-functioning markets" (Royce, 2009, p. 7). However, taking into account that ratings have to be used for regulatory reasons, and that market participants' over reliance on them "derives from decades of regulatory dependence of ratings," and ratings ultimately became part of the financial culture (Partnoy, 2009b, p. 11). To the extent that investors are concerned, a rating can be legally tantamount to investment advice. In this context, however, the rating agencies explicitly point out that their ratings are merely expressions of their points of view (Dennis, 2009). Sanctions for wrong rating assessments would thus, given this and the legal protocols established, be possible only in cases of clear and willful wrongdoing (Theurl and Schaetzle, 2010). This view has been consistently supported and applied by US Courts, effectively excluding the ratings issued by rating agencies from legal liability (Lipszyc, 2009).

NRSROs' responsibility had been overlooked for decades to such an extent that there are serious obstacles of a legal nature to any party prosecuting and litigating against rating agencies, even though their role is pivotal to material damages incurred by investors (Freeman, 2008). It seems unlikely that rating agencies facing claims of negligence would be prosecuted, as they could easily defend themselves by saying that their business is the dissemination of information rather than issuing qualitative judgments on matters. The law makes a distinction between "apparently factual information" and statements containing "the quality of a judgment" (Hunt, 2009, p. 195). Even in cases where the restatement law does apply, rating agencies defend themselves based on the argument of "absence of duty to investors," and the conveniently hedging statement that their ratings "are not investment recommendations" (Hunt, 2008, p. 195). Due to the lack of accountability for rating agencies, institutional investors are now vulnerable because rating agencies cannot be held responsible given that any claim based on "reliance on ratings is weakened" (Partnoy, 2009c, p. 6). This is the case because it can be argued that ratings become less reliable when "rating agencies are not accountable for fraudulent or reckless ratings" (Partnoy, 2009c, p. 6).

In addition to investors, another group that can claim wrongful doing on the part of the rating agencies is the issuers. Damage can occur as a result overly pessimistic ratings (Mühl, 2010). In this case, the initial consideration is whether the credit rating was solicited (requested by the issuer) or unsolicited (initiated by the rating agency themselves or by a third party). The question of liability consequently arises from a contractual or non-contractual standpoint. With solicited ratings, the rating agency's obligation is to conduct an assessment of creditworthiness by analyzing relevant market and business data (Theurl and Schaetzle, 2011). A rating set too low by the rating agency would therefore turn out to be detrimental to the issuer as a result of the correlation between default risk and interest payable (i.e. the risk-return relationship) (Partnoy, 2009c). In this context, it has been shown that, even with contractual agreements regarding a rating assessment, the agencies cannot necessarily be called to account for incorrect evaluations (Hunt, 2009).

Rating agencies have (by way of exception) also made rating assessments without being instructed to do so by the company concerned (Poon and Firth, 2005). Such a rating can, for example, be initiated by a large potential investor who would like to assess the risk of a planned investment (Mühl, 2010). Motivated by the self-interest of the rating agency, a rating can be made, for instance, to win a new client, or to maintain or expand market share (Burnie and Langsam, 2004). The publication of such an unsolicited rating can result in material and immaterial damages for the rated company, especially if the credit rating is negative. Along with a loss of image and reputation, a less than favorable rating could seriously disrupt the financial plans or performance of the company in question. In this case, it is in the interest of such a company to make a stand against the unsolicited rating by making liability claims (e.g. claims for damages) against the rating agency (Mühl, 2008). In cases of any damage to the issuer caused by erroneous ratings, tortious claims for damages are recognized in all legal systems. Although there are no general exemptions from liability clauses, there are a number of obstacles to successfully obtaining legal rulings in favor of the claimant, such as the proof of fraudulent intentions (Blaurock, 2007), and thus far it has proven to be very difficult to initiate legal proceedings against rating agencies (Hunt, 2009).

Despite the rare cases in which rating agencies were sued, an Australian ruling could provide a decisive precedent for others to present their cases (Watkins et al., 2012). The Australian court decision[11] marks the first time that a rating agency (S&P) "has been held accountable for its rating opinion that it is paid to assign to financial products" (Banton and Theodorou, 2013). The implications of the ruling "are global and widespread within the financial industry" and "highlights the capacity for a duty of care to arise [...] between investors and the parties involved in structuring and rating financial products that they purchase" (Banton and Theodorou, 2013). The crumbling Amendment defense is ever more obvious in light of current developments in litigation against rating agencies. More recently, in February 2013, the US Justice Department sued S&P for ignoring its own standards for rating mortgage-backed securities that led to the collapse in financial markets (Eaglesham, Neumann, and Perez, 2013). Rating agencies' liability is one of the issues that will be addressed in the empirical part of this research, discussing if and how this could be made applicable.

2.3.4 Lack of Transparency in the Rating Process

Following the collapse of the market for structured products, concern spread around the globe about the ability and preparedness of the credit rating agencies to keep pace with innovations in the financial markets (Kotecha, Ryan, and Weinberger, 2010). Critics argue that conflicts of interest, combined with a lack of transparency, have produced a flawed system (Issing Committee, 2008). It can alternatively be posited, however, that transparency is an important and integral part of improving the functionality of a market (Issing Committee, 2008). The crisis made it clear that the rating agencies did not provide market players with sufficient information, and they therefore could not fully understand the assumptions underlying the ratings (Hassan and Kalhoefer, 2011). It is the function of the rating agencies, though, to reduce existing information asymmetries (Baresa, Bogdan, and Ivanovic, 2012). The lack of transparency in the rating process and the rating models led to doubts about the validity, reliability, and objectivity of the ratings (Hunt, 2008), particularly against the background that the ratings for structured products did not clearly reflect the quality of the

11 In a landmark decision the Federal court of appeal in a first instance decision ruled that S&P had breached its duty of care and had misled or deceived investors by assigning AAA ratings to volatile structured finance products.

underlying assets. This gave rise to false impressions about the true risks inherent in the various tranches of these securities (Kotecha, Ryan, and Weinberger, 2010). Thus, market players increasingly found the quantitative assumptions underlying the ratings to be obscure, and complained that that the rating agencies were "acting like a black box" (Kotecha, Ryan, and Weinberger, 2010, p. 68).

2.3.5 Deficiencies in the Rating Method and in the Rating Process

The credit rating agencies' lack of experience with the new financial instruments that developed from the securitization of subprime loans was identified in several reports (e.g. Issing Committee, 2008; FSA, 2009) as one of the main reasons for the errors of judgment made by the agencies. Experts criticized the rating agencies' methods and identified the following main shortcomings in the rating process: faulty methods, model risk, inadequate disclosure of information relating to models and their assumptions, inadequate attention to market and liquidity risk, misinterpretation of related issues, and rating agencies' terminology (Hunt, 2009).

Faulty methods. A number of official reports in the United States[12] and Europe[13] ascertained weaknesses in the rating process that contributed to the crisis. These included not only considerable underestimation of the risks involved with the structured products, but also flaws in the methods used (Utzig, 2010). The development of structured products led to an increase in innovative rating methods; at the same time, the volume and complexity of mortgage-backed securities (MBS) and collateralized debt obligations (CDOs) also grew (Kotecha, Ryan, and Weinberger, 2010). The accuracy and completeness of assessing the methods underlying the new financial instruments, nevertheless, were overestimated by the rating agencies (Hunt, 2008).

The rating of these financial products is based on mathematical-statistical models, and the results of these mathematical models used depend heavily on assumptions regarding the probability of default of the elements of the portfolio and their correlation with one another (Brabänder, 2008). The reason given for the failure of the rating agencies is that the ratings for MBS and CDOs were based on cash flows from a portfolio of assets that correlated with each other,

12 See, for example, US Securities and Exchange Commission (September 2009) Annual Report on Nationally Recognized Statistical Rating Organizations, As required by Section 6 of the Credit Rating Agencies Reform Act of 2006.

13 See, for example, Financial Stability Forum (2008). Report of the Financial Stability Forum on Enhancing Market and Institutional Resilience.

instead of concrete corporate risk. This led to substantial corrections of the ratings for these products during the crisis (Jorion, 2009). If corporate bonds and MBS/CDOs carry the same rating, the expected loss is interpreted to be very similar. With regard to unexpected losses in the case of structured products, the negative variance from income value[14] differs significantly from a corporate bond, and is strongly dependent on the correlation structure between the underlying asset positions. This correlation was simulated by the agencies in quantitative models (Bannier and Müsch, 2008). It was thus possible to create securities rated as very safe from loans with poor credit ratings and low correlations (Fender and Mitchell, 2005). However, it is misleading to regard the relationship to bond prices (or spreads) as a reference for the quality of a rating, since various factors come into play here (Frost, 2006).

Calculating expected losses and default probabilities for structured finance products is an important task for rating agencies, as the losses will critically depend on the tranche size and its position in the loss distribution of the underlying securitized asset pool (Fender and Mitchell, 2005). One additional aspect in this respect is that portfolios of traditional structured financial products (ABS of credit card receivables, for instance) consist of large, well-diversified, homogenous asset pools, whereas more sophisticated new financial products, such as CDOs, consist of less diversified, heterogeneous asset pools. This displays a significant difference that needs to be considered in choosing the approach to loss determination and thus the rating (Fender and Mitchell, 2005). With conventional financial instruments (ABS), idiosyncratic risks thus play a significantly smaller role. In this case, the calculation of expected and unexpected losses (default risk) is typically evaluated using the so-called actuarial approaches (e.g. on the basis of Monte Carlo simulation) (Morkötter and Westerfeld, 2008).

The agencies' assumptions about the default risks for all financial products were mapped in line with historical data. However, there was very little data available for subprime loans and other complex products, if any at all, and then only from short periods of time (Hassan and Kalhoefer, 2011). Most rating agencies relied on loan data from 1999–2000, and applied this information to

---

14 In the context of risk control (e.g. at financial institutions), the unexpected loss (UL) defines the possible loss from loans that exceeds the expected loss. The expected loss (EL) is derived from loan loss experience and statistical probabilities, i.e. it is assumed *a priori* that a certain percentage of loans will default. The UL is, so to speak, an expected value and is taken into account a priori. The UL can thus be defined as a variance (negative) from the income value and aggregates the fluctuations (loss volatilities) around the income value. (Finanzlexikon.de.).

calculate default probabilities of subprime loans in a pool. The data used had little in common with innovative subprime mortgage products (Dennis, 2009). The correlations between the various mortgage loans were significantly higher than that which had been assumed by the rating agencies, and it eventually became obvious that they had underestimated the default risk (Hassan and Kalhoefer, 2011). One of the reasons for this was that until 2006, real estate prices in the United States had steadily risen. Based on this trend, it had been erroneously assumed that a pool of loans from different regions of the United States could be regarded as sufficiently diversified (Brabänder, 2008). The missing data, however, highlighted the weak points in the quantitative models applied (Bannier and Müsch, 2008). In reality, the methods applied by the credit rating agencies resulted in unjustifiable potential losses and default probabilities, and there is evidence suggesting that this led to high credit ratings that were fundamentally unwarranted (Dennis, 2009).

Model risk. The default risks of a structured financial product depend strongly on the position of a tranche in the underlying pool of receivables (security pool). The default correlation, which acts as an indicator for the same type of default behavior of the underlying security pool, is closely related to the distribution of the cumulative portfolio losses around their income value (Coval, Jurek, and Stafford, 2009). In the event of a change of the correlation, the loss distribution over the individual tranches will shift. The higher the correlation, the higher the default probability will be. As a result of this, the higher-ranking tranches (investment grade) will bear higher risk, but the lowest tranches (equity piece/first loss piece) stand to profit because the risk results are spread more widely (Amato and Gyntelberg, 2005). In this situation, a reversion effect takes place, given that the probability for the first loss piece rises of incurring no losses or any losses hardly can occur (Fender and Mitchell, 2005). This effect is possibly amplified by problems in terms of governance, and "the question of who, if anyone, should take responsibility for restructuring the portfolio" becomes even more relevant should part of the underlying assets in a portfolio become distressed (Fender and Mitchell, 2005, p. 71). The owner of the equity piece might have a greater incentive to increase interest rates and returns, while senior tranche holders would be incentivized to minimize default risks in the pool portfolio. Governance issues might therefore lead to erroneous model inputs, as the equity piece holder would prefer asset pools that are composed of obligors displaying high default correlations at the detriment of the senior tranche holders (Fender and Mitchell, 2005). For tranches in the middle range (mezzanine tranche), this effect is difficult to determine. In addition, problems for correlation management can still arise from the inclusion of CDOs of CDOs (so-called squared CDOs) in an existing pool (Fender and Mitchell, 2005).

The factors outlined above contributed decisively to the fact that the estimates of risk and yield react very sensitively depending on the assumptions of default correlations in the underlying asset pool (Ubide, 2008). This implies, in turn, that each individual rating agency's estimates can differ from one another. This can be accounted for by differences in the methodology applied as well as by differing assumptions. This gives rise to the risk that the measures taken by rating agencies to improve the creditworthiness of a particular tranche (and thus its rating) will only very imprecisely reflect the actual risk of the tranche. Accordingly, in order to enable the investors to evaluate the risk, they would have to know the model risk – otherwise they cannot claim the risk-related interest payments for their investments (Fender and Mitchell, 2005). The limited historical data available in the structured product area cannot serve as a basis for a solid correlational calculation, and will thus increase the model risk (Hunt, 2009).

Inadequate disclosure of information relating to models and their assumptions. The credit rating agencies' practices of disclosure are considered inadequate (Partnoy, 2009c). The information disclosed by the rating agencies has proved to be incomplete, as important evaluation criteria and their weighting within the rating itself remain unclear (Issing Committee, 2008). Corporate bonds and structured financial products exhibit different risk characteristics (Utzig, 2010). Ratings are thus particularly important because they enable market players to scrutinize securities in terms of their probability of defaulting. With corporate bonds, investors are in a position to obtain extensive information about the issuers concerned, and are therefore not dependent on the information provided by the rating agencies (Elamin, 2011). This constitutes a significant distinguishing criterion for bond ratings and the ratings of financial products (Frost, 2006). During the course of the crisis, market participants increasingly found that the quantitative assumptions underlying the rating agencies' ratings had not been made sufficiently transparent (Kotecha, Ryan, and Weinberger, 2010). This point is extremely important: without enough information, it is not possible to verify the ratings issued by the rating agencies (Elamin, 2011).

Inadequate attention to market and liquidity risks and misinterpretation of related issues. The crisis made clear that the credit rating agencies had underestimated the impact of market and liquidity risks as key factors in the valuation of structured products; they were not included in the analyses to determine default probability (Gopalan, Song, and Yerramilli, 2009). Nevertheless, even when there is no risk of default, there can still be a number of market and liquidity risks (White, 2009). So long as these risks do not pose an insolvency risk, liquidity risk is not reflected in the agencies ratings (Buiter, 2007). The repercussions of the collapse of the real estate market and the ensuing loss of confidence in structured products were thus factored into their ratings far too late. The rating agencies had also overlooked the fact that the subprime sector continued to grow despite rising interest rates and falling house prices. Contradictory market signals should have resulted in the rating agencies undertaking a more cautious appraisal. In addition, the risk arising from maturity transformation at the level of special purpose vehicles (SPV) should have been recognized as such by the rating agencies[15]. Maturity transformation poses a big threat to the static equilibrium of the financial system, and is now regarded as one of the major factors contributing to the financial crisis (Gray, 2009). The particular risk in maturity transformation is that the refinancing of non-matching maturities results in liquidity squeezes when the securities issued by the SPVs (as part of follow-on financing) can no longer be placed on the market (Bannier and Müsch, 2008).

Terminology of the credit rating agencies. The evaluation of the rating agencies is released to the market in the form of a rating. This assessment is usually expressed in the form of a rating symbol. For further differentiation within the individual classifications, modifying factors such as +/- or 1/2/3 are added to the letters (Gras, 2003). A rating scale is characterized by its ordinality, meaning that all ratings on the scale are comparable (de Haan and Amtenbrink, 2011). The global credit rating agencies, such as Moody´s, Standard & Poor's and Fitch, are strictly geared towards maintaining consistency across all categories of issuers, industries, instruments, and regions, and the same scale is used for corporate bonds, debentures, sovereign bonds, and structured securities (de Haan and Amtenbrink, 2011).

Although the risk features, rating stability, and rating process for structured financial products are clearly different from those of conventional bonds, the credit rating agencies use the same scale for both product categories (Coval, Jurek, and Stafford, 2009. The fact that yields of structured products lie above those on normal bonds with the same rating creates an investment incentive for investors (Dionne, 2009). The risk that is then associated with such investments is significantly higher than that assumed by the investor. The

---

15 Maturity transformation using SPVs is practised primarily in the context of so-called asset-backed commercial paper programs, in which long-term loans (often mortgage loans) are repackaged into short(er)-term ABCPs (Acharya and Schnabl, 2010).

International Monetary Fund's 2008 report (IMF, 2008) came to the conclusion that for many investors, ratings constituted a decisive factor (key input) in the evaluation of structured products, as they were perceived to be a uniform evaluation scale for all fixed-income instruments. Especially in the absence of reliable price quotes, the prices of structured products were often determined by means of conclusions drawn from the prices and credit spreads of similarly rated comparable products for which there were quotes available. Thus, the price of a triple-A ABX subindex maintained by Markit Group Ltd.,[16] for example, could be used to determine the price of a triple-A mortgage tranche; a triple-B subindex could therefore be used to determine the value of a triple-B MBS-tranche, and so on (de Haan and Amtenbrink, 2011). Nevertheless, the rating agencies themselves continue to point out that their ratings represent a uniform measure of credit quality, globally, across all types of debt instruments (de Haan and Amtenbrink, 2011). The ranking of the highly complex and difficult-to-grasp products on the same scale (and thus in the same category of creditworthiness) is therefore criticized because of the differing risk structure (Kotecha, Ryan, and Weinberger, 2010).

The credit rating agencies Moody's, Standard & Poor's, and Fitch divide their rating scales into two large sections. For example, Standard & Poor's has a quality section between the ratings BBB and BB and one between B- and CCC (Kräussl, 2005). Financial instruments rated BBB- or higher are considered 'investment grade,' whereas ratings falling between BBB- and BB+ marks the transition to the speculative section. Ratings with the first letter C mark the start of poor credit quality; a D rating indicates that payment defaults have already occurred. Even if the calibrations of the scales of the large rating agencies look very similar, they are nevertheless *de facto* different, and many small differences make each scale very specific (Langohr and Langohr, 2008). Even if the alphanumeric symbols in each scale look similar and represent the same ranking by all three global rating agencies, the underlying key indicators signify quite different things (Langohr and Langohr, 2008). This means that the same symbol at each agency means something different. As Everling (1991) has already established, the manifold diversity of rating symbols makes it difficult

16 The ABX set up by Markit Group Inc. measures the overall value of mortgage returns on subprime CDOs and is based on 20 bonds with initial ratings of AAA. The index allows financial institutions to determine if the market for subprime related securities is improving or worsening (Longstaff, 2010). In order to increase liquidity in the asset-backed-market and to bring more price discovery to the market, a penultimate sub-index was added (Goodman et al., 2008).

to determine the differences in the various ratings. While Moody's ties its ratings to losses in the event of default, ratings from Standard & Poor's and Fitch focus only on the *possibility* of default (Salmon, 2011). Inconsistent rating definitions undermine comparability. Due to regulatory requirements, a downgrading from 'investment grade' to 'speculative grade' can have a major influence on investor behavior.

The SEC commissions conducted a study, as required by Section 939(h)(1) of the Dodd-Frank Act, "on the feasibility and desirability of the standardization of rating terminology, so that all credit rating agencies issue ratings using identical terms" (SEC, 2012). The study by the SEC commission noted that standardizing the terminology might better facilitate the comparison across all rating agencies and "result in fewer opportunities for manipulation credit rating scales to give the impression of accuracy" (SEC, 2012, p. 3). It also found that the standardization of ratings terminology is problematic, given the differences in the rating methodologies themselves (SEC, 2012). However, since not all rating agencies "use the same definition for their ratings" and given that "investors are confused by or even unaware of what a given credit rating agency's rating means," a uniform definition is, nevertheless, highly desirable (Blumenthal, 2008, p. 3). The following tables provide a summary of the three major rating agencies' ratings symbols, including modifiers and the associated interpretation of risk classification adopted by each agency.

Table 1: International Long-term Rating Comparison

	Standard & Poor's	Moody's	Fitch
Interpretation			
Investment Grade			
Extremely strong/best quality/ highest quality	AAA	Aaa	AAA
Very strong/high quality/Very high quality	AA+ AA AA-	Aa1 Aa2 Aa3	AA+ AA AA-
Strong/upper medium grade/high quality	A+ A A-	A1 A2 A3	A+ A A-
Adequate/medium grade/good quality	BBB+ BBB BBB-	Baa1 Baa2 Baa3	BBB+ BBB BBB-

	Standard & Poor's	Moody's	Fitch
Interpretation			
Non-investment grade			
Speculative – less vulnerable/low grade/ speculative	BB+	Ba1	BB+
	BB	Ba2	BB
	BB-	Ba3	BB-
More vulnerable/low grade/highly speculative	B+	B1	B+
	B	B2	B
	B-	B3	B-
currently vulnerable/substantial risk	CCC+	Caa1	CCC+
	CCC	Caa2	CCC
	CCC-	Caa3	CCC-
currently highly vulnerable/highly speculative/ very high default risk	CC	Ca	CC
imminent default/extremely poor/exceptionally high default risk	C	C	C
In default/in default/in default	D	C	D
Under regulatory supervision/ -/ – /	R		
Selective default/ – /restricted default	SD		RD
Not rated/ – / -/	NR		

Source: adopted from Voizey (2006) as summarized in Duff & Einig (2007); Fitch Ratings (2013); Standard & Poor's (2013).

Short-term ratings are assigned to debt obligations or issuers in corporate, public, or structured finance with an initial maturity of one year or less (< 360 days). Table 2 summarizes the comparison of the international short-term rating scale and the corresponding designation of default of the major three rating agencies. These rating definitions correspond in their reflection of default probabilities to the long-term rating scale. Short-term, investment-grade ratings signal a very low probability of default, and speculative ratings signal that there is a high probability of default, or that a default has already occurred (Duff and Einig, 2007).

Table 2: International Short-term Rating Scale Comparison

	Standard & Poor's	Moody's	Fitch
Interpretation			
Investment Grade			
Strong/superior/highest	A1	P1	F1+
Satisfactory/good/strong	A2	P2	F2
Adequate/acceptable/fair	A3	P3	F2
Non-investment Grade			
Speculative/not prime/speculative	B	Not Prime	F3
Vulnerable/ – /high default risk	C	–	B
Default/ – / default	D	–	C
			D

Source: adopted from Voizey (2006) as summarized in Duff & Einig (2007).

Since the start of the subprime mortgage crisis, it has been debated worldwide as to whether structured financial products should be rated on a separate scale – especially given that factors such as price risk or liquidity risks continue to be excluded in the ratings of these products. Meanwhile, rating agencies are required to draw a distinction between structured finance products and traditional bonds by the International Organization of Securities Commission's code of conduct (IOSCO, 2008b), for instance.

2.3.6 Quasi-Regulatory Role of Rating Agencies

Regulatory requirements[17] have meant that there is a great dependence on ratings and thus also on credit rating agencies, particularly on the big three players

17 In 1936, in an attempt to ensure that banks only invested in safe bonds, US regulators prohibited banks from investing in 'speculative investment securities' – as determined by 'recognized rating manuals.' This prohibition is still in effect. 'Speculative' securities are defined as bonds that are below 'investment grade,' meaning that since 1936, banks have been restricted to holding only bonds that are rated BBB- or higher.
In 1975, the SEC decided to set minimum capital requirements, and so again tied the requirements to the rating agencies judgments (White, 2009b, p. 390–391). In 2006, Congress enacted the Credit Rating Agencies Reform Act (CRARA), which required rating agencies to disclose their procedures for issuing ratings and have policies in place to manage conflicts of interest. The Act also gave power to the SEC to suspend or revoke an agency's designation as an NRSRO for violations of the Act. (Dennis, 2009).

in the ratings industry. This shift of responsibility by the supervisory authorities of the US government to third parties has led to ratings and rating agencies gaining quasi-legal power (White, 2009b). This was further supported by the SEC regulation requiring that all bond/security issues must be rated by at least one NRSRO (Beaver, Shakespeare, and Soliman, 2006). In addition, regulatory requirements limited the supervisory authority of the SEC over the NRSROs, particularly with the prohibition of "regulating the substance of the credit ratings or the procedures and methodologies by which any NRSRO determines credit ratings" (see U.S.C.S. § 780–7(h), 2008) cited in Dennis (2009, p. 1115). Although organized on a commercial, private-sector basis, rating agencies are accorded a market-supervisory function. They thus have a quasi-public status or, it can be argued, the status of a quasi-state entity (de Haan and Amtenbrink, 2011). Accordingly, these privately managed businesses themselves assume the role of the regulator. This dual role played by the agencies has, in light of the financial crisis, prompted calls for the agencies to be controlled more tightly, or to decrease the power of their role in the financial markets (Gras, 2003).

2.4 Conclusion

This chapter has highlighted the main points of criticism leveled at the rating agencies since the onset of the subprime mortgage crisis. Their increasing role in the global financial markets and the reliance of many institutional and private sector investors on rating agencies' risk assessments demonstrates the dependency of many players in the market on these private-sector entities. In view of their pivotal role in the marketplace, and the massive downgrades of previously high-rated securities, regulatory authorities and others claim that conflicts of interest, above all stemming from their business model, paved the way for biased and inflated ratings. In order to promote their own business interests and to foster their market position, rating agencies were incentivized to offer high ratings to their customers. In turn, originators/issuers had the possibility to obtain (shop for) ratings from different rating agencies, but only published the most favorable rating to them, which further perpetuated the creation of mispriced securities. This was further supported by the complexity and opaqueness of securitized transactions, giving even more room for manipulation and ratings inflation. Moreover, rating agencies were accused of advising their clients on how to structure transactions in order to meet the criteria to obtain the highest possible rating.

The Act went into effect in June 2007, but according to Kotecha Ryan, and Weinberger (2010), it failed to improve the quality of ratings in the run-up of the subprime crisis.

Combined with the market demand for investment grade ratings, these factors led to exposure to high credit risk. The oligopolistic market structure where the largest three rating agencies have a combined 95% market share played a not insignificant role in creating this environment, which was further fostered by the requirement that securities or the entity to be rated needed a rating obtained by at least one NRSRO. This has all given rise to questioning of the independence of the rating agencies, and what the future status of rating agencies in financial markets should be.

The lack of transparency in the rating process raises serious questions about the integrity of the rating agencies, and the validity and reliability of their ratings. In the fallout of the crisis, it became apparent that apart from ratings themselves being biased, the rating agencies' methodologies were not adequate for the risk assignment of such complex securitization transactions. Their methods were based on historical loan data and did not adequately reflect the risk of subprime loan-based structured finance transactions, leading to complaints that rating agencies acted as if in a 'black box'. Following the collapse of the subprime market, market participants discovered that rating agencies methodologies and their assumptions regarding default correlations were not adequate and did not reflect the true value of the underlying asset pools. The result was a massive downgrading for investment-grade ratings, not least due to regulatory rules and requirements, with banks, pension funds, institutional investors and private investors facing huge losses. The question then arose as to if and how rating agencies should be held responsible for false and misleading ratings. However, until recently, rating agencies successfully defended themselves, calling upon the First Amendment first and foremost. In light of their activities in the structured finance sector, it is, however, questionable whether rating agencies' ratings are indeed only 'opinions,' and whether ratings actually do fall under the protection of constitutionally protected free speech.

Following the debacle, rating agencies' responsibility for the crisis has been analyzed, and there are increasing calls for reform of the rating industry and reduced reliance on credit ratings. As part of the wider debate, it has also been argued that excessive reliance on ratings in US and European legislation might have discouraged banks and institutional investors to exercise their own due diligence. When assessing the rating agencies' role in the financial market – in an environment where the growing complexity of financial instruments had led to greater reliance on ratings – investors need to reassess their own reliance on ratings. Regulatory authorities and financial institutions should be encouraged to reduce their dependence and reliance on rating agencies, as there might be a need for alternative standards. This could help address the question of whether other business models for rating agencies or alternatives to credit ratings could mitigate existent problems. Rating agencies are being called upon to explain and release the criteria they use for their risk assessments to the public so as to increase transparency for all financial market participants. However, despite these warranted criticisms and the fact that rating agencies bear a great responsibility for the crisis, rating agencies have adamantly defended themselves against the accusations made and continue to deny any responsibility. The defense submitted by the rating agencies is dealt with in the following chapter.

3. The Rating Agencies' Defense – A Critical Review

There seems to be widespread agreement that there is a need for governments and regulatory authorities to intervene, as the US subprime crisis raised concerns about financial stability (Rousseau, 2009). Thus, rating agencies have, to a great extent, become the target of several regulatory investigations and legislative reforms (SEC, 2011a). A number of suggestions and proposals have been made to address the criticisms leveled, as well as what can be accepted and tolerated (SIFMA, 2008). Confronted with criticism and suggestions for improvement, the rating agencies have presented a plethora of responses. Senior managers of the rating agencies have tended to criticize the optimization proposals whilst also defending their approach in evaluating structured financial products in their submissions of testimonies and evidence in hearings of the Senate, House of Representatives, Financial Crisis Inquiry Commission (FCIC) hearings, as well as in comment letters to the SEC. In their defense, Vickie Tillman, at the time Executive Vice President of Standard & Poor's Credit Market Service, stated the following in her *The Wall Street Journal* article on August 31, 2007:

> "The fallout over subprime mortgages has provoked a rush to judgment, and some are now blaming the credit-rating agencies for the recent market turbulence. These charges reflect both a misunderstanding of the work carried out by rating agencies, and a misrepresentation of the overall credit performance of securities backed by residential mortgages." (Tillman, 2007a, para. 1)

Unless critics do not fully understand the depth and sheer volume of information that rating agencies produce, one should not criticize them from an insufficient informed position (Clark, 2012). Rating agencies outlined a variety of factors to try and explain how they failed to predict material downgrades, argued against conflicts of interest, and addressed concerns relating to competition in the rating industry and with reference to the liability issue (Mullard, 2012).

3.1 The Role of Rating Agencies and their Rating in the Capital Markets

In order to counter possible misunderstandings, the rating agencies emphasized that their role in the market is one of an opinion provider, and more particularly, providing an opinion of default risk – regardless of whether they should provide a rating for structured securities, municipal securities, sovereign issuances, or corporate bonds or securities (Clarkson, 2010). They neither participate in the origination of loans, nor do they receive or review individual loan files. They also do not perform any due diligence or audits (Kanef, 2007). Moreover, they neither structure securities nor do they provide any assistance with regard to drafting, editing, or fine tuning legal documents or the terms of debt contracts. In short, "CRAs do not participate in the marketing of a security" (Clarkson, 2010, p. 3). Rating agencies argue that their ratings are public opinions based on qualitative as well as quantitative information, and that their ratings address one issue, and one issue only: the credit risk associated with the rated security (Langohr and Langohr, 2008). Thus, ratings are designed to focus only on the probability that a rated security will default (Tillman, 2007b).

Two of the major rating agencies (Moody's and Standard & Poor's) have pointed out that they are merely expressing a view of the credit quality or general creditworthiness of an issuer's debt security or financial obligations (Wessendorf, 2008). Accordingly, rating agencies emphasize the fact that their role in the structured finance market is ultimately identical to the role that they have played for decades in the corporate bond market (Kanef, 2007). Rating adjustments (whether upwards or downwards) result from deviations in performance based on assumptions and expectations held at the time when the initial rating was assigned. In the case of structured finance products, rating agencies' expectations and assumptions regarding the performance of the underlying asset pool are used to determine the rating, and in the case of corporations' assumptions and expectations (in terms of realized financial plans or business), this constitutes the basis for the rating (Kanef, 2007).

In addition, rating agencies emphasized that they do not actually give any investment advice, and that their ratings do not constitute a recommendation to buy or sell any security or financial instrument (Hunt, 2009). Rating agencies also noted that the ratings themselves do not predict the likely market performance of a security – they *indicate* only the relative likelihood of a debt issuer to repay debt in a timely manner (Tillman, 2007b). Thus, they claim that ratings do not address "whether a rated security is in line with the investor's risk appetite", nor "whether the price of a security is appropriate or even commensurate with its risk"; or if "factors other than credit risk should influence that market price and to what extend" (Tillman, 2007b, p. 4). On the contrary, they claimed to have *discouraged* market participants from using their credit ratings "as indicators of price, [and] as measures of liquidity" (Kanef, 2007, p. 3). However, taking into account that ratings are hardwired into the financial system in the form of contracts, investment processes, and regulatory frameworks, the rating agencies' decisions do have far-reaching, systematic consequences – and viewed from this perspective the matter does indeed look different (Deb et al., 2011).

3.2 Managing Conflicts of Interest

3.2.1 Rating Agencies Business Model

Rating agencies have been accused of having been too lax in their ratings for structured finance products, and for many commentators, the main reason can be traced back to the fundamental conflict of interest generated by their business model: the model in which the issuer pays (Mathis, McAndrews, and Rochet (2009). Responding to this criticism, the rating agencies submitted that the conflict of interest inherent in the issuer-pays model does not present a problem (Hunt, 2009). Concerns regarding this model, they maintain, are not substantiated, referencing the large number of studies that have established that potential conflicts of interest in this business model had either not materialized, or else had been dealt with effectively before the crisis (Tillman, 2007b). However, Strobl and Xia (2012) show that there is evidence that the issuer-pays model bears potential for conflicts and creates incentives for inflated ratings. Managing the conflict in the business model requires rating agencies, as they admit, to balance the competing interests of the two groups (Witt, 2010).

According to He et al. (2012), the conflict-of-interest hypothesis stipulates that rating agencies may assign better ratings to issuers where this behavior may have a substantial influence on their current or future business. In addition, the conflict between the rating agencies' reputation for objectivity, and the promotion of its own activities, coupled with their special status as Nationally Recognized Statistical Rating Organization (NRSRO) in regulation, may further distort incentives on both sides (Altman et al., 2011). This would especially be the case if one considers that under current regulations, holding highly rated securities reduces the burdens for capital requirements (He et al., 2012). If there were straightforward rules, guidelines, and criteria for rating assets, and if "all rating agencies must rate an asset the same way," then from a rational point of view, ratings would be expected to be unbiased (Skreta and Veldkamp, 2010, p. 261). However, rating agencies take the view that it would not be desirable to standardize approaches to ratings, as investors benefit from different experiences, perspectives, and methodologies (ASF, 2011). Furthermore, ratings are to some extent based on "qualitative factors that would be difficult to standardize" (SEC, 2012, p. 10). Nevertheless, there are other factors contributing to ratings inflation.

According to Buiter (2007) agencies face a dilemma because they are subject to multiple conflicts of interest. Senior managers of the rating agencies, in their submission of testimonies at various House of Representatives and FCIC hearings, tended to argue that issuer fees were introduced decades ago into their revenues model and have since then functioned perfectly well. In his testimony on September 30, 2009, Stephen Joynt, President and Chief Executive Officer of Fitch Inc., admitted that the majority of Fitch's revenue came from fees paid by the very issuers they rate, but that these are supplemented by the fees paid for research subscriptions that they offer to different market players (Joynt, 2009b). Rating agencies argue that their business model benefits market participants, as it allows analytical coverage of every asset class in every capital market – a model that allows market participants to freely and fully access the quality of their work in real time (Tillman, 2006). Delivering his testimony before the Financial Inquiry Commission on June 2, 2010, Raymond McDaniel, Chairman and Chief Executive Officer of Moody's Corporation, summarizes this as follows:

> "[...] we believe that offsetting public policy benefits need to be considered. The issuer-pays model of the rating business serves the public policy objective of broad, contemporaneous dissemination of credit rating opinions to the public without charge." (McDaniel, 2010, p. 8)

The issuer-pays model thus promotes and simplifies the exact analysis of the ratings by the market itself, as Hunt (2009) notes. Moreover, rating agencies have a vested interest in avoiding conflicts of interest, since the quality of their credit ratings is their most important capital: their reputational capital (FAZ, September 5, 2007). This in turn guarantees the objectivity and credibility of their ratings and, as a general principle, ensures the reduction of potential influence on the part of the issuers (Sy, 2009). In response to questions as to whether the issuer-pays model has led to rating agencies issuing more or less vigorously analyzed ratings in order to garner more business, Tillman (Standard & Poor's) clarified their position on this question, saying "First and foremost, there is no evidence – none at all – to support this contention with respect to S&P, [...] it would be clearly against S&P's self-interest as well as its cornerstone principles" (Tillman, 2007b, p. 15). It would thus follow that if rating agencies do not deliver sound and objective assessments of a security, they would harm their reputation and in turn, suffer long-term declines in their profits (Pagano and Volpin, 2010).

Defending the issuer-pays model, the major rating agencies emphasized (e.g. in congressional hearings) that the investor-pays model holds potential for conflict, too. Investors, for example, would prefer lower ratings at the time of issuance to obtain higher yields – unlike short sellers of any other security of the issuing company (Richardson and White, 2009). In this case, the investor would benefit from a rating upgrade, whereas, the short seller would lose, and as with the rating upgrade, the securities' prices would rise. This practice permits the short seller, who does not own the stock at the current market price, to cover the transaction at a later date by buying the stock at a lower price and pocketing the difference (Ceresney, Eng, and Nuttall, 2009). This ordinary short selling practice is not prohibited[18] (Jarrow, 2012) as long as regulators (such as the SEC, or Federal Reserve Bank) are satisfied, and the short sales do not convey negative information to the markets, giving the impression that the shorted stock prices are overvalued (Ceresney, Eng, and Nuttall, 2009). If short sellers create the appearance of a declining market by spreading false market rumors to increase their own profits and indeed cause the markets to decline, their activities would be illegal (Frankel, 2006). In terms of rating agencies' announcements, one must consider that these also produce a significant market response (Hooper, Hume and Kim, 20082). Given that short selling enables market participants to achieve financial gains "through *speculating on falling asset price*[s]", it becomes evident that rating agencies' downgrades also "send a crystal clear signal to financial markets, meaning it is time to speculate on the price fall" of securities and "therefore sell short" (Andreff, 2013, p. 20). According to Andreff (2013, p. 20), this illustrates that "rating agencies look like a referee whistling the kick-off of a *definitely winning downward speculative game*". Regulators and the financial market itself ban short selling transactions during times of crisis in order to stabilize the market, as it is argued that short selling encourages price manipulation and speculation, leading to unjustified reductions of asset values that could potentially "contribute to self-perpetuating price spirals in times of panic" (Hendershott, Namvar, and Phillips, 2013, p. 5). However, the short-selling ban in the stock sector in 2008 "did not extend to derivatives market makers", creating possibilities for false rumors (i.e. short selling-speculation) and "opportunities for the migration of short-sale order flow to options and credit default swap (CDS) markets" (Hendershott, Namvar, and Phillips, 2013, p. 6).

When considering conflicts of interest, rating agencies underline that it is in the economic interest of many market participants (investors, issuer and government) that ratings are assigned to securities (McDaniel, 2010). Some now argue that replacing the current issuer-pays model with an investor-pays or dealer-pays model would not only remove potential conflicts of interest, but would also result

18 "Short-selling requires the short-seller to borrow the debt from third party and to sell it on the market" (Jarrow, 2011, p. 13).

in better quality of the ratings (McDaniel, 2010). In this context, rating agencies emphasize that it should be taken in consideration that in cases of possible subsequent changes in securities ratings, investors would prefer upgrades and would not favor downgrades, as the situation on the short seller side would be the other way around (Richardson and White, 2009). This would create an environment in which investors could influence markets, as they might be tempted to force the issuance of biased ratings in order to move markets in a certain direction (Deb and Murphy, 2009). Rating agencies have occasionally proven their vulnerability to conflicts of interest and manipulation (as in the Enron/WorldCom scandals; Carneiro, 2009). This behavior is not consistent with their original role as reliable financial gatekeepers (Partnoy, 2009c), particularly when considering that they should act as reputational intermediaries for evaluating securities (Pinto, 2006). This point is especially relevant, given that it should be their role to improve markets' efficiency by increasing the transparency of securities (Beaver, Shakespeare, and Soliman, 2006).

Rating agencies argue that proposals to replace the issuer-pays model ignore the fact that the rating agencies' ratings in other sectors performed well even during the extremely challenging market conditions of the past few years during and after the crisis (McDaniel, 2010). The issuer-pays model might not be the only workable model, but the advantages and benefits offered by this model may not be available to the market with other business models. In their congressional submissions, rating agencies' senior managers made their position known, arguing that rating agencies whose only source of revenue would be subscription fees would generally limit access to their rating announcements to their subscribers. The result would be a limitation of the free flow of rating analysis to the marketplace (e.g. Tillman, 2006). Developing and maintaining models and hiring experienced analysts are costly, and an approach that would cover the costs by subscription-fees, without receiving issuer-fees, would be very problematic (Tillman, 2007b). Joynt (Fitch) argues that a move from the issuer-pays model to a complete investor-pays model, making the ratings business a purely subscription-based product, could lead to the disappearance of ratings in the public domain (Joynt, 2009b). This would lead to the question of how to access credit risk in the absence of rating agencies' guidance. Without their guidance, it is very likely that investors would see a significant impact on their administrative costs, along with higher levels of uncertainty stemming from a lack of experience in this area (Schüler, 2008). Therefore, as Schüler (2008) notes, and as will be discussed in the following sections, market participants should explore alternative possibilities and methodologies for risk assessment of financial products prior to the removal of ratings in laws and regulations.

The major rating agencies also acknowledged the more benign risk of error, but downplayed its significance, stating that their reputation is far too valuable to the success of their business. The importance of their reputation means that that they would not succumb to the biases inherent in the issuer-pays model or to issuing inaccurate ratings (Lynch, 2010). As reputation and integrity are their most valuable long-term assets, as Tillman stated, it would be imprudent for Standard & Poor's to provide anything other than fair, objective, and independent ratings opinions (Tillman, 2006). She points out that a report by Covitz and Harrison, two Federal Reserve Board economists, published in December 2003, concluded that there was "no evidence" of rating agencies acting in the interest of issuers which would signify a conflict of interest (Tillman, 2007b, p. 16). This, as she said, is indeed the case, and the report concluded that "rating agencies appear to be relatively responsive to reputation concerns and so protect the interests of investors." (Tillman, 2007b, p.16). In her view, this result has since been confirmed by a number of other studies that have come to similar conclusions (Tillman, 2007b).

3.2.2 Individual Conflicts of Interest

Commenting on individual conflicts of interest, the rating agencies stress that they have adopted wide-ranging policies and procedures to avert such conflicts of interest (Elkhoury, 2009). In their defense, the agencies argue that they keep business development strictly separated from credit analysis, so as to make sure that each group is focused on its own core business. In addition, rating agencies' employees are not permitted to own securities in institutions that are rated by the agency. Analyst are, moreover, neither evaluated on the basis of revenues associated with the entities they rate, nor is their compensation based upon the ratings assigned to issuers they cover (Kanef, 2007).

Confronted with increased concerns about structuring the transactions they later rate, rating agencies have argued in congressional hearings that this leads to false assumptions about their independence. Their communication with the originator/issuer is only an open dialogue that ultimately benefits the marketplace. This is certainly not, as is frequently wrongly assumed, a kind of structuring of the transaction (Kanef, 2007). Admittedly, their analysts talk to issuers of structured products, as this is indeed part of the rating process (Cantor, 2009). However, this is of importance in complex structured finance transactions, where contrary to corporate bond transactions, less information is publicly available. Through these dialogues, their analysts get deeper inside the transactions to be rated – including modifications to such transactions that may occur throughout the rating process (Kanef, 2010). In fact, these dialogues support the idea of a transparent rating process, something that regulators have demanded on various occasions (Tillman, 2007b). This point is certainly questionable, as it involves the interplay between private dialogues and disclosure to the public (Lander et al., 2009). Nevertheless, rating agencies state that these types of discussions should not lead to distrust, as some issuers structure transactions to achieve a specific rating outcome. Furthermore, they maintain, without their discussions and reflection, issuers would come forward with one proposal after another, so that, in the end, the structure would meet the issuers' goals, and this would certainly make for anything but a transparent or efficient market (Tillman, 2007b).

3.2.3 Rating Shopping

Since the crisis, growing concern has focused on rating shopping (Utzig, 2010). Regulatory proposals discussed to reform rating agencies have focused on increased competition and the formulation of new rules that would make it mandatory to disclose rating shopping – with the aim of banning it (Deb and Murphy, 2009). Commenting on this point, Moody's pointed out that they share market participants' concerns over the practice of rating shopping (McDaniel, 2010). Further, rating agencies admitted that this was indeed the practice that allowed issuers to choose the rating agencies offering the highest rating for a proposed transaction prior to 2008 (Levine Coburn Report, 2011). Skreta and Veldkamp (2010) looked for triggers that could explain why rating shopping did not come to light until the crisis. The authors stressed that this was possible since, on the one hand, the originator/issuer decides which ratings are going to be publicly disclosed in almost all cases, and because of the increased asset complexity on the other (Skreta and Veldkamp, 2010). The reason for the latter is that for simple assets, rating agencies come to nearly identical estimates. Issuers in such cases publicly disclose *all* rating estimates received to reduce investors' uncertainty. In contrast, for more complex assets, the rating agencies' individual ratings may differ, thereby creating incentives for issuers to shop for the best available rating (Skreta and Veldkamp, 2010). A recent study by Sangiorgi and Spatt (2011) questioned if the enforcement of information disclosure would guarantee unbiased ratings, and showed that rating shopping is harmless when ratings valuation is publicly disclosed, as investors can infer the true value of the financial product from the number of ratings initially solicited. The rating agencies thus argued that rating shopping is not the result of the business model applied, but the result of insufficient disclosure of relevant information for the purposes of assessing a security (McDaniel, 2010). However, in his statement before the Financial Crisis Inquiry Commission (FCIC), Gary Witt, a former Managing Director of the CDO Group at Moody's, argued that it is important to understand that "no single rating agency can address this problem" (Witt, 2010, p. 10).

With a view to contributing to the implementation of appropriate measures, the SEC proposal of December 20009 suggested that rating agencies should be required to make any initial consultation with issuers public, even if the obtained rating is not used. According to the SEC, this would allow investors to ascertain whether any rating shopping occurred, and, moreover to determine whether any rating inflation occurred between the preliminary rating and the final rating obtained by the issuer as a result of shopping around (SEC, 2009). In addition, it would allow investors to better understand the risk inherent to the securities they are buying, and also, as Deb and Murphy (2009) note, effectively ban rating shopping. Fitch reacted to the disclosure issue in its comment letter to the SEC dated September 9, 2011, on Rule 17g-5 under the Securities and Exchange Act of 1934 (as amended) (Brown, 2011). Commenting on the rule that requires NRSROs to disclose certain conflicts of interest, Fitch responded that they suggested strengthening the rule for greater disclosure requirements for *all* rating agencies. This would entail requiring all rating agencies to publicly disclose all transactions, regardless of whether or not the final ratings were actually provided by them. Making this kind of information public would allow investors to make comparisons and identify which NRSROs reviewed the transaction and which one ultimately rated the transaction, thereby significantly increasing the transparency surrounding the originator/issuers selection process of NRSROs ratings (Brown, 2011).

The new SEC requirements are further intended to strengthen the disclosure of information that rating agencies request from the originator/issuer regarding the underlying collateral of structured securities (SEC, 2011c). The amendments were finally adopted to ensure greater disclosure of rating agencies' methodologies in determining credit risk. The desired increased transparency in rating agencies' processes is intended to simplify market participants' independent risk analysis by using the information provided by NRSROs (SEC, 2011c). Such transparency would ultimately benefit parties, investors, and the originator/issuers. (Frost, 2006). However, rating agencies argue that disclosure of preliminary ratings would not prevent rating shopping for originator/issuers, and instead they would be motivated "to shift their rating shopping to an earlier stage in the process" (Zarin, 2013, p. 5). Although Moody's cannot tell, as Zarin (2013, p. 2) notes, what would be the "right" business model, nor do they "take a position on what the correct industry structure should be", they do believe that ratings should only be treated as probability analysis of credit risk. It follows that regulators should not use ratings for the oversight of other sectors or industries (Zarin, 2013). These issues are addressed in Chapter 6.

3.3 Competition Amongst Rating Agencies

A number of commentators have criticized the oligopolistic market of rating agencies and the regulatory environment in which they operate, (White 2009a). In their comments on this issue, Joynt (Fitch) pointed out that many market participants and commentators argue that there are no difference between the major three agencies. Indeed, the media coverage of the rating agencies and related regulatory inquiries tend to characterize the rating industry as being "dominated by the big three" (Joynt, 2009a, p. 2). However, he emphasized that "not all credit rating agencies are the same", and on issues like credit culture, he would like Fitch to be judged on its own merits (Joynt, 2009b, p. 2). Although their processes and methodologies look similar, there are indeed differences (Rona-Tas and Hiss, 2010). Fitch's internal audit processes were robust and their staff level appropriate for keeping pace with the growth in business. Allegations that are related to another NRSRO are specifically related to individual NRSRO, and should not therefore be commented upon by any other one (Joynt, 2009b).

In his comments, Michael Rowan, Managing Director of Moody's Investors Services, pointed out that there are over 100 rating agencies around the world, only ten of which are registered with the SEC as NRSROs (Rowan, 2011). Moody's competes in a large field of opinion providers, but sees other rating agencies not only as competitors, but also as providers of purely quantitative and market-based measures of credit risk, such as bond price indicators and credit default swaps. Moody's, Rowan said, had continuously been supporting regulatory initiatives to encourage competition and thereby increase the number of diverging, occasionally contrary opinions (Rowan, 2011). Moreover, healthy competition amongst the various opinion providers is good for the market overall, as it provides incentives to improve the quality of opinions and hence the quality of ratings over time. However, healthy competition, as Rowan (2011) noted, is not best achieved by increasing the number of rating providers, if the diversity of rating opinions declines at the same time.

Rules for competition need to be rigorously applied to make sure that rating agencies compete on the basis of the reliability and usefulness of differing and independently formed judgments to support an efficient information capital market. In Moody's view, regulatory demands or proposals for having a sole predictor would be unhealthy for the markets (Rowan, 2011). Rowan further argued that Moody's thinks that markets thrive when the regulatory landscape allows for, and encourages, differing views. Hence, it would be equally important not only to tolerate, but rather encourage adverse perspectives. Moody's has been a strong advocate of competition in the industry – as long as that competition occurs on the basis of credit ratings quality (Rowan, 2011). Fitch shares this view, and has also emphasized that the markets would benefit from different viewpoints, expressed in different ratings from different rating agencies (Joynt, 2009a). All the rating agencies have pointed out that their unsolicited ratings should, in this context, be seen as a benefit to the market, as unsolicited ratings contribute to generating greater competition amongst rating agencies as they enable smaller rating agencies to compete with the 'Big Three' (Van Roy, 2006).

Tillman expressed that in Standard & Poor's view, the right path towards more competition would be for the SEC to adopt a more inclusive, transparent, and streamlined NRSOR designation process – but not by tearing down a system that worked well for decades (Tillman, 2006). While supporting initiatives to create a more transparent and streamlined NRSRO system, Standard & Poor's is against any legislative or regulatory scheme to further increase the number of designated rating agencies that would compromise the quality of protection provided by the existing NRSRO system. This, in Standard & Poor's view, would provide poorer service to investors and the market, as NRSROs' ratings are a crucial proof of quality. However, Tillman admits that the existing process by which NRSROs are designated by the SEC can be seen as a barrier to entry (Tillman, 2006). For this reason, Standard & Poor's explicitly supports activities to allow more *qualified* rating agencies in the market.

Deven Sharma, President of Standard & Poor's, welcomed the fact that the recently adopted Credit Rating Agencies Reform Act (CRARA),[19] lowered the barriers of entry for other rating agencies to register as NRSROs. The new agencies that have registered since then[20] include rating agencies that operate with different business models, such as the investor-pays model and/or apply different processes and methodologies to determine their ratings, a development that provides increased information and a larger number of points of views for investors

19 The Credit Rating Agencies Reform Act of 2006 (CRARA) was enacted into law on September 29, 2006. (Congress, S. 3850 – 109th).

20 The 2011 Summary Report of Commission Staff's Examinations of each Nationally Recognized Statistical Rating Organization (NRSRO) from September 2011 names another seven registered credit rating agencies in addition to Moody's, Standard & Poor's, and Fitch (SEC, 2011a).

to choose from within the marketplace (Sharma, 2010a). Although more competition can give market participants access to more information about credit risks, it would be against regulatory efforts to mitigate conflicts of interest and rating shopping and might aggravate the situation as was noted with reference to existent academic literature in Chapter 2. In this context, Bolton, Freixas, and Shapiro (2012), as well as Becker and Milbourn (2011), find that increased competition actually exacerbates the phenomenon of credit shopping, as it gives issuers even more opportunities to shop around for the best rating. The latter argument was also brought forward by Witt (Moody's) in his statement on the Credit Rating Agencies Reform Act of 2006, focusing on increased competition among rating agencies to combat rating shopping. In his view, this has even worsened the situation (Witt, 2010). Furthermore, when arguing that more competition could decrease rating inflation and resolve conflicts of interest, it is often overlooked that the reward of maintaining one's reputation is considerably less important when the market is divided by numerous rating agencies (Camanho, Deb, and Liu, 2012).

3.4 Liability

Confronted with the accusation of not being called to account for their errors of judgment associated with the US subprime loans, rating agencies cited the constitutionally protected First Amendment right to freedom of speech (Harper, 2011). Rating agencies argue that they have the same free-speech rights to comment on matters of public concern as any other person or entity. This freedom of speech extends to include making informed and well considered predictions about the future (Joynt, 2009a). The position they took is that they are financial publishers, and their published opinions are thus analogous to newspaper editorials, for instance (Krebs, 2009). The latter argument is also put forward when they are sued by issuers who claim that they have been injured by the actions of the rating agencies (White, 2010), and as ratings are matters of public interest, the 'actual malice' protection (as established in landmark 1964 Supreme Court ruling New York Times Co. v. Sullivan)[21] is the correct legal criterion – and most courts have recognized this argument (Kettering, 2008).

In court proceedings and questions of guilt (this is rarely the case)[22], the rating agencies routinely pointed out (and continue to point out) that there

21 See Kettering (2008), supra note 449.

22 See Rosenblatt and Golvin, 2009: U.S. District Judge Shira Scheindlin refused to dismiss a lawsuit against the two major Rating agencies Moody's and S&P, rejecting arguments

was no breach of obligation on their part to aggrieved investors with whom they had no express contractual agreement (Kettering, 2008). They stress the disproportionateness of investors' excessive reliance on ratings, when the investors were in fact warned that these ratings comprised merely an expression of opinion – not investment advice (Partnoy, 2009c). Ratings are only assessments, not legally binding statements (Harper, 2011). Their most common response to the First Amendment defense is therefore that one cannot fault them for their opinion (i.e. congressional hearings). Nevertheless, this is not the only defense strategy of the rating agencies. In cases where investors claim that their dealings with rating agencies were established by contract and would like to take action against rating agencies, they will find that the rating agencies not only negotiated the terms of such contracts, but explicitly disclaimed any liability (Krebs, 2009). The agencies accordingly claim that they are not responsible for any errors or omissions (Harper, 2011). In addition, the argument that rating agencies act as a fiduciary for investors fails, as in the investment sector, fiduciary duties "are implied only where there is a more specialized relationship than that which exist between a rating agency and its subscribers" (Krebs, 2009, p. 156).[23] Moreover, their disclaimers inform and advise investors

---

that investors cannot sue the rating agencies over deceptive ratings of private placement notes with the argument that those opinions are protected by free-speech rights. "The ruling may affect Fitch Group Inc. and other raters [...] '[I]t's the first major ruling upholding fraud allegations against an arranger and the rating agencies on the instruments that are at the heart of the financial crisis' said lawyer Patrick Daniel[s]"; see Stempel, (2012) "[J]udge Shira Scheindlin refused to dismiss claims accusing Moody's Investors Service and Standard & Poor's of negligent misrepresentation over their activities regarding Cheyne and Rhinebridge structured investment vehicles. She also dismissed claims alleging aiding and abetting fraud, breach of fiduciary duty and negligence. A third rating agency, Fitch, is also a defendant it the Rhinebridge case." Her decisions were issued on Friday, May 4 and issued on Monday, May 7, 2012. Tony Mirenda, a Moody's spokesman, said that the cases are without merit, pointing out that remaining claims against Moody's will be dismissed. John Piecuch, an S&P spokesman, said that the ruling on negligent misrepresentation is inconsistent with decisions of other courts and that S&P will defend itself against the claim. Fitch spokesman Daniel Nooan made a similar comment, saying that Fitch will continue to defend the case.

23 Krebs (2009) as cited in supra note 195: "Husisian, supra note 33, at 457. In his article, Husisian notes that „As parties' relationship changes from one of private counseling to one of public offerings of information, the client's fiduciary interest declines, and the publisher's first amendment protections increase. Once the publication reaches the level of general publishing, where the clients are known to the publisher only by names b a mailing list, the publisher's fiduciary duty diminishes to zero. Thus, Standard &

not to rely on their ratings (Langohr and Langohr, 2008). Rating agencies claim that their ratings are not irrefutable facts, but rather mere expression of views (Krebs, 2009). Exposing rating agencies to litigation by investors, issuers, and others when these disagree with the rating, might, therefore, have a not-insignificant effect on the agencies' willingness to publish their independent opinions (Langohr and Langohr, 2008).

The major rating agencies support the concept of greater accountability for their work, but disagree that more liability would be the best way to achieve this goal. In their defense, the rating agencies claim that they are already liable under current securities law to the extent that they intentionally – or with gross negligence – make material misstatements or omissions (Harper, 2011). Moreover, under the anti-fraud provisions of current US securities law, any plaintiff may make claims against a rating agency. The anti-fraud provision provides a legal mechanism for investors who are injured by violations of law. The argument provided by these rating agencies, however, fails to take into account the fact that 'secondary actors' are exempted from the anti-fraud provision. Such actors that can fall within this category are accountants, attorneys, securities analysts, to name but a few – and rating agencies themselves (GAO, 2011). From the rating agencies' standpoint, however, separate and additional liability standards for designated rating agencies (NRSROs) are both unprecedented and unnecessary (Joynt, 2009b). Given that current and pending legislation regulates only NRSROs, it is very difficult to believe that unrecognized rating agencies would try to gain their reputation and status as NRSROs, particularly as such a status would subject them to greater accountability and liability than would be the case without this designation (Coffee, 2010; Harper, 2011). In his prepared statement, Stephen Joynt argued:

> "What rational rating agency would continue to be part of the NRSRO system if there is compelling reason to do so, yet be willing to incur the significant costs and enhanced liability associated with it? In terms of competition and new entrants, what firm not currently recognized as an NRSRO would ever apply for the designation?" (Joynt, 2009b, p. 4)

The arguments put forward by the rating agencies did not consider the fact that exclusion from the anti-fraud provision is available to rating agencies that

---

Poor's has ample support for its contention that '[ratings] do not create a fiduciary relationship between Standard & Poor's and users of the ratings sine there is no legal basis for the existence of such a relationship."

are regulated under section 15E of the Securities Exchange Act as 'NRSROs' (SEC, 2011b).

3.5 Trancperency in the Rating Process

Lack of transparency was a further point of criticism addressed with regard to the rating agencies. There is little knowledge as to how ratings are made (Benmelech and Dlugosz, 2010), as the major rating agencies make their rating determinations in secret, as part of their propriety process of evaluation (Partnoy, 2006). Hence, the secretive nature of the evaluation process makes it difficult to evaluate their ratings (Ellis, Fairchild, and D'Souza, 2012).

To counter concerns relating to the lack of transparency in the rating process, Joynt (Fitch) argued that Fitch has always stressed the importance of transparency and the integrity of its ratings and credit opinions. These targets are even more important than other implications and have precedence over any revenue-generation strategy (Joynt 2009b). He further emphasized:

> "Those in the market that allege that our ratings are a 'black box' must not be fully aware of the information we make available, or they do not fully appreciate the concept that the rating is not a simplistic mathematical output, but rather a committee decision based on a range of quantitative and qualitative factors." (Joynt, 2010a, p. 13)

Similar comments were made by the other major rating agencies in testimonies before the Senate, House of Representatives, and the FCIC (Sharma, 2011a). Increasing transparency, however, could create confusion and fear in the markets, as many funds invest in structured finance products without being required to disclose such investments, thus making it unclear where different interrelated assets are held. This, in turn, could lead to a "crisis of confidence" – and it is a matter of enlightened self-interest to the rating agencies to enhance transparency in the area of "who holds what" (Kanef, 2007, p. 24).

3.6 Perceived Weakness in the Rating Process

In debating whether the rating agencies contributed to the crisis of 2007, critics emphasized failures in the methodologies employed by the rating agencies. The SEC staff examined rating agencies and their practices, arriving at the conclusion that rating agencies struggled significantly with the increase in volume and the complexity of RMBS and CDOs (SEC, 2008b).

Faulty Methods. Confronted with criticisms about their methods and the quality of their ratings, the rating agencies defended themselves with the argument that their assumptions were based on historical data (McCleskey, 2010).

They had no prior experience to draw on, and no kind of information as to how MBS portfolios/bonds would behave in difficult times. In this context, they pointed out that until 2005, real estate prices in the United States had climbed continuously, and that there had been no nationwide depression in this market sector before the housing bubble burst (Weill, 2010).

For MBS issued before 2005, there were only very minor adjustments registered; for post-2005 MBS, however, there were historically high downgrades averaging three to ten rating notches (Ashcraft, Goldsmith-Pinkham, and Vickery, 2010). In their defense, the agencies argued that the actual performance and the sharp reduction on MBS reflected unexpected exogenous shocks, as the drastic decline in housing prices in 2007 took most market players by surprise (Mullard, 2012). Nevertheless, the decline in house prices in the United States was accompanied by rating agencies' downgrades on asset-backed securities from AAA to below investment grade, causing great uncertainty in the global financial markets, and confronting investment banks with a need to provide additional collateral (Mullard, 2011). In 2007, the rating agencies adjusted their ratings for MBS worth USD 1.9 trillion, most of them facing a downgrade from risk-free to junk status (Gupta, Mittal, and Bhalla, 2010). A more comprehensive study by the Financial Inquiry Commissions Preliminary Staff from June 2, 2010, reported that at the time of preparing the report, securities downgraded amounted to USD 2.5 trillion in RMBS and USD 564 billion in CDOs (FCIC, 2010).[24]

Commenting on such findings in their submissions of testimonies and evidence, the rating agencies' senior managers tended to argue "the case that their decision to downgrade to below investment grade of US$4 trillion of asset-backed securities value that they had previously rated as AAA did not represent a failure of the rating agencies", but reflected market forces in a wider context (Mullard, 2012, p. 78). In the rating agencies' comments on complaints about the accuracy and completeness of their methodologies used to assess the risk underlying structured products like residential mortgage-backed securities (RMBS), Tillman emphasized that Standard & Poor's had had an excellent track record in assessing RMBS default probabilities (see Table 1) (Tillman, 2007b). These default statistics are a critical measure in rating analysis. However, ratings do not address factors such as supply and demand, which influence securities' prices, as ratings reflect only assumptions about timely repayment (Tillman, 2007b).

24 According to the staff report, "these are the total principle amount of securities that were *ever* downgraded; securities that were downgraded multiple times are only counted once" (see supra note 31, p 33).

Once again, the rating agencies pointed out that they do not rate the mortgage loans underlying a mortgage pool; they evaluate only the credit characteristics of the mortgage pool as part of their RMBS rating process (Krebs, 2009). Thus, the rating agencies' role in the process of establishing a rating consists of reaching an opinion as to what extent and by what amount they believe the underlying loans are likely to generate earnings (Tillman, 2007a).

Response to Deterioration in the Subprime Market. In their testimonies with reference to questions concerning whether they reacted too slowly to the deteriorating situation in the subprime market, the rating agencies countered by saying that they believed these questions resulted from an incomplete understanding of the facts (Tillman, 2007b). Contrary to what is expressed sometimes they had begun to issue warnings to the market starting in 2003 (Kanef, 2007). Moody's warned that there would be a crash in house prices, resulting in a significant double-digit decline (Mullard, 2012). All three major agencies further argued that in response to the increase in riskiness, they enhanced the levels of credit protection on pools of subprime loans, and repeatedly informed the markets of their views. However, they did admit that as no one can see the future, and they had "not anticipate[d] the magnitude and the speed of the deterioration in mortgage quality" (McDaniel, 2009, p. 3).

In their submissions, rating agencies furthermore argued that they should not be held solely responsible, as a variety of factors contributed to the deterioration in the subprime market. As argued by the rating agencies, these factors have been well debated and documented, and include "historically low interest rates; policies that promoted home ownership; a sudden and sever nationwide decline in home prices; and an equally sudden and severe contraction of refinancing credit" (Clarkson, 2010, p. 2). As explained by Clarkson, "taken together, these factors had the effect of increasing default rates among borrowers to levels far higher than Moody's and others in the market anticipated" (2010, p. 2). Another major factor that contributed to the housing bubble and the sharp corrections that came later resulted from the constant erosion of underwriting standards that had taken place between 2003–2006. Many market participants have also suggested that fraud stemming from misrepresentations made by mortgage brokers, appraisers, and the borrowers themselves played a significant role in the deterioration and exacerbated the problem, as the rating agencies emphasize in their defense (Kanef, 2007).

Model Risk. The Financial Stability Forum (FSF) report published on April 7, 2008, criticized the inclusion of inadequate historical data as a key factor for significantly increased model risk (Utzig, 2010). The major rating agencies were criticized for their inadequate correlative risk assumptions (Levine Coburn Report, 2011). Witt (Moody's) reacted with the following statement:

> "[A]ll CDOs backed by RMBS have performed very poorly as the US has sustained the largest nationwide decline in house prices in its history. This is not a result of lower rating standards at Moody's." (Witt, 2010, p. 27)

Analysts at Moody's and Standard & Poor's used various models to determine the probability of default within MBS. As it was not their duty to perform analyses of individual entries, the data received from third parties used to calculate the default probability was assumed to be correct (Kanef, 2007; Mullard, 2012). However, the quality of their rating opinions could be influenced during the input process in cases where the data received was erroneous, for instance as a result of misrepresentation or incomplete information that did not reflect real market conditions (Kanef, 2007).

Witt observed various correlation problems with Moody's CDO model, and he told the Subcommittee[25] that he felt uncomfortable with the lack of correlation and the methods applied by Moody's. Furthermore, a Bloomberg article from September 2008 criticized Moody's, claiming that the Correlated Binominal Model (which Witt had worked on from 2004–2005) allowed securities firms to sell more top-rated subprime mortgage bonds than ever (Smith, 2008). As the Financial Crisis Inquiry Commissions staff and other governmental investigators had used this article, which Witt maintained was misleading, as the main source of information about Moody's rating practices, Witt too referred to this article in his prepared statement given before the Financial Crisis Inquiry Commission (FCIC). Witt responded to the issue by pointing out that the purpose of the Correlated Binominal Model was not to eliminate the diversity score problem of the BET model, but to explicitly integrate correlation into the model (2010). However, the new methodology introduced by Moody's did not go as far as Witt had proposed. He pointed out that he had no doubt that Moody's were doing something wrong for CDOs with RMBS as underlying assets (Levine Coburn Report, 2011). Thereafter, Moody's had adopted a new model in June 2005: a simpler Correlated Binominal Model called CDOROM. The model was updated in September 2005, and was made easier to use as a Normal Copula simulation (Witt, 2010). Further key model adjustments were made by the major rating agencies in 2006 (for their RMBS and CDO models), which were designed to improve their ability to predict

25 Subcommittee interview of Gary Witt, Former Managing Director, Moody's Investors Service (10/29/2009), cited from Levin, C. (Ed.) Wall Street and the Financial Crisis: Anatomy of a Financial Collapse (2011: supra note 1140).

expected losses and defaults for mortgages with higher risk (Levine Coburn Report, 2011). Since the Bloomberg article made the assumption that the former BET approach was superior to the later-used correlation-based model (CDOROM) for "ABS CDOs modeling the highly correlated subprime RMBS," Witt clearly stated that he disagreed with these assumptions in general, and especially the notion "that the large volume of subprime CDOs would not have been issued, had Moody's continued to use the BET for rating ABS CDOs" (Witt, 2010, p. 28). In elucidating this point further, he questioned why investors continued buying ABS CDOs at increasingly lower spreads if rating standards were declining, as the Bloomberg article had asserted (Witt, 2010). However, in the follow up to the developments in the subprime loan sector, rating agencies adjusted their models and their assumptions to take the growing risk into account, specifically with regard to loss expectations and credit protection. Kolchinsky (Moody's) delivered one possible explanation for this when pointing out that the increased use of synthetics transactions has changed the nature of the ABS and CDO market, and thus changed "the nature, the role and the incentives of the players in our market" (Kolchinsky, 2010, p. 3). He stressed that this new way of trading, with the ability to go short, evoked "a new class of 'investors' whose goal was to maximize losses" and that rating agencies' models and assumptions never anticipated the impact of the new players (Kolchinsky, 2010, p. 3). Unfortunately, as they emphasized, they did not anticipate the magnitude of the downturn, but they were "far from alone in that regard" (Clarkson, 2010, p. 2).

Within the framework used to analyze RMBS and CDO transactions, Standard & Poor's uses in an initial step: their so-called LEVELS® model (Loan Evaluation and Estimate of Loss System). Based on individual loan characteristics, the LEVELS® model calculates probabilities of default and (expected) loss realized upon default. However, rating agencies do not dictate the terms of loan contracts; they only collect the data from the originator/issuer and do not perform any review. Standard & Poor's argues that they rely on these participants (originator/issuer) to fulfill their roles and obligations to verify and validate the information before these are passed on to the rating agencies (Tillman, 2007b).

Richard Gugliada, a former head of the Standard & Poor's Global CDO Group, admitted that the underlying assumptions about correlative risk in S&P's models were wrong, but that this was only part of the reason for the inaccurate RMBS and CDO ratings issued by Standard & Poor's (Levine Coburn Report, 2011). Standard & Poor's used (and still uses) a Monte Carlo simulation model called CDO Evaluator – a model designed to estimate the default-rate distribution in collateral portfolios. To determine a rating, the model takes into account the borrower's credit rating, the probability of default, and the maturity and correlation between each asset pair, and then presents the default rate probability distribution of the aggregated portfolio as a result (Picone, 2002). However, Gugliada emphasized that Standard & Poor's considered higher default rates in their models, since they believed that underlying assets defaulting together was more likely to happen for MBS than for corporate bonds held in CDOs) (Levine Coburn Report, 2011). Moody's also continuously increased loss expectations for subprime loan pools and the credit protection level in its models. In the end, rating agencies had to discover that even these increased credit protection measures were not sufficient to maintain the stability of their ratings in an environment of market upheaval where unprecedented levels of mortgage defaults were coupled with declining house prices (Clarkson, 2010).

Disclosure of Rating Methodologies. With the growing concerns about the rating agencies' methods, rating agencies publication policy also came under criticism (Frost, 2006). Although rating agencies generally support the concept of greater disclosure, they do believe that the responsibility for disclosing such information should rest entirely with the issuers and the underwriters – *not* with rating agencies. Furthermore, disclosure of additional information is of questionable value in the rating agencies' view, if the accuracy and reliability of such information is doubtful. This refers directly to due diligence, and due diligence is not, and should not be, the responsibility of rating agencies (Joynt, 2009a).

Defending their approach, the rating agencies argued that they had used proven modeling, made material process disclosures, and carried out appropriate ongoing monitoring. Furthermore, their models and methodologies were accurate and valid on the date when the ratings were prepared and published, even if they were later downgraded (Kanef, 2007; Rom, 2009). Moreover, they further claimed that their methods are publicly accessible through the Internet on their websites (Sharma, 2011a; Tillman, 2007b). The rating agencies also emphasized that they make announcements to the public about any changes to the applied models, meaning that their basic criteria are available for public criticism and comments (Tillman 2007b; Joynt 2010a; McDaniel 2010).

As articulated by Teresa Wyszomierski, Vice President of Structured Finance Derivatives at Moody's, their "methodologies and models which made public online are fully transparent [...] making any digression immediately obvious to market participants" (Wyszomierski, 2007, p. A15). It was also argued that the rating agencies hold the rights to their methods. Demand for publication of their methods would attract free riders (see Darcy, 2009), undermining the individual quality of the rating agencies' risk analyses, and all incentives to innovate would be lost. This would effectively leave the market with a smaller number of similar ratings instead of larger pool of ratings based on different methods and analyses (Partnoy, 2009c). In such a scenario, credit ratings would no longer represent a rating agency's differentiated perception of credit risk based on its independent assessment; it would also reduce the transparency of the securities market to the detriment of investors. Deven Sharma (Moody's) highlights that the independence to develop their own methodologies lowers the systematic risk that one rating could no longer be distinguished from another (Sharma, 2011a). Pressure from the regulatory side to use a common methodology throughout all rating agencies would not only deprive investors and other market participants of a variety of differing approaches to information, but also hinder advances in analytical methods (Sharma, 2011b).

In this context, the rating agencies emphasized that they already publish extensive information about their procedures and methodologies to enable outsiders to understand how rating agencies arrive at their rating opinions. This information includes their opinion of each rating category, the time horizon used in determining a rating decision, and the definition of default (Kanef 2007, Tillman 2007). Furthermore, the rating agencies disclose reports describing the development of individual rating opinions in accompanying releases (e.g. Cantor, 2009). In addition, studies of historical default rates of different rating categories are also published. Full disclosure, however, could result in issuers structuring their financial products in accordance with the published methodologies – which could entail adverse effects on the quality of ratings issued. Another consequence of this could be reduced flexibility, as changes in rating methodology would be more difficult to adopt as they would immediately impact outstanding ratings, a further negative effect (Witt, 2010). Following the proposed additional rules on disclosure (SEC, 2008a), the major three rating agencies announced that they would implement measures to improve the accuracy and integrity of the data underlying their rating decisions (Rom, 2009).

Market and liquidity risks. The rating agencies argued that ratings are designed to be stable and, unlike market prices, do not fluctuate on the basis of market conditions (Tillman, 2007). They argued that understanding what a rating constitutes is critical, particularly as this must be seen against the background that the market turmoil was not the result of widespread defaults of rated securities, but was instead based on the tightening of liquidity and significant falls in market prices. Moreover, ratings do not speak to what the market value of a security should be or the potential volatility of its price, which could be significantly influenced by other factors underlying credit quality (Sharma, 2011a). Michael

Kanef (Moody's) commented in his testimony that Moody's was developing additional financial tools to measure fundamental values and potential volatility in securities prices, and that such tools could respond to unmet market needs (Kanef, 2007). Adopting such measures could also lighten the burden on the existing rating system by potentially reducing misuse of ratings for purposes other than what they are designed to do. However, as he stressed, given that for the time being such models do not exist, they do not know whether they would be successful in developing such models or if financial market participants "are interested in – and would benefit – from using them" (Kanef, 2007, p. 23). The 2010 Dodd Frank financial oversight law is intended to ban any reliance on NRSROs ratings in banking rules, yet struggled to provide feasible alternatives (Clarke, 2011).

Terminology. Some suggestions contained a number of provisions that appeared to be redundant, contradictory, or overly formulaic from the rating agencies' point of view (Joynt, 2009b). For example, the House Bill of December 11, 2009[26] required drawing a distinction in the symbology of fundamental securities and structured finance products, as well as the requirement that rating agencies standardize rating terminology and approaches across all asset classes. The rating agencies were willing to continue to implement reasonable and balanced steps to enhance the market's confidence in the rating agencies and their ratings (Joynt, 2009b). In this regard, rating agencies continued to communicate with market participants and public sector authorities in order to garner a better understanding of the different concerns raised, and the resultant recommendations proffered to enhance transparency. They share the belief that many of the proposed changes would be likely to enhance greater accountability, but they remain concerned that some of the proposed measures seem to be contradictory in nature, as "some would promote diversity of opinions, others would discourage it" (McDaniel, 2010, p. 2). Mandating standardized rating definitions would promote the application of homogenous analysis among all rating agencies, undermining the value of different approaches and opinions in the market. Such approaches would be against reforms of improvement and could provoke unwelcome effects. Standardization would "effectively 'shoehorn' all credit rating agencies into taking the same approach to analyze creditworthiness" – an approach that would lead to one uniform view of credit risk to make investment decisions (Sharma, 2011b, p. 2).

---

26 Wall Street Reform and Consumer Proection Act of 2009, 'H.R. 4173', in 111th Congress (ed.), (House of Representatives 2009), passed the House on December 11, 2009, URL: http://thomas.loc.gov/cgi-bin/query/r?r111:@OR+(+@1(H.R.+4173)++@1(H.+R.+4173)++) (Retrieved June 15, 2012).

In responding to this statement and associated measures, Deven Sharma,[27] President of Standard & Poor's, expressed the view that standardization of terminology used by the rating agencies would not be wise or desirable; commenting:

> "Having multiple assessments based on different methodologies, conveyed in a transparent fashion, provides more information to investors and other market participants. Standardization would deprive investors and other market participants of a diversity of approaches and information and [...] would hinder analytic advancement. Mandating a uniform terminology [...] would have the effect of stifling competition within the credit rating business by restricting opportunities for innovative approaches that differ from the standard." (Sharma, 2011b, p. 2)

Although the three major rating agencies utilize a rank ordering as the general theme for their rating system design, there are differences as to what they rank. Standard & Poor's focus lies on attachment probability, whereas Moody's focus is on expected losses, whilst Fitch's is a combination of both: attachment probability and expected loss (e.g. Prince, 2005). According to the rating agencies, this has been seen as a benefit for the markets because having multiple ratings in the marketplace that express different interpretations of creditworthiness afford market participants greater insight. Further, as the nature of rating agencies' opinions differ, rating symbols should not be standardized, either, and regulators should, therefore, encourage rating agencies to adopt distinctive symbols.

Against the background of the intensified debate about the rating agencies' approaches to assessing structured products, Fitch announced on April 29, 2008, that it would evaluate and define an additional rating scale for structured financial products in order to enhance transparency. Fitch, however, emphasized that these rating scales would not replace the existing ones. Fitch, as well as Standard & Poor's, announced plans to add the letters "SF" to their ratings to facilitate identification. This indicator was introduced at the end of 2011 to identify a bond as a structured product. However, this does not entail any kind of change in the rating agencies' opinion or definition of ratings (Fitch, 2011b).

3.7 Regulatory Role of Rating Agencies

The importance of rating agencies in financial markets was compounded by their legal status, one that entrenched their influence in millions of financial transactions (Segal, 2009). Hardwired into financial contracts, the judgments of the major rating agencies on the safety of different bonds was an *official* determinant for

27 Comment letter on File No. 4–622, dated February 7, 2011.

most American financial institutions' bond portfolios (White, 2009b). From the rating agencies' point of view, removing any reference to NRSROs in all federal statutes, while at the same time seeking to significantly increase the federal regulatory requirements and the overall burden on NRSROs seems contradictory (Joynt, 2009b). In congressional hearings, the rating agencies tended to argue that they themselves are asking to be freed from their quasi-regulatory role (FT Editorial, July 26, 2011). Sharma (Standard & Poor's) said in a *Financial Times* article from July 25, 2011 that reducing "what some perceive as the excessive influence of ratings in financial markets and the financial policy process" would be a more thoughtful way as commentators have requested (Sharma, 2011c, para.4). He also pointed out that "rating agencies do not claim to be the sole voice expressing reasoned views about the future" (Sharma, 2011c, para. 11). The more relevant question for the financial system would be how ratings are used by regulators and policymakers, and how their reliance on ratings in determining their decisions may contribute significantly to their focus on rating agencies' opinions (Sharma, 2011c).

Rating agencies responded to the issue of a perceived over-reliance on ratings by stating that the market would be best served if legislation and regulation of the credit rating industry were consistent with the role these companies play in the market (Rowan, 2011). Proposals on how to reduce such over-reliance by eliminating the use of ratings in regulations, or eliminating the whole concept of NRSROs, may appear simple in principle, but this elicited several strong responses from the rating industry. Ratings are an important benchmark used constructively in many places in regulation: as Joynt (2009a) underlines, they are used as benchmark to assess the relative credit risk of a debt issue, and are widely used in legislation, in the rules of regulators, and in private financial contracts. These rules distinguish between whether securities or the entities issuing them have received investment grade ratings from NRSROs, or if the benchmark has not been reached. Therefore, as the rating agencies emphasize, the NRSROs system plays an important role in the regulatory landscape that would otherwise not be available. Abolishing the system without creating a suitable replacement or substitute for the NRSROs system (a system that frees savings and loans, pension funds, and others from the limitations imposed on them by the regulators, both at the Congressional and state level), would create a regulatory vacuum that could expose investors to unjustifiable risks (Tillman, 2006). Further, if regulators were to eliminate the use of ratings of designated rating agencies (NRSROs), and thereby permit financial entities to make their own credit risk assessments without reference to the benchmarks provided by the NRSROs, market participants would develop their own guidelines, which in effect would be a continuance of a rating system, albeit in another form. Considering the fact that regulators would like to increase competition in the rating industry and thereby foster improved rating results, they concluded that such moves would ultimately have negative effects (Joynt, 2009a). What may look simple and appropriate is, in reality, impractical, as there is still no organization in the position to take on the rating agencies' role in financial markets. The only practical way to increase accountability would, in the view of the rating agencies, be "mandating minimum credit standards," as this would "put a floor on market share motivated free-falls in methodologies and restrict completion to where it belongs – price and services" (Kolchinsky, 2010, p. 5).

3.8 Conclusions

The primary focus of this chapter has been to critically highlight and discuss rating agencies' responses to the accusations made against them that emerged during the course of the crisis of 2007–2008. Senior managers of rating agencies repeatedly stressed that "all major market participants, including the CRAs, did not predict the depth of the crisis," and that the crisis was a result of exogenous events (Mullard, 2012, p. 77). Rating agencies recognized the anxiety and frustration in the financial market resulting from unprecedented market conditions in the subprime mortgage market. They stressed that their role in capital markets is only that of providing opinion, arguing that market participants should not use ratings as indictors of price or measures of liquidity, nor as an explicit or implicit recommendation for buying or selling securities. However, against the background of regulatory requirements for which ratings have to be used as a benchmark for capital adequacy rules, many investors are thus required by law to rely on ratings. In light of this, the argument is not as convincing as the ratings agencies portray it to be.

The ratings agencies downplay accusations that they face conflicts of interest in terms of their business models. Such concerns are groundless, they maintain, as their business models benefit market participants, and enable for the contemporaneous dissemination of ratings opinions to the general public without charge. From a purely economic point of view, delivering anything other than sound and objective risk assessments would compromise their reputation, resulting in long-term declines in profit. Moreover, a change to the investor-pays model would also bear possible conflict potential, as investors would prefer lower ratings at the time of issuance in order to raise profits with rating upgrades at a later date. It is a major issue for rating agencies to balance the interests and concerns of both groups – the issuers and investors. Given that any feasible business model bears potential conflicts, rating agencies believe that any such potential or possible conflict must be assessed together by counterbalancing the public benefits that arise from them. Efforts that attempt to improve the utility and reliability of rating agencies' 'products' should begin to recognize the limitations of a market-based business model, as the challenge lies in achieving safe and sound (ratings) results through the practice of using independent rating agencies for the estimation of risk in financial investments.

Rating agencies claim that the accusation that they structure transactions to their benefit is a misunderstanding of the business model. Their communication with the issuer is of particular importance in the structured finance market, as less information is publicly available in this market sector. These dialogues support what is required: greater transparency. Their interaction with the issuer, however, raises another point of criticism: the rating shopping behavior of issuers, which pushes rating agencies to inflate ratings. It was claimed that it is this ease to move from one NRSRO to another NRSRO that largely contributed to that rating agencies assigning inflated ratings. This was possible given that there was no requirement (though changes are currently under discussion or have already been implemented) to publicly report the rating agencies issuers had contacted to obtain their rating, nor the ones they were compensated by for their service. In their defense, rating agencies argue that it is that behavior of sophisticated issuers of clandestine operations that contributes to the problem, and that no rating agency alone could address the problem. Meanwhile, new rules require greater disclosure, and *all* rating agencies are now obligated to publicly report any ratings activity, regardless of whether the final rating was provided by them or not. In light of the fact that the rating agencies have proven their occasional exposure to conflicts of interest, this does not seem to be consistent with their original role of serving as reputational intermediaries in the financial markets.

Furthermore, many complain about a lack of competition in the rating industry and advocate for greater competition as the market is dominated by the 'Big Three' agencies. In response to this particular criticism, the rating agencies argue that they compete in a large field of opinion providers and that they support initiatives to increase the range of opinions in the market. However, healthy competition in the rating market would not be best achieved by increasing the number of rating providers. Proposals to standardize methodologies and terminology and to have one sole predictor would be counterproductive, as it would lead to limited quality and compromise the accuracy of ratings. They believe that greater flexibility to incorporate new information or conditions relating to credit risk in their methodologies, a larger diversity of views as to how such information should be applied, and more transparency with respect to underlying assumptions and methods, would be of greater benefit to investors. This flexibility, in turn, would also help to ensure greater competition. The challenge, in their collective view, is therefore striking the right balance between the desire for more reliable risk-assessment opinions based on reliable methodologies for the financial markets, the desire to reduce reliance on the 'Big Three' ratings agencies, and guaranteeing independent competitors in the rating industry.

The methodologies and terminologies used by rating agencies have been closely scrutinized by academics and other commentators. While rating agencies and some advocates argued that rating agencies did not anticipate the massive downgrades of asset-backed securities as their mathematical models did not capture the new mortgage loans, it turned out that "their models [...] did not capture the new mortgages", but instead continued to use historical data (Mullard, 2012, p. 93). Rating agencies claim that regulators, banks, and other market participants all made the same errors in risk management, given the fact that they all missed the economic downturn in the US housing sector. Rating agencies argue that they do not rate the individual mortgage loans in the underlying asset pool of structured securities; they only evaluate risk characteristics as part of their rating process, establishing an opinion as to what extent and to what degree the underlying loans are likely to perform. Unprecedented defaults in the underlying mortgages and the subsequent massive downgrades of securitized assets led to questions as to whether rating agencies reacted too slowly. From the rating agencies point of view, such questions result from an incomplete understanding of the facts. They began warning the markets in 2003 that there would be declines in housing prices, repeatedly updated their assumptions, and enhanced the levels of credit protection on pools of subprime loans. However, they did not anticipate either the speed or magnitude of the deterioration in the mortgage sectors. Their decision to downgrade a larger number of securities that were previously highly rated does, as they emphasize, not constitute a failure of the rating agencies, as these downgrades resulted from a wider context of market forces and reflected the actual situation on the market.

Given the pivotal and quasi-regulatory role that rating agencies play in today's financial markets, along with the fact that rating agencies' opinions are hardwired into financial contracts, their judgment has far reaching consequences. Some proposals advocate for reduced reliance on ratings and removing any reference to NRSRO in federal statutes. From the rating agencies' standpoint, this seems contradictory when at the same time it is argued that regulatory requirements and the overall burdens for rating agencies should be increased. A more relevant question in their opinion is how the ratings are actually used by regulatory authorities. It may look simple to reduce overreliance on ratings, or to even eliminate the whole NRSROs concept, but without a suitable alternative, this would create a regulatory vacuum that would expose investors to unwanted risks.

The rating agencies' faulty methodology did lead to enormous losses and ultimately, the collapse of the global financial market – not least due to the regulatory use of ratings. Not surprisingly, rating agencies have been sued by many institutional and individual investors, state attorneys general, and governmental authorities not only in the United States but around the world for fraudulently inflating ratings for structured finance products, effectively hiding the inherent risk of default (Zhou and Kumasr, 2012). Nevertheless, rating agencies relied and continue to rely on the First Amendment defense, classifying their ratings as opinions and claim their protection under NRSRO status when defending accusations. They argue that given that ratings represent only their view, no one can fault them. Exposing them to greater liability when market participants disagree with ratings would reduce their willingness to publish their judgments, which in turn would reduce the number of rated securities. It is, as Harper notes, "unrealistic to hold CRAs liable for the full value of issues they rate because it could subject them to crushing liability" (2011, p. 1970). Thus, as Harper argues, "liability must be limited to a fraction, or at most a small multiple of the fees CRAs earn" (2011, p. 1970). This defensive behavior is actually at a 'tipping point' as the Australian Federal Court ruled that Standard & Poor's had engaged in misleading and deceptive conduct with investors and was therefore liable for the investor's losses (see Chapter 2). Never before had rating agencies been found to owe a duty of care to investors, but they continued to hide behind their First Amendment defense.

When considered together, the conflicts of interest faced by the rating agencies, the methods they use for assessing the risk embedded in sophistic structured financial instruments, and the actual liability standards applied to rating agencies, there remains substantial room for suspicion regarding the evaluation of credit risk, the methods they apply, and the rating process in general. To provide a better understanding of what rating agencies do and do not do when rating structured finance products, the rating process as it is practiced must first be evaluated, and it is this issue that is outlined in Chapter 4.

4. The Rating Process

As one of the most important forms of financial innovation that has developed in recent years, asset securitization plays a major role in capital markets (Lapanan and Anchev, 2011). The rapidly growing market for these innovative financial instruments was one of the main factors that contributed to the crisis of 2007–2008 (Solomon, 2012), and has since been a main focus of attention. A considerable number of rating downgrades on structured finance products, such as mortgage backed securities (MBS) and collateralized debt obligations (CDOs), have given rise to doubts about the nature of these products (Fender, Tarashev, and Zhu, 2008). In addition, concerns have been raised relating to the quality of ratings and the integrity of the rating process (Hunt, 2009).

The intense interest of market participants in how rating agencies conduct the process of rating a structured finance product can be attributed to the high number of subprime mortgage-backed securities and CDOs issued (Hu, 2007). As there is excessive reliance on external ratings provided by rating agencies such as Moody's, Standard & Poor's, and Fitch, it is important to understand how credit ratings for structured finance instruments are developed – and what they mean (Carter and Watson, 2006). For this reason, this chapter covers the process used to rate structured finance products in order to provide the background information necessary to gain a greater understanding of the structured finance transaction.

All three major rating agencies apply a common set of basic analytical principles to all sectors: a rating decision is made by a rating committee for both traditional bonds and structured finance instruments, based on information and documentation specific to the instrument to be rated. In the case of structured finance products, market participants must be aware of any risks arising from the transactional structure. For instance, default risks not directly related to the underlying assets in the pools are designated as collateral, which may affect the risk of the structured finance products' tranches (Fender and Kiff, 2005).

The reliability of structured finance ratings is dependent on two primary factors: the rating agencies' ability to carry out effective risk assessments for the underlying asset pool, as well as the accuracy of the modeling of the cash–flow distribution from an underlying pool of exposures used to service different stratified risk positions or tranches. For this reason, the major rating agencies follow a two-stage approach (Fender and Kiff, 2005). Given the fact that they dominate the market, their methods can be regarded as representative, as variances in individual rating criteria are of little practical relevance (Serfling, 2007). The following discussion is (primarily) based on publications issued by the three major rating agencies and focuses on the basic structure of how they compile and process their ratings for structured finance transactions.

A fundamental differentiation needs to be made between unsolicited and solicited ratings. The key difference, as van Roy (2006) notes, is that solicited ratings are obtained through a cooperative dialogue with the issuer, where non-publicly accessible (confidential) information also plays a role. In contrast, unsolicited ratings solely rely on all publicly available and relevant information that rating agencies can gather (Adair and Hutchison, 2005). This chapter presents an overview of (1) rating agencies' rating definitions; (2) how structured finance products are created; and (3) the basic rating process for structured finance products. Since each of the major rating agencies uses their own methodology to determine ratings (Rona-Tas and Hiss, 2010), however, this chapter should be seen as a general overview of the various factors commonly applied to structured finance transactions rather than looking at specific nuances.

4.1 Rating Symbols, Definitions and the "SF" Modifier

Rating agencies utilize a ranking order that is meant to indicate the likelihood of default within a defined range from extremely safe to highly speculative. To do this, they use a system of symbols from AAA down to D. These symbols are defined by adding modifiers (plus or minus), or other modifications to the grading scheme[28]. Rating symbols used by the major agencies roughly correspond, since they use the symbol BBB or above (including modifiers) for products carrying an investment grade rating, thereby establishing a uniform definition (Cantor and Packer, 1994).

Rating agencies define their ratings as a forward-looking opinion about the relative credit risk inherent in issued financial obligations (Moody's 2012b). In many cases, as Coval, Jurek, and Stafford (2009) observe, structured finance instruments are rated in bunches of multiple tranches of liabilities, where the tranches represent the various credit quality and seniority. Ratings assigned to such liabilities deal with the probability of the specific tranche performing in accordance with the policies of the relevant documentation. Although rating definitions look similar, it is important to distinguish between the meanings assigned to for the relevant transaction by each rating agency. Ratings typically

28 As described in detail in Chapter 2.

reflect a particular probability of default. However, some agencies' ratings may also include "an expected recovery rate given default, that is, an expected net loss, rather than the probability of a loss occurring" (Carter and Watson, 2006, p. 89). The description of the rating type assigned to a specific tranche is included in any pre-sale or new issue report, and in some cases requires that any non-rated aspects or carve-outs in the transaction have to be disclosed in the legal opinions and the offering circular (Carter and Watson, 2006).

The major rating agencies distinguish between short-term and long-term financial obligations. Short-term ratings are normally assigned to issues where the rating agencies' opinions take into account the originators'/issuers' ability to honor their short-term financial obligations. Such obligations normally carry a maximum life span of 13 months and are designed to reflect the likelihood of a default for committed payments. In contrast, long-term ratings are generally assigned to issues with an original maturity profile of one year or more (Moody's, 2012a). These ratings reflect not only the likelihood of default on payments contractually agreed upon, but also the financial losses that investors would incur in the event of a default (Moody's, 2012a).

In the wake of the financial crisis, both the European Union Regulation for Credit Rating Agencies (EU CRA Regulation) and the International Organization of Securities Commissions Code of Conduct Fundamentals for Credit Rating Agencies (IOSCO Code) required that ratings for structured finance ratings be differentiated from corporate bonds, preferably through a different rating symbology (IOSCO, 2008b). Since 2010, the major rating agencies have differentiated structured finance products from other fundamental ratings[29] by adding the modifier "sf" to such products. The identifier, added to all asset-backed securities,[30] has two main objectives. First, its function is to eliminate any presumption that ratings for such products and regular securities carrying the same letter rating will behave in the same way. Secondly, it ensures that similarly rated structured finance products and regular securities can have different risk characteristics (Moody's 2012b). However, the modifier "sf" does not change the meaning or definition for such instruments, nor does it change the risk of any particular structured finance instrument. Expectations about the performance

29 That is, ratings on non-financial corporates, financial institutions, and public sector entities; see Moody's "Rating Symbols and Definitions" (2012a).

30 Including residential mortgage-backed securities (RMBS), commercial mortgage-backed securities (CMBS), collateralized debt obligations (CDOs), and asset-backed commercial papers (ABCPs), Fitch (2011b).

of structured finance instruments should not be interpreted as having been adjusted in any way by the "sf" modifier (Fitch, 2011b).

4.2 Creation of Structured Finance Instruments

Rating agencies contribute something to the creation of structured finance products that would otherwise not exist. This lies, as the rating agencies explain, in the very nature of structured finance, and the degree of their interaction with the originator/issuer. The interactional process "is not only beneficial to the structured finance market but almost certainly a perquisite to having any kind of structured finance market at all" (Standard & Poor's, 2007, p. 2). Structured finance products such as ABS, MBS, and CDOs are created by means of the securitization of assets that are, by virtue of their nature, non-tradable and therefore non-liquid. The key element of securitization is the fact that repayment is based on the assets and cash flows generated by the underlying collateral – not the overall strengths of the originator (Vink and Thibeault, 2008). Securitization enables the issuer to aggregate cash flows from assets transformed into a package of securities backed by these assets, to structure the priority of payments, and sell the securities with ratings that are in accordance with investors' tolerance for risk (Coval, Jurek, and Stafford, 2009; Standard & Poor's, 2007).

Securitization determines a product whose special characteristics distinguish it from other forms of risk transfer, as it shifts the risk of the underlying asset pool via tranching of claims (Fender and Mitchell, 2005). A key objective of the tranching process is to create different security classes with various risk-return profiles (BIS Working Group, 2005). The specific characteristic of tranching for such products is that their performance and their ability to ensure timely payment of interest and ultimately, repayment of the principal, are separated from the performance of the originator. Although such securities differ in terms of their form and degree of complexity, they do have much in common in terms of their senior-subordinated structure, where the various tranches of the debt-instrument issued are paid by the pooled cash-flow generating assets in line with their seniority. While a distinction can be made between ABS, MBS, and CDOs, when looked at in economic terms (Vink and Thibeault, 2008), all structured finance securities are either cash flow or synthetic transactions (Khadem and Parisi, 2007). In cash-flow transactions, the ownership of assets is transferred to a special purpose vehicle (SPV), whereas in a synthetic transaction, only the risk associated with the assets is transferred. Furthermore, in cash-flow transactions, principals and interest are transferred along with the risk (Khadem and Parisi, 2007), see Figure 1 below.

Figure 1: Securitization Process.

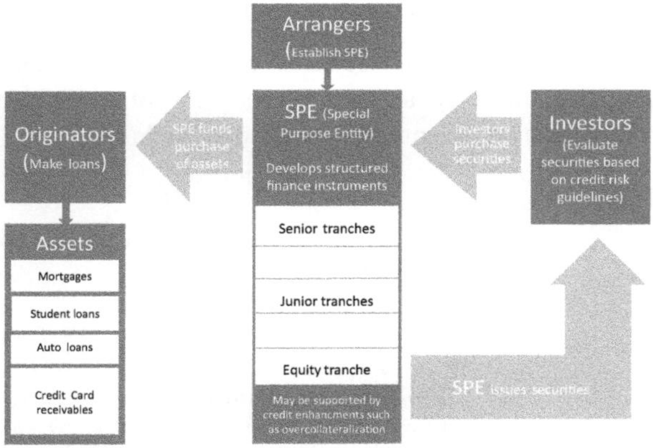

Source: adopted from Standard & Poor's (2012a).

For sliced financial products, such as CDOs, the claims against the underlying asset pool are ranked in order of their priority. These tranches contain the following levels of seniority: senior and mezzanine tranches, and an equity piece (the so called 'first-loss piece'; Fender, Tarashev, and Zhu, 2008). Whereas one of these securities may be considered nearly risk-free from default with a AAA rating, others are often high-risk, as the payments generated by the underlying asset pool are initially used to make the required payments to investors holding AAA bonds before any funds are available to the holders of the other, riskier bonds (Kanef, 2007). In case of default, "the equity/first loss tranche absorbs initial losses, followed by mezzanine tranches which absorb some additional losses, again followed by more senior tranches" (BIS Working Group, 2005, p. 1).

Matching available risk and the markets' appetite for risk provides the structured finance market with the possibility of obtaining and accessing cheaper pricing in all financial markets. This all can be achieved by adopting a simple device such as tranching, which allows for greater symmetry between both parties in the transaction: the sellers of risk and the buyers of risk (Standard & Poor's, 2007). The securitization and tranching of assets can enhance an issuers' creditworthiness. However, as it might be difficult to assess the constructional structures for each tranche risk-return characteristic, credit ratings assessed by rating agencies may have limitations with regard to their ability to fully reflect the risk of sliced securities (Fender and Mitchell, 2005).

4.2.1 How Rating Agencies Conduct the Rating Process for Structured Finance Instruments

While the process for rating structured finance instruments is generally similar to the process that rating agencies use for rating corporate and government issues, there are some key differences, as outlined in Table 3.

Table 3: Structured vs. Traditional Credit Ratings

Structured finance versus traditional credit ratings: commonalities and difference

Issue	Structured finance	Traditional
Rating process	Basically identical: analyst review, credit committee	
Rating concept	Identical rating basis: expected loss (EL) or default probability (PD)	
Structural features	Tranching can create securities with same expected loss, but much different unexpected loss properties	Expected loss may be a reasonable proxy for credit risk
	More "complex" - extensive analysis of "moving parts" required	Structural features, such as bond covenants, exist - but analysis less extensive
Credit risk analysis	Controlled environment enables more model-based, quantitative analysis of asset pool; emphasis on the relatively easily definable cash flow generated by the underlying asset pool; known maturity	More limited scope for quantitative analysis of overall balance sheet/franchise; emphasis on the cash flow generated by the obligor's ongoing business activities (issuing entity is going concern)
Conflicts of interest	Exist in both cases	
	Between originators, investors, third parties - more transparent, easier to control, requires structural mitigants	Between shareholders, different debt holders, management - more difficult to control (covenants)
Nature of rating	Pronounced ex ante nature (targeted ratings, iterative process, rating issued at inception); more model-based; greater flexibility to adjust structural factors	Ex post, though with ex ante elements (pre-rating feedback, issuer first rated in mid-life); more judgmental; limited issuer ability to adjust credit characteristics
Performance	More stable on average, but larger changes - significant instability of particular asset classes	Benchmark for structured finance ratings via EL/PD mapping

Source: BIS Working Group (2005, p. 15).

Whereas rating agencies establish their ratings based on quantitative models in the first case, in the latter, their assessment requires the separation of criteria regarding a company's performance in terms of its long-run condition and likely competitiveness throughout its lifetime (Ashcraft and Schuermann, 2008). These differences not only influence the way in which the rating process is initiated and carried out, but they also have a significant impact on the kind of information rating that individual analysts review (Standard & Poor's, 2012a) process. In structured finance transactions, the primary focus of the analysis is on the financial instrument rather than conducting an in-depth analysis of the originator/issuer's liquidity risk profile (as is the case for corporate or governmental bonds). Given the nature of structured finance transactions, another form of dialogue is required (Standard & Poor's, 2012a). The reason for this is that in contrast to traditional non-structured transactions, structured finance transactions require rating agencies to be involved in the structuring process. This stems from the fact that "a tranche rating reflects a judgment about both the credit quality of the underlying collateral asset pool and the extent of credit support that must be provided through the transaction's structure in order for the tranche to receive the rating targeted by the deal's arrangers" (BIS Working Group, 2005, p. 2). The process thus requires the assistance of rating agencies.

The issuer of a structured finance instrument has a desired rating outcome and will be tempted to compose the underlying asset pool and structure the transaction so as to meet the criteria published by the rating agencies (Standard & Poor's, 2012a). This involves, *inter alia*, obtaining the rating agencies' structuring opinions, at least to the point of using their publicly available models to pre-structure the transaction. In addition, this also entails engaging in an iterative dialogue with rating agency analysts in order to obtain a pre-evaluation of the rating agencies' opinion and to decide on the final form and structures to be used (BIS Working Group, 2005). The pre-evaluation helps rating agency analysts to determine if additional information is required, as well as to identify specific matters and arguments the issuer needs to put forward at the management meeting. The purpose of the management meeting is to give rating agencies the opportunity to probe for pertinent information in greater detail (Standard & Poor's, 2012a).

There is typically some reciprocal action between the originator/issuer and the rating agency during the rating process regarding the applicable criteria concerning the composition of the asset pool and the transaction structure (Standard & Poor's, 2012a). This, along with the fact that the originator/issuers may adjust structures to meet the rating agencies' criteria, has led some commentators to question whether the ratings analysts assume an advisory role (Standard & Poor's, 2007). It would, as the rating agencies point out, be an entirely wrong to conclude that they serve as advisors because such an interpretation would be based on fundamental misunderstanding of their service (as already mentioned in Chapter 3). In this context, it should be remembered that in non-structured finance transactions, the rating process also involves a dialogue with the rating analyst. This is because it is the rating analyst who routinely discusses the rating agencies' preliminary views on the matter with the issuer (Standard & Poor's, 2007).

The rating agencies' perspective is deliberately based on reviewing public and private documentation and information, and is aimed at establishing the deal's subordination levels (described more fully below) to achieve a particular security rating (e.g. Fitch, 2011b). They compile the information and data forwarded to them in order to determine credit worthiness. The purpose of a credit rating for structured finance instruments is to provide a tool for the investor, to the extent of helping them to make appropriate assessments of the issuers' ability to fulfill the contractual payment obligations (Carron, Dhrymes, and Beloreshki, 2003). However, the rating agencies' rating does not reflect risk factors[31] such as prepayment risk, which may affect investors' returns. It is instead the rating agencies' opinion about the credit risk associated with the transaction (Forti and Iaconelli, 2001).

Ratings do not address any possible potential losses of the market value of structured finance products that may arise from illiquidity and interest rate risk, which can, in addition to credit risk, have a negative impact on investors' returns (Hu, 2007). Liquidity risk, is as Matz and Neu (2006, p. 100) note, prospective – a risk calculated on the probability "that future events produce adverse consequences" (the same counts for interest rate risk). Structured finance products are generally not listed or are only thinly traded on a stock exchange (Roxana, Oana, and Alexandru, 2010). As a consequence of this, there is no secondary market for this type of product; an investors' ability to sells these securities prior to maturity is therefore low or non-existent (Acerbi and Scandolo, 2008). Although structured finance can generate higher yields during periods of low interest rates, investors are exposed to risks that predominantly arise through changes in interest rates. This is the case when there is a mismatch of fixed/floated interests between the assets and liabilities of the structure (e.g. fixed-rate paid asset coupons and floating paid liabilities; Culp, 2011). This means that securities with a long maturity are subject to higher liquidity risk *and* interest risk. Overall, though, rating agencies' risk assessment is a systematic mechanism for identifying and evaluating events that could affect structured finance transactions (Forti and Iaconelli, 2001).

31 Described in greater detail in section 4.4.

The rating process generally involves the following steps: initial evaluation, pre-analysis, proceedings of the rating process, the committee process, the communication of a decision and the assignment of the final rating (Carter and Watson, 2006).

4.2.2 Request for Rating

With regard to structured finance transactions, the rating process is typically initiated when a rating agency has been contacted by, or on behalf of, a securities originator/issuer (Reiss, 2006). In the initial phase that follows, the formal request is made from the originator or issuer and a discussion is held via conference call (or brief meeting) in order to present an overview of the proposed transaction (Khadem and Parisi, 2007). The originator or issuer presents all information on pertinent issues (including background details, strategies, operational systems, historical performance data, and any other relevant information regarding the originator/issuer) to the rating agency (Reiss, 2006). The rating process will be initiated after an informal discussion with the originator/issuer concerning the proposed securitization transaction and structure, (Forti and Iaconelli, 2001). The subsequent rating procedure followed by all major rating agencies starts in a similar way and ends with the publication of the rating for the rated originator/issuer and issues (Khadem and Parisi, 2007). Once a rating is assigned, it is monitored by an analyst at the rating agency (Siddaiah, 2011).

4.2.3 Pre-Analysis

The major rating agencies generally follow a two-stage rating approach, which is applied equally to CDOs and traditional ABS (BIS Working Group, 2005). In the first stage, rating agencies assign a primary analyst (PA) who coordinates all analytical matters and is responsible for formulating a rating recommendation. After this, the rating agencies review the information package provided by the originator regarding the assets proposed for securitization, and the proposed terms and conditions of the securities to be issued. At this point, the rating agency will also discuss the parameters and the transaction type, the applicable transaction criteria, timing, and documentation of the transaction, its legal structure, as well as cash-flow models with the originator or issuer, as needed (Moody's, 2012a; Standard & Poor's 2012c). A rating agency's review of the documentation does not include any audit, and the rating is based on the representations made by the various parties involved in the transaction (Khadem and Parisi, 2007).

The rating agencies determine a stabilized net cash flow, the value of the asset pool, and calculate estimates of how much debt may be rated based on the selected range of parameters. This can help the originator/issuer to evaluate the proposed transaction and to assess whether or not it is satisfactory from an economic point of view (Forti and Iaconelli, 2001). The tools applied to analyze the asset pools may differ between the major rating agencies according to the nature of the underlying assets (Fender and Kiff, 2005).

4.2.4 Proceeding of the Rating Process

Based on the outcome of these dialogues, the originator is free to decide whether or not to further proceed with the rating process (e.g. Standard & Poor's 2012a). If a rating agency believes that the public and private information provided is not reliable or sufficiently detailed, no credit rating will be assigned or maintained by the agency (e.g. Fitch, 2011c). When the preliminary results are accepted by the originator/issuer, and a signed engagement letter has been received, an analyst team will then be assigned to rate the transaction. The decision to proceed initiates a more detailed review. This is the beginning of the second stage in the rating process (Forti and Iaconelli, 2001). In the case of a multi-seller conduit[32] the second step will be repeated many times over, whereas this may occur only once in a single-seller case (Moody's, 2012b).

The second stage of the process involves structural analysis (Fender and Kiff, 2005). In this phase, which significantly depends on the deal specifications detailed in the structured finance documentation (Fender and Kiff, 2005), rating agencies supplement the previously received information by asking the originator/issuer for more specific details relating to the assets and/or the transaction (Griffin, Nickerson, and Tang, 2013). Generally, this requires rating agencies to have a detailed cash-flow model and to conduct site inspections, and undertake a legal evaluation of third parties involved in the transaction, such as servicers and asset managers (Fender, Tarashev, and Zhu, 2008; Standard & Poor's, 2012a). The result of the extended cash-flow analysis may in turn feed back into the applied models in the form of adjustments made to the assumptions used in the first model. At the end, all the information is aggregated and mapped together into a single, alphanumeric tranche rating, which is chiefly orientated on the historical performance of corporate bonds (in case of CDOs) or historical loan data (e.g. Fender and Kiff, 2005). The findings are then presented to a rating committee for further discussion.

32 A multi-seller conduit is a special-purpose entity that regularly buys a variety of assets from many sellers. For this reason, a multi-seller conduit provides more diversification and is potentially less risky than a single-seller conduit. A single-seller conduit buys assets only from one originator.

4.2.5 The Committee Process and Communication of Decision

The rating agency's analyst in charge of the transaction (typically the primary analyst [PA], who often works together with other analysts who have already evaluated similar transactions) completes the evaluation of the principal analytical considerations based on both quantitative and qualitative factors. The results from the information review, incorporated into the credit analysis and loss determination, are then recommended by the PA to a rating committee (Forti and Iaconelli, 2001). This committee has a safeguarding function in that it limits the influence that any one individual person may have on a rating agency's rating opinion.

The rating committee has more than one role in the rating process. First, it reviews and assesses the primary analyst's rating recommendation for a new rating or rating changes. Second, it ensures that there are checks and balances against conflicts and undue influence. Finally, it assures consistent application and adherence to standards of rating criteria (Standard & Poor's, 2012a). The rating committee fully discusses the asset pool's issues relevant to the deal, particularly the credit analysis, risk factors, model output, relevant legal issues, the performance history and trends of transactions with similar collateral (Fitch, 2011c). Its evaluation is based on a discussion of the main analytical factors, which are summarized in an internal report presented by the PA. The report explains the background for the long-term rating, short-term rating, and the outlook for the specific issuer (Standard & Poor's, 2012a). This ensures that the final ratings are consistent with the ratings that have hitherto been issued for similar structured finance transactions (Hu, 2007). However, the structure is analyzed by more than one rating committee in some cases and for some asset classes. In such instances, the final rating is determined by a subsequent committee (Fitch, 2011c; Hu, 2007; Standard & Poor's, 2012a).

Standard & Poor's may thus, for example, hold more than one meeting in cases where a presale report is published. The published pre-sale report includes a preliminary rating that has been voted upon by the committee. Even when a preliminary rating committee is held, the final rating will ultimately be determined following discussions in a final rating committee's meeting (Standard & Poor's, 2012a). The issuer is first notified of the rating decision before the rating is communicated to the public. This enables the originator/issuer to present their opinion, should they not be satisfied with the decision (Cantor and Packer, 1994). If the issuer is not satisfied before the rating is assigned, they can submit new and significant information to support their view. If an appeal is granted, the rating agency once again convenes a committee meeting to review the new information provided and vote again (Fitch, 2011c).

4.2.6 Assigning the Final Rating

After the rating decision is made, the rating letter and pre-sale reports and rating action commentary (RAC) are drafted (Fitch, 2011b, 7). The final report summarizes the main expectations reflected in the rating, along with any conditions that may lead to a raising or lowering of the rating in the future (Standard & Poor's, 2012c). Once the rating committee has made its final decision, the result is communicated to the originator/issuer. Final ratings may differ from the preliminary rating results conveyed in rating agencies' pre-sale reports due to changes noted in the provided or obtained information and/or the transaction structure. In cases where the final ratings do not differ from the expected rating outcome in the pre-sale report, no subsequent notification to the originator/issuer is needed. The final published rating is then subjected to an ongoing monitoring process (SEC, 2008c).

4.3 Areas of Analysis

The estimation of risks associated with securitized assets is carried out in different ways depending on various factors. These factors include, but are not limited to the following areas:

- Default risk – the inherent risk of default in the underlying mortgage portfolio in which the default would result in a payment shortfall for the securities investors who will then "not receive their due interest and principal" (Buckberg et al., 2010, p. 6). To assess the risk of default, the rating agencies focus on the issuers' financial strengths (Pottier and Sommer, 1999).
- Financial asset maturity – the risk of default rises with the length of maturity, as the likelihood of potential hazards occurring increases over a longer period. It thus follows that the probability of default increases the longer the expected time to maturity or the higher the weighted average lifetime of the structured finance transaction is (Carter and Watson, 2006). Rating agencies therefore calculate expected reductions of yields and the limitation of the maturity to integer values (Raynes and Rutledge, 2003).
- Prepayment risk – the risk that a security can be prepaid at any time, thereby reducing the weighted average lifetime of the security and exposing investors to a high degree of uncertainty surrounding future cash flows (Fabozzi, Davis, and Choudhry, 2006). If the investor of a fixed-rate mortgage security were to

be repaid much sooner than anticipated, the investor would face a loss, as he can now only reinvest in lower interest rated securities (Buckberg et al., 2010). For this reason, rating agencies analyze the impact of fast and slow prepayment rates, along with the issuers' ability to meet their obligations in accordance with the terms of the transaction (Standard & Poor's, 2012c).

- Substitution criteria – there are many transactions that involve either revolving assets or contain re-investment periods. For such transactions, rating agencies require exact specifications to be made in the transaction documentation, defining the criteria for assets that can be newly acquired, the maximum maturity of the transaction, and other factors. Credit enhancement is then adopted to take its exposure under the worst-case scenario into account (Carter and Watson, 2006)

4.3.1 Analyzing the Financial Structure of the Transaction

In order to ascertain the potential for loss in structured finance products, rating agencies must evaluate several factors (Reiss, 2006). The senior-subordinated debt structure plays a central role, where the distribution of the cash flows from the underlying asset pool amongst the different tranches follows particular rules. This structure enables rating agencies to develop low-risk securities that help to solve the "asymmetric information problem" (Allen, 2008, p. 42), as investors rely on rating agencies' "quality certification [...] and ascertain credit quality differences between different tranches based mainly of their ratings" (Allen, 2008, p. 45). This is important, as from an the issuer's perspective, the least possible subordination would be the preferred option (as they can sell subordinated tranches only at a discount, but the more senior tranches at a premium), whereas investors buying senior tranches prefer as much subordination as possible in order to receive default protection. For a structure of this kind, the subordination levels represent key variables, as they indicate the proportion of credit support the senior tranches gain from the subordinated levels. Rating agencies thus play an important part with regard to price determination and risk management for structured finance products, (Xudong et al., 2008). These associated issues are discussed in greater detail in Chapter 5.

Subordination is a critical point in the analysis, as it constitutes a cushion from default for the higher seniority tranches (Xudong, 2011). The term '"subordination" describes "any hierarchical payment relation in general parlance, but in the context of CE [credit enhancement] it usually signifies priority in the allocation of principal" (Rutledge and Rayes, 2010, p. 62). Assuming that the senior tranche has 20% subordination means that this slice has the rights to the first 80% of cash flows due from the underlying collateral asset pool. Considering subordination as the only credit enhancement in the structure, the senior tranche will not face any losses unless the limit of 20% of the scheduled principal is reached (Buckberg et al., 2010). As the default risk of subprime collateral is higher compared to the collateral of standard real estate finance, securities with subprime collateral are designed by applying a variety of mechanisms "called 'credit enhancement' to mitigate and reallocate the default risk" (Buckberg et al., 2010, p. 6). The most common forms of credit enhancement are tranching, over-collateralization and excess spreads (Buckberg et al.2010). However, rating agencies experienced a "learning by doing" approach in this rapidly growing market sector, and there is no standard subordination design (Xudong et al., 2008, p. 11). It is typically the originator/issuer who proposes the framework and structure for the debt, after which the rating agencies draw up their independent evaluation to determine whether the structure can achieve a particular rating for each tranche (for instance AAA, AA, A, and BBB). Each rating agency uses its own model to determine the level of subordination, though the individual assessments are generally conducted under similar framework conditions (Xudong et al., 2008).

The actual model applied in the rating process depends to a large extent on the transaction type. In cases of more complex structured transactions, which differ from straightforward transactions with fixed payments, the payments are passed through to the investor in a 'waterfall' structure (Hu, 2007) The waterfall payment structure provides structural protection and dictates how the cash-flow payments from the collateral are distributed amongst investors (Buckberg et al., 2010). Rating agencies' simulations incorporating waterfalls are designed to provide protection to tranches with a higher level of seniority and to investigate the financial product's performance under particularly extreme situations (Crouhy, Jarrow, and Turnbull, 2008). This is important because in order to assign ratings to structured finance products, the rating agency must be in a position to model the entire portfolio, and the dependence structure of defaults (Coval, Jurek, and Stafford, 2008). The loss distribution gives rating agencies the opportunity to determine the credit enhancement (CE): the amount of loss on the underlying collateral that can be captured before the respective tranche absorbs any losses (Ashcraft and Schuermann, 2008).

Based on the collateral analysis and stress tests of the proposed structure, rating agencies define the amount of CE needed to receive a particular credit rating for an issue (Fabozzi, Davis, and Choudhry, 2006). CE offers the advantage of additional protection against default for all or any part of the securities (Standard & Poor's 2012a). In order to determine the adequacy of the CE, rating agencies use cash-flow simulation models in which each of the major rating agencies uses its own model (Crouhy, Jarrow, and Turnbull, 2008). Moody's for instance, evaluates the credit enhancement by using "the 'so-called' expected loss approach" to determine the expected loss in an asset pool based on different scenarios (Güttler and Wahrenburg, p. 756). Standard & Poor's and Fitch go further, basing their evaluations on "the so-called weak link" approach (Batchvarov, Collins, and Davies, 2004, p. 38). In this technique, "rating agencies look at the confluence of different entities or assets in the structure" in order to pinpoint the weakness, that means the point where the structure could break down (Batchvarov, Collins, and Davies, 2004, p. 38). The advantage of this method is that the final rating cannot be higher than the weakest link in the chain. This enables rating agencies to determine what they describe first-dollar lost – another rating approach determines the likelihood that a security will lose its first dollar of principal, in contrast to the expected loss assessment (Batchvarov, Collins, and Davies, 2004). Rating agencies determine the presumed severity of losses and fix an approximate frequency and probability with which such losses may occur (Krebsz, 2011).

Methodology for Collateral Analysis. There are a number of methodologies to estimate the default properties of the underlying asset pool (Fender and Kiff, 2005). Ratings for structured finance products are normally determined by the application of at least one mathematical-statistical method (Krebsz, 2011). Where applicable, rating agencies apply basic components, including prepayment, interest rate, default timing, probability recovery rate and asset correlation scenario assumptions as described in their published asset-specific and global criteria, as input factors into the models (Hu, 2007; Standard & Poor's 2012c). In addition, rating agencies may apply sensitivity analyses using defined stress tests to key rating assumptions that would substantially reduce the relevant rating, for instance scenarios that would lead to a full category reduction of the rating (to a non-investment grade of substantial risk) (Fitch, 2011c). The results of the different analyses are then presented to the rating committee (Fitch, 2011c).

The currently method generally used by the major rating agencies is the Monte Carlo simulation approach.[33] In this method, a time series of macroeconomic variables is simulated through a stochastic process in order to calculate the estimated probability of default (SEC, 2008c). Each Monte Carlo trial simulates default and recovery upon defaults for each obligation in the reference pool. The simulated losses on each of the tranches are then computed for each trial,

33 The information is gathered from the following websites: http://www.stadardandpoors.com, http://moodys.com, and http://fitschratings.com.

together with the attachment and detachment points for the tranches (Hu, 2007). Attachment and detachment points represent the critical levels of default in the underlying asset pool of the transaction as Fender, Tarashev, and Zhu (2008) note. They reflect the points at which the tranche holder will begin to suffer losses and where a tranche is exhausted (Mitchell, 2005). Multiple repetition of a large number of simulations leads to an estimate of the expected loss by each tranche (Hu, 2007). Once the loss distribution of the pool is known (or a specific distribution can be assumed on the basis of these simulations), the amount of the future expected cash flows from the assets can then be calculated (Rutledge and Raynes, 2010). The rating process, however, not only considers the loss distribution, but also cash-flow simulations (Ashcraft and Schuermann, 2008).

4.3.2 Initial Evaluation

In order to understand the objective of the transaction with regard to the underlying cash or synthetic reference obligations, the rating agency engaged by the involved parties (originator/issuer and third parties and, if applicable, other involved services) reviews a general description of the components of the desired securitization transaction. This is usually the point at which a rating agency's deal team manager provides the originator/issuer with relevant information, such as how long it will take to assign a letter rating for the transaction and the portfolio information required to be submitted to the agency in order to continue with the planned deal (Carter and Watson, 2006). If an originator/issuer is frequently in the market and has already negotiated the documentation and the rating requirements with a rating agency for one or several prior transactions, it will only take a few days to obtain a reliable rating indication, but not the final rating. In cases of more complex transactions, such as whole business securitizations or first-time collateral debt obligations (CDOs), the process of obtaining a rating takes longer (Carter and Watson, 2006; Fitch 2011b). Following the preliminary discussion between the rating agency and the issuer, the rating agency will go into further detail and a process of more precise analysis begins.

4.3.3 Cash Flow Analysis

A cash flow analysis is typically associated with transactions in which assets have been transferred via true sale to a special purpose vehicle (SPV). Rating agencies analyze if, and to which extent, the collateral can generate the cash flows needed to service all the obligations of the transaction. Payments that must be performed from the cash flows of the collateral include interest and principal repayment (Fabozzi, Davis and Choudhry, 2006). In such transactions, "losses that exceed the available excess spread (the difference between the gross rate received on the underlying assets, and the total cost of liabilities issued by the SPV, including assumed expenses) and the first loss tranche are allocated in the reverse sequential order" of the contracted payment waterfall structure of the transaction (Carter and Watson, 2006, p. 90). The loss distribution starts with the junior tranches, followed by the subsequent mezzanine tranches and finally the senior tranches, "thereby, the mezzanine and junior notes (tranches) together with the first lost piece provide credit enhancement to the senior notes in form of subordination" (Carter and Watson, p. 90). The results of the quantitative models applied are then compared with the priority payments (the waterfall) of the security tranches specified in the legal documentation. The waterfall structure is the result of the translation of complex legal documents, allowing the determination of the order and the amount of payments or losses to be directed to the holder of the issue.

The waterfall documentation may contain specifications regarding "over-collateralization and excess spread triggers that, if breached, [...] [through reallocation shifts the] principal and interest payments from lower tranches to higher tranches until the minimum levels of over-collateralization and excess spreads" are effectively reestablished (SEC, 2008c, p. 8). Given that the rationale behind the waterfall structure is to provide protection to more senior tranches of the transaction, subordination levels play an important role, as they determine the amount of credit support senior tranches require from the subordinated tranches (Xudong et al., 2008). In cases where the collateral of the transaction does not experience credit losses, the subordinated and equity tranche holders obtain a higher return on investment than the more senior tranche holders (Guegan and Houdain, 2005). However, the sequential payment process means that the subordinated and equity tranches are at much greater risk in the event of a default in the asset portfolio (Krahnen and Wilde, 2008). The subordination would serve as a safeguard against such losses, as it means that the senior tranches of the transaction would receive first of all the cash flows generated by the underlying assets, and as such, the subordinated tranches would be served last (Krebsz, 2011).

The equity/first loss tranche bears the highest risk and is generally unrated (Franke and Krahnen, 2007). This tranche absorbs initial losses until the level where these notes are depleted is reached (Fender and Mitchell, 2009). To further support and assure that the transaction will perform within expectations, in most cases, the originator holds the equity or first loss piece, as he would face losses first (Krebsz, 2011). Nevertheless, this might not be seen as a guarantee that the transaction actually behaves as expected (Krebsz, 2011). Furthermore, the tranche retention might solve moral hazard problems in securitization transactions (Franke and Krahnen, 2007). The logic behind the moral hazard problem in securitization is clear, according to Bubb and Kaufmann: "lenders that sell loans they originate to dispersed investors may bear less of the cost when loans default, and hence they may have less incentive to screen borrowers" (2009, p. 1).

The aim of the cash flow analysis is to test whether there is sufficient CE and liquidity support available for ratings to endure under certain stress scenarios. The determination of the rating of the various tranches, for instance from AAA to BB, is dependent on the transaction and based on the probability of default (Carter and Watson, 2006). Once all parameters are clearly mapped out, Moody's for instance, calculates the probability associated with each level of loss that may arise from the underlying assets in CDO transactions on the basis of the number of defaulted comparable assets by using a simple algorithm. The correlated binominal default distribution achieved by this can then be used, in connection with a cash flow model that explicitly incorporates the CDO waterfall structure, to generate an evaluation of the probability-weighted loss for each CDO across all specific scenarios for default (Moody's, 2005).

In certain cases, rating agencies classify the expected loss based on confidence intervals for defined rating categories. For mortgage backed securities (MBS), cash flow tests are used to measure the effect of cash flows generated by such securities when variables such as prepayment speed, interest rates, default and recovery rates, weighted-average margin compression, recession timing, and delinquencies are stressed (Carter and Watson, 2006). In the case of MBS, it must also be considered that senior and subordinated tranches with an over-collateralization structure are hybrid instruments that combine the use of excess interest[34] in order to cover losses and create over-collateralization (Ashcraft, Goldsmith-Pinkham, and Vickery, 2010). These financial instruments have a capital structure in which the value of excess interest is determined by the cash flow analysis. In these cases, excess interest displays the difference between the amount of net interest paid on the loan (the borrower's side) and the interest paid to the security holder. This analysis mainly serves as a means to cross-check how much excess interest is available to absorb losses over the maturity of the security (Khadem and Parisi, 2007). The applied tests allow rating agencies to

34 "[I]nterest payments from the mortgage loans underlying the deal will typically exceed the sum of servicer fees, net payments to the interest rate swap counterparty, and coupon payments to MBS issued" and serve as additional support for the issued securities, and thus provide a buffer in case of any losses (Ashcraft, Goldsmith-Pinkham and Vickery, 2010, p. 6).

model scenarios for cash flows received from mortgages and other asset-backed transaction sources and their reallocation with particular deal structures. Stressing these variables can show how modifications can have a drastic impact on the results and lead to corresponding changes in the probability of default (Carter and Watson, 2006). If these tests produce the required results, they show that the "payment of current interests can be maintained and that the losses adequately absorbed" (Khadem and Parisi, 2007, p. 557). Thus, "while ultimately paying the rated class, the transaction will meet the stress test" to fulfill the requirements (Khadem and Parisi, 2007, p. 557).

However, the models applied by the rating agencies are not designed to deliver infallible answers about credit risk, but to support the conclusions made by rating analysts (Raynes and Rutledge, 2003). The basis for the preparation of cash flow estimates is a summary of financial characteristics based on data normally provided to the analyst by the originator/issuer. It is the task of rating agencies' analysts to synthesize the pool performance characteristics from the raw data that has been supplied, keeping in mind that there are different approaches that can be used to model cash flow modeling, and that each rating agency applies its own procedures (Rutledge and Raynes, 2010). Nevertheless, all three major rating agencies rely and focus heavily on stress-test scenarios; Moody's may also add *ad hoc* stresses to the basic assumptions of their simulations of probability distribution. It is also important to remember that in practice, not all aspects of asset risk might be analyzed and modeled, and distortions of the pool performance may arise that had not previously been considered. Cash flow performance is not only influenced by the microstructure of the risk, but is also decisively influenced by macroeconomic factors. This means that even models with modulated losses or simulations based on the Monte Carlo model could lead to false impressions about fair representation of default dynamics (Raynes and Rutledge, 2003).

4.3.4 Synthetic Transactions

In synthetic transactions, unlike other structured finance products, the securities payoffs do not primarily depend on the cash flows generated by a distinct pool of assets. Instead, they depend on assets or securities that are not held in a particular pool (Bethel and Ferrell, 2006). In synthetic transactions, the risk of the assets is separated from the ownership of the assets, and as such, only the risk associated with the exposure is transferred. With this metaphysical separation of risk, the synthetic CDO market was born (Rutledge and Raynes, 2010). The synthetic CDO market contains a broad range of products with different risk profiles (Carter and Watson, 2006). At the outset of this market from 1997–1999, such transactions included a set of several tranches (equity, mezzanine and senior), whereby the entire notional amount of the tranches usually corresponded to the notional amount of the reference portfolio. Currently, most of these activities comprise so-called single tranche CDOs, where only one tranche of a CDO's capital structure is sold (each tranche in the structure has a notional amount and a coupon). The essential aspect of such transactions is that the originator/issuer buys protection in return for a premium that promises to compensate the investor for the default risk in the reference credit portfolio. A common CDO structure involves slicing the credit risk of the underlying reference pool into different risk levels. In addition, synthetic tranches can be funded, partially funded, or unfunded (Fender and Kiff, 2005; Gibson, 2004).

A fully funded transaction transfers the credit risk of the entire asset portfolio to the SPV via credit default swaps (Eales and Choudhry, 2003). In the case of fully funded CDOs, investors pay the notional amount of the security in advance. In turn, investors are entitled to payments from the cash flows, depending on availability, throughout the lifetime of the transaction (Buckberg et al, 2010) – generally at LIBOR plus a spread reflecting the inherent risk of the respective tranche (Gibson, 2004). The investor's money is normally re-invested in securities with lower risk characteristics. In a funded synthetic transaction, the investor has no obligation to make any further investments, even if defaults are rapidly becoming more widespread. In the case of a 100 % default and loss of the underlying CDO debt, an investor only faces the loss of their original investment (Choudhry, 2010). A disadvantage of a fully funded transaction is that the fully funded tranche is more expensive in comparison to the same risk sold in the form of partially funded or unfunded credit default swaps (Eales and Choudhry, 2003).

In partially funded transactions, the premium that the issuer has to pay is lower than in a fully funded transaction, which is to the issuers' advantage compared to the fully funded structure (Choudhry, 2010). In a partially funded structure, only the portfolio segment carrying the highest risk is transferred (Eales and Choudhry, 2003). In case of a default in the underlying assets, the required amount of collateral will be disposed of and the proceeds of the sale will be paid to the issuer as compensation for the loss (Fabozzi, Davis, and Choudhry, 2006). A critical point is that only a smaller amount of notes (typically 5%–15%) is issued from the notional amount of the entire portfolio. "Thus, only the first 5%–15% of losses of a particular portfolio are funded [...] which leaves the most senior risk position unfunded" (Fabozzi and Goodsman, 2001, p. 145). Prices are lower because the issuer "is not required to cover the difference between the yield on the collateral and the coupon on the note issue (the unfunded part of the transaction)" (Choudhry, 2010, p. 458). Fabozzi and Goodman argue that given the quality of the underlying reference portfolio "there's only a remote probability that the loss might exceed the 5–15% of the exposure that has been unfunded" (2001, p. 150), as in essence the unfunded note is better that a AAA credit risk. In this structure, investors are also responsible for covering a default, if only in proportion to 'their share' of the portfolio (Schweimayer, 2010).

In contrast to fully funded or partially funded structures, no payment is required in the initial period for unfunded transactions. The risk investors face lies in "their obligation to compensate buyers of the protection if sources from the funded class subsequently prove insufficient" as severe credit losses occur (Buckberg et al, 2010, p.15). The investors therefore take on the role of an insurance company. Investors receive periodic premiums in return for their guarantee (with lower coupons than the holders of the funded notes), but such transactions expose investors to potential future payments in times of financial instability and crisis (Chance and Brooks, 2009).

All of these synthetic CDOs have three principal risks in common: "the first is the risk that losses in the reference portfolio exceed the tranche attachment point (the percentage of the pool at which point the investor will experience losses) or the credit enhancement" of the tranche (Carter and Watson, 2006, p. 94). All three major rating agencies apply a Monte Carlo simulation using a random number generator for the estimation of the default properties of the underlying CDO pool and a large variety of stress scenarios (Fender and Kiff, 2005). The second risk may arise from charged assets in a funded synthetic CDO deal. Fitch defines a charged asset as "the collateral in which note proceeds are invested in a funded synthetic CDO" (Kabahar and Gambel, 2005, p. 3). In case of default, investors may face losses. The potential risks for these products are default, early-termination, counterparty risks, and market risk. Rating agencies discuss these obstacles and address them through their modeling. The third type of risk comes from the default of the credit default swap (CDS) counterpart. The case of a swap counterpart default may call for the liquidation of the security representing the charged assets prior to maturity. In such an event, investors run the risk of losses arising from the market value of the assets (Carter and Watson, 2006). To mitigate market and default risks, rating agencies use structural protections (Kabahar and Gambel, 2005). Such protections are supported by credit enhancements, including mechanisms as guarantees and collateral, developed to limit the potential risk of specific risk assessment issues (Standard & Poor's, 2012a). In addition to the abovementioned types of risk, rating agencies also face a number of risks that may arise in other areas of the transaction.

4.3.5 Assessing Operational and Administrative Risks

While the key part of the rating process is to analyze the credit quality of the underlying collateral, risk that may arise by operational weakness often does not appear in the characteristics of the collateral, but manifests in the performance of the asset pool (Fitch, 2011b). For that reason, rating agencies conduct reviews of the entities (originator or servicer) responsible for servicing or managing the assets securitized. This allows rating agencies to determine indications of risks in structured finance transactions attributable to the competence, capability and quality of the servicers in managing the operation in presale or new issues, as well as post-closing (Fitch, 2011b; Moody's, 2012a; Standard & Poor's, 2012a.). The reviews are conducted for all asset classes of major structured finance transactions. Such reviews may include, depending on the agency, the evaluation and analysis of corporate stability, management and staff experience, technological capabilities, operational capacity, policies and procedures, controls, and its proven track record in the market (e.g. Fitch, 2011c; Moody's, 2012b).

It is the duty of the servicer or manager to collect asset payments, to work with delinquent obligators, and to track cash receipts and disbursements, as well as being responsible for the disposing of collateral and providing timely and accurate investor reports (Standard & Poor's, 2012a). Fitch assesses the information gathered throughout the review process, and when applicable, incorporates the agency's transaction surveillance data in order to foster the servicers' analysis. Once the process is completed, an opinion is derived based on the review of the aforementioned key points and a servicer's rating is assigned. The rating assigned to the servicer "is separate and distinct from the credit rating and reflects the servicer's operational strengths and weakness" (Fitch, 2011b, p. 6). In cases where the servicer is rated lower than the securitized assets, rating agencies consider scenarios in which the original servicer is unwilling or unable to perform its duties for the transaction. In such cases, a rating agency may anticipate the likelihood that an alternative or backup servicer would be able and willing to step into the servicing function for the transaction in their analysis (as Standard & Poor does). This scenario may be influenced by a rating agency's opinion about the sufficiency of the servicing fee to attract a substitute servicer, as well as by the seniority of the servicing fees in the payment waterfall of the transaction. The servicer's fee may be senior to or on a *pari passu* basis to the rated noteholder payments and should be sufficient to motivate a substitute servicer (Standard & Poor's, 1999). Other factors that might hinder the orderly transition of the servicing function from the original servicer to the replacement servicer may also be taken into account. Such factors include the availability of an alternative servicer in the transactions sector or region, as well as certain asset specific characteristics (Standard and Poor's, 2012a). Rating agencies established these reviews in order to provide investors and other market participants with an indication of the servicer's capabilities and capacities (Fitch, 2011b).

4.3.6 Analysis of Counterparty Risks

What all structured finance transactions have in common is their exposure to counterparty risks, either through operational reliance or in the form of credit dependency based on payment obligations, or a combination of both. As the timely repayment of structured finance products depends on counterparties delivering the funds under agreement, rating agencies assess the risks associated with counterparties and the role they play as part of their analysis of structured finance transactions (Fitch, 2011b; Moody's 2012a, Standard & Poor's, 2012b). Every possible measure needs to be taken into account and needs to be monitored by the rating agencies for as Gregory notes, the risk "at the portfolio level is complicated by uncertainty of exposure as well as the problem of measuring default correlations" (Gregory, 2010, p. 393). The major rating agencies have similar descriptions of their rating process for structured finance where third parties are involved. These criteria are designed to reflect whether a security transferred via a vehicle (SPV) remains AAA, or at least investment grade rated, until the last equal-ranking liability (senior tranche) is repaid in the event of the SPV's liquidation (Kim, 2012).

The servicer assumes servicing the responsibilities "when a loan defaults or encounters certain other negative events" (Forti and Iaconelli, 2001, p. 12). Its ability to successfully handle transactions under potential difficulties is the key criterion to determine the relevant risk exposure factors of the transaction. It is also a key factor to reduce the assumptions regarding the loss of default in the rating models of most of the rating agencies. If these tasks can be fulfilled effectively, the servicer contributes to the successful reduction of the overall risk by minimizing losses and maximizing the value of the remaining defaulted loan (Forti and Iaconelli, 2001).

4.3.7 Legal and Transaction Document Risks in Structured Finance Transactions

The clarification of the legal aspects associated with structuring asset securitization is considerably more intensive than it is in the case of corporate or governmental finance transactions (Hu, 2011). The legal analysis of structured finance transactions comprises a critical function in the rating process. This stems from the fact that any cash-flow projecting model would be interrupted if a borrower were to go bankrupt. Applied to structured finance rating transactions, this would mean that if the obligations of the deal were not enforceable against the counterparty, such as principal and interest payments, investors would discover not only interruptions to their scheduled interest payments, but also potential losses with respect to the principal (Forti and Iaconelli, 2001). For this reason, the major rating agencies' analysts work with the originator or issuer and review legal matters with their own legal advisors to make certain that unexpected legal issues will not have negative effects on the transactions' cash flows. Analysts therefore review the representation provided by the involved transaction parties corresponding to the characteristics of the underlying asset pool.

The objective of the review is to determine whether the securitized assets have been isolated from any participating entities' risk of bankruptcy or insolvency in an appropriate manner. Rating agencies are especially invested in ensuring that an involved entity's bankruptcy or insolvency would not have an impact on the rights of the securitization structures (Fitch, 2011b; Moody's, 2012a). The main aim of the rating agencies' legal review is to ensure that the probability of loss calculated on the basis of various models is not underestimated owing to an oversight of potential legal matters that "may interfere with the projected cash-flow" (Forti and Iaconelli, 2001, p. 12). The review typically focuses on the entity that owned or originated the assets prior to the securitization (Standard & Poor's, 2012a). In most cases, rating agencies look for a true sale of the assets from the originator to the bankruptcy-remote entity (SPV).

It is the intention of the rating agencies to ensure that the likelihood the SPV will go bankrupt could be regarded as at least remotely connected with the requested rating and jurisdictional issues (Standard & Poor's, 2012a). Therefore, rating agencies review all documents and the dossier of any SPV that is part of the securitization structure before assigning a credit rating (Standard & Poor's, 2012b). These measures are taken to assure that the rating agencies' decision can be passed with confidence that there are reliable facts about the transaction collateral and the involved parties (Fitch, 2011; Standard & Poor's, 2012a). The representations and warranties provided by the originator/issuer also play an important role in the agencies' due diligence processes. Any expectation thereto and/or derogation from the applied standards "put rating agencies on alert with regard to loans that may not meet customary standards and, depending on the nature of the expectation, could have a negative impact on the rating" (Forti and Iaconelli, 2001, p.12). In the final analysis, rating agencies compile all reviewed information relevant to the credit rating and present the developed rating to the final rating committee (Fitch, 2011c).

4.4 Rating Action Commentary and Supporting Guidelines

As soon as the primary analyst has received and reviewed the offering memorandum, a presale report and/or rating action commentary is drafted in which the expected rating is announced (Morkötter and Westerfeld, 2009). A series of measures implemented by the Dodd-Frank Act and associated EU regulations to improve transparency require distinct disclosures relating to key rating drivers, cash-flow assumptions, default and loss analyses, and a number of other factors that may affect the rating. These measures have been taken to improve the ability of market participants and regulators to assess the quality and objectivity of the credit rating (Elkhoury, 2009). In addition to codifying rating agencies' existing practices for ensuring transparency, these rules set forth defined time frames for originator/issuer notification and the disseminating of the rating (Fitch, 2011b). These regulatory periods of 12 hours notification before publication of the credit rating reflect the balance between giving the rated entity sufficient time to react and to review the factual accuracy of the data presented, and ensuring a timely publication of the rating (EU, 2009). This also applies to the dissemination of expected and new issue ratings, as well as actions taken on existing ratings (Fitch, 2011a). These rules should ensure that the issuer has enough time to react to the rating[35], while at the same time providing adequate and timely access to the information for other market participants.

4.5 The Role and Function of Credit-Quality Monitoring

The monitoring of the performance of structured finance transactions once issued is a critical part of the role undertaken by rating agencies in rating structured finance products. Rating agencies are obliged to monitor the accepted and published

35 The current 12-hour rule for notification will be replaced by new rules in order to ensure that the issuer notification takes place during working hours (European Commission Memo, "New rules on credit rating agencies (CRAs) – frequently asked questions", 16 January, 2013b, IV, 9. para. 4).

ratings over the lifetime of the instrument (Carter and Watson, 2006). This is especially important in the field of structured finance, where issuers of structured finance products do not make available information relating to due diligence and the underlying loan performance to the public (SEC, 2008c).

Whilst rating agencies' analysis focuses on the evaluation of historical data, the ratings are designed to be a forward-looking statement on credit quality. However, credit ratings are not static. The reasons why ratings change vary, as a number of factors may influence the rating assessment. Such adjustments may be related to overalls shifts in the economy, e.g. growing inflation that affects interest rate levels, or unforeseen erosion in the credit markets. Changes may also occur as a consequence of growing or shrinking debt burdens (especially with stringent capital spending requirements) and regulatory changes. Another reason would be a change in the credit quality of the issue or the issuer that had not been anticipated by the rating agencies when they assigned the initial credit rating. These factors may result in a rating adjustment to reflect the new information. The monitoring process ensures that the rating assigned reflects a rating agency's view on the issues/issuers credit risk in an appropriate manner (Fitch 2011c; Moody's 2012b; Standard & Poor's, 2012c). These follow-up procedures imply an implicit contract between the agency and the issuer, whereby the latter implicitly promises to undertake actions to mitigate possible deteriorations in its credit standing – and of course, its rating (Boot, Milbourn, and Schmeits, 2006). Rating agencies' predictions and risk prognoses are not an exact science, and since ratings are intended to be forward looking, they are not construed as statements about absolute default probability, but rather relative indications of credit risk (Standard & Poor's, 2012c).

In order to determine the appropriateness of the current rating, rating agencies surveillance analysts routinely perform analyses similar to the ones carried out for the initial rating (detailed in section 4.3.2.). These analyses are based on the most recent collateral performance data available as well as prevailing market conditions (Hu, 2007). Structured finance transactions are monitored to detect variations in performance that fall outside of the agreed-upon normal range for that obligation from the initial performance expectations (Fitch, 2011b). Depending on the structure of the transaction, remittance reports are received and reviewed at monthly intervals (Carter and Watson, 2006). Reviewing the composition and performance of structured finance portfolios on an ongoing basis enables rating agencies to forward timely information and commentary to their subscribers. The monitoring procedure provides either confirmation of the assigned rating, or leads to adjustments in the form of upgrades or downgrades. In accordance with the EU Regulation on Credit Rating Agencies (CRA) 1 that has been in force since December 2010, such actions occur at least once every 12 months. Rating actions may, however, take place more frequently if the performance of the underlying asset pool exhibits rapid deterioration (Carter and Watson, 2006; Fitch, 2011b). Monitoring of rating performance is valuable for the rating quality in structured finance transactions, and rating agencies should maintain sufficient resources and organizational flexibility to ensure that this can be carried out (CESR, 2008). The timely monitoring of the relevant factors is important because it creates the conditions necessary for carrying out required adjustments of credit risk. However, these adjustments can trigger accelerated price adjustments, which are likely to turn out to be higher if the prices were overvalued (Adrian et al., 2013).

4.6 Conclusion

The structured finance market has raised particular interest in the methodology applied by rating agencies to structured finance products. Ratings are designed to offer market participants an uncomplicated and simple way of comparing the credit quality of different obligations and looking at expected volatility over time (Carter and Watson, 2006). This is especially important in the case of complex structured financial instruments, as these products may reduce volatility within the investment portfolio. The structuring of financial assets into several risk classes makes it possible to meet the different expectations of various investors. Subordination levels are an important factor as they determine the credit support the senior tranches receive from the subordinated tranches and define investors risk exposure. Subordination is a determinant factor for pricing and risk management. There are indications that subordination levels systematically declined over time as a reason of rating agencies "learning by doing" in subordination design, and it is argued "that this decline is a result of rating agencies being overly conservative" in the early stages of the market development for such products (Xudong, Yongheng, and Sanders, 2008, p. 46). Recent research suggests that "subordination levels observed in the market levels are higher than their estimates and [...] that markets will likely see further reductions in subordination" (Xudong et. al., 2008, p. 5). As the current crisis has demonstrated, the opacity and complexity of modeling different risk positions or tranches opened the door for opportunism in terms of the input assumptions and estimation methods used in the rating process, and it turned out that rating agencies had failed to follow their prudential standards in assessing the underlying asset pools and the various debt tranches of structured finance deals (Kim, 2012).

Furthermore, while rating agencies use the same or similar scales to distinguish between different default risk degrees, "they need not necessarily be equivalent in meaning" (Ellis, 1998, p. 40). Although the major rating agencies publish ratings and research reports about an issuer's creditworthiness and the credit quality of a specific debt instrument, which do look similar at first glance, there are differences, such as the methodologies or approaches used, or the scope of their coverage (Standard & Poor's, 2012c). Since ratings are subjective assessments of default probabilities ratings, using two rating agencies for an issue may result in different ratings being given due to differences in opinion. Such differences are not only likely to create differences in regulatory and risk-weighting requirements (van Roy, 2006), and this may mean for investors that financial instruments can carry a different risk than that which was expected.

Due to the complexity of structured finance products and the role these instruments play in global capital markets, effective surveillance is very important. Surveillance of structured finance instruments normally consists of monitoring actions and the ongoing interpretation of observed data (Alcubilla and del Pozo, 2012). Although it is important that rating agencies put their ratings for structured finance products on their watch list, there is a moral hazard problem inherent to this activity, as the monitored clients are simultaneously the rated issuers (Ory and Raimbourg, 2008). With the developments that have occurred in financial markets over the last two decades, the role of rating agencies in the process of rating structured finance products has gained ever-greater significance. Rating agencies should, as Hu (2011) notes, provide investors with useful information about their chance of receiving contractual payments (principal repayments and interest) in a timely, transparent and predictable manner. However, the mispricing of credit risk was not the first time that rating agencies failed to fulfill their role (e.g. the WorldCom/Enron scandals). Therefore, investors should not unconditionally rely on credit ratings, especially with regard to complex structured finance securities. Rather, they should inform themselves about the methods employed to be aware of the kind of risk that rating agencies address with their assumptions. This is particularly important in light of the fact that capital market prices, as the crisis has shown, are heavily affected by uncertainty and volatility. To understand just how significant rating agencies' ratings of securities are in the price discovery process of financial markets, it is helpful to understand the measures and effects of establishing prices according to the theory of price, as well as understanding the characteristics of financial markets. Accordingly, the characteristics of financial markets and how prices are determined are discussed in the next chapter.

5. Rating Agencies and Price Determination in Financial Markets

This chapter addresses the process of price determination in the financial markets. It presents an overview of the theory of price and how prices are established, discusses the characteristics of markets and credit markets, and examines the role of rating agencies in the pricing process, focusing on the significance of rating agencies in the field. Financial markets play a key role in society and economics by simplifying the exchange of information, goods and services, and by facilitating payments. By doing so, they generate economic value for market participants such as buyers, sellers, and society more generally (Bakos, 1998). In line with the approach adopted by Aspers and Beckert (2011), financial assets as discussed in this research are subsumed under the notion of goods, except when otherwise indicated, even though economists usually distinguish between goods markets and financial markets.

Rating agencies determine the cost of capital and, in many cases, whether capital can be raised effectively (Duarte et al., 2008). The specific nature "of credit markets as markets for information explain why they need consumer and rating agencies to act as intermediaries and market enablers by anchoring prices" (Rona-Tas and Hiss, 2011, p. 223). With the help of mathematical models, rating agencies transfer the abstract value of creditworthiness into a letter rating, which in turn determines credit costs (Hiss and Rona-Tas, 2011). Ratings are indicators of prices, and thus provide useful information for determining the quality of the underlying assets (Jorge, 2012). Nevertheless, the weakness of the translation process highlighted by the subprime crisis has shown that rating agencies have not always been able to establish prices sufficiently close to the real value of the underlying financial assets (Hiss and Rona-Tas, 2011). Inaccurate credit ratings and evaluation models were responsible for the unstable prices of structured finance products (Collins, 2008). However, credit markets do provide a coordinating mechanism between market participants and support measures for risk sharing schemes. Rating agencies play a central role in this process, as market participants use ratings to overcome information asymmetries (Coval, Jurek, and Stafford, 2008). Asymmetric information occurs in a lending relationship (Kräussl, 2005) when one party in the transaction has more or better information regarding future prospects than the other(s) (Bharath, Pasquariello, and Wu, 2009). This is especially the case in the market segment of structured finance products (Fender and Mitchell, 2005). Akerlof (1970) stressed that in accordance with the asymmetric information theory, the seller knows the quality of the good that is going to be traded better than the buyer in any transaction. For the credit market this means that the lender is penalized by moral hazard and adverse selection problems resulting from a lack of information (Stiglitz and Weiss, 1992).

5.1 Price Theory and Prices

From the viewpoint of economic theory, prices are determined by supply and demand (Hiss and Rona-Tas, 2011). In contrast, from a socio-economic perspective, prices are determined as a result of market transactions being embedded in social networks and institutions, or as a consequence of them being defined in "culturally anchored frames of meaning" that structure the market (Beckert, 2011a, p. 757). According to political economist Adam Smith, individual preferences are the determining factor of social welfare (Schneider, Gräf, and Peter (2010). In addition, the *homo economicus* model describes humans as rational and self-interested beings capable of making judgments based on subjective reasons in order to maximize their well-being (Nyborg, 2000). This fundamental assumption provides the basis for the majority of economic models and approaches (Brennan and Buchanan, 1998). However, in trying to keep pace with the growing complexity of the markets around them, consumers' decision-making capabilities are severely tested. In reality, their decisions are not based "on established preferences and complete information", and thus the attempt for a rapprochement with regard to a decision by approximation contradicts the *homo economicus* model (Schneider, Gräf, and Peter, 2010, p. 1). "As a rule", as Schneider, Gräf, and Peter argue, "these approximation methods deliver serviceable results, but they often also lead to distorted perceptions and systematic flaws" (2010, p. 1).

Arguments claiming that prices are affected by institutional influences do not challenge economic price theory, for the latter is based on the assumption of perfectly informed market actors operating with full rationality (Beckert, 2011). However, against the background of increasing regulatory structuring and the application of institutional rules that influence price determination, the supply/demand orientated price-determining mechanism stands at the very end of a long series of price-determining factors that are shaped by market structures and cultural frames representing the perception of the value of goods (Beckert, 2011). Certain major events, such as the Japanese Bubble Economy of the mid-1980s and the US stock crash of 1987, resulted in a large number of studies focusing on the re-assessment and re-evaluation of the traditional methods and models of price determination affecting real-world markets, and above all, asset markets.

These studies led to the development of a number of new theoretical models that took the actual characteristics of contemporary financial markets into account (Kortian, 1995). Modern financial markets are key drivers of innovation in the world economy. These markets, global as they are in their scope, not only face increased international competition, but also offer increased access to finance and transnational distributions of capital, thereby delivering diversification effects for monetary policy purposes (Huber, Rueschemeyer, and Stephens, 1999).

Pricing plays a central role in conveying information about values, particularly those related to intangible products or services like financial products (Berry and Yaday, 1996; Jarobe and Ellis, 2010). Further, prices are a source of reference and guidance to make heterogeneous objects and services comparable (Aspers and Beckert, 2011). From the point of view of market participants, prices are indicators of costs to be paid or revenues to be collected or gained from a good or service, and are thus directly connected to the distribution of wealth (Beckert, 2011). From this viewpoint, in economic sociology — an approach that traces its origins back to the nineteenth-century political economist Max Weber (Swedberg, 2007) — prices do not "mysteriously emerge from the market but are a result of established rules of the game" that producers implicitly follow (Beckert, 2011, p. 760; Velthuis, 2005, p. 10). One of the prerequisites for the determination of prices is, therefore, that market actors are able to assess the value of the products offered (Beckert, 2011). In order to determine price, the value of a good (asset) needs to be transformed into economic value (Hiss and Rona-Tas, 2011). In economic theory, prices reflect the interaction between supply and demand, and are set to achieve a balance between the quantities supplied and demanded (Marshallian approach).[36] According to the equilibrium markets theory, these quantities are determined by the marginal utility of assets to different buyers and sellers (Hicks, 1946). From this perspective, buyers and sellers act in order to maximize their total utility. One essential assumption behind the marginal utility analysis is that buyers seek to maximize their utility in all circumstances. In its pure form, the *homo economicus* model asserts that individuals are fully informed at all times, thereby abstracting them from the presence of uncertainty and the cost of information (Schneider, Gräf, and Peter, 2010). However, as Schneider, Gräf, and Peter (2010) emphasize, this does not necessarily mean that they know what the future holds for them. In the neoclassical theory, which is dictated by Marshall's view on economic science, the basic assumption is founded on

36 Alfred Marshall's approach propounded that price is determined by the interaction of the forces of supply and demand. The point at which demand is equal to supply is the so-called equilibrium point, and the price prevalent at that point is the equilibrium price.

the concept of prices functioning through decentralized decision-making (Rumelt, 2003). However, even Marshall, whose work formed the basis of neoclassical economic theory, considered the equilibrium model to be only an interim step toward further developments in the social sciences (Shelby and Morgan, 1996).

Apart from the neoclassical approach[37], which concludes that markets are always in equilibrium or moving towards equilibrium, Keynesians show how economies tend to go beyond Marshall, as they do not limit the analysis to marginal relations, and rarely, if ever, attain equilibrium (Neisser, 1968). The neoclassical approach follows classical assumptions of price flexibility and competitive equilibrium with interminable rationality, but also takes rational expectations into account. Nevertheless, just how rapidly prices and price expectations adapt to changes in demand seems to "be an important point of disagreement among theories of price determination" (Kahn, 1984, p. 17). Although there is no universal price determination formula (Davis, Panas, and Zariphopoulu, 1993), Kahn defines it as follows: "while no theory of price determination can claim to explain [...] price behavior completely, Keneysian, monetarist, and new classical theories have emerged as the leading contenders" (1984). According to price theory, the price for any specific good or service represents the relationship between the forces of supply and demand for that particular good or service (Smith, 1979). The theory postulates that the most optimal market price for a good or service is achieved at the point when the benefit gained from those whose demand meets the supplier's marginal costs (Lange, 1936). The concept of marginal cost plays a central role in pricing theory, as the equality of marginal cost and price is one of the key factors for efficiency (Hall, 1988). One of the main concerns of the price theory is to explain economic activities (trade) with respect to the creation and transfer of value – value related to trade in goods and services amongst different actors in the economy (Weber, 2012). In these market activities, the monetary value of goods or services is represented in the form of a price (Murad, 1958).

5.2 Distinguishing Between Price and Value

Price and value represent the worth of goods in our society (Aspers and Beckert, 2011). Price and value may deviate from each other in a wide variety of cases in which prices may misrepresent the underlying value. Generally speaking,

37 Approaches to economics focusing on the determination of price are known as neoclassical economics, a term introduced by Thorstein Velben (1899) to distinguish the so-called marginalists in Alfred Marshall's tradition from those of the so-called Austrian school.

though, "the two are interconnected and shape each other" (Rona-Tas and Hiss, 2011, p. 224). Markets establish the economic value of a good (asset) in the form of a price (Aspers and Beckert, 2011). The sustainable functioning of a market economy is only possible by means of coordination through a price system in which the price of goods reflects their value to those who actually utilize them. Alternatively, the price of a good reflects a buyer's willingness to pay (Beckert, 2011). All costs of production—that is, all costs ultimately incurred (e.g. payment to a worker for the work he provides instead of taking a vacation or spending money for one purpose and thus making it impossible to use the same amount of money for another purpose) are reflected in the price at which goods are sold (Friedman, 1990, part 2). Prices and values are the focal point for free trade and markets are required for conducting trade (Krugman, 1993). In order to stand out and stay afloat, markets need to overcome the problem of valuation, "a task different form and a precondition for price formation" (Rona-Tas and Hiss, 2011, p. 224).

The existence of markets is linked to competition at least on one side of the market: demand or supply (Aspers and Beckert, 2011). In order to permit competition to develop, concerned actors must not only have the desire to obtain the offered goods (assets) and the necessary ability to purchase these goods, but must be able to assess the quality of these goods (assets) relative to each other and compare them with regard to their value (Aspers and Beckert, 2011). According to Frisby (2004), such interaction in markets constitutes a form of indirect conflict. Interaction (trade) in markets requires decision-making and acting under uncertain conditions. The difficulty of judging the quality of products offered in the market and predicting their value leads to uncertainty. If this uncertainty is not resolved, the prices attached to a good would appear to be completely random. Markets can only coordinate the distribution of economic goods if these difficulties and issues are resolved.

The value and price of goods are the outcome of people's interactions while trading, but are also the outcome of specific institutional structures (Aspers and Beckert, 2011). Uncertainty and the imperfectness of information are displayed in the form of asymmetric information where the seller knows the true value of a good, but the potential buyer does not. Producers and intermediaries (rating agencies) have the common objective of assigning the correct values to goods (assets) by mitigating this information problem, and through so doing, facilitating trade (Clerides, Nearchou, and Pashardes, 2008).

The price of a good or service is a strong reflection of what people would sacrifice to obtain benefit or pleasure from something (Friedman, 1990). Value refers to the perception of benefits received for what someone must give up (Farber et al., 2002). Only if market participants are in a position to distinguish the value of goods can they overcome the uncertainty regarding the value of objects that are substituted (Hiss and Rona-Tas, 2011). This is not possible without assessing the price in relation to the utility obtained from the products. The possibility of judging prices is hampered if the value and price of a good are independent (Aspers and Beckert, 2011). This leads to the question of how value and price are evaluated, along with their status in society.

5.2.1 Evaluation of Value and Price for Financial Products

The worth of goods and services in society is expressed in terms of values and prices, where prices that are established by the markets, which are governed, to a large extent, by values upon which the market is based. Contrary to prices, values may exist outside the sphere of markets. Rona-Tas and Hiss use the examples of housework and childcare – both of which are valued irrespective of whether they are traded and priced on the market or not (2011). The price of housework and childcare in markets could differ substantially from the values attached to them since "whether prices truly reflect the underlying values strongly depends [...] on the question of how values are counted and measured: not as a precondition for market creation [...] but as an ongoing effort to converge prices and values" (Rona-Tas and Hiss, 2011, p. 225). The identification of various dimensions through which a purchaser assesses the value of a good or service does not indicate how market participants arrive at their assessment. This question is central to the evaluation of goods since it is associated with a level of uncertainty that actors in financial markets must confront when making a choice among different goods and services. In order to define what constitutes the economic value of a good or service in relation to other goods or services offered in the marketplace, their symbolic qualities must be shaped (Aspers and Beckert, 2011).

In financial markets, an apparent convergence of value and price takes place, since the only thing that matters for financial market actors is money in its most abstract from (Hiss and Rona-Tas, 2011; Frisby, 2004). Profits and losses depend on the price mechanism in such markets. Market participants must be capable of evaluating the prices offered in the market in terms of whether they are appropriate, i.e. too high, or too low. Thus, in order to evaluate prices, actors in the financial market must refer to something that is more fundamental than the price – namely the value of the good or service. Financial markets assess the value behind the price by utilizing a set of instruments, including analytical and organizational aids (Hiss and Rona-Tas, 2011). Where these assessments are incorrect, prices may lose their relationship to the underlying values. In turn, this may lead to far-reaching and severe economic consequences and market shake-outs. Intermediaries such as rating agencies (and their ratings) thus fulfill an important function in the evaluation and determination of prices for structured finance products (Coval, Jurek, and Stafford, 2008).

In order to enable customers to understand the evaluation of products such as financial instruments, it is important to examine how market intermediaries such as rating agencies form their opinions about these products. Rating agencies use a number of variables and factors to reach their judgments. These variables and factors were discussed in Chapter 4. Taking into account the fact that the different assets underlying financial products may often be heterogeneous, market participants are also confronted with innumerable financial products within each category if they wish to make an investment (Aspers and Beckert, 2011). Solving financial problems requires tools, for example, in the areas of credit scoring, loan evaluation, and ratings. To this end, such tools (e.g. mathematical models to evaluate cash-flows) support the financial sector where predictions and classification are required in terms of accuracy, robustness, effectiveness, and efficiency (Wong and Selvi, 1998). This implies that the most important aspect in the evaluation of goods is their classification (Aspers and Beckert, 2011).

Through classification systems, purchasers can categorize, evaluate, and authoritatively rank financial products (Schneidberg and Berk, 2010). Karpik (2010) describes a number of 'judgment devices' to inform consumers about the quality of the product they wish to buy. Judgment devices are tools that help market participants to orient themselves in markets, including trust and delegation mechanisms, cognitive supports, and active forces (Anastasoaie, 2012) like experts or rankings (Hiss and Rona-Tas, 2011). Thus, rating agencies serve investors in more ways than one: they help to overcome the uncertainty that arises from the asymmetric information in markets and standardize securities (Sy, 2009). Their experts also analyze and evaluate risk and express their findings in a ranking order (a simple linear rating scale) to allow market participants to assess the value of a product (Beckert, 2011; Sy, 2009). Rating agencies must ensure that the prices of assets reflect the real economic value and derive prices from values in order to do so.

5.2.2 Deriving Prices from Values

The main instruments for deriving prices for structured finance products from their value are calculative practices supported by mathematical methods. The central concept underlying calculative practices is interpreting reality through numbers (Dillard, Brown, and Marshall, 2005). The supposed reproducibility of numbers is a fiction, however, as measurements and numbers are always based on assumptions; thus, the results for assets compared may differ. In other words, rating agencies may provide different ratings for the same company or product even on the basis of the same calculation factors used to assess creditworthiness. Moreover, the limits of what may be calculable and what may not have been extended with the capabilities of modern risk-management systems (Hiss and Rona-Tas, 2011). Innovation in information technology was a key driver in the development of financial instruments and has gained a considerable influence in the financial market sector (Lupica, 2009). Rating agencies enabled the development of structured finance products, and thus the establishment of a structured finance market (Sinclair, 2011). Even if these products do not reduce the risk attached to real assets, the new technology has made it possible for highly complex financial products to be exchanged in the global financial marketplace (Lupica, 2009). Financial development supports the expanding diversity of investment opportunities and performs a fundamental distributive function by improving the allocation of capital in financial markets (Wurgler, 2000). However, there is no generally acknowledged and accepted model of how markets function (Besley, Coate, and Loury, 1994).

5.3 Markets, Credit Markets, and Prices

The concept of marginal utility has shifted from differentiating between market price and value. The new theory, which emerged in the late nineteenth century, focuses on the marginal benefit instead of objective measures (like labor) to assess the economic value of a product and plays a crucial role in the so-called marginal revolution. Amongst the most prominent representatives of this theory from which the revolution evolved are William Stanley Jevons, Carl Menger, Leon Walras, and John Bates Clark (Aspers and Beckert, 2011). The marginalists of the revolution were concerned with problems where neither risk nor uncertainty played a role (Manicas, 2007). In accordance with this tradition, economics and finance theory had been influenced for decades by the belief that markets operate in a perfect manner, with prices being completely flexible and changing immediately in response to any shift in demand or supply (Kahn, 1984). Thus, following the logic of this theory, the market ensures the optimum allocation of goods or services through the coordination of prices that reflect all available information. In other words, prices reflect the value they represent in a perfect manner (Hiss and Rona-Tas, 2011).

The view that prices in a perfect world – with perfect market prices and values – would be equated to the real value of a good or service is also supported by Hayek (Rona-Tas and Hiss, 2011). Hayek believes that prices should be derived by competition in the market, instead of being guided or fixed by authorities (Hayek, 1940). Furthermore, Hayek considers markets to be a communication system and asserts that the market process can convey dispersed information, which can result in better allocation of resources. (Holtmann and Neumann, 2003). Hayek also claims that better resource allocation can be achieved with more competitive mechanisms rather through a centralized allocation mechanism (Zappia, 1999). Hayek identified this problem long before Akerlof, Stiglitz and Spence (all Nobel Prize winners in economic science) started working on the problem of asymmetric information. A key example often used for this situation is "the classical metaphor of the 'Walrasian Auctioneer', where assuming perfect information is inadequate to explain the price functioning of a market" (Holtmann and Neumann, 2003, p. 84). According to Hayek's "marvel of the market", with the help "of the forces supply and demand prices aggregate the dispersed knowledge about a commodity in a way unrivaled by central calculation or any other form of market coordination" (Rona-Tas and Hiss, 2011, p. 225). For Hayek, the aggregation of dispersed knowledge is a social procedure and cannot be substituted by formal calculation. However, the problem with this approach is that it fails in credit markets, where market participants need to make choices under conditions of uncertainty, as the future is unpredictable (Beckert, 2007; Knight, 2006). Credit and financial markets are characterized by predictions regarding the future; this is particularly true for financial derivatives that rely solely on such predictions (Rona-Tas and Hiss, 2011).

Nevertheless, price behavior in markets does not always follow the principle of market equilibrium. Perfect markets exist in theory, but rarely in reality, as noted by Ackerman (2002). The efficient market hypothesis (EMH) can, in essence, be considered an extension of the classic equilibrium theory insofar as this hypothesis takes into account dynamic price behaviors in speculative markets under conditions of uncertainty (Jensen, 1978). In the 1950s and 1960s, research on stock markets began to examine if there were patterns in (share) prices so that future movements could be predicted based on that what had occurred historically (Russel and Torbey, 2002). These studies suggested that there was little or no correlation between successive movements in these prices, hereafter referred to as the random walk theory (Leuthold, 1972). Based on these findings, it seemed that at any point in time, all available information was reflected in the price indicated; therefore, the next move could not be predicted based on the last, since each new piece of information was already implied in past prices (Malkiel, 2003). The central feature of the EMH is that while stock markets are not perfect, they are at least efficient.

If markets are not perfect, price distortion may occur and prices will then not necessarily reflect the true value of the goods. In appearance, this discrepancy is true in many markets. The situation is aggravated by the fact that prices are interrelated and when mortgage credit is cheap, prices for housing will be cheap too, even if house prices are rising (as shown by the housing bubble). The misinterpretation of prices in one market then spreads to other markets, making market contagion more likely and expanding the effect to adjacent markets. This phenomenon was observed in the subprime crisis (Rona-Tas and Hiss, 2011).

Real markets are imperfect by definition; perfect and complete information therefore does not exist (Thomas, 1998). Markets that depend on predictions and forecasts lack complete information, and such markets include credit and rating markets. These markets are not only characterized by time uncertainty – whether the beneficiary (borrower) reimburses the entire outstanding balance of the debt – but also the uncertainty surrounding rational information asymmetry (Hiss and Rona-Tas, 2011). The borrower has better knowledge of their own creditworthiness than the lender does, and since creditworthiness is not directly apparent, lenders need to make estimations about a borrower's capability or willingness to fulfill his repayment obligations (Standard & Poor's, 2012d). Consequently, prices may not only reflect but also influence value, as some mortgage delinquencies in one area might affect the credit score in the entire area.

Unlike in the ideal-typical scenario, prices in perfect markets are thus not determined in the same manner as in markets where creditworthiness plays a role. In these markets, prices are not agreed upon through negotiation between buyers and sellers until a consensus is reached (Hiss and Rona-Tas, 2011). Given the fact that creditworthiness is not a directly apparent characteristic, the lender normally has to estimate it from observable attributes using various approaches. This can be done either by conducting their own analysis, or by using information supplied by third parties, such as rating agencies (Standard & Poor's, 2012d). This leads to the conclusion that intermediaries such as rating agencies are required for such markets to function as they reduce information asymmetry (Hiss and Ron-Tas, 2011).

5.3.1 Price Determination in Credit Markets

A distinction must be made between two ideal-typical forms of markets: standard markets and status markets (Aspers, 2009). Consumer markets are identified as status markets, while a production market is defined as a standard market

(Aspers, 2005). In standard and credit markets, the assessment of the value and price of what is offered in the market is entrenched with standardized evaluation scales. These standardized scales might be created by market intermediaries. However, the relevance of status orders is primarily subject to consumer markets, but not limited to them. Since status markets also face uncertainty regarding the value (for example: what establishes the quality in art?), these markets involve expert judgments (Aspers and Beckert, 2011).

Financial markets are driven by supply and demand for credit (Lillo, Farmer, and Mantegna, 2003), thereby determining and setting prices for different credit risk classes. Lenders also make efforts to understand the perceived riskiness of borrowers before making lending decisions. Both the lender and borrower take trust and credibility into consideration. In general, the equilibrium supply of and demand for, financing credits at a specific level of risk results in the establishment of an equilibrium cost of capital for the borrower (Partnoy, 1999). However, in reality, contrary to the neoclassical theory, there are great discrepancies among the various actor groups (Banerjee, 2001). As price determining mechanisms might be biased in generating and shifting financial surpluses from the transaction for a specific actor, an independent third party is used to provide a credit check to reduce buyer or seller uncertainty (Kambil and Van Heck, 1998). Therefore, credit markets determine prices by consulting intermediaries such as rating agencies. The emergence of new financial instruments (e.g. MBS and CDOs) facilitated the transfer of credit risk among investors and made the transfer more efficient. The result is that the transfer of credit risk became associated with innovations in securities design (Duffie, 2008).

Rating agencies assume a central role as intermediaries in price determination in real estate loans and their securitization (Wainwright, 2009). Rating agencies evaluate creditworthiness and the probability of default. With the booming housing market through 2005 in the United States, banks packed a large proportion of their real estate loans as mortgage-backed securities, thereby transferring credit risk to capital market investors. Credit ratings played a central role in this, as the ratings display the creditworthiness of the securitized financial products and affect the price for which such structured products can be sold. This implies that ratings show similar characteristics to prices (Hiss and Rona-Tas, 2011). Hence, ratings can fulfill a coordinating function for markets as they have a signal effect as well as a communicating function; thus, ratings can be considered tools for attaining desired market equilibrium (Boot, Milbourn, and Schmeits, 2006). If the rating agencies' evaluation of creditworthiness and probability of default are incomplete, imprecise, and inaccurate, though, then ratings will not reflect the actual value of the structured finance product (Hiss and Rona-Tas, 2011).

The significant negative effects and the economic consequences arising from errors in the credit assessment of securities were illustrated by the subprime crisis (Orlowski, 2008). Experience has demonstrated that there is a spillover effect into other sectors and the globalization of financial markets has only exacerbated this problem. Financial markets converted themselves from a series of narrow national markets into a single, highly integrated, independent global economic market sector with huge volumes of financial transactions. To limit credit risk, ratings were implemented in regulations as measures of risk, and were designed to limit risk-taking on the part of investors. Credit ratings were (and still are) considered to serve a standardizing, coordinating function, setting expertise-based rules to overcome transparency as well as accountability problems (Kerwer, 2001). The steadily growing complexity of financial markets, particularly in credit markets (Samolyk, 2004), has, however, led to dramatic changes in the financial services industry (Baker and Mansi, 2002). Since ratings play an essential role in investment decisions, the activities of rating agencies put them at the very heart of the global financial system (ECOFIN, 2008). Ratings have a direct influence on the price-determination process in markets (Brunner, Pieter, and Weber, 2000), which in turn leads to the question of the role played by rating agencies in this process.

5.4 Rating Agencies and their Role in the Determination of Prices

In the neoclassical approach to price determination – where equilibrium and information efficiency prevail – all market participants are informed extensively and free-of-charge. However, it is possible that this traditional approach overlooks some more complex measurement problems. In neoclassical world of economic models, there is no place for rating agencies (Rudolph, 2004). However, if the assumption of complete information is relaxed and information efficiency is seen in light of Fama's efficient market hypothesis (1970), where it is proposed that there are three types of efficiency (strong-, semi-strong, and weak efficiency), conditions may be derived for the scope of information of ratings in order to provide beneficial information to market participants (Schätzle, 2011). The underlying definition of information efficiency is that it abstracts the costs of obtaining information as well as the cost of trading securities, and thus implies all market participants' agreement as to the impact of the information content on the current price and the future price distribution (Schätzle, 2011). According to Fama, in the weak form, the information set is the historical price that can be predicted from historical price trends; thus, it is impossible to profit from it (Le Roy, 1976). Fama's semi-strong form requires all publicly available information to be reflected in the price (for example, through company announcements), whereas in the strong form, *all* information, including private information, is incorporated in the price (Fama, 1970). This implies that changes in the price of a security are the result of new information in the market (Malkiel, 2003). When applied to rating agencies, security prices reflect a number of factors, including factors such as supply and demand, maturity, liquidity, and non-payment risk. Over the course of time, regularly traded securities will therefore reflect all available information (Everling, 2008).

Capital market efficiency is characterized by prices that fully reflect all available information (Pinches and Singleton, 2012). Rating agencies establish information on the creditworthiness of borrowers in the form of a rating and make it available in the market. Therefore, they are predominantly considered to be information intermediaries (Beaver, Shakespeare, and Soliman, 2006; Kerwer, 2001). This leads to the question of if and in what manner information on borrowers' creditworthiness (expressed in the form of a rating) enhances the efficiency of financial markets (Heinke and Steiner, 2007). Kerwer postulates the question of "whether the role of rating agencies can be reduced to that of efficiency enhancing financial markets intermediaries" (2001, p. 4–5). In order to answer this question, neoclassical finance theory attempted to determine the influence of ratings on the price of assets. The most significant assumption of these theoretical models is that all potential market participants have access to perfect information, as previously noted. Additional information would increase the efficiency only in rare cases in which there is not perfect (complete) information. One case in point is when a rating effectively conveys insider information. If this were to happen, rating agencies would compromise the effectiveness of financial markets since their service is expensive without any significant tangible benefits. In contrast to this approach, the neo-institutional finance theory adopts a generally benevolent attitude toward rating agencies. According to the assumptions of this theory, "all credit relationships are characterised by a principal-agent problem," with the most important conclusion being that there is an information asymmetry to the disadvantage of the lender (principal) (Kerwer, 2001, p. 5).

In order to compensate for this disadvantage, the lender would ask for a risk premium, which in turn would increase transaction costs. Here, rating agencies enhance efficiency by assuming the role of an honest intermediary and help to reduce the lenders' costs. Apart from this perspective, there is another additional consideration, as outlined by Sinclair (1994), that rating agencies only sell specific information to the market. This opinion is based on his hypothesis that rating agencies cannot remain external to the relation with either party (borrower and lender), as they cumulatively create the credit relationship. Rating agencies effectively shape the expectations that each party has from the other. The role of rating agencies is partly justified by the mutual agreement that there is no alternative to the rating in the credit relationship (Kerwer, 2001).

Price discovery plays a pivotal role in the economic system, as "prices consolidate the knowledge scattered around a commodity through supply and demand in a manner otherwise unmatched (Rona-Tas and Hiss, 2011, p. 225). In financial markets, price discovery is of overriding importance (Bakos, 1998). Market participants face uncertainty in more than one way, as there is more than one source of risk that they need to quantify and assess in terms of cost (Greenspan, 2004). Moreover, limited information can be considered a source of risk (Barry and Brown, 1986). Limited information-acquisition ability on the demand side involves the notion of uncertainty regarding the value of a good or service and, hence, indicates the need for information procurement. The buyer is uncertain regarding the price and value and must actively gather information before making any trade-off to arrive at a decision. Since information acquisition is costly and time-consuming, the buyer approaches the decision-making process with the support of rating agencies as intermediaries (Holthausen and Leftwich, 1986).

Rating agencies facilitate transactions in credit markets as they provide support to market participants in their decision-making process (Kräussl, 2005). Further, these agencies establish and strengthen a certain level of trust as intermediaries, a role which protects both buyers and sellers from the opportunistic behavior of market actors (Bakos, 1998). Until the subprime mortgage crisis, rating agencies enjoyed the reputation of being neutral information providers (except in the Enron case), objectively assessing the risk inherent in a certain entity of debt security (Cinquegrana, 2009). With respect to the discussion outlined above, it is necessary to examine what a rating agency actually does when abstracting and reducing reality.

5.4.1 Abstraction and Reduction of Reality

To enable credit markets to emerge, the complexity of reality needs to be reduced to a seemingly manageable level for market participants (Best, 2010; Turhan, 2010). All current rating systems are based on generalizations and abstractions of reality (Key and Key, 2005). By reducing credit risk to a single symbol – the rating – rating agencies allow market actors to participate in credit markets, thereby making the functioning of these markets possible. Without rating agencies (and investment banks), along with their models for abstracting and evaluating structured finance products, this market form would not exist (Hiss and Rona-Tas, 2011). Bearing in mind their task of transforming highly complex factors into a single measure of credit risk, it can be said that rating agencies provide a means of converting uncertainty into calculable risk; it can even be stated that rating agencies convert uncertainty into calculable risk (Kerwer, 2001). It is the business of rating agencies to produce stable expectations that serve as a safeguard for contingencies. Using the findings of rating agencies as a base, it has become possible for actors in global financial markets to make sound decisions, even when confronted with unknown factors (Strulik, 2002). Thus, in terms of functionality, rating agencies transfer and translate a number of concerns and factors into a language that is understandable by market actors. This language is a form of standardization, as the rating agencies make such factors measurable, calculable, and quantifiable (Avetisyan and Gond, 2012). However, it should be remembered that "every rating carries a calculable margin for error," as they are merely estimates (Herring and Kane, 2009, p. 31). The US mortgage crisis is a vivid illustration of market failure where the abstraction of complexity extended into an excessively widening dimension (Hiss and Rona-Tas, 2010). Although there were also other factors contributing to the crisis (Schwartz, 2009), the transformation and translation of credit risk in modern financial markets was only made possible through calculative tools and technologies (Langley, 2009).

5.4.2 Calculative Tools and Judgment Devices

One prerequisite for qualifying products is to determine what exactly needs to be valued. In all cases, market participants must know how to value the products offered to the market. Standardized and status markets follow a different approach in valuing goods; however, they are both social devices that enable various offers in the market to be classified into different categories, which also allows for uncertainty to be reduced at the same time (Aspers, 2005). The two approaches may be considered the principles of the categorization of goods, and provide markets with an opportunity to submit their offers. This leads to the question of how such standards are set and how their status might be assessed. A considerable number of studies in this field have been undertaken in recent years, exploring the role of mathematical models as tools for evaluating the value of financial products (Aspers and Beckert, 2011). Apart from MacKenzie, Muniesa, and Siu (2007), Karpik (1999), and Preda (2006), the study by Callon (1998) is among the most important investigations in this field of research, particularly for his calculative tools for the calculation of equivalence through the application of formulas (Aspers and Beckert, 2011; Beckert 2011).

As part of one of these studies, MacKenzie and Millo (2003) focused on the Black-Scholes model of derivatives pricing for the evaluation of structured financial products. They argued that the derivatives market was primarily very limited, as there was neither the appropriate technology nor the relevant know-how for the pricing of such products. Therefore, the accurate calculation of derivatives prices has only been possible since the 1970s, with constant developments in computerization and progresses in the option price theory, such as the Black-Scholes model. Given these substantial changes in this field, it has become possible for traders to implement theoretical insights from finance theory into their trading practices – and utilize them for their operational advantage (Beckert, 2011).

In a more recent research, MacKenzie (2011) examined and analyzed the evaluation practices of rating agencies conducting risk assessments of structured finance products such as collateralized debt obligations (CDOs) and asset-backed securities (ABS). He discussed these matters on the basis of the valuation method typically applied to determine the implied default correlation in CDOs and ABS: the Gaussian copula model. The Gaussian copula model enabled the calculation of the credit risk inherent in financial products such as CDOs, as the model "relies on a correlation number that expresses the interdependencies of the securities pooled in one CDO" (Aspers and Beckert, 2011, p. 19). According to MacKenzie, the market for such products would have been very limited if participating in the market required an understanding of such models (2011). This is where rating agencies and their ratings come into play: ratings compare the economic value of the highly complex, structured products with less complex securities, such as corporate bonds.

In contrast to scholars focusing on calculative tools, it was Karpik's aim to develop a conceptual framework for the mechanisms used for the measurement and assessment of quality factors that mostly apply to singular goods (2010). He terms these mechanisms 'judgment devices'. According to Karpik's concept, the idea constitutes a signpost and serves as an aide for individual and collective actions to remedy the lack of transparency in markets where market participants show weakness in the appraisal of product quality resulting from insufficient knowledge. Karpik established a range of devices through which judgments on products in markets are made. In the sociology of economics, much research has been influenced by the keyword 'judgment device' when focusing on the classification of goods (Aspers and Beckert, 2011). Customers' expectations regarding the quality and value of goods are built upon the recommendations of guides, experts, and rankings — to name but a few. To manage values in credit markets is one of the challenges of driving economic growth. This management is conducted by market participants through judgment devices that are produced and applied by intermediaries such as rating agencies (Beckert, 2012). This leads to the question of how such judgment devices impact price formation (Beckert, 2012).

One of Karpik's devices is his so-called *cicerones*, a term used to designate critics and guidebooks exerting gentle pressure in the form of authority, which may influence the evolution of the qualities of various offers (Aspers and Beckert, 2011). He conducted a study on the *Guide Michelin,* which selects, compares, and rates restaurants (Karpik, 2000). The *Guide Michelin* developed its own quality evaluation criteria, and applies this set of criteria to judge and ultimately classified restaurants based on the Guide's own opinion. The Guide establishes the principles for quality, but it does leave room for the manifold possibilities and perceptions of worth that may be attributed by different customers by providing the reader with information on various other aspects and categories beyond quality alone. Apart from the critics and guidebooks, Karpik also uses the term *cicerones* for experts in a market sector, as they create judgments on goods with their assessments. As applied to financial markets, this means that analysts in this market sector present their assessments of financial assets as experts on the issue, thereby exercising at least mild pressure on investment decisions by their judgment (Aspers and Beckert, 2011).

Another of Karpik's judgment devices is 'rankings,' that apply, for instance, to bestseller lists for music and books, as well as to academic journals, lawyers, and wine. Rankings are particularly important in the wine market, as they have a major influence as a judgment device. The same is true for the financial market and rating agencies, as even the rankings of the major rating agencies can no longer be considered satisfactory by investors with regard to reliability (Amenc and Le Sourd, 2007). Contrary to the soft authority of *cicerones,* with the possibility of including more than just one principle of worth, rankings create an order in which the complexity of goods offered in the market is reduced to one single scale at the level of order. The American wine critic Robert Parker implemented a ranking system on a scale of 50 to 100. In terms of impact, the scale imitates an objectivity standard while ultimately being subjective by nature. However, a number of studies demonstrated the influence of the Parker ranking in the wine market (Aspers and Beckert, 2011). The same holds true for rating agencies and their influence in the financial markets (Kerwer, 2001).

In his article on the economy of price and status formation in the Bordeaux wine market, Hay (2010) examines the role of wine critics as 'rating agencies' and places special emphasis on the globalization of the price-determination process in the context to the institutional character of this market, and the extent to which international wine critics could be considered agents of standardization (Hay, 2010). In the credit and financial markets, it remains crucial to emphasize that the value of standardization is defined by rating agencies using comparable classification methods (Cisneros, Lizaraburu, and Salguero, 2012). However, there are concerns regarding the independence and objectivity of critics, as the critics in wine markets (who are quite often assisted by a team of colleagues) are, in many cases, sponsored by wine producers (Combris, Lecocq, and Visser, 2003). This is comparable to financial markets, however, when rating agencies are paid by the issuer (Deb and Murphy, 2009). Similar to the financial market, the wine market is one that lacks information; in financial markets, consumers speculate on anticipated increases in the market value of goods – or at least on no losses in their investment. As is not only the case in financial markets, "speculation in future prices is the dominating preoccupation of the participants" (Tobin, 1978, p. 157). For this reason, the wine and financial markets are heavily dependent on expert ratings – wine critics in the former case and rating agencies in the latter –. This situation in each respective industry may adversely affect the price at which wine or securities can be sold (Hay, 2010). In his study, Hay demonstrates that these markets require information to operate. More precisely, the markets need "a series of proxies of quality which international investor-consumers can use" to make choices for their investment despite inherent uncertainties regarding the quality of their investment decisions (Hay, 2010, p. 705). This also applies to the role of rating agencies in the global financial market (Kerwer, 2001).

In light of the parallelism noted between the financial and wine markets, another of Hay's findings should be taken into consideration within the context of this research. Hay compared the 2005 global consumer boom in the wine market, which was characterized by higher-than-anticipated prices for so-called investment grade wines, with the 2008 campaign that took place during an economic downturn. He demonstrated the critic's (Parker's) role in the price formation process in both cases, and found that Parker had a tremendous impact and influence on pricing. Parker had, like the rating agencies, "become part of the institutional embedding of this market", and played a key role in the price and status determination process (Hay, 2010, p. 685). Applied to rating agencies, this means that they not only play a central role in the process of price determination as they rate the majority of all financial products, but also that any of their rating downgrades become, in the end, a self-fulfilling prophecy, leading to price erosion (Partnoy, 1999). Such parallels in behavior were further confirmed given the fact that the wine industry, like the financial market, witnessed a boom in 2005 and a bust in 2008 (Hay, 2010).

5.5 Conclusion

As price and value may deviate but affect each other, pricing plays a central role in communicating the values of goods and services, as well as serving as a tool with which to make heterogeneous objects comparable. Nonetheless, prices may misrepresent the underlying value (Rona-Tas and Hiss, 2011). For decades, economic and finance theory operated under the assumption that prices in the market reflect all available information (Adams, Mullins, and Thornton, 2011). This perception did not consider that credit markets are markets where choices need to be made under conditions of uncertainty, as the future is unpredictable. Derogating from this theory, real markets are imperfect by definition; markets with perfect and complete information do not exist (Thomas, 1998). As a further consequence of the uncertainty caused by asymmetric information in credit markets, prices are not only a reflection of value, but they also influence the value itself, which poses a problem in estimating creditworthiness. These markets therefore need to overcome the problem of valuation and judging the quality of goods/services offered, especially in the area of financial derivatives.

Faced with the difficulty of judging the quality of the goods/services offered, along with the fact that price formation may be biased in generating and shifting surpluses of the transaction to a specific actor, these markets need an independent intermediary and 'judgment devices' in order to solve the problem. These judgment devices are, similar to mathematical models for the evaluation of financial products value, another means of improving comparative evaluation. Since managing values in credit markets is a challenging issue of driving growth, judgment devices are established and applied by intermediaries to simplify the pricing of financial instruments. One judgment device able to exert a great influence in valuating and pricing financial instruments is a ranking order.

As intermediaries, the objective of rating agencies is to reduce asymmetric information resulting from the uncertainties and imperfections of information faced by market participants. Rating agencies' assessments of creditworthiness facilitate transactions in credit markets and establish certain levels of trust for both buyers and sellers, which are attributed to the regulatory use of credit ratings. However, their independence is doubtful despite the fact that their information provides utility and the fact that they have become increasingly powerful in global financial markets (Kerwer, 2005). The rating affects the price for which a security can be sold, and thus displays similar characteristics as prices. Thus, rating agencies take over coordinating and communicative functions, as they have a signal effect.

The significant negative effects arising from incomplete and imprecise creditworthiness assessments have been revealed in the subprime crisis, since rating agencies mistaken perceptions drastically affected securities prices. Although rating agencies were overwhelmed by the complexity of financial instruments they rated (Eggert, 2009), they nevertheless play a unique role in the price determination process driven by existing regulatory framework provisions. However, given the enormous risks and the high degree of uncertainty in securities markets, the role they play as reliable market intermediaries has come under increasing scrutiny.

Particularly in times of uncertainty about the real value of securities experienced by market participants due to a financial crisis and general loss of confidence in the marketplace, price determination for structured finance products in capital markets may be limited insofar as the confidence in the quality of ratings representing the underlying value is shaken. Better understanding of how prices are set is required, particularly of the respective roles of the various factors influencing prices, as well as the ratings agencies' role in price formation in the financial markets. Increased understanding, in turn, will help to determine the necessary action, as regulators have a significant impact on pricing and market participants' behavior. Indeed, there have been calls for reforms to discipline rating agencies and in terms of financial market regulation. The next chapter will outline regulatory authorities' role, as well as regulatory provisions, and their impact on the price determination process of the financial markets.

6. Regulators, Regulations, and Price Determination in Financial Markets

The foundations of a stable, informed, and functional financial market place is based upon a combination of regulatory oversight and private sector reporting policies and standards. These principals were largely disregarded by the authorities, who underestimated the extreme volatility and the risks involved in trading complex and speculative financial instruments. Based upon early theories of equilibrium and rationality in stock market trading and investor decision-making, government oversight in major markets has largely been limited to a reactive role in which bubbles and crashes have resulted in significant legislative and control-oriented modifications to operational oversight. One area in which regulatory agenda setting has inconsistently addressed the link between information and investor decision-making is the scope of rating agencies. A recent study by Ziebart and Reiter (2010) underscored the importance of the role of information and ratings in the securities pricing process, as they are the main indicators for investors to evaluate the price charged for a specific security.

At the core of rating agencies' regulatory agendas, policy makers have continued to concentrate on predominately 'micro-prudential issues' that focus on limiting conflicts of interest, encouraging competition, and improving transparency (Sy, 2009). Given such limitations, there has now been a significant shift in attention towards more explicit regulation of rating agencies and their relative powers within the marketplace. This has particularly been the case since the recent market crash of 2007–2008. From uncertainty to inefficiency, the role of information in investors' decision making is an important determinant of future market behavior (Levy, Levy, and Solomon, 2000). However, given the risk proclivity of credit ratings, and 'irrational exuberances' (Shiller, 2009), the link between regulatory oversight and rating agencies information sharing, and its impact on prices, is assessed in this chapter in order to highlight areas of deficiency and opportunity.

After providing an overview of the reasons governing the introduction of regulatory authorities in financial regulation that evolved during the last two centuries, and the objectives of regulations in financial markets, this chapter offers a brief account of how regulators attempt to regulate capital markets along with the impact of regulatory, deregulatory, and liberalizational measures. The second part of the chapter discusses regulatory approaches to price setting and addresses the question as to what extent they influence price determination in financial markets. Finally, the chapter provides an overview of the most important key regulations recently implemented, with regard to rating agencies and credit ratings.

6.1 Regulation of Financial Markets

6.1.1 History of Regulations in Financial Markets

Following the historic market crash of 1929, a number of rules and objectives were put into place to protect investors against fraud and other irregularities, as well as to promote the development of standards and procedures designed to prevent price manipulation (Hess and Frost, 2012; Kadish 1963). These formed the basis of market protection for the major part of the 20th century. However, the 1987 crash, which has gone down in history as 'Black Monday', turned into a global financial crisis (Sandoval and Franca, 2012). In its aftermath, many called for a revamping of regulations so as to attain greater stability in the financial markets (Harris, 1988). It is this legacy of the late 1980s that has shaped much of the present-day regulatory framework.

6.1.2 Objectives of Financial Market Regulation

As Barth, Capiro, and Levine (2002) as well as Reinhart and Rogoff (2010) note, there are, generally speaking, three objectives of financial regulation: (1) fostering macroeconomic stability; (2) ensuring a high, effective and consistent level of prudential regulation of intermediaries; and (3) transparency in the market of intermediaries to ensure investor protection. To meet these objectives, it is appropriate to incorporate relevant rules to control market powers and structures, particularly by focusing on controlling financial intermediaries, such as rating agencies (Barth, Capiro, and Levine, 2002). To determine how these objectives can be implemented, it must be asked who, how, and what should be regulated (Lastra 2003).

Every country has its own national regulatory authorities, while in Europe, the European System of Financial Supervision (ESFS) has an additional general oversight. Within the ESFS, the European Supervisory Authority (ESA) plays a fundamental role. In the United States, the financial markets get general regulatory oversight from the Securities and Exchange Commission (SEC) and the Commodity Futures Trading Commission (CFTC). In addition to these bodies, the Financial Industry Regulatory Authority (FINRA) is responsible for oversight in the securities market, but none of these three bodies have complete authority over the market. Regulation of the US monetary system is left to the Federal

Reserve Bank (Fed). At a global level, the Group of Twenty (G20) constitutes the key-forum for exchanging views, information, discussions and recommendations that aim to overcome the global financial downturn. Other authorities acting on a global level are the International Organization of Securities Commissions (IOSCO) and the Financial Stability Board (FSB), established in 2009. The common aim of all of these authorities is to link their activities within an area of increasingly complex regulation of financial markets along with the objectives of financial regulation. In order to achieve these goals, financial regulations subject financial market participants to certain requirements, restrictions, and guidelines, including the supervision of banks and financial service providers, as well as the supervision of investment management.

Regulatory authorities are traditionally active in financial markets and in the governance of financial intermediaries. As a consequence, financial markets are accustomed to regulation and regulation itself is seldom questioned, specifically why regulation of rating agencies has become of such primary concern (Cecchetti, 1999). While Goodhart et al., (1998) consider these questions and provide details on the scale and nature of regulatory problems globally, with special attention to specific sectors, Danielsson et al. refer to the failures of supervisory authorities in the Basel II proposals to address the principal shortcomings of the financial regulatory system. In so doing, they give particular attention to the "heavy reliance on rating agencies for the standard approach to credit risk" (2001, p. 13). Given the strong dependence on external ratings, the role played by governmental authorities in the financial sector, their interventions in the pricing and allocation of credit, and their role in the regulation and supervision of financial intermediaries such as rating agencies gained considerable attention (Barth, Capiro, and Levine, 2002). Ideally, regulators would develop a number of policies and procedures relating to investor protection and reducing systematic risks (Cecchetti, 1999). However, in discussing how to achieve the issues and targets of regulation, Barth, Capiro, and Levine (2002) argue that there is no uniform method, theoretical model, or a single practical approach that can be applied to the regulation and supervision of financial markets.

6.1.3 How Regulators and Regulations Regulate Financial Markets

Ribstein (2003) argues that it appears that regulators only react after market mistakes take place, rather than preventing similar mistakes in the future. Moreover, according to Ribstein, regulators in post-bubble times disregard the advantages of market flexibility, and in so doing lose sight of the risk-taking and innovation in markets that will be likely to launch the next boom. Particularly worthy of emphasis are previous moves towards soft touch regulation, as this was an important causal factor in the current crisis driven by narrow sectional and political interests. French, Leyshon, and Thrift argue that "[t]his race to bottom in terms of regulation was facilitated by a general sense that financial markets and products were too complicated to be regulated by those outside the market" (2009, p. 292). Furthermore, the authors underline that it was believed "that financial institutions were sufficiently sophisticated and forward thinking to develop risk assessment models that would [...] avoid systematic financial crisis" (French, Leyshon, and Thrift, 2009, p. 292). The idea was that the scientific techniques used were effective tools for managing risks, and were robust enough for the evaluation of rare financial events (Taleb and Martin, 2012). Moreover, regulators permitted financial institutions to estimate risk and set capital requirements assuming that large losses could not occur (Crotty, 2009). However, the recent crisis of 2007/2008 demonstrated that the implemented regulations were not adequate in the area of financial innovation (Crotty, 2011). Sy further emphasizes the extent to which the rating industry that played a key role in financial innovation and the origins of the current crisis predominantly relied on self-regulation (2009, p. 3); and self-regulation has long been regarded as an important factor in the governance of financial markets (Miller, 1985).

6.1.4 Regulation, De-Regulation, Liberalization, and their Impact on Globalization

From the 1980s onwards, states opened the door for the globalization of financial markets by "granting freedom to market actors through liberalization" (Helleiner, 1995, p. 1). The process of deregulation, liberalization, and privatization of financial services from nationalized regulated markets created the infrastructure for a fast-growing capital market (Lütz, 2002). Jeon and Chiang cite deregulation and liberalization measures, fast-changing developments in communication technology, and computerized trading systems, along with innovations in financial products and services, and increasing activity of multinational companies as factors that contributed to the world market integration of stock (security) markets (1991).

The introduced reforms of the regulatory framework improved access to credit through a reduction of borrowing costs, and sharply increased the variety and complexity of financial products. These financial products, specifically securitization, triggered the crisis of 2007–2008, and some of the more recent economic theories suggest that innovation can cause instability in both financial and economic environments in circumstances where investors neglect the associated smaller threats in such investments (Gennaioli, Shleifer, and Vishny, 2012). In addition, investors can have "biased expectations or institutional preferences and constraints," such as institutional investors' and pension funds' demand for AAA-rated securities (Shleifer and Vishny, 2010, p. 306). The latter is important here, as ratings are implemented and used as parameters for investment decisions. An aspect of the mechanical use of ratings is that it can reinforce pro-cyclical behaviors in markets (CGFS, 2010). However, the unexpected effects of such governmental policies were felt in the crisis of 2007–2008 as regulatory authorities considerably underestimated the potential price effects of market liberalization.

Associated with the globalization of financial markets, regulators, quasi regulators (such as rating agencies), and regulations changed and influenced the risk perceptions associated with complex forms of financial products. The mindset and ideology that assumed that markets are by some means rational, logical and, most importantly, self-correcting, had a profound impact on how financial markets and financial institutions were regulated and governed (Awrey, 2012; French, Leyshon, and Thrift, 2009). This ideology and way of thinking were institutionalized in the international regulatory framework of Basel II, which, as noted in greater detail below, is a program based on the concept of prudential regulation. This approach "displaced the regulatory gaze from financial risks themselves towards the risk assessment systems employed by financial institutions" (French, Leyshon, and Thrift, 2009, p. 292). In addition, the internal risk assessment procedures and systems of financial institutions were delegated to privatized quasi-regulatory bodies, such as rating agencies (Sinclair, 2005). In light of the structural changes in the securities sector, especially in the mortgage sector, and the growing global financial markets, politicians and lobbyists urged further deregulation (Immergluck, 2009) – an approach that gave rating agencies a remarkable boost for their activities.

Although Stiglitz (1993) recognized that there is a role for government in financial markets, he maintains that governmental interventions in this area lead to mixed results on the whole. Concurring, Mayntz observed that market discipline and efforts of self-regulation do not appear to have worked to prevent the current crisis (2012). Mayntz stressed that "the existing rules had significant gaps and created incentives for circumvention and deviation" (2012, p. 7). She cites these shortcomings as evidence as to why markets have been inflated with toxic assets, and argues that the unregulated spaces have paved the way for the development of new practices (Mayntz, 2012). This, so the author's argument goes, "holds for the construction of 'innovative' financial instruments, such as structured asset-backed securities and credit default swaps" (Mayntz, 2012, p. 7).

The pressure on self-regulatory frameworks increased during the course of the crisis of 2007–2008. As a consequence of this, forces such as the development of stronger statutory regulatory authorities, the consolidation of financial service industry regulatory bodies, and the ongoing globalization of capital markets affected the scope and effectiveness of self-regulation (Carson, 2011). As private rating agencies failed to adequately assess the risk in the new financial products with their models, regulators are now working on measures regarding prudential supervision and rating agencies' activity and role in financial markets in order to restore normality, thus allowing capital market prices to regain stability. Financial market liberalization must not endanger financial stability, and there is every reason to question whether government intervention and restructuring concepts will lead to softened economic liberalization policies.

6.2 Regulatory Impact on Price Determination in Financial Markets

6.2.1 Prices and Regulation

As noted in Chapter 5, prices are a reflection of supply and demand and the relationship between the two factors underlines the forces that make markets work. In equilibrium – where supply and demand intersect – the interaction in free market forces determines the price and quantity of any good or service traded (Lo, 2004). The underlying assumption behind financial market regulation was that financial markets are rational *and* efficient. A primary concern of financial regulation is to remove the impediments that may cause inefficient and illiquid markets (Ball, 2009). These regulators aim to ensure that market participants comply with the various rules and regulations introduced by the authorities. Financial markets are among the most strictly regulated sectors in the economy, with regulations designed to safeguard the soundness of the sector Governmental oversight plays an important role in ensuring well-functioning markets. The vast majority of regulatory policies in existence relate to money markets, and as far as the credit and stock markets are concerned, governmental intervention has, historically, relied almost exclusively on self-regulation (Dodd, 2002).

In debating the issue of modern financial theory, Fox (2011, p. 137) alleges that the US Congress gave a major boost to the concept of modern finance with the implementation of the pension-reform legislation of 1974, an act which has had many "interesting consequences." One of the consequences was that risks tended to be vague and an unquantifiable threat which could only be defined with judgment. Fox cites this development as a curious fact, since "[t]he same finance scholars who claimed that you couldn't predict future stock price movements by looking at past stock price movements were embracing the idea that future stock volatility could be predicted by looking at past stock volatility" (2011, p. 146). Regulators, therefore, supported not only the price determination for risky financial instruments, but also enforced private risk-taking (Awrey, 2012). However, the changing financial landscape and the complexity of financial markets and innovation have brought about regulatory challenges at various levels of the existing regulatory framework (Awrey, 2012). In commenting further, Cerny stresses that the essential feature of markets "is that they are arenas for the setting of prices" (1994, p. 332) and that efficient prices adjust markets. He further argues that the concept of self-regulating markets can only work under conditions where the mechanisms for price-settings are sufficiently efficient to clear those markets. The author considers that the setting of efficient prices is characterized by the clearness and precision of the price signals conveyed by and exchanged between the purchasers and sellers. Extrapolating the limitations of an equilibrium-based price determination model, Smith, Suchanek, and Williams argue that if markets are indeed at equilibrium, then "stock prices should change only when there is new information that changes investors' dividend expectations", as the "theory of common stock valuation holds that a stock's current market value tends to converge to the (risk adjusted) discounted present value of the rationally expected dividend stream" (1988, p. 1119). It is within this force-based variability and market adjustments that the authors identify three primary processes including changes in the assets' dividend value, evolution of agents' price expectations, and an adjustments to an assets' price (Smith, Suchanek, and Williams, 1988). In debating the role of regulations and system adjustments during the most recent financial crisis, it is essential to address these particular values, especially in relation to the ambiguity, high risk, and heterogeneity of speculative investment vehicles.

Asymmetric Information. As a result of market forces, stock/securities prices change every day, and movements in the stock/securities markets are likely to be unpredictable. The theory of price relations based on the concept of asymmetrical information was only very rarely used in guiding asset pricing and portfolio allocation decisions (Biais, Bossaerts, and Spatt, 2010). Bisin and Gottardi (1999) discussed the influence of asymmetric information on competitive equilibria in economics under conditions of 'sufficiently' complete markets (as asset markets are), and where all individual positions are pooled together and securitized. The authors showed that two prices (bid and ask price) for financial contracts are sufficient to ensure the existence of competitive equilibrium in markets where trading takes place based on asymmetric information. While in an efficient capital market a trader will not have the overall chance to improve his speculative gain through obtaining access to publicly accessible information and "evaluating that information intelligently in determining which stock to buy or sell", paradoxically, market efficiency results from "competitive efforts of securities analyst and investors who strive to earn superior returns by identifying mispriced securities, securities that are either overvalued or undervalued" (Fischel, 1978, p. 2–3).

Financial innovation and price setting in financial markets. Financial markets should be efficient and transparent. Regulation should therefore pursue a strategy aimed at enabling investors to determine prices easily and rapidly on the markets. The fact is, however, that financial markets are more complex than other markets, and they play a critical role in the price determination process due to their own institutional and economic structures (Dodd, 2012). In financial markets, the price for a debt is predominantly set by the rating of the debt issue (Capital Markets Division, 2009). However, ratings for debt need to show accuracy over time in order to prove that they are adding value going beyond the market price (Ekin and Calabria, 2012). In addition, credit ratings contribute to the determination of interest rates (Gavras, 2012), which is particularly important with regard to payment obligations relating to the purchase or selling of securities.

Finance and capital markets are subject to a number of factors and forces affecting the level of interest rates and prices. From the investor's perspective, such 'affecting factors' (not only interest rates, but also the risk of default for instance) can cause severe losses. In addition, as financial markets are always sensitive to risks that can arise, they should be subject to regulatory mechanisms developed to support a robust financial market structure (Borio and Zhu, 2011; Knight, 1998). In this context, Stiglitz and Walsh argue that long ago "[e]conomic theory – and historical experience" proved the necessity of regulation in financial markets, [...] [b]ut ever since the Reagan presidency, deregulation has been the prevailing religion" (2005, p. 3). Deregulation was considered to support the efficient market theory (EMT), according to which financial markets are "informationally efficient" (Ferguson et al., 2011, p. 19).

This interpretation, according to Davis (2011, p. 11) is not entirely correct, as the EMT and Fama's Efficient Market Hypothesis (EMH) "simply asserts" that prices reflect all available information, but does not state that "prices are right nor that the information is correct". Furthermore, Davis points out that theory has "little to do with the conventional wisdom regarding financial regulation" (2011, p. 11). Although the author agrees that the efficient market hypothesis is relevant insofar as price signals reflect available information, he argues that this approach to financial regulation was based on the "longstanding hypothesis that competitive markets will generally, through the price signals generated" reach an optimal utilization of resources (Davis, 2011, p. 11).

Financial markets are not only regulated by governmental authorities, but also by the rating agencies, which are *de facto* regulators in this market segment. Rating agencies not only influence the price level by expressing their risk estimates for risks to which investors are exposed in the form of ratings, but also specify which regulatory measures apply (Kerwer, 2005). The regulatory use of ratings unveils their double role in financial markets, as they are used both for valuation purposes and for contractual use. Financial instruments assigned 'low-risk' (investment grade) are subject to lighter regulatory requirements, whereas instruments assigned 'high-risk' (speculative grade) are subjected to higher regulatory requirements.

In response to artificial market shifts, bubbles, sunspots, and so on, McCallum (2001) offers quantitative evidence to reject the foundations of price level determination, suggesting that two dimensions, including the monetary price of consumption and monetary holding, are in constant competition. This results in inefficiencies that are under-addressed in the price determination model. Woodford also contends that the expectation of "exact homogeneity of the equilibrium" is an errant interpretation of a Keynesian aggregative model, whereby variations in the money supply and the heterogeneity associated with open market operations (rather than taxation or transfers) cannot be considered as resulting "in the increase of decrease in the money supply necessary to accommodate a given change in the current price level" (1994, p. 372–373), ultimately affecting consumers budget constraints. Specifically, Woodford (1994, p. 345–346) takes a fiscal theory stance regarding price determination, suggesting that "price level is determined by the ratio of nominal debt to the present value of real primary surpluses" (cited Bloise, 2005, p. 1037). As Bloise argues, "the controversy ultimately relies on the interpretation of intertemporal public budgets constrains" (2005, p. 1038). As the author further stresses, if we follow conventional classic point of view, "the intertemporal public constraint imposes a restriction on fiscal plans, which can only be stet subject to such a constraint" (Bloise, 2005, p. 1037–1038). In contrast, in the fiscal theory of price levels it is maintained that "fiscal plans can be set exogenously and the intertemporal public budget constraint only holds as an equilibrium condition" (Bloise, 2005, p. 1038). Such a Non-Ricardian hypothesis identifies the intertemporal balanced public budget as a consequence of private budget constraints, whereby at equilibrium, a surplus in the public budget corresponds to a positive net transfer in the budget constraint of the "representative individual" (Bloise, 2005, p. 1038). By definition, at equilibrium, speculative bubbles "cannot occur on securities that are in positive net supply" and thus equilibrium cannot exist with unbalanced transfers across individuals, whilst speculative bubbles can be sustained on securities in zero net supply (Bloise, 2005, p. 1038).

In spite of the quantitative justification for this Non-Ricardian hypothesis introduced by Bloise (2005), it is evident that such systemic models are based upon an anticipation of rational actors and market conditions. Harris and Spivey (1990), however, introduce an exemplary realization of irrationality and uninformedness in trading activities. With specific reference to 1987's Black Monday, the authors suggest that "panic selling by irrational or uniformed investors [...] implies rejection of the rational expectations model of stock price determination" (Harris and Spivey, 1990, p. 59). Under the rational expectations model of security prices, Harris and Spivey explain that predictions are made that stock prices will "reflect the value of expected future pay-outs of the underlying assets" (1990, p. 60). Yet, with such an accelerated crash as the one witnessed on 'Black Monday,' the researchers emphasize that there is sufficient, compelling evidence to reject the market efficiency and rational expectations models, suggesting instead that "stock prices are irrational in the sense that they reflect emotional, animal spirits, or the appearance and collapse of speculative bubbles" (Harris and Spivey, 1990, p. 60).

As evidence of the irrationality of stock prices, Harris and Spivey (1990) assert that under rational conditions, stock prices would not decline uniformly during a crash condition, whereby the closing prices of the Standard & Poor's 500 fail to reflect the appropriate individual stocks' betas. Resolution of such systemic variability has been strategically accomplished through price determinations and limitations, particularly in speculative markets. Westerhoff (2003) suggests that a price limitation is the maximum range within which prices are allowed to move within a single day, based upon a percentage determined by the previous day's closing price. Yet there are two schools of thought relating to price limitations. The first school "supports the overreaction hypothesis", where price limits serve as a necessary cooling off period to reduce reactionary, irrational investor decision-making (Westerhoff, 2003, p. 497). In contrast, the second school "believes in the information hypothesis" where price limits slow the adjustment of prices to a new equilibrium and have no real effect on volatility (Westerhoff, 2003, p. 497). Through a critical empirical analysis of such price limit adjustments, Yeh and Yang (2010) demonstrate how investors will continue to adjust the stock prices in the following trading periods due to an incomplete information cycle, regardless of efforts to reduce volatility in the immediacy.

6.2.2 Effects of Regulatory Rules on Insider Trading and Price Formation in Financial Markets

At the core of investment decision-making, Wu cites liquidity as a precondition of exchange, with which investors are able to dispose of shares "without undue delay" and without "incurring an unreasonable loss caused only by lack of potential buyers" (1968, p. 263). Within the actualization of liquidity, Wu considers that the federal regulation (e.g. the SEC in the United States) of capital markets and the requirement of "full disclosure" strengthens public confidence through improved public knowledge and "fair price determination" (1968, p. 264). Given that the true, intrinsic value of a given share is difficult to ascertain accurately, stock prices are intrinsically determined by supply and demand factors, whereby the "state of confidence" plays a significant role in short term price movements (Wu, 1968, p. 265). Citing insiders as an example of "fair price determination", Wu (1968, p. 266) suggests that insider speculation reflects an allocational and promotional efficiency, whereby pricing is predictable due to the low entry and high exit points of the insider. Such considerations argue against the SEC's initiative to vigorously apply rule 10b-5 (16, b) to short term trading restrictions on corporate insiders, as it may ultimately preclude the exchange of information and disclosure that is necessary for achieving equilibrium conditions in the marketplace (Wu, 1968).

The anti-competitive nature of insider trading cannot be discounted, and efforts by the SEC in the United States to regulate this behavior have comprised an important step towards developing a market-based (rather than insider-based) foundation of price-setting determinations. As investment management firms have become core components of the financial market, the FSB (2010.) emphasizes that the potential for risk-based deficiencies and mechanistic investment decision-making continues to present a challenge for public investment confidence across global markets. From the failure to appropriately manage and supervise risk, to inadequate disclosures and public reporting measures, to an intrinsic reliance on the recommendations of credit reporting agencies, the liabilities associated with institutional investment platforms are perpetuating an inefficient information cycle, which has had significant impacts on market performance and inefficiency (FSB, 2010).

Exemplifying the challenges associated with regulatory oversight and their potential implications for investor behavior in the market, Linsmeier et al. (2002)

cite the SEC issuance of the Financial Regulation Release No. 48 (FRR No. 48) as a particular influence upon volume-sensitive investments and risk-based disclosure agenda setting. Following a string of massive derivative-related debacles in the 1990s, FFR No. 48 was introduced to mitigate potential market-based risks associated with adverse changes in market rates and price changes, "mandating forward looking quantitative market risk disclosure in companies' 10K- reports" (Linsmeier et al., 2002, p. 344). The intention of this provision is to inform investors through a formalized public disclosure of firms' exposure to market-based risk (Linsmeier et al., 2002. The researchers empirically demonstrated that prior to the introduction of FRR No. 48, investors exhibited uncertainty and a range of diverse opinions regarding the effects on firm value from changes in varying market rates/prices associated with interest rates, foreign currency exchange, and commodity prices. Following the introduction of FRR No. 48, the relative value of this information was immediately apparent, resulting in declines in trading volume sensitivity relative to interest rates, exchange rates, and energy prices (Linsmeier et al., 2002). Although such findings are far from universal – and are ultimately inconsistent when considering the scope of reporting standards and outcomes in global financial markets – they are indicative of the information-based influence of regulatory oversight, corporate controls, and the equalization of information resources across the investment marketplace.

In the context of regulation of insider trading and FFR No. 48 on derivative and market risk disclosure, it should be kept in mind that rating agencies do acquire confidential (inside) information from their clients. As this information is, by its very nature, sensitive to stock/securities prices and is not available to the public, having access to this information poses a dilemma for the rating agencies. To resolve this dilemma, rating agencies assess all information without disclosing the inside information on which the rating is based (Langohr and Langohr, 2008). Rating agencies were in legally safe harbors as the SEC's ruling specifically exempted rating agencies from its fair disclosure regulation (FD) adopted in 2000 (Poon and Evans, 2011). Regulation FD prohibits companies from selective disclosure of material non-public information to analysts, institutional investors, and others without simultaneously making the information available to the public at large (Harris, 2002). This rule reflects the regulators' perspective that all investors should have equal access to material disclosures at the same time. Although the SEC removed the exemption of rating agencies from Regulation FD as required under Section 939B of the Dodd-Frank Act of 2010 (the revised rule was made effective with publication in the Federal Register on October 4, 2010), rating agencies continue to be exempted under Regulation FD. Rating agencies are exempted from Regulation FD if the agency has expressly agreed with the issuer to maintain confidentiality of the disclosed information. Exemption also applies in cases where communications made between persons owe a duty of trust or confidence to the issuer (SEC 2010). This means that investors have to consider whether rating agencies are among the non-exempted persons, or whether rating agencies opted for another exemption from Regulation FD available whenever non-public information is provided to them.

The exception of rating agencies from fair disclosure requirements illustrates their specific position within the regulatory framework, "and some evidence suggest that this exception increased rating agencies' importance in valuating securities" (Dwyer, 2010, p. 3–4). While the expectations and agenda of the SEC may be much broader than establishing an equal investment field through a risk mitigation platform, efforts to mitigate shocks and constrain the potential for uncertainty (relatively speaking) are indicative of a progressive regulatory tradition. Ultimately, these challenges will have significant implications for information-providing services in the financial markets, especially rating agencies, as will be discussed in the subsequent sections of this chapter.

6.3 Regulatory Issues Related to Rating Agencies

6.3.1 A Regulatory Paradigm for Rating Agencies

By definition, a credit rating is designed to reflect the "rating agency's opinion, as of a specific date, of the creditworthiness of a particular company, security, or obligation" (SEC, 2003, p. 5). Revised in 1990, Section 203 of the OCC handbook emphasizes that under Law 12, USC 24, a security must be marketable and not predominately speculative in order to qualify as an investment (OCC, 1990). Citing specific rating agencies' ratings, including Standard and Poor's BBB and Moody's Baa-1 and Baa, these guidelines validate the relevance and importance of rating agencies in determining investment opportunities for large US banking institutions (OCC, 1990). This establishes a benchmark of rating-based determinations, which inherently extends to the financial market itself. At the level of large institutional investors, such as pension funds, the rules of regulatory legislation, which include a cap on the holding of asset rated at speculative grade, are followed (Canuto, dos Santos, and de Sá Porto, 2012).

Although, these rating agencies' assessments were primarily designed for private financial markets, they have increasingly guided investors through their investment decisions with information on creditworthiness, thereby directly contributing to the determination of interest rates or prices (Canuto, dos Santos, and de Sá Porto, 2012; Gavras, 2012). Given the ever-increasing recognition of ratings in regulations, ratings have become fixtures on the global financial landscape. In support of this assertion, Canuto, dos Santos, and de Sá Porto argue that if rating agencies' ratings serve as an instrument for determining credit risk, then "ratings tend to be reflected in the price of assets" (2007, p. 12). However, ratings have a considerable impact on the operation of markets, and unanticipated rating changes do have significant effects (Hau, Langfield, and Marques-Ibanez, 2012).

The assumption of relative rationality (Smith, Suchanek, and Williams 1988; Bloise 2005), characterized by systemic regulation and explicit disclosure-based controls by the SEC and other regulatory bodies, fails to address the nature of inconsistent or inadequate information – a dimension of disequilibrium that will ultimately facilitate the manifestation of bubbles or crashes in the market. If rating agencies are indiscriminate in their ratings or management of investment-based information, as demonstrated by Partnoy (2006), the likelihood of irrationality is exacerbated. This may result in inefficient trading movements that can disrupt the equilibrium of the marketplace. Accordingly, it follows that if upgraded or downgraded, the price of a bond or security will move following the upgrade or downgrade (Canuto, dos Santos, and de Sá Porto, 2007).

In discussing the effect of rating announcements, Claessens and Embrechts (2007) contend that the easiest way for measuring rating agencies' impact on financial markets is to test the causal connection from ratings to spreads. The majority of research on the impact of rating agencies is on securities prices, so claim the authors, and this research is conducted in the sphere of corporate bonds, equities and commercial papers, dealing largely with the question of whether rating changes "convey information not already incorporated into the price" (Claessens and Embrechts, 2003, p. 7). Claessens and Embrechts further assert that the findings obtained illustrate a "more significant effect from downgrades rather that from an upgrade" and perhaps even more importantly, "the largest effect[s]" arise from unexpected rating changes (2003, p. 7). The same holds true for structured finance products, as Micu, Remolona, and Wooldridge (2006) demonstrate in their study on Credit Default Swaps (CDS) spreads.

Attempting to clarify the specific role of rating agencies within the financial industry, Kerwer (2005, p. 455) argues that as profit seeking firms, they fail to qualify as "non-majoritarian regulators," yet simultaneously wield a form of "illegitimate power" which is manifest in the force and influence that they possess over the formalized ratings process. Basing fact-gathering research on a condition of "legitimacy" and its absence within a system that fails to regulate modern rating agencies adequately or strategically, Kerwer (2005, p. 455) suggests that the identification of a satisfactory regulatory solution may actually be more difficult than is often anticipated in academia. Kerwer (2005) maintains that accountability itself, in the pursuit of a reputation-branded business (e.g. rating agencies are successful because of their infallible reputations), is largely within the construct of a ratings system that is enterprising (e.g. maintaining a code of ethics), or is purposefully misleading (e.g. attempting to improve position through issuing more favorable ratings for payments). Ultimately, determining intention is a difficult task, and one which is unlikely to be successfully pursued. However, it is evident from a variety of recent reports (e.g. FSF, 2008; FSA, 2009) that efforts to prevent possible fallibilities through regulatory interventions are under way.

In a critical assessment of the role and responsibilities of rating agencies during the past two decades of credit crises, Sy, emphasizes that historic evidence has shown significant increases in systemic risk that operates on a pro-cyclical plane, fuelling investments during "good times" and "accelerating market losses during bad times" (2009, p. 3). In spite of such influence, Partnoy (2006, p. 4) argues that credit ratings offer limited informational value to investors and fail to assist in the management of risks, even in light of widespread reliance on ratings outputs and variations. The primary reason for this determination is that the ratings outputs are unjustified and largely reflective of the opinions of the credit rating gatekeepers, rather than a quantifiable justification according to corporate or market baselines (Partnoy, 2006). In order to maximize the merits of a regulatory platform for rating agencies, Sy (2009) stresses that the procyclicality of rating agencies' rating systems and the inherent systemic risk associated with such variable and inconsistent outputs must be strategically monitored and controlled. Although it is well known that ratings may involve systematic risk, there is no formal procedure for assessing the impact their use has on financial markets. One of the great challenges will therefore be finding the best possible way to manage it once the systematic risk associated with ratings is assessed (Sy, 2009).

6.3.2 Private Securities Litigation Reform Act of 1995

The Private Securities Litigation Reform Act (PSLRA) of 1995 serves as a mechanism for resolving the severity and arbitrary nature of litigation against public corporations and auditors in relation to securities fraud (Lee, Mande, and Son 2009). Specifically, the PLSRA imposed limitations on the collection of damages in response to securities fraud, constraining liability to those instances in which auditors and firms "knowingly violate securities laws" (Lee, Mande, and Son, 2009, p. 86). The PSLRA (1995) outlines a variety of conditions relating to the discovery and determination of intention including the 'required state of mind' clause and 'safe harbor clause'. Of particular importance when discussing the responsibilities and liabilities of rating agencies the safe harbor clause, which places an emphasis on the disclosure of 'meaningful cautionary statements' that serve as indications of the potential unreliability of information shared in published reports. Both oral and written forward-looking statements (when adequately noted in accordance with the safe harbor clause) are protected under the PSLRA (1995), which thereby limits the potential liability of the disclosing individual(s) or entities (Lee, Mande and Son, 2009).

In order to systematically demonstrate the net impact of the PSLRA (1995) on the equity performance of firms within the US stock market, Lee, Mande, and Son (2009) conducted a critical, quantitative analysis of the cost of capital and its evolution over time in relation to the reduction of fiscal liabilities. Lee, Mande and Son (2009) conclusively state that in spite of its primary intentions to reduce frivolous lawsuits against firms and auditors, the PSLRA (1995) actually resulted in a decrease in litigation for justifiable lawsuits as well. Further, the overall cost of equity capital for organizations covered by the PSLRA (1995) increased, while the audit quality of the largest audit firms in the US simultaneously declined. The output of lower quality information arising from the PLSRA (1995) controls is consistent with a risk-averse standard of exchange. However, it is also indicative of strategic information governance and a decline in the exchange of quality auditor evidences within the public sector (Lee, Mande and Son, 2009).

The role of informational controls in market-based preferences is an important, predictive determinant of what tangible outcomes might arise from a more constrained credit reporting assessment standard. Citing the strategic response to the Mexican financial crisis in the late 1990s, Fischer (2003) emphasizes that the need for improved informational transparency, particularly in relation to cash reserves and liquidity, had a direct influence on the pursuit of a more uniform, global 'Code of Good Practices'. Whilst such research stresses the role of central banks in the surveillance and governance of market adjustments and transparency (Fischer, 2003), the relevance of such outcomes is consistent with institutional deficiencies during the most recent financial crisis of 2007–2008 (Utzig, 2010). In fact, Utzig (2010) offers similar conclusions to Fischer's (2003) assessment of centralized banks in relation to the more recent 2007 crisis. The former argues that rating agencies were not only methodologically un-prepared for resolving credit risks, but were also responsible for failing to adjust their ratings quickly enough in order to resolve 'deteriorating market conditions.' Such observations re-orientate the arguments surrounding regulation and monitoring to a position of accountability – one which the rating agencies have yet to fully realize in their private self-interest operations.

It is also noteworthy that the PSLRA, designed as it was to discourage frivolous litigation, not only protected auditors but also rating agencies against monetary damages arising from legal actions taken against them. In light of the recent crisis, rating agencies emerged as a target for investigations and possible litigation. However, any potential plaintiff faced great hurdles before they could successfully litigate against rating agencies (Freeman, 2008). First, Freeman (2008) explains that investors must demonstrate that the First Amendment protection of public opinion does not apply; once they are over this first hurdle, they must then demonstrate that a primary violation of the securities law has been committed by the rating agencies (or another secondary party). In other words, plaintiffs must seek to establish damages with reference to the market price of securities (Freeman 2008). With the heightened pleading standards of the PSLRA, however, it is very difficult for investors seeking damages to prove such a violation occurred, since they have no insight into the rating agencies' internal work processes (Freeman, 2008). Furthermore, the PSLRA provided a safe-harbor for forward-looking statements; what was particularly advantageous for rating agencies, as in the case the results predicted fail to materialize, liability cannot be based on forward-looking statements if those statements are identified as such and accompanied by meaningful cautionary language (GAO, 2011). Growing criticism of rating agencies' liability resulted in lowered pleading requirements in securities law actions for fraud under Rule 10b-5[38] introduced by the Dodd-Frank Act of 2010 (Zhou and Kumar, 2012). Nevertheless, even as reforms to rating agencies' First Amendment protections are underway, they still remain protected under the PLSRA's safe harbor provision.

6.3.3 The Sarbanes-Oxley Act of 2002

Following the bankruptcies of organizations such as Enron, WorldCom, Waste Management, and Tyco, the US Congress passed the Sarbanes-Oxley Act on July 25, 2002 (Coates, 2007). Underlining a new distinction between gatekeeper responsibilities and corporate reporting, this act serves as a mechanism for establishing transparency and prescribing accountability within a system that had become lax and lenient with its regulatory controls (Coates, 2007). According to the Securities and Exchange Commission, "the primary purpose of the Sarbanes-Oxley Act was to ensure the integrity of the United States capital markets and

---

38 See Chapter 3.

restore investor confidence in the wake of financial scandals" (SEC, 2003, p. 3). Coates (2007) recognizes that this Act served to incentivize organizations to invest in corporate controls. Furthermore, the Act promises long-term benefits by reducing investors' risk of losses from fraud, along with improving accountability and transparency of reporting standards (Coates, 2007). Following the introduction of the Sarbanes-Oxley Act of 2002, the Securities and Exchange Commission (SEC, 2003) engaged in a critical assessment of rating agencies and their role in the market crisis following the collapse of Enron and WorldCom (Sy, 2009). The SEC (2003) endeavored to make determinations as to whether there were deficiencies in key areas of information flow, potential conflicts of interest, anticompetitive or unfair practices, regulatory barriers to entry, and ongoing oversight.

6.3.4 Credit Rating Agency Reform Act of 2006

The Credit Rating Agencies Reform Act of 2006 was enacted by the 109th US Congress with the objective of improving the quality of ratings to ensure the protection of investors and to improve accountability, transparency, and competition in the credit rating agency industry more generally. The act is primarily concerned with the issuance and use of credit ratings. Moreover, the act placed Nationally Recognized Statistical Rating Organizations (NRSROs) under a new framework of regulation, providing explicit guidelines for determining which credit rating agencies will qualify as NRSROs (Sy, 2009). The NRSRO status of rating agencies has a number of implications following regulations in connection with certain investment decisions, as NRSROs ratings are a benchmark for whether the securities or the rated entities carry an investment grade rating (issues which are dealt with in greater detail in Chapters 2 and 3). By codifying the designation process, the Act seeks to increase competition among rating agencies; the SEC designated NRSROs through a no-action letter procedure prior to the introduction of the act (Coskun, 2008). While the act made it easier to obtain NRSRO status, it also tightened the criteria rating agencies must meet with the aim of preventing the misuse of material, non-public information (Utzig, 2010). NRSRO status profoundly affected rating agencies business, and the major rating agencies were challenged to assert their validity as NRSROs for the first time since the 1970s in accordance to the new requirements (Wolfson and Crawford, 2010). In response, Standard & Poor's, for example, published its formal NRSRO application in 2007, along with a variety of formal institutional exhibits (documents which have been updated regularly in order to reflect the policies and procedures for ratings determinations applied by S&P in the marketplace).

Of these exhibits, Standard & Poor's (2014) offered an unprecedented insight into its credit rating process, which involves several key stages – from the initial rating request, the assessment of information, and the review and committee process, to publishing the results, as well as their surveillance procedures (issues which are described in more detail in Chapter 4). Although the act gives the SEC the legal right to issue certain oversight rules for rating agencies that register as NRSRO, the act does not empower substantive regulation of the rating process applied by NRSROs.

The 2006 Act failed to fulfill its purpose of improving the quality of ratings in the wake of the subprime crisis. Based on the apparently inadequate efforts regulators had undertaken at level of the rating agency, a number of provisions and rules followed, with the aim of tightening regulation on rating agencies (Rousseau, 2009). On September 17, 2009 the SEC released in its Open Meeting Agenda of additional proposed rules that they were considering. These proposed rules would require rating agencies to provide further information on credit history and to disclose conflicts of interest in order to address concerns relating to the integrity of rating agencies' methodologies and procedures. This was initiated for the background that investors often consider ratings as an indication of whether or not to buy or sell a particular security. These proposals were followed by a number of acts passed in 2009 to strengthen the reliability of credit ratings (Wolfson and Crawford, 2010).

In 2011, the SEC published 17 CFR, its final rule in the Dodd-Frank Wall Street Reform and Consumer Protection Act (Dodd-Frank) to remove references to credit ratings in rules and forms under the Securities and Exchange Act. This assessment was based upon the Congressional ruling (939A) that each federal agency must "(i) review its regulations and identify any regulation that requires the use of an assessment of the creditworthiness of a security or money market instrument and (ii) any references to or requirements in such regulations regarding credit ratings" (Federal Reserve, 2011, p. 1). Specifically, the SEC intends "to reduce [...] reliance on credit ratings for regulatory purposes" (2011, p. 4). The assessment seeks to make determinations of methods by which the agency could "avoid using credit ratings in a manner that suggests in any way a 'seal of approval' on the quality of any particular credit rating or rating agency" (SEC, 2003, p. 4).

Underscoring the foundations of the Dodd-Frank Act (specifically Subtitle C, Section 936), the US Congress (2010) emphasized that regulations had evolved out of the systematic importance of credit ratings and the reliance placed on credit ratings by individual and institutional investigators, as well as financial regulators. The implications of S943 are significant for NRSROs, for they must include "in any report accompanying a credit rating for an asset-backed securities offering, a description of (A) the representations, warranties and enforcement mechanisms available to investors; and (B) how they differ from the representations, warranties, and enforcement mechanisms in issuance of similar securities" (US Congress, 2010, p. 497). As the FSB (2010) recognizes that many investment managers and institutional decision makers have come to rely on rating agencies as a primary source of risk-based information, the efforts of the US Congress (2010) to establish regulatory mandates for informational transparency and accuracy are an important step towards achieving more efficient informational management standards.

6.3.5 Basel I to II framework

The first accord, Basel I, was established in 1988 by the Bank for International Settlements (BIS). It set out minimal capital requirements for financial institutions, aiming to minimize credit risk. However, the Basel I principles have revealed certain inadequacies over time, such as focusing primarily on credit risk, failing to provide risk-orientated measurements with regard to the creditworthiness of counterparts, and giving financial institutions few incentives for developing and strengthening risk-management systems (Cannata and Quagliariello, 2009). The Basel II Accord, drafted in 2004 and implemented in the European Union in 2006, was intended to overcome the deficiencies of the first accord by ensuring more up-to-date, prudent regulations in line with the evolution of the financial markets (Mostert, 2013). In his European Commission-sponsored review of the differences between Basel I and Basel II, Holmquist (2007) argues that a core oversight in Basel I necessitated the rehabilitation of framework standards to reflect a more explicit distinction between credit quality gradations and the identification of deterioration in asset quality. Specifically, many researchers recognize that Basel I grouped all ratings of bonds under the same category of "capital arbitrage," failing to address the capital requirement necessary to account for operational risk (Holmquist, 2007, p. 3). One major theme throughout this particular review was the concept of 'risk sensitivity', a dimension of the Basel II framework that was proposed to align capital requirements with the specific ways in which banks actually manage risks (Holmquist, 2007). Such disclosure requirements are an important step towards a regulatory approach that both balances proprietary information and provides public disclosure of strategies that are needed to determine investor portfolio definitions.

While Basel II may have been heralded as a solution to issues of accountability and transparency, the focus of these guidelines on model-based risk measurement and ratings failed to sufficiently assess the potential for crisis conditions and market shocks (Pattanaik, 2009). Following the 2007–2008 crisis, it became evident that such quantitative modeling was unable to estimate risk exposure adequately and ultimately increased vulnerability amongst institutions to market shocks and liquidity demands (Pattanaik, 2009). In response, a critical review by the FSB (2010) proposed that there must be adjustments to Basel II in order to achieve a more salient and transparent model of prudential supervision for banking institutions. Specifically, the FSB proposed that banks should publicly disclose information about their approach to credit assessment (Pillar 3 of Basel II), and that there should be greater control imposed on the relationship between minimum capital requirements and the use of rating agencies' ratings by banks. It is evident that the FSB (2010) believes that all institutions should reduce their reliance on rating agencies, and instead focus their valuation and risk assessment models on a more comprehensive assessment of risks and exposures that is based on a systematic review of corporate finances and performance.

6.3.6 The Rating Agencies Paradox and the Consequences of Under Regulation

In a critical analysis of the link between rating agencies and potential abuses of power within the financial reporting industry, Partnoy (2006) emphasizes that the significance of the conflicts of interest which arise from the tradition of rating agencies being paid for the ratings they generate is of particular influence in future regulatory agenda setting. The 2002 Sarbanes-Oxley Act was designed to resolve conflicts of interest at the core of the accounting industry (Coates, 2007). Partnoy (2006) argues that the true conflict of interest in rating agencies' operations is the direct result of the lack of regulation, which affords a variety of unique consulting opportunities and compensation possibilities that are beyond the scope of traditional accounting and investment guidelines. Further, a 2008 report published by the Financial Stability Forum (FSF, 2008) highlights how rating agencies' ratings are vulnerable to model risks due to substantive methodological shortcomings and inadequate historical data. From insufficient monitoring of securitized products to inconsistencies in the rating of structured finance products and corporate bonds, the failure of rating agencies to operate as a prudent and effective gatekeeper was a direct indication of the unregulated influence held by these organizations over the investment population (FSF, 2008). Exemplifying the potential conflicts associated with the rating agencies' tradition of both solicited and unsolicited ratings, the conditions of ratings practices have yet to be standardized or sufficiently regulated within the context of informational responsibility.

Citing the 'meltdown' of various innovative financial instruments following a broad spectrum of defaults within the sub-prime mortgage industry, Pattanaik reflects that the potential for this "global systemic meltdown" was largely ignored as a direct result of a widely held perception amongst policymakers that "free markets and globalization together had succeeded in delivering a prolonged period of high growth and low inflation for the world economy" (2009, p. 21). Citing a broad spectrum of instruments and the downward spiral of market stability over a rapid period of time from 2007–2008, Pattanaik emphasizes that the loss of market trust itself became a catalyst for financial instability, and ultimately, for policymaking to be "held hostage to market needs" (2009, p. 29).The extreme and unexpected volatility in the financial markets "exposed many financial and non-financial entities to a new threat" (Pattanaik, 2009, p. 29). This demonstrated the danger of a globalized world with integrated markets and weak regulations that are limited in their diversity and highly inefficient when faced with the potential consequences of a severe crisis scenario (Pattanaik, 2009).

6.3.7 The de Larosière Report and the FSA Turner Review

Rating agencies' shortcomings, specifically, their ratings standards and methodologies, which came to light during the 2007–2008 crisis, were challenged by the de Larosière Group (de Larosière, 2009), and the Financial Services Authority's Turner Review (FSA, 2009). These investigations concentrated on issues that reflect the core inaccuracies in financial markets. The de Larosière Report of 2009 contained an analysis of the causes of the crisis, along with recommendations on how to respond to it (Masera, 2010). The Turner Review (FSA, 2009) put forth arguments regarding the responsibility of rating agencies in the unfolding of the financial crisis beyond the more intangible arguments of 'opinion' based reporting and the advocacy of transparency. Specifically, the Turner Review concluded that the models employed by rating agencies raised concerns regarding the potential for raters to structure the rating in such a way as to allow for issuances and institutions to clear a specific rating hurdle. Further, it was determined that due to this securitized form of credit intermediation, the pro-cyclicality of the system actually increased as investors pursued reassurance from the ratings, and based investment decisions on "rating-based triggers" (FSA, 2009; Sy, 2009). Utzig (2010) summarizes the findings of the FSA (2009) and the de Larosière

Group (2009) to reflect the following limitations of quality and transparency in the rating agencies' outputs:[39]

- Overreliance on mathematical and statistical methodologies based on inadequate data;
- Insufficient consideration for market and macroeconomic developments as factors that influence ratings;
- Failure to account for interdependencies;
- Disregard for conflicts of interest;
- Inadequate disclosure practices with regard to models and assumptions used in models.

These findings led both the de Larosière Report and the Turner Review to argue that a fundamental review of the way ratings for complex structured securities are hardwired into financial legislation is necessary, particularly within the Basel II framework. The Turner Review argues that rating agencies should be subject to registration and supervision in order to ensure conscientious management of conflicts of interest. Additionally, as the unexpected degrading of securities frustrates investors' confidence, the review suggests that ratings should be only applied to securities that have a certain ability to maintain their credit rating. Finally, communications with investors should make clear that ratings are designed to carry an inference of credit risk, not liquidity risk or market risk. Both came to the conclusion that a fundamental review of the rating agencies' business model should be conducted, specifically their "economic model" (de Larosière, 2009, p. 9).

The de Larosière Report and the Turner Review partially addressed similar issues to build up a sounder financial system, particularly in the context of proposals for reform at the European level, and to some extent also on a global level. They set out a framework for regulatory authorities towards a new regulatory agenda. Although the report and the review addressed many shortcomings and found significant answers, the question remains whether this will lead to a truly different regulatory structure (House of Lords, 2009). This is something that only time will reveal.

6.4 A Regulatory Future for Rating Agencies

In order to establish a more concrete regulatory framework, Sy (2009) proposes three key stages to address the system risks associated with credit ratings including the introduction of rating maps, a formal stress-testing agenda for institutions'

39 These points has been dealt with in greater detail in Chapters 2 and 3.

balance sheets and off-balance sheet positions, and the introduction of liquidity controls that are designed to protect institutions vulnerable to abrupt ratings downgrades. At the core of the debate regarding the influence of rating agencies on financial markets and investor confidence, Partnoy (2006) notes that within the United States, immunity from prosecution or criminal liability has evolved out of a First Amendment protection specifically because rating agencies present their ratings as opinions rather than binding recommendations or investment-based advice. From a market-based standpoint, Utzig (2010) proposes that the primary objective for regulating rating agencies should primarily be to make these ratings more reliable, while at the same time reducing potential conflicts of interest – factors that were directly reflected in the Sarbanes-Oxley Act, and the subsequent Dodd-Frank Act. Each of these policy-based standards place emphasis on controls to establish accountability for rating agencies in a similar fashion as those imposed on audit agencies.

Utzig (2010) concludes that regulation of rating agencies is an essential and necessary first step towards more functional and informed financial markets. Utzig (2010, p. 11) highlights the dangers relating to pro-cyclicality and the potential for a "chain reaction" associated with credit ratings quality, i.e. default probabilities, as witnessed during the 2007 crisis. Emphasizing an adaptation of the credit agency standard towards a more functional, risk-adverse system, the Federal Reserve (2011) suggests that lower levels of risk sensitivity have had a direct impact on the risky nature of bank assets, resulting in institutional incentives for holding riskier exposures (e.g. no capital requirements). Utzig (2010) contends that the choice by firms and investors to be guided by a rating scale when making investment decisions can trigger destabilization under conditions in which downgrades and rating shifts trigger mass selling behavior, write-downs, and additional capital requirements. Basing their determinations on a market-based model of credit rating, the Federal Reserve (2011) concludes that both supervisors' and market participants' views should be considered in the rating process, allowing for consistency and improved accuracy across the expanding breadth of corporations and institutions.

6.5 Conclusion

The responsibility of regulators in today's globalized, unpredictable, and complex financial marketplace is expanding significantly. The recommendations of the FSA (2009), Turner Review, and a broadening scope of academic insight (such as Sy, 2009; Utzig, 2010) are challenging the claim of First Amendment protections towards a much more rigid and explicitly defined support mechanism. The interests of the many are being affected by the financial and reputational interests of a few leading authorities in the areas of ratings and financial analyses. While most investors will likely seek multiple sources of information, there is, as Utzig (2010) notes, a high degree of value placed on rating agencies – a perspective that may ultimately bias the risk-based determinations made on an independent level.

Be it psychological, systemic, or reputational, it is the degree of influence exerted by rating agencies within the modern financial architecture that must be addressed. Governmental agencies around the globe have already taken new measures and are introducing new regulations (Brewer, Gough and Shah, 2010); these will be discussed in the next chapter. Even though these reforms that are underway will most likely result in significant changes to financial regulations, they may fail to meet the target of fundamentally altering widespread over-reliance on disclosure. They may therefore also fail to find a solution to deter and prevent future financial crises if there is no sufficient international cooperation. Brunnermeier et al. assert that even when regulators with new powers do intervene, "when a regulatory mechanism has failed to mitigate boom/bust cycles, simply reinforcing its basic structure is not likely to be a successful strategy" (2009, p. 11). For policymakers, the challenge lies in creating reliable, robust framework conditions that can ensure stability and efficiency in the financial system, while avoiding the need for costly, disproportionate interventions (Vittas, 1991). Accordingly, ongoing efforts must proceed towards promoting transparency in the rating process and ensuring adequate reporting and information not only for regulators, but for all market participants, as ratings play a key role in the price discovery process for securities.

7. Responses to Rating Agencies Shortcomings

For decades, the regulation of rating agencies was not seriously addressed, as regulatory authorities and the rating agencies themselves operated under the belief that reputation alone would ensure that they maintained high quality standards (RMI, 2011), but the severity, depth, and scope of the recent crisis has changed this perspective. The impact of the crisis on the global economy is still being widely felt. Although different views have emerged as to who should be held responsible, rating agencies must shoulder a large part of the blame (CGFS, 2008). The Levin-Corburn Report (2011) argues that the crisis was a result of complex and highly risky structured finance products, undisclosed conflicts of interest, failures on the part of rating agencies and regulators, and failures of the market itself to restrain reckless behavior on Wall Street. Legislative and regulatory gaps are seen as primary factors that contributed to the global financial downturn and as factors that encouraged faulty, risky, and unproven practices in the rating industry (RMI, 2011). In order to restrain and counter the negative impact of the rating agencies, politicians, governments, and other organizations have called for restrictions to be placed on the role of rating agencies in the market and for stricter regulatory and supervisory requirements (Ryan, 2012). In the meantime, Europe, the United States, and other countries have taken steps towards increasing the efficiency of national regulatory frameworks and facilitating the integration and implementation of international standards into their own regulatory frameworks in order to improve governance of the rating industry. This chapter will highlight the major regulatory initiatives undertaken in Europe and abroad (outside the United States).

A number of studies and reports have revealed the weaknesses of rating agencies and regulatory oversight authorities. Gupta, Mittal, and Bhalla (2010) examined the diversification of rating agencies and came to the conclusion that there is a need for strategies to be adopted to change the regulatory framework so as to avoid the repetition of such financial crises in the future. Since 2004, rating agencies have been primarily governed by the International Organization of Securities Commissions' (IOSCO) code of conduct, which was based on voluntary compliance, and did not include enforcement mechanisms (de Haan and Amtenbrink, 2011). Following the G20 summit held in Washington, D.C., in November 2008, the G20 leaders agreed to enhance sound regulation and to ensure strong oversight of rating agencies in the Washington Declaration (G20, 2008). This declaration establishes the goal that in the future, no financial institution, financial product, or financial market – whether at European or international level – should be unregulated (EC, 2013). The role of rating agencies has become an essential component in global financial markets. Within the course of the globalization of financial markets, rating agencies have played an increasingly key role in the international allocation and pricing of capital (Levich, Majnoni and Reinhart, 2002). As a reputation-branded enterprise, rating agencies have established a firm foothold as an informal, and indirect advisor to investment decision makers, basing their determinations on variable and oftentimes obscure methods and models (Utzig, 2010).

However, it has been demonstrated that in reality, rating agencies are exposed to conflicts of interest, and the reputational mechanism does not seem to function adequately. The shortcomings of the rating agencies and of the rating process itself were clearly revealed in the 2007–2008 global financial crisis. The crisis has invalidated "any argument that reputation guaranties high quality" (Hunt, 2008, p. 163). The adjustments of ratings for securities that were widely held in institutional and private-sector investor portfolios resulted in panic and market decline (Welfens, 2010). Against this background, policy makers in the United States, the European Union, and elsewhere have sought ways to bolster the effectiveness of the functioning of the reputational mechanism through other means than the once in use (Hunt, 2009). In light of market deterioration and uncertainty, there have been significant tensions in financial markets (Duff and Einig, 2009a). Tabellini (2008) addresses this issue, arguing that it was in part a result of the fragmented nature of the US regulatory system. It seems that regulatory authorities and governments were unpleasantly surprised by the sudden and prolonged fall in the market for asset-backed securities, and therefore the "assumption that only private forces are to blame for the crisis seem[s] to be incomplete" (Bondarouk, 2010, p. 3). The special feature of structured finance products to repack risk and "to create 'safe' securities from otherwise risky collateral" led to a sharp rise in the issuance of such structured products (Coval, Jurek, and Stafford, 2009, p. 3). Rating agencies labeled securitized structured products with their ratings, and most of them were then considered by investors as "virtually risk free and certified as such by the rating agencies" (Coval, Jurek, and Stafford, 2009, p. 3). These led to questions about who triggered the crisis and why regulatory authorities did not intervene (Bondarouk, 2010), as well as what regulatory authorities did actually do as the crisis unfurled (Helleiner, 2011).

Blame lies not only with rating agencies, but also with the regulators (Helleiner, 2011). Initial controls imposed on ratings agencies, as discussed in Chapter 6, were imposed in the early 1930s, and offered incentives to institutions that received high ratings from ratings agencies (Ekins and Calabria, 2012). Throughout the radical expansion of financial markets, rating agencies retained their traditionally privileged position as providers of information to the investment community. The consequences of the incentivized credit rating system in financial markets have been far reaching: following the 2007–2008 global financial market crisis, it is evident that additional regulatory measures are needed to prevent agency-based opportunism and ongoing financial incentivization. The following chapter offers an overview of several of the world's leading financial markets and their strategic responses to the 2007–2008 crisis.

7.1 The European Position

Following the Enron debacle, research was carried out by The Committee on European Securities Regulators (CESR, 2006) for the European Union Commission (EC) in 2005. The study recommended that the adoption of new "legislation was not necessary to address the failings" of rating agencies (Rousseau, 2009, p. 19). The Commission relied on self-regulation instruments to ensure rating agencies accountability implemented through the IOSCO Code of Conduct. Given that the CESR were directly responsible for the monitoring of rating agencies' compliance with the Code, it is remarkable that the Commission concluded that the need for specific legislation was not confirmed (Rousseau, 2009). After the market turmoil of 2007–2008, calls for reforms intensified, leading to initiatives seeking to enhance the regulation of rating agencies at the EU level (Manaigo-Vekil, 2012).

7.1.1 Regulation and Reform of Rating Agencies after the 2007–2008 Crisis

The Financial Stability Forum (2008) challenged rating agencies and their activities in light of the US subprime crisis, and recommended changes to the role and use of credit ratings. In their critical overview of proposed regulatory measures at a European level, de Haan and Amtenbrink (2011) argue that the FSF recommendations were not far-reaching enough as they did not propose a supervisory system that was more stringent for rating agencies. On the contrary, the FSF "advised that competent authorities should 'monitor, individually or collectively, the implementation of the revised ISCO code by CRAs, in order to ensure that CRAs quickly translate it into action'" (de Haan and Amtenbrink, 2011, p. 18). In Europe, the "rejection of a comprehensive regulatory approach was supported by the European Securities Market Expert Group (ESME)" and the CESR (de Haan and Amtenbrink, 2011,

p. 18). Efforts and measures to improve the regulation of rating agencies at the EU level have only begun, since ongoing difficulties in the financial markets continue to persist (Utzig, 2010). De Haan and Amtenbrink argue that "while the European Commission considers the revised IOSCO Code to be 'the global benchmark', it maintained that its substance had to be made more specific" (2011, p. 19) in order to make the practical application easier and more efficient. From the Commission's perspective, they have "opted for more stringent and enforceable rules" (de Haan and Amtenbrink, 2011, p. 19). The Commission concluded that "EU legislation appears to be the only option that could sufficiently protect investors and European financial markets against the risk of malpractice by credit rating agencies" (EC, 2008, p. 6). According to the Commission, such a uniform approach could create a framework in which the competent authorities of the Member States can ensure that rating agencies adhere to the new set of requirements consistently throughout the European Union. The introduction of a uniform framework would eliminate the inefficiency of non-comprehensive registration and surveillance measures (given that any of the member states has a degree of flexibility in deciding how to adopt national legal orders), and help ensure that market participants' confidence in ratings is restored as quickly as possible (EC, 2008).

Addressing the problem of credit rating agencies more specifically, Credit Rating Regulation No. 1060/2009 (CRR) was passed by the European Commission and introduced mandatory registration guidelines for all credit rating agencies in the EU in addition to various oversight and regulatory standards (Seibt and Schwarz, 2011). There were three clear tenets of this particular regulation: (1) the registration and supervision of rating agencies; (2) stringent requirements for the issuance of ratings for structured finance vehicles; and (3) the establishment of a framework of equivalence and endorsement (RMI, 2011). Seibt and Schwarz (2011) suggest that revisions to this model are evidence of the need to customize the CRR framework to reform the European supervisory bodies, establishing the European Securities and Markets Authority (ESMA) as the primary oversight authority for these entities. From an intermediary-based perspective, Seibt and Schwarz (2011) propose that this move towards more centralized control will re-establish investor confidence and introduce a set of standards that will transcend the spectrum of investment vehicles and institutional interests. As part of Europe's response to its commitments to the G20 agreement of 2008, the EU Regulation of Credit Rating Agencies (CRA Regulation) entered into force on December 7, 2010, and was amended in May 2011 in order to adapt it to the creation of the European Securities and Markets Authority (ESMA) (EC, 2011).

Given that the Commission proposed the amendment to Regulation 1060/2009 (CRR) shortly after it was enacted, de Haan and Amtenbrink argue that this can hardly be seen as "a sign of sustainability of EU financial market legislation" (2011, p. 19). The Commission could have made plans for much more profound reforms of financial market supervision in the EU, thereby improving the efficiency of the present system by reviewing and reforming the Lamfalussy framework and its committee structure (de Haan and Amtenbrink, 2011; Lastra, 2003). The Lamfalussy approach was applied in the securities sector following a decision of the European Council in Stockholm in March 2001, with the aim of providing the European Parliament with two legally binding methods of controlling the activities of the Securities Committee. However, the financial crisis revealed gaps in financial supervision. As a result, a group of independent, high-level experts was set up by José Manuel Barroso, President of the European Commission, and chaired by Jacques de Larosière, to make concrete proposals to strengthen European supervisory arrangements. The de Larosière Group report (2009) recommended that it should be the task of the Committee of European Securities Regulators (CESR) to license rating agencies and also advocated for the establishment of a new authority that would be in charge of registering and supervising rating agencies (a strengthened version of the CESR). In light of these recommendations, the European Commission adopted a package of legislative proposals intended to strengthen macro-prudential supervision through the establishment of a new body at the EU level in September 2009: the European Systemic Risk Board (ESRB). The new system of financial supervision was intended to transform the current committees (CEBS, CEIOPS, CESR)[40] into three new European authorities: (i) the European Banking Authority; (ii) the European Securities Authority; and (iii) the European Insurance Authority (European Parliament, 2013). Moreover, the European Financial Stability Facility (EFSF) was created in the first quarter of 2010 as a temporary rescue mechanism in order to safeguard financial stability, supplemented by the European Stability Mechanism (ESM), which was created as a permanent mechanism and has been in force since October 2012 (EFSF, n.d).

Reflecting on the 2007–2008 crisis as a "powerful incentive for change", the Chairman of the European People's Party in the European Parliament, Joseph Daul (2009, p. 21) suggested that the 'European reaction' would ultimately set the tone for financial regulation and responsibility for the coming century (2009).

40 Committee of European Banking Supervisors (CEBS), Committee of European Insurance and Occupational Pensions Supervisors (CEIOPS), and Committee of European Securities Regulators (CESR).

Citing a pre-crisis standard of self-regulation among rating agencies via the International Organization of Securities Commissions (IOSCO), Daul (2009) emphasizes that future agendas will need to include a formal foundation of regulation and supervision. On the basis of a mirrored model between the United States and the European Union, Daul (2009) proposed a four-tiered strategy for rating agencies' regulatory responses, which includes the following dimensions:

- Ensuring that credit rating agencies avoid conflicts of interest in the rating process (or manage them adequately)
- Improving the quality of the methodologies used by credit rating agencies and the quality of ratings
- Increasing transparency by setting disclosure obligations for credit rating agencies
- Ensuring an efficient registration and surveillance framework, avoiding 'forum shopping' and regulatory arbitrage between EU jurisdictions (EC Regulation No. 1060/2009 of September 16, 2009 on credit rating agencies).

To limit the rating industry's influence and to act effectively against conflicts of interest, the EC pointed out that stricter regulation is needed to promote competition for the so-called 'Big Three' rating agencies. A corresponding proposal was submitted by Michel Barnier, the European Union's chief of financial services, in a committee meeting on November 27, 2012 (Brunsden, 2012). The proposed legislation is intended to update existing regulation on credit rating agencies and "will limit the stakes that investors can have in rating agencies, so as to ensure their independence" (King, 2012, p. 1). To foster competition, issuers will be obliged to rotate the rating agency they use to assess their debt. The rules on the rotating use of agencies will be limited to re-securitizations that fall under the scope of repacked securities, such as CDOs, which are used to back up other securities' debt agreements (Brunsden, 2012).

7.1.2 The "Basel" Perspective

From a regulatory perspective, the principles associated with Basel II are directly tied to the implementation of more rigid governance standards in the European Union in relation to risk and capital management. Yet, Welfens (2011) erroneously emphasizes that banks are predicted to succeed if they can establish an equity capital-loan ratio that is sufficiently high – a factor that fails to address the pro-cyclicality of core factors such as credit ratings and investment vehicles. Although traditional price determination has been based upon an assumption of markets in equilibrium, Welfens (2011) maintains that asymmetric information and moral hazard problems directly interfere with such stability predictions, resulting in an inefficient market perspective. In response, Seibt and Schwarz (2011) cite EC proposals regarding specific market and investment resources such as derivatives, which are oriented towards enhanced transparency and broader spectrum supervision.

The idea behind Basel II was to create international standards that could provide protection to the global financial system, especially with regard to problems that may arise if a major bank or a number of banks collapse. As the crisis has shown, however, Basel II ultimately did not protect them (Kovanis and Kvalem, 2012). In order to counter the existent weaknesses in the regulatory framework, the Group of 20 (G20) endorsed the decision to revise Basel II in 2010, strengthening the banking sectors' ability to absorb economic and financial shocks (BIS, 2012). The new regulation, Basel III, was adopted at the EU level in 2013 and entered into force in January 2014 through two legislative acts: the Capital Requirements Regulation (CRR) and the Capital Requirements Directive (CRD), combined as 'CRD IV' (European Banking Authority, EBA, n.d.). As a 'regulation', CRR offers the advantage of being binding and directly applicable to all member states. The directive (CRD) requires EU member states to install compliant legislation nationwide by December 31, 2013, allowing them to implement the new EU requirements in a form or manner that is reasonable to them. Additionally, CRD addresses issues not covered by Basel III, such as implementing sanctions and reducing the reliance on external credit ratings. During a transition period (until 2019), banks will have to meet new minimum capital requirements expressed in risk-weighted assets, as outlined in the Basel III accord. The new framework contains measures to address the gaps and flaws of Basel II. The Basel III accord addresses the reduction of cyclical effects in the Basel II accord and the reduction of systematic risk (Ojo, 2012). Moreover, the new rule increases the requirements with regard to counterparties' credit risk arising from derivatives and securities financing activities, and addresses liquidity and leverage ratios. Finally, the most significant changes in Basel III result from strengthening the supervisory standards of the second pillar and the heightened standards for disclosure to the market as introduced in pillar three of the Basel II accord (Kovanis and Kvalem, 2012). Given that the implementation of CRR/CRD in the European Union generally applies to all credit institutions and investment firms, these firms and institutions are subject to a wider scope of regulation under Basel III at the EU level than is the case in the United States.

7.1.3 Current Regulatory Efforts (2013)

The most recent communiqué from the European Commission was published on January 16, 2013, and reflects a presentation of new rules on credit rating agencies (EC, 2013a). This EU summary focuses on three primary dimensions of EU regulation: registration, conducting business, and supervision via ESMA (EC, 2013b, section 4). Viewed as a supplement to the Capital Requirements Directive (IP/11/915), the European Union emphasizes that both initiatives are designed to reduce the general reliance on ratings for investment decision-making (EC, 2013b, section 5). Consistent with the recommendations of the FSB (2010), this new directive places emphasis on the removal of references to rating agencies' ratings from laws and regulations, and compels institutions and investors to make their own credit assessments, meaning that they should not rely solely on the evaluations and ratings provided by the rating agencies (EC, 2013b, section 6). Beyond this particular agenda item, the EC (2013a) also rejects the ongoing absence of liability on the part of rating agencies and the lack of independence and objectivity in ratings' determinations due to commercial commitments. In this respect, it should be noted that current EU regulation of rating agencies does not cover the use of ratings. The conditions for the use of external ratings by financial institutions are regulated in sectoral financial legislation, such as the Capital Requirements Directive (EU, 2013b).

7.1.4 The European Rating Agency Case

To address rating agencies' shortcomings, the European Union introduced not only the legislation as hitherto noted, but also considered a publicly funded European Credit Rating Agency to combat the perceived US bias of the Big Three rating agencies (Tichy, 2011). The setup cost "could be 'wholly or partially covered by the public sector' although over time 'public investment could be phased out'", which could be accomplished by a partially "publicly-funded pan-European independent agency" (Ryan, 2012, p. 17). The proposal to establish an independent and autonomous European Credit Rating Foundation was not followed by the European Commission. The idea of a European Rating Agency remains vague since European officials have not been able to reach an agreement on how it would be funded or when and where it might be established. In addition, there are concerns that such a governmental sponsored rating agency may have difficulties in establishing both credibility and independence in the market (RMI, 2011).

The underlying concept behind establishing a European rating agency is that such an agency could "increase competition in the sector and combat the perceived US bias of the 'big three' rating agencies" (Ryan, 2012, p. 17). In this context, Ryan (2012) argues that it is fair to question the Big Three's influence on Wall Street and the US government, considering the market power of the US-based rating agencies. In light of the European sovereign debt crisis, European leaders called once more for a European rating agency that would be credible and transparent (Böcking, 2011). However, addressing the issue of a European Rating Agency raises the question of whether such an agency could operate independently and guarantee clear and transparent ratings (Müller, Sauga, and Schult, 2011). Kemmer (2012) argues that there are several obstacles for such a European agency to overcome; a key issue would be how the objectives associated with such a project could be achieved. One major goal is improving the quality of ratings. Kemmer (2012) observes that the assessment of the quality of a rating depends primarily on the interests of the market participants involved, and that 'quality' is thus unable to be precisely defined. Furthermore, the author argues that while the issuer would consider a higher rating – an AAA instead of AA – as an improvement, any potential investors' criteria to judge its quality will be based on how precisely the rating reflects the probability of default. Kemmer added, "whatever competitive impetus a European credit rating agency were able to provide, it would not necessarily lead to better ratings from everyone's perspective" (2012, p. 2). This, in turn, means that a European rating agency would not resolve the debate over the quality of credit ratings (Kemmer, 2012). In debating the issue of an independent European rating agencies and the associated improvement of ratings quality, Snower (2011) further suggests that such an innovation would not resolve the existing rating agency problem. Rather, he posits, it would even have the opposite effect: a single rating agency for all of Europe would establish a *de facto* monopoly, further aggravating the situation. It would be more advantageous (and of greater benefit to the financial markets) if there were, instead, increased competition between rating agencies models, methods, and ideas (Snower, 2011).

7.2 The Chinese Position (and an Emergent Russian Ally)

The financial crisis, although detrimental to many economies across the world, had a variable influence within China, as domestic capital protections strove to reduce financial sector impacts. Spence (2009) recognizes that while other developing nations such as India, Brazil, and Russia experienced an outpouring of capital and a rapid decline in the exchange rate of their respective currencies, China utilized its $3.6 trillion in reserves to stop the appreciation of the Yuan against the US dollar until they could assess the real implications of the crisis.

Based upon this strategy of monetary controls and financial prudency, Spence (2009) suggests that China would weathered the financial crisis much better than other developing countries. Following the free fall of the global economy, the growth of China's economy declined from 13% in 2007 to 6% in the fourth quarter of 2008 (Spence, 2009). In light of the reduction of growth rates, the Chinese government took actions in November 2008 to escape from the global downturn (Yongding, 2010).

Following the financial crisis of 2007–2008, a number of efforts to reform the regulatory landscape have been made. In order to respond to the severe problems experienced, core principles for effective banking supervision were modified and requirements for risk management strengthened. China welcomed the new rules on regulation (e.g. the Basel standards) as an important step in the process of establishing a more robust global financial system. In order to write the new Basel standards into law, the Chinese Banking Regulatory Commission published its "*Guiding Opinions*" in 2011 (Min, 2012, p. 3). Min describes the underlying goal as follows: "To implement international financial regulatory reform and improve China's banking regulatory regime is not only the international obligation of China as a member of the G20, FSB and Basel Committee, but also a necessary measure to facilitate the transformation of bank's development mode, improve the capability of the banking sector to tackle external impact, ensure the banking sector's long-term robust operation, and fend off systematic financial risk" (Min, 2012, p. 4). Chinese banking regulators realized that the rationale behind the Basel standards could contribute decisively to the quality of capital supervision. With the implementation of these standards, the capital adequacy, the size and quality, and the profitability of Chinese banks saw substantial advances (Sun, 2009).

When reviewing the factors that worked best to insulate economies from the crisis, Dooley (2010) identified one key factor: "the degree of government supervision of the financial sector" (cited Conway, 2010, p. 6). Countries where the financial markets were subject to strict supervision, whether with advanced economies such as Canada, or emerging economies like China, largely escaped from the financial shocks experienced throughout the entire global financial system on the whole, as well as the wider economy. Supervision in these countries discouraged not only speculation in risky financial instruments such as CDOs, but also the over-leveraging that intensified the crisis in other countries (Conway, 2010). In this context, Liao Min, director-general and acting head of the general office of the China Banking Regulatory Commission, used a very striking phrase:

"Chinese financial institutions needed CBRC[41] approval to launch individual product types, making it nearly impossible for exotic financial instruments, such as the ones blamed for the subprime crisis, to exist in China" (Crotty and Epstein, 2008, p. 11).

However, China's market, like numerous other emerging markets, has also seen consistent activity in the volumes of securitized products. Securitization provides benefits for the welfare of these countries, as it allows the originator/issuers to gain access to capital, and "as a new asset class, emerging market ABS/MBS allow investors to construct more diversified portfolios" (Mostowfi, 2011, p. 58). Although countries such as China have active local rating agencies, in light of the globalization, the implementation of international standards such as Basel II can foster the domestic rating industry by stimulating the demand for "regionally-oriented financial services and products" where Asian agencies seek greater collaboration to overcome the dominance of the Big Three (Asian Development Bank, 2008).

In a more recent critique of rating agencies and their relative value in China, Poon, Chan, and Firth (2013) revealed that credit ratings have a direct, positive influence on accuracy outcomes that from a price setting perspective. However, due to inconsistencies in the rating scales used within the domestic sector, it is the act of receiving the rating itself, rather than the actual rating that is the most important outcome. For this reason, the findings of Poon, Chan, and Firth (2013) may simply indicate a robust platform of investor mistrust, particularly following the past three years of regulatory agenda setting, uncertainty, and fragmentation within the industry. Adequately addressing these issues and using domestic ratings for regulatory purposes may only be possible by developing a globally comparable tool to measure default risk (Dale and Thomas, 2000).

As a committed member of the G20, FSB and the Basel Committee, China has been actively involved in international regulatory reform since 2008. Nevertheless, China has drawn lessons from the crisis, and Chinese regulators will continue to act cautiously, focusing on comparatively simple yet effective rules (Min, 2012). Given China's large size and significance in the world economy, its response to the crisis is of particular importance (Yang et al., 2008).

In 2011, Jianzhong, President of China's Dagong Global Credit Rating Co. Ltd., argued that a credit system consisting of the debtors of different nation creditors' would require a highly independent rating system. He describes the

41 The China Banking Regulatory Commission (CBRC) is agency of the People's Republic of China (PRC) authorized by the State Council to regulate its banking sector.

path towards an international rating system as "establishing a supra-sovereign independent international rating agency composed of all domestic rating agencies in each country; establishing a new international rating regulatory organization based on all countries' regulators and that "the international rating agency will develop a brand-new international rating standard according to the planning of international regulatory organization" (Jianzhong, 2011, p. 2). Jianzhong stresses the importance of the new international rating power of Dagong Global Credit Rating Co., Ltd. which was acknowledged in the international community. He also highlighted its objective credit rating ideas, theories, methodologies, its technical strengths and its independent rating stand by not pursuing any policies in the interest of any one specific nation. All these factors speak for China's ability to contribute to the establishment of a new international rating system, and for that reason "China can come up with more professional proposals during the reform progress" (Jinazhong, 2011, p. 3).

In China, there are concerns about the potential impact of the Big Three rating agencies on the Chinese national economy (RMI, 2011). Chinese officials are concerned that the Big Three and US-focused rating agencies are not informed or knowledgeable enough about China's economic situation to make informed rating assessments and judgments (Poon, 2003). Experts in China argue that the country needs to have its own successful rating agency in order to combat the influence of the Big-Three, would also afford China greater international pricing power (RMI, 2011). The RMI report cited that Xian Songzuo, Deputy Director of the Center for International Monetary Research at the Renmin University of China, "believes that countries other than the US should develop their own credit rating agencies in order to reduce the Big Three's dominant power for securities and other financial assets" (RMI, 2011, p. 27). Given that the judegment of the major agencies can create great shifts in value, greater international pricing power would be a significant factor, especially for China, as Chinese entities are increasingly listed in foreign markets, along with the fact that China has extensive foreign exchange reserves in oversea assets (RMI, 2011).

In mid-2012, significant progress was made towards mitigating reliance on the 'Big Three' rating agencies in China and Russia through the expansion of a joint international credit rating body. The "Beijing Declaration" reflects a commitment to a "multilateral, independent, international credit rating agency which does not represent the interest of any particular country or group" (Yoshioka, 2012, p. 1). The proposal, if it can successfully be enacted, would result in a centralized, operational headquarters and an international supervision system that would be introduced over a period of five years (Ruan, 2012). The three rating agencies (Bejing-based Dagong Global Rating, Russia's RusRating and the US-based agency Egan-Jones) are uniting together to create the Universal Credit Rating Group (UCRG), with the aim of providing a system of comparable, global credit ratings in financial markets. The UCRG was launched in June 2013 in Hong Kong. It is the group's task to promote reform of the international rating system and to develop a new international rating system in accordance with the Beijing Declaration. A further mission of the group is to develop new international ratings criteria, establish an independent supervision system for credit ratings, and disseminate impartial rating information to global markets. To support their statements, Sean Egan, President of Egan-Jones Rating, explained that "overly optimistic credit ratings have led to an economic crisis, almost to a catastrophe that was only avoided thanks to unprecedented central bank intervention. The credit system urgently needs to be reformed" (Caijing, 2012, p. 2). Information is a key factor for the proper functioning of global economic markets, and according to Jianzhong, ratings are indispensable in this sector: the need to reform the current rating system and introduce new ways of thinking is clear (Hume, 2013). The new agency's aim is to supplement the current rating system: the current system is, according to Sean Egan, "New York centered" and the UCRG would bring in new geographical perspectives, meaning that the "UCRG will get different rating results from the big three" (Changxin, 2013, p. 1).

At the core of this controversial yet strategic internationalization agenda, Egan-Jones has recently undergone SEC scrutiny for issuing a downgrade rating on US debt, a punishment that critics associate with the failure of the independent agency to 'play ball' within the scope of the Big Three domination of the industry. The SEC has complained that the agency overstated its rating expertise in its accreditation application (Ruan, 2012). At the same time while Egan was downgrading US debt, Dagong (China) encountered its own range of controversies, introducing a superior rating for a debt-ridden Railways Ministry, while also downgrading China's sovereign debt to an inferior status (Ruan, 2012). Such controversy represents an ominous forecast for the partnership; however, it also establishes justification for a more competitive, non-consensus forming assessment protocol that could circumvent the pitfalls of the existing, more homogenous rating agency platform. However, President of Rus Rating Richard Hainsworth stressed that given the complexity of the world and "competing interests among countries" it is "not sufficient" for the rating industry "to be dominated by just a tiny number of analysts sitting in one town, in one city" (Ruan, 2012, para. 5). With the strategy to launch the new united rating agencies in Hong Kong, UCRG will gain a foothold in the international bond/securities rating business, given that Hong Kong is one of the primary markets for such activities. Apart from this, Dagong "has also set up an alternative rating system for local governments based on its study of local governments in 105 countries and regions around the world" (Mu, 2013, para. 29). The new system is fundamentally different from the systems used by western firms, as it is based on a solvency assessment of debtor's wealth-creating capability, instead of focusing on their capacity to borrow. According to Dagong, this system will be "revolutionary", as it will be a better warning tool for local debt risk and help to avoid the "Big Three's mistakes of assigning "wrong credit ratings" (Mu, 2013, para. 32).

7.3 The Indian Position

In the wake of the financial crisis, India's High Level Coordination Committee on Financial Matters (HLCCFM) held a meeting on January 11, 2008, and decided that "the legal and policy framework for regulating the activities of CRAs should be revisited in order to take a larger view of the entire policy with respect to banking, insurance and securities market" (HLCCFM, 2009, p. 10). Within India's controlled institutional framework, credit rating agencies have continued to play an important role in supporting investors' decision making, establishing comparative benchmarks, and "rectifying information asymmetry between borrower and lender, thereby lowering cost[s]" (Bhushan, 2013, p. 38). In India, the credit rating sector began with the introduction of the Credit Rating Information Services of India (now CRISIL Ltd.). The CRISIL project was promoted by leading Indian financial institutions and by 2009, four more rating agencies had been registered by SEBI in addition to CRISIL.

There are six primary agencies in the Indian market today. The global Big Three (Moody's, Standard & Poor's, and Fitch), are all represented through subsidiary operations, as required by India law. In 1999, the Securities and Exchange Board of India (SEBI) established its operational definition for rating agencies as "a body corporate which is engaged in, or proposes to be engaged in, the business of rating of securities offered by way of public or rights issue" (SEBI, 1999, p. 3). The SEBI was in fact "one of the first few regulators, globally, to put in place effective and comprehensive regulation for CRAs" (HLCCFM, 2009, p. 24). Although the SEBI's (1999) initial regulations regarding rating agencies were implemented in order to establish a variety of general guidelines relating to registration and governance, the most important components (with regard to the most recent crisis) are tied to monitoring and review. Specifically, rating agencies were compelled to engage in ongoing monitoring practices and to disseminate information regarding newly assigned ratings to the public in order to maintain a constant state of communication (SEBI, 1999).

Multiple controls were also introduced in order to prevent conflicts of interest, which have prohibited rating agencies from generating ratings for those securities or organizations in which they hold a vested interest (SEBI, 1999). Finally, the SEBI established liability guidelines for cases involving defaults on rated securities, focusing primarily on failure to comply with conditions under the act, and imposing penalties (such as suspension or cancellation of registration), in addition to other financial penalties in accordance with the 2002 Securities and Exchange Act. With the implementation of the new guidelines, SEBI was granted the power to inspect and investigate rating agencies' books of account, records, and documents as well as the power to "to investigate complaints received from investors, clients or any other person concerned with the business of credit rating agencies" in order to detect punishable violations (Bhushan, 2013, p. 47). With these rules, the SEBI was ahead of other countries in holding rating agencies liable. The SEBI requirements are intended to regulate the functioning of rating agencies, with the aim of protecting investors' interests and making the system even more valuable and more helpful to them (Bhushan, 2013). SEBI's requirements were far more stringent than pre-crisis SEC regulations and were designed to protect the system against manipulation, while also considering liability issues.

One of the most valuable dimensions of the 1999 (Credit Rating Agencies) Regulation Act was the introduction of a formal code of conduct for rating agencies that highlights a number of operational expectations (SEBI, 1999). According to this act, rating agencies are required to protect the interests of investors, conduct their business with high standards of integrity, dignity and fairness, and to operate ethically and professionally. Under the act, rating agencies must exercise due diligence and professional judgment in order to maintain objectivity during the rating process and pursue an adequate, reasonable basis for their rating evaluations. Moreover, the act requires that rating agencies do not to make untrue or exaggerated statements and that they prevent the use of privileged information for price rigging or manipulation. The act also states that they should not engage in unfair competition. In order to ensure continuity, rating agencies are required to undertake regular rating reviews and a monitoring process.

The above-mentioned requirements were designed to protect investors' interests in the securities market, and to ensure a clearly formulated dissemination process for ratings. Thus, the act stipulates the terms and conditions to be followed while assigning a rating, as well as an internal auditing process that must be conducted. SEBI regulations also set force requirements with regard to the terms and conditions for establishing a rating agency in India, the conditions and processes for receiving certification and registration, restrictions on ratings, and a number of transparency and disclosure norms. The SEBI regulation thus ensures that only credible market players enter this business sector and that rating agencies behave and operate in a manner that enables them to issue objective and fair rating opinions (SEBI, 1999).

Given the far-reaching influence of ratings, the High Level Coordination Committee on Financial Markets (HLCCMF) looked at steps to improve the functioning and accountability of rating agencies in 2009. The committee focused on rating agencies' existing business models, current regulatory activities underway, global experiments, and the Indian efforts undertaken in the aftermath up of the crisis 2007–2008. Despite all the shortcomings identified, the committee felt no immediate concern about rating agencies' operations and activities in India. Nevertheless, the committee recommended greater disclosure for revenues received by rating agencies from particular issuers, as well as from non-rating activities, such as advisory services. Moreover, the committee recommended India's voluntary compliance with the existing and emerging regulations such as the IOSCO Code (HLCCMF, 2009).

Although not comprehensive, the 1999 code of conduct is indicative of the general expectations the SEBI (1999) has imposed upon rating agencies. A formal amendment to these regulations was adopted in 2010. It placed a greater emphasis on disclosure and transparency among rating agencies' ratings practices, which had not existed in the same from hitherto (Business Standard, 2012; TNN, 2012). This particular circular introduced record keeping requirements for rating agencies, focusing on the justification of particular ratings. In addition, it requires them to "disclos[e] their compensation arrangements with the issuers [...] and their shareholding patterns" (RMI, 2011, p. 22). Furthermore, historical evidence regarding rating agencies' default rates (one year, cumulative, three year) must be published and released to the public in order to ensure that investors are aware of the success and longer-term performance of these rating guidelines. For structured finance products, rating agencies are required to disclose track records of the originator/issuer and "the nature of the underlying assets when assigning the credit ratings", along with the requirement to "disclose the performance of the underlying asset pool at least once every six month" (RMI, 2010, p. 22). The debate regarding conflicts of interest that emerged in India following the 2007–2008 financial crisis centered upon regulatory guidelines that would constrain participation in marketing or business development between rating agencies and issuers (SEBI, 2010). The aim of the proposed and introduced measures is to tackle any possible room for maneuvering in favor of their customers by rating agencies when assigning ratings. Moreover, these requirements are seen as a means of increasing the level of compliance with the norms and achieving a greater level of investor confidence with credit ratings. In the face of changing business dynamics, the SEBI sees a need for safeguarding standards in order to prevent any manipulation in the area of credit ratings – a concern that came to light since the 2007–2008 financial crisis (The Hindu, 2013).

As a supervisory institution, the SEBI is limited to securities issued by public entities or rights issues, including public/rights/listed issue of bonds, initial public offering (IPO) grading, capital protection oriented funds, and collective investment schemes (Bhushan, 2013). Supplementing such oversight, the Reserve Bank of India is responsible for regulating the rating of other financial instruments, including commercial paper, bank loans, security receipts, and securitized instruments (Bhushan, 2013). Through the adoption of the Basel II standard, Indian institutions have been able to withstand capital shocks by implementing a provisioning scheme that incorporates risk weights into asset management strategies (Bhushan, 2013).

By keeping the recent crisis in mind, India's regulation policy also focused on unsolicited ratings. Rating agencies claim that there is market demand to justify publishing unsolicited ratings. However, as Poon (2003) argues, empirical results demonstrate that unsolicited ratings tend to be lower than solicited ratings. Many companies find such ratings offensively and unfair, as they believe rating agencies cannot justify the unsolicited rating without having undertaken a comprehensive analysis based on information received from the company's management.[42] In order to address the issue, under India's new regulations, rating agencies have to disclose and monitor their ratings, as it is required for solicited rating. The new regulatory approach requires that rating agencies accompany the security's name with the word 'unsolicited' in the same font size. Rating agencies are also obliged to rate the issue during its lifetime (Bhushan, 2013).

The disparity between solicited and unsolicited credit ratings has been critiqued by Partnoy (2006) in relation to what was viewed as a retaliatory rating introduced by Moody's in 1999 during a public-sector bond issuance. The expectation for unsolicited ratings under India's new standards is that they are

42 According to Poon (2003, p. 596), "Moody's does not differentiate unsolicited and solicited ratings." Quite to the contrary, the agency "refuses to release the names of its clients, claiming a confidential agency-client relationship." Such ratings are used rather as a punishment, as the author stresses, for firms that would otherwise not commission a rating process with a rating agency.

explicitly reported as such, so as to enhance the overall transparency of the rating issuance and to prevent investor confusion. Further, Indian rating agencies are expected to generate a taxonomy of issuer and rating history for these securities, thereby allowing investors to pursue opinions and ratings reviews from beyond this single source (SEBI, 2010). Importantly, such new guidelines impose what the RMI recognize as a valuable solution to the process of ratings shopping, which issuers once used to access higher-level ratings prior to their acceptance of a particular determination (RMI, 2010). Through such disclosure guidelines, rating agencies are now required to publicly reveal their rating procedure, their rating history, and their default rates through traditional and online channels, generating a historic overview of the rating process (SEBI, 2010). With these measures, SEBI aims to ensure that the market is provided with information that will allow market participants to judge and assess the rating agencies' activities, as well as their performance and reliability.

The SEBI (2010) agenda for rating agencies' regulations introduced important controls that may ultimately do little to establish more robust accountability despite fostering greater support of a more transparent rating environment. In furthering this viewpoint, Bhushan empathizes that the CRA's made money by manipulating the ratings, "they knew that, had they not rated the instruments highly, people would not have bought if" (2013, p. 41). This controlling of fee-based contracting is an important step forward for the ratings industry, as Bhushan (2013) notes, particularly in relation to its century-long history of providing commercial stimulus and partnering with issuers This is because with the conflicts of interest revealed that the SEBI intends to make sure that rating agencies do not offer fee-based services that go "beyond credit ratings and research" (SEBI, 2009, p. 26). Further, the SEBI is committed to addressing any regulatory oversights through a more controlled dynamic that places emphasis on consistency and a framework of control, rather than a framework of litigation and courtroom debate. Although India has recently amended the regulation that it adopted, "concerns about conflicts of interest prevail" (Philipose, 2013, para. 2). Regulators, not only in India but also in other countries, should encourage market participants to perform "their own independent appraisal" of borrowers' quality and capabilities, and should not require mandatory use of ratings any longer (Philipose, 2013, para. 4).

7.4 The Canadian Position

While the global crisis brought down financial institutions across the world and led to the creation of government bail-out packages for distressed banks and countries, Canada's banking sector survived without a tax-payer financed bailout program and its banks remained stable. The reason for this lies in Canada's capital adequacy standards, which are among the most rigorous in the world (Gill and Raiser, 2008). In Canada, the crisis was most felt most by the collapse of the asset-backed commercial paper (ABCP) market, and from the Canadian point of view, the subprime crisis had a fundamental impact on the ABCP market (CSA, 2008). At the outset of the crisis in summer 2007, "investors holding ABCP began to realize" that the underlying assets of the securities they held "included RMBS and CDOs" (Rousseau, 2009, p. 12). As a result "their confidence was seriously challenged, even more so given the uncertainty surrounding the degree of exposure of commercial paper to the subprime mortgage market" (Rousseau, 2009, p. 12). The decisive aspect here is that rating agencies "provided the ratings the exempted ABCP from prospectus requirements" (Chant, 2009, p. 4).

As in other countries, Canadian regulations distinguish investment-grade securities from speculative securities, and ratings are used to identify the securities in which certain types of institution can invest without consent or authorization (Rousseau, 2009). According to Rousseau, despite a relatively broad us of credit ratings, Canada has "no principle approach with respect to CRAs" (2009. p. 17). In fact, Rousseau maintains that rating agencies activities and organization are *per se* not regulated, yet "regulatory regimes only recognize ratings issued by 'approved' or 'recognized' rating agencies, these expressions are only defined through a rudimentary listing of large CRAs" (Rousseau, 2009, p. 17). While Canadian authorities only recognize ratings issued by "approved" or "recognized" rating agencies, "these categories are not defined except through a simple listing of large CRAs that is based on undisclosed criteria" (Rousseau, 2012, p. 3). In addition to the two major Canadian rating agencies – Dominion Bond Rating Services (DBRS) and Canadian Bond Rating Services (CBRS) – the Canadian segment of 'approved' rating agencies also includes the three major rating players: Standard & Poor's, Moody's, and Fitch (Rousseau, 2009).

In the wake of the 2007–2008 credit market turmoil, the Canadian Securities Administrators (CSA) released a consultation paper that called for enhanced regulations, largely based on the IOSCO code of conduct. In its 2008 consultation paper, the CSA proposed regulatory reforms that were consistent with international developments and initiatives, such as the IOSCO, the SEC, the CESR, and the FSF, among others (CSA, 2008). More recently, the CSA published the notice of the adoption of *National Instrument 25–101 Designated Rating Organizations* (NI 25–101) in March 2012, along with amendments consequently relating to Instrument 25–101. The Instrument and all subsequent amendments entered into force on April 20, 2012 (Grewal, 2012). NI 25–101 sets out requirements for designated rating organizations (DRO) relating to filing, disclosure, and other applicable features that will be set out in legislation to DROs. In order to satisfy legal requirements of the securities, rating agencies are required to apply for DRO status, and the same applies to NRSROs as defined under the Securities and Exchange Act of 1934. Under the new regulatory framework of NI 25–101, rating agencies that apply for DRO designation will have to maintain, enforce, and comply with the code, which is compatible with the IOSCO code. In Canadian securities law, a number of rules include the concept of the 'approved credit rating' of 'approved rating organizations', and such 'approved credit rating organizations' like the DBRS, Moody's, Standard & Poor's, and Fitch (Grewal, 2012). Neither of them "have ever been required to apply to be 'approved' or 'designated', which means that the instrument will at the current stage not have any impact on these agencies at the current stage. There is no proposal to change these definitions (Grewal, 2012).

Although there have been numerous reports identifying failures on the part of rating agencies, the C.D. Howe Institute argued that those are not sufficient to enhance accountability and effectiveness of the rating agencies. Professor Rousseau, Chair in Business Law, Université de Montréal, said "Canada's response so far, like those in the US and EU, doesn't go far enough and arguably goes in the wrong direction by adding another layer of cumbersome regulation" (C.D. Howe Institute, 2012). The report recommends that reforms to address the shortcomings should be pursued in three major areas in the regulatory framework: eliminating regulatory reliance on rating agencies, developing due diligence obligations for institutional investors with regard to issuers' creditworthiness, and disclosing information on the assets underlying issues of structured finance products (Rousseau, 2012).

7.5 The Australian Position

Like Canada, the Australian financial system was much more resilient to the financial crisis, and, like Canada, the Australian banks did not require any infusions of governmental capital. However, the Australian economy was not fully immune from the crisis, and there was a substantial decline in equity prices, reducing the wealth of the economy by nearly 10 percent by March 2009 (Australian Bureau of Statistics, 2009). Nevertheless, Australia largely escaped the global downturn and was less affected than other countries (Brown and Davis, 2010). In light of the crisis, the Australian Government initiated major changes to existing regulations. On November 13, 2008, Nick Sherry, Australia's Minister for Superannuation and Corporate Law, announced that the Australian Securities and Investment Commission (ASIC) would remove rating agencies' exemption from holding an Australian Financial Services License (AFSL) (Sherry, 2008). The exemption protected the 'Big Three' agencies from any liability for ratings that they had published by in prospectus documents (Yeates, 2009). In addition, all rating agencies acting in Australia would be required to hold such a license in future and would be required to routinely outline how they comply with the updated IOSCO code. Sherry pointed out that "ASIC will also ensure that as part of the new Australian regime there will be no diminution of CRAs' adherence to the regulatory measures currently in place, or likely to be put in place, by the United States Securities and Exchange Commission, which include such issues as strengthened surveillance arrangements, limits of prohibitions on securities trading by staff of CRAs and rules on the receipt of gift" (Sherry, 2008, p. 1).

These measures would, in line with the SEC, allow market participants "to analyze the [financial] instrument and verify the accuracy of the data" (Bunjevac, 2009). This is a wide-ranging amendment, as up to that time rating agencies in Australia operated largely outside of the regulatory environment (Yaetes, 2009). Under the changed framework, Australian's regulators require special licensing conditions and disclosure rules of rating agencies' methodologies and their assumptions behind a ratings opinion. Thus, these requirements should ensure more consistent application of rating methodologies and full compliance with the regulatory framework. Through the new regulatory framework, Australian's government aims to expose rating agencies to a greater degree of scrutiny, and to scare off investors from taking ratings as a simple tool for measuring credit risk. The new regulations should help the authorities to assess whether rating agencies comply with the ASCI requirements and with provisions of the IOSCO Code.

In 2011, the ASIC released a consultation paper "on the form and content" of the annual compliance report in which each rating agency is required to give a written commitment (ASIC, 2011b, p. 1). The aim of this report is to "boost the integrity and standards" of Australia's financial system (ASIC, 2011b, p. 1). ASIC's chairman, Greg Medcraft, pointed out that by establishing reporting standards in combination with the Australian Financial Services (ASF) licensing conditions contributes to a wide-ranging surveillance of the ratings industry, and thus, the ASIC is a key tool for the regulatory supervising of rating agencies. The background for the 11–111MR ASCI proposal for credit rating agencies' compliance reporting is formed by the parameters of the governments' announcement of November 13, 2008 (ASIC, 2011b). However, in their comments on the Australian requirements, international rating agencies claimed that reporting requirements in the United States and the European Union are specifically tailored to specific regulations in these regions, and that it would therefore be inappropriate to base the Australian compliance report on the reporting requirements of the European Union. Nevertheless, rating agencies *must* comply with the terms and conditions for Australia's AFS licenses requirements and financial service laws. This is something that is unique to Australia (ASIC, 2011a). The efforts undertaken on the regulatory framework and the introduced measures endow Australian authorities with "sufficient powers to enable effective supervision and enforcement of credit rating agencies, including the power of sanction CRAs in breach of the applicable rules" (EC, 2012, p. 1). The ASIC is also endowed with the power to "stop unlawful behavior by a CRA or to impose fines where it has contravened any of its obligations under the relevant financial services legislation" (EC, 2012, p. 1). The ESMA has concluded a cooperation agreement with the ASIC to provide information exchange with regard to "enforcement and supervisory measures taken cross border CRAs" (EC, 2012, p. 1).

7.6 The Japanese Position

Investors in financial transactions in the domestic and foreign markets increasingly rely on what Schwarcz calls the "substantial comfort regarding the risk associated with the full and timely payment of debt securities" (Schwarcz, 2002, p. 3). Countries such as Japan or the United Kingdom, which have a unified regulatory structure, did not avoid the 2007–2008 crisis (Jickling, 2010). The major Japanese banking groups were also hit by subsequent turbulence. However, because the Japanese banks booked the relating losses in the business year 2007, the future burdens related to losses from the subprime-loans were limited (Takahara, 2008). A further reason why Japan was less affected was because the Japanese financial sector's exposure to opaque, toxic assets was significantly less than that of other nations. Sato (2009) argued that the awareness of risk management practices of the part of Japan's financial firms had been increased as part of the lessons learned from weathering the Asian crisis in the 1990s, which probably also helped here, too (Sato, 2009).

The main statute codifying Japanese securities law and regulating securities companies is the Financial Instruments Exchange Act of June 14, 2006 (Osugi, 2007). In addition, Japan implemented the Basel II framework at an early stage. Nevertheless, Japan also took measures in response to the market turmoil (Sato, 2009). However, according to Sato "the measures taken in Japan in response to the current financial stress, [...] differ somewhat from those in the United States and Europe" (2009, p. 285). According to the author, this different approach "reflects the fact that Japan has suffered in the current turmoil exogenous. In other words, Japan's financial system suffered from external injury, not from a disease of internal organs" (Sato, 2009, p. 288). Sato (2009) emphasizes that regulators must strike the right balance between short-term stabilization and medium-term stabilization measures. However, in its efforts to keep up with regulatory developments in other nations, Japan's government implemented a number of provisions governing rating agencies under the amendment of the Financial Instruments Exchange Act, enacted on June 17, 2009. In this context, it is necessary to consider the extent to which the new rules influence rating agencies' operations. Whereas rating agencies with a "well-established operational system in place" could obtain their admittance through a newly introduced mechanism from Japan's Prime Minister (RMI, 2010, p. 23), under the new provision, foreign corporations like Standard & Poor's, Moody's, and Fitch are now required to establish a base in Japan. Moreover, rating agencies must ensure the quality of the information used in their rating activities. They must also monitor this information and keep track of rating changes while also preventing conflicts of interest. Registered rating agencies are subject to the supervision by the Financial Service Agency. The Financial Service Agency does, however, not supervise the rating business operation itself; rather, it performs oversight of the adequacy of the rating agencies' operational systems and procedures with respect to the regulations in place by collecting reports or by carrying out on-site inspections (Yamaguchi, 2013).

Reflecting international discussions on the regulation of rating agencies following the crisis, Japan adopted a registration system for rating agencies in April 2010 that aims to protect the interests of investors; registered rating agencies are subject to rules requiring information disclosure on rating policies, and must establish operational control systems and prohibitions (provisions of rating service to stakeholders whose issue is rated by the rating agency, or any consulting service to the rated entity). The new rules established have similarities to requirements in the United States and Europe. Although the CSRS report from June 9, 2010, identified some differences, the CRSR concluded that overall, the legal and regulatory framework that Japan adopted in June 2010 could be considered comprehensive, and in many cases equivalent to the European Union's regulatory regime. The CRSR report marked a major step as the report assessed the "equivalence between 3rd country legal and supervisory frameworks and the EU regulatory regime for credit rating agencies" (CRSR, 2010, p. 11).

More recently, in 2011, the Financial Service Agency of Japan (FSA) and the ESMA exchanged letters in relation to rating agency supervision and information sharing. The so-called 'Exchange of Letters' (EOL) established a cross-border co-operation mechanism among rating agencies (RMI, 2011). This EOL with Japan is ground-breaking, as it the first cooperation agreement between Europe and "a supervisory authority from a so-called third country" (RMI, 2011, p. 24). This agreement is not simply an expression of market growth, but it also reflects the "progress that is currently made in ensuring the supervision of CRAs at an international level" (RMI, 2011, p. 24).

7.7 Rating Agencies and the Future of Regulatory Oversight

For nations like China, India, Korea and Russia, the net impact of credit ratings on investor confidence and market participation has been significant, as noted by Rajya Sabha (2009), resulting in strategic initiatives that were designed to decrease the risk of exposure to systematic events and information asymmetries. This reflected the primary goals of equilibrium planning and was based upon what Bloise (2005) views as a network of rational actors and informed trading decisions. Yet the failsafe measures implemented by regulators (such as Basel II) have proven to be inadequate in overcoming the informational power of the rating agencies' consortium. Researchers such as Yeh and Yang (2010) and Westerhoff (2003) attempt to describe an equilibrium response associated with either investor panic or regulatory intervention. However, it is evident that even under the most comprehensively controlled systems, such as that in India, the potential for a crash is directly tied to the asymmetrical nature of information and investor-expert exchange. The challenge lies in rectifying asymmetrical information and boosting financial and economic coordination.

Pro-cyclicality in the rating agency debate was robustly debated by Sy (2009) in an effort to address the implications of information, rating downgrades, and investor behavior. Such arguments suggest a "good times-bad times" relationship, whereby stock price movements could be quantitatively tied to both rating agencies' reports and downgrades, indicating a higher anticipation of risk in a given issue (Sy, 2009, p. 24). Ultimately, this argument was proven false within the derivatives and speculative instrument-based investment strategies employed prior to the 2007–2008 crisis. In response, India, took action against rating agencies and the commercialization of their interests, and in so doing solidified the regulatory agenda through a more controlled, more focused position of responsibility and transparency within the existing investment framework (Rajya Sabha, 2009).

In the European Union, O'Donnell (2012) cites regulatory commitments to improving transparency across rating agencies. Yet such regulations presuppose the objectivity of rating agencies and strive to deliver a more explicit governance scheme, which imposes restrictions on the varied exposure of these organizations to the financial interests of their rated issuers (EC, 2009: L 302/1-L302/3). The European sovereign debt crisis has further advanced the debate on rating agencies and the mutual dependence that exists between different financial markets. Rating downgrades resulted in "significant widening of sovereign bond and credit default swap (CDS) spreads" and put substantial pressure on stock markets (Alcubilla and del Pozo, 2012, p. 245). Several studies supplied evidence for the spillover effects on sovereign ratings, which in part contributed to the growing discomfort about the undue influence of rating agencies' decisions on the stability of the European economy. While much of the research in this field focuses on commercial paper and bond issuances, there are other factors at stake in the rating agencies' agenda, such as sovereign ratings. Kräussl (2003; 2005) reflects on the potentially negative impact of sovereign credit ratings on in-country positions as investors assess the implications of downgrades and comparative credit scoring. He notes that rating agencies "interpret sovereign credit ratings as forward-looking indications of the relative risk that a sovereign debt issuer will not have the ability and willingness to make full and timely payments of principle and interest over the life of a particular rated financial instrument" (Kräussl, 2003, p. 3). Divided into investment grade and speculative, non-investment grade credit ratings, the downgrade of sovereign debt may have significant implications for managers of bond portfolios who must trade following specific classification guidelines (Kräussl, 2003). Through a critical, quantitative analysis of country-specific evidence, Kräussl (2003) describes the contagion effect of rating agency-driven sovereign rating actions, particularly in relation to interwoven downgrade events. Such findings are indicative of a spillover effect, which is also the case for the structured finance market in which "rating changes in in a ground zero country have a (statistically) significant impact on the financial markets of other emerging market economies although the spillover effects tend to be regional" (Kräussl, 2003, p. 1). Ultimately, the sensitivity to such effects is directly tied to market stability and interdependencies between nations; however, generalizations based on credit ratings may exacerbate investor concerns and result in market withdrawal or resistance.

A number of aspects for the governance of rating agencies are on regulatory agendas, advocating policies for international regulatory standards, robust official regulation, capital controls, and the greatest possible decentralization in the regulatory environment (Helleiner, 2009). Masters highlights that part of this agenda includes a measured assessment of rating agencies' operations and ratings outcomes, whereby regulators will not be "rating the ratings", but will be assessing their models in order to ensure that they are sound and properly researched (2012, para. 5). Such agenda setting is not only data and time-intensive strategy, but it also places an emphasis on the expertise of the reviewer and the regulator to ensure that their understanding of rating agencies' methodologies are consistent with the actual ratings themselves. It is evident that the Indian attempt to reduce and eliminate commercialistic principles embraced by rating agencies might better benefit the European Union and its diverse spectrum of investment-related interests. To a large extent, US and European regulators accepted the conflicts of interest inherent within the issuer-pays model as an explanation for unreliable ratings, and while they have undertaken steps to reduce such conflicts, "they have made few systematic changes, and they have not restricted the trading of complex instruments, such as mortgage-backed securities" (Kirshner, 2013, p. 2).

7.8 Conclusion

Changes to the regulation and supervision of financial markets and rating agencies have been proposed and implemented globally in response to the financial crisis of 2007–2008. This chapter highlighted regulatory efforts undertaken in several of the worlds' leading financial markets. The improvement of financial regulation is necessary "in order to encompass all market participants (including rating agencies [...]) and to dampen pro-cyclical impacts of accounting and prudential rules" (Noyer, 2009, p. 2). Rating agencies damaged their reputation as a result of their perceived role in the financial crisis, and are now challenged to revive their reputation and standing as reliable players in the field (Noyer, 2009).

The pre-crisis regulatory paradigm (which relied first and foremost on self-regulation) has been reversed by the financial crisis of 2007–2008. In order to provide better supervision, the European Union installed several EU regulatory authorities providing vehicles that served to ensure coordination between national regulatory authorities and the European body. Nevertheless, "details regarding the governance structure and enforcement of powers remain scant" (O'Brien, 2010, p. 64) In the European Union, the implementation of the Basel II accord has introduced key rules for the regulation of rating agencies for the first time (Pagliari, 2012). This was followed in the case of the recent crisis by a number of provisions providing the European Union with a comprehensive regulatory framework for the regulation and supervision of rating agencies. However, there are concerns that even though the proposals for further improvement go into the right direction, some of them are not be far reaching enough (Wishart, 2013)

Parallel to regulatory measures taken and developments underway at the European level, many countries in the Asian-Pacific region have explicitly signaled or have already taken actions to strengthen their regulatory framework relating to the governance of rating agencies. The Asian-Pacific countries recognized that it was essential for their economies to establish provisions that set out rules comparable to those of western countries in light of the internationalization and globalization of financial markets. Emerging markets implemented Basel II standards to contribute to the quality of capital supervisions. However, concerns about the independence of rating agencies and the negative impact of the 'Big Three' for Asian countries led China to establish a joint venture rating agency, Universal Credit Ratings Group (UCRG), not only to compete with the major US-centric rating agencies, but also to offer a different point of view.

Although a number of regulatory changes have been made or are underway, there is still ongoing debate as to whether these are sufficient or far reaching enough. Such discussions generally center upon whether regulations should standardize the ratings themselves, along with whether or not the rating agencies should be required to 'fully' disclose their methodologies. However, the very recognition that reforming the regulatory framework requires more coordination and integration at a global level became clear in light of the economic consequences of the recent crisis. The Indian regulation of financial markets and rating agencies could provide to be a global guide for how intensive regulations of financial markets should be performed – and by whom (Kirshner, 2013). Supervision with an appropriate level of governance, measures, regulations, and joint efforts targeted to guarantee sound management of financial markets and rating agencies are needed in order to restore confidence in both the economy and the rating agencies themselves. The challenge for governments and regulators is to define what an 'appropriate' level of transparency, disclosure, and necessary accountability in the ratings industry would be.

8. Empirical Research: Design and Methodology

The role of rating agencies in the financial crisis of 2007–2008 raised questions regarding their methodologies, the quality of their ratings, their role in financial markets, and their responsibilities. In response to these issues, stakeholders including regulators, investors, governmental authorities, and commentators, have considered a number of measures and proposals relating to improving the quality of ratings information and regulatory issues pertaining to framework reconfigurations. As noted in the literature reviewed, and addressed in the previous chapters, a great deal of debate, has accompanied such proposals. Despite the intensity of the debate, however, some areas remain in which a general consensus on how to move forward has not been reached. To date, there are only a few empirical studies that have focused on debt market participants' perceptions in relation to rating agencies. For instance, Duff and Einig (2007, 2009a, 2009b) assess the factors that influence 'ratings quality' (based on pre-crisis interviews conducted in 2005), and Fennel and Medvedev (2011) focus on different forms of rating agencies' 'compensation model'. In the context of market participants' perceptions, Duff and Einig (2009b) refer to Francis (2004), who stresses the importance of stakeholder perceptions with respect to quality and credibility, and argue that the quality of rating agencies as gatekeepers is difficult to verify. Furthermore, Duff and Einig (2009b) refer to Watkins, Hillison, and Morecroft (2004) when suggesting that quality is subject to a set of definitions that mostly depend on a degree of market perception. This research focuses on the information quality of ratings and the liability aspects of rating agencies. In so doing, it also identifies a range of possible remedies to existing problems.

8.1 Purpose and Research Approach

This research considers the views of financial market participants after the 2007–2008 meltdown in the financial markets. It explores alternative approaches relating quality issues for financial products and managing the liability of rating agencies. The opinions of top management respondents from the banking sector, investment banks and other financial institutions in Germany, Switzerland, and the United Kingdom were collected through personal interviews. The aims of this research are to identify (1) if there are other ways to assess the quality of financial instruments and to express varying degrees of risk factors; (2) whether rating agencies should be an autonomous state agency; and (3) what nature and form a possible liability regime for rating agencies should take. This research contributes to the growing discussion about rating agencies' role both before and during the recent crisis by adding the viewpoints of the market participants who were, and continue to be involved in this industry. The empirical part of this research presents and describes the findings from these interviews.

8.2 Research Approach

There are four broad scientific methods used to arrive at a conclusion: the deductive, inductive, retroductive, and abductive approaches (Blaikie, 2007, p. 3). The deductive and inductive methods are probably, as Blaikie (2007) notes, the most familiar. The main difference between these is that the deductive approach is aimed at testing the conceptual and theoretical structures (the theory), whereas the inductive approach generates conclusions from the empirical observations. In qualitative research, the focal points – collecting, analyzing and interpreting data – are not necessarily conceptualized on a chronological scale (Gibbs, 2008). This interaction between theory and research is what Babbie describes as "a never-ending alternation of deduction and induction" (2008, p. 52), something that is actually common practice. In addition, according to Bryant and Charmaz "abductive reasoning resides at the core of grounded theory logic: it links empirical observations with imaginative interpretation, but does so by seeking theoretical accountability through returning to the empirical world" (2007, p. 46). In qualitative research, the objective is attributed to words and meanings and takes into account the participants' views. By applying a qualitative approach, the investigator comes closer to social reality, resulting in a narrowing of the gap between reality and representation. This approach attempts "to generate theory with its inductive logic" and provides a rich and in depth source of data" (Bapir, 2012, p. 6–7).

For the reasons given above, this research has primarily utilized the inductive approach which has been considered alongside grounded theory so as to examine the fullness of the analysis provided by the research. The reasoning behind this dual approach is that it seemed to offer the best analytical linkage with the research method, as the interview guidelines were based on and created with the help of a theoretical framework. Thereafter, through an analysis of the empirical data with respect to the theory, a number of reasoned conclusions are advanced at the end of this empirical section.

8.3 Research Strategy

In economics, qualitative research has long been considered less important compared to quantitative research. There are areas of research, such as economics and its closely related fields, where this research method has, according to Starr, shown "a small explosion" in the last 10–15 years (2012, p. 238). The author emphasizes that "well-done qualitative work can provide scientifically valuable and intellectually helpful, ways of adding to the stock of economic knowledge", which is particularly the case "when applied to research questions for which they are well suited" (Starr, 2012, p. 238). However, Starr argues that economists have "the tendencies to associate 'good' research qualities (representativeness, rigor, objectivity, explanation) with quantitative data methods, and corresponding 'bad' ones (un-representativeness, informality, subjectivity, description)" (2012, p. 240). Yet, according to the author, "both the 'good' and the 'bad' research qualities occur in both types of research" (Starr, 2012, p. 240). In qualitative research, different types of approaches are available, such as case studies, phenomenological research, and grounded theory. In grounded theory, the researcher "derives a general, abstract theory of a process, action, or interaction grounded in the views of participants" (Creswell, 2009, p. 13). The constant comparison of the data with emerging categories and the theoretical sampling of refined (data) groups in order to maximize the potential similarities and differences that can be found in the information are the primary advantages of this method (Creswell, 2009).

8.4 Selected Research Method

According to Yin (2008), the best method to choose depends on the purpose of the research and associated questions. For this study, the qualitative research approach was chosen for a number of reasons. First, given that the main objective of this research is to find out stakeholders' perceptions, it was useful to apply a qualitative approach, as it enabled more 'in-depth' responses to be analyzed. Second, "because of the differences in the data, how data is collected and analyzed and what the data and analyses are able to tell us about our subject of study", the knowledge obtained through such investigations is "more informative, richer and offers enhanced understandings compared to that which can be obtained via quantitative research" (Tweksbury, 2000, p. 38). As the aim of this research is to garner rich, detailed answers from the participants, the in-depth understanding calls for a qualitative approach. Third, the qualitative research approach is an appropriate strategy for situations in which data is collected from cross-border or cross-cultural settings (Ghauri, 2004). For these reasons, qualitative interviews were selected as the method of data collection.

The openness and flexibility inherent to the qualitative research approach might contribute to other understanding beyond that found in quantitative studies. Quantitative data may be useful in surveys where a large number of respondents are involved, and a large number of attitudes across the sample is desired. To find out and learn about an individual's perceptions regarding a particular survey topic, grounded theory is a useful tool, as the methodological framework is aimed to gather individual, in-depth views (Martins and Nunes 2011). Using qualitative research and grounded theory provides the opportunity to discover principles relevant to the subject under investigation. Following such arguments, the qualitative approach, in conjunction with grounded theory, is most applicable for fulfilling the purposes of this research, as the analytical focus lies in how the topic under study is experienced and viewed by the participants.

8.5 Methodology Interviews

There are two types of data sources: primary and secondary. Primary data refers to sources for which the researcher gathers original data for the research topic, such as by using interviews or questionnaires (Bryman and Bell, 2007). Secondary data refers to sources for which the data has been contributed by other researchers or institutions in the form of articles, books documents and other relevant literature (Ghauri, 2005). Both primary and secondary data were collected in this study. The primary data was collected within the framework of qualitative research interviews. For the secondary data, a literature search was conducted to identify relevant academic, industry papers, journal articles, governmental reports, books, databases, and Internet sources. They were all, thereafter, critically evaluated. The theoretical framework of this research is constructed on the basis of the analysis conducted on this secondary data, which also served as the foundation to support the empirical part of the research. The literature review also helped to formulate the research questions.

There are different types of qualitative research interviews: structured, semi-structured and unstructured. Structured interviews are defined by having a rigorous questionnaire, in which fixed format interview questions are asked and presented in a particular manner, allowing little or no variation (Gill et al., 2008). In contrast, unstructured interviews are more conversational and do not include a list of prepared questions, and in unstructured interviews, the interviewee "takes an active role in constructing the interview" and has a major influence on the direction the interview goes in (Bryman and Bell, 2007, p, 504). Semi-structured interviews consist of pre-determined "key questions that help to define the areas to be explored" but permit derogations to pursue an idea or response in order to have a more detailed look on the issue (Gill et al., 2008, p. 291). The method used in this study was based on a semi-structured interview approach with open-ended questions. According to Damgaard, Freytag and Darmer, (2001) the semi-structured interview form should neither be a highly structured questionnaire, nor a free conversation. Semi-structured interviews have a flexible, fluid structure and contain consistent questions that the researcher ensures are asked to every person who is interviewed (Mason, 2004). Semi-structured interviews are the most widespread interview method in qualitative research and can be conducted either individually or in groups (DiCicco-Bloom and Crabtree, 2006). Moreover, they are conducted only once, with each individual or group and generally take between 30 minutes and one hour to complete, though in some cases the timeframe can be extended to several hours (DiCicco-Bloom and Crabtree, 2006). The interviewee is seen as an expert in his field and the term "expert-interview" has become synonymous with semi-structured interviews (Weßel, 2010, p. 929). Semi-structured interviews enable the interviewer to control the interview flow and direction, while encouraging respondents to speak freely about each topic. In addition, semi-structured interviews create more scope for aspects that the interviewer had previously not thought of to be explored (Gill et al., 2008). Semi-structured interviews with open questions are effective for gaining insight to what Sykes (1990)) refers to as the possibility of finding "meaning behind numbers", allowing flexibility without large samples (cited Sinkovics, Penz and Ghauri, 2008, p. 691), and "offer[ing] a clear and holistic view of the context" (Sinkovics, Penz and Ghauri, 2008, p. 690).

This research uses semi-structured interviews, with a cross-section of respondents from banks, investment banks, and other financial institutions. This combination of experts was selected from investment banks and other financial institutions located in Germany, Switzerland and the United Kingdom. Collecting and combining the views of respondents from different market locations allowed for an extended (cross-border) view to be garnered. The participants of the survey were assured of the anonymity for themselves personally, as well as for their institutions, in accordance with both university and market protocols. The personal details of interviewees are not revealed in this research due to confidential and ethical concerns (Orb, Eisenhauer and Wynaden, 2001). In order to further ensure anonymity, individual names were replaced with uniquely assigned codes. To maintain confidentiality and anonymity, individual statements are presented in the form of quotations with a clear reference to the corresponding interviewee (referenced by their unique code).

The interviewees were chosen for their knowledge, insight, and active interest in ratings and rating agencies' roles and functions. All interviews were conducted face-to-face at locations determined by the interviewees. Face-to-face interviews have a number of advantages compared with other forms of interviewing that could have been used (e.g. telephone interviews). This is because the face-to-face encounter builds greater confidence between both the interviewee and interviewer, as noted by Earl-Slater (2004).

The following professionals working in the financial industry were regarded as experts for the purposes of this research:

- Executive Directors
- Vice Presidents
- Managing Directors
- Head of Research

The participants were approached via telephone and/or e-mail and were asked if they were willing to participate in the study. Interviews were then arranged with the interviewees directly.

8.6 Data Collection

The research used qualitative methods, and the data was collected through semi-structured interviews from June–September 2011. 19 individual interviews were carried out, as well as two group interviews, one interview with two people, the other with three respondents. All interviews were conducted face-to-face. The applied format for the questions was an interview-guide in which the wording of questions was predetermined, but depending on the 'pre-determined' flow of the interview, the sequence was altered during the conservation. This approach has the advantage of allowing the data collection to be more systematic, ensuring that each topic is covered without disrupting the content (Patton, 2002).

The interviews varied in length from 45 minutes to one hour and 50 minutes. The interviews were audiotaped (digital), as this allowed the interviewer to concentrate solely on the interview at hand, rather than being distracted by the need to take notes. Using audio recording tools had a further advantage: the outcome of the data collection is more accurate because the exact words used by the interviewee are captured, along with vocal expression, such as inflections in tone. In accordance with ethical research guidelines, permission was sought and obtained from each interviewee before their comments were recorded. The importance of this is further discussed by Bauer and Gaskell (2000). Prior to beginning the interview, each of the interviewees was informed of the objective of the study and given a copy of the list of questions that were to be asked during the interview. Considerable efforts were made by the interviewer not to influence the interviewees' views with either his own personal views or opinions. The interviewees were encouraged to present their perspectives and to expand upon the answers they gave when they thought that the area warranted further comment. The interviews were then transcribed and analyzed using qualitative techniques and the text analysis computer software (MAXQDA). The transcriptions of the interviews were transcribed verbatim[43]. For this research, relevant passages of the interviewees' responses to the questions are cited with the unique code assigned to each individual interviewee.

8.7 Quality Criteria

A key issue in qualitative research is the reliability and validity of the research strategy. Traditional criteria for the evaluation, validation, and recognition of qualitative research are reliability, objectivity, and internal and external validity (Klenke, 2008). However, there are alternatives, such as the four criteria proposed by Lincoln and Guba (1985): credibility, transferability, dependability and conformability. This is an approach that Morse et al. consider "an interesting shift for 'ensuring rigor' from the investigator's action during the course of the research, to the reader or consumer of qualitative inquiry" (2008, p. 13). They cite this as an approach where trustworthiness and utility are going to be implemented once a study is considered to have been completed. However, Morse et al. emphasize that "reliability and validity remain appropriate concepts for attaining rigor in qualitative research" (2008, p. 13). Bashir et al. assert that qualitative researchers "have to salvage responsibility" (2008, p. 35) for the reliability and validity of their research. This would be best achieved by "implementing verification strategies integral and self-correcting during the conduct of inquiry itself" (Morse et al., 2008, p. 13). This system, in addition, according to Bashir et al. ensures the "attainment of rigor using strategies inherent within each qualitative design" and shifts back the responsibility of "incorporating and maintaining reliability and validity from external reviewers' judgment to the investigators themselves" (2008, p. 35).

43 Where necessary, translation was undertaken to reproduce the foreign phrasing faithfully, rendering the sense of the original language.

Reliability and validity are important factors when carrying out qualitative research, as these factors help to determine the objectivity of the research. To illustrate this, the trustworthiness, reliability, and validity are separated into internal and external measures (Bryman and Bell, 2007). In this context, Bryman and Bell (2007) propose a strategy of adapting a similar role as the original investigator to recreate and replicate the initial research. Internal validity refers to the congruence of an investigator's findings with reality. A strategy that can help to ensure that the investigator's "interpretation of 'reality' being presented is as 'true' to the phenomenon as possible" is, for example, tri-angulation, using "multiple methods to confirm the emerging findings" (Merriam, 1995, p. 54). Merriam therefore suggests that, "if the researcher hears about the phenomenon in interviews, sees it taking place in observations, and reads about it in pertinent documents, he or she can be confident that the 'reality' of the situation [...] is being conveyed as 'truthfully' as possible" (1995, p. 54). As in qualitative research, the 'sample' is a relatively small part of the population that can be regarded as a problem (Bryman and Bell, 2007). In this context, it is important that "the investigator needs to provide 'sufficient descriptive data' to make transferability possible (Merriam, 1995, p. 225).

The generally small sample size utilized in qualitative research comes from a wider population, and external validity refers to how well the sample (population) surveyed represents the wider population (Anderson, 2010). There is no rule in qualitative research specifying an ideal sample size; the sample size depends on what the researcher wants to know, the purpose of the inquiry, and what will be useful and provide credibility, along with "what can be done with available time and resources", as the validity and meaningfulness have more to do with richness of the information obtained and the capabilities of the researcher "than the sample size" (Patton, 2002, p. 224, 245).

8.8 Questionnaire Development

The development of the questionnaire was based on the literature that considered the criticism of rating agencies in light of the financial crisis of 2007–2008 and its aftermath. The questionnaire items were created to identify characteristics of rating agencies and ratings pertaining to information quality and potential liability issues. The questionnaire contained six main questions, supplemented by "follow-up questions in order to clarify the respondent's meaning [...] and get beyond superficial responses" (Barker, Pistrang, and Elliot, 2005, p. 97). This approach is helpful because qualitative research intends "to explore the complex set of factors surrounding the central phenomenon and present the varied perspectives or meanings that participants hold (Creswell, 2009, p. 127–128). The main questions focused on ratings terminology, methodology, liability aspects, and as to whether rating agencies should be governmental institutions. The aim of asking these questions is to discover participants' perception in order to develop inductively derived theory grounded in the data. The follow-up questions focused on the omission of reference to credit ratings in mandatory guidelines (given that the regulation of rating agencies at US and European level attempted to remove mechanistic reliance on ratings), and the lack of competition amongst credit rating agencies. These questions were grouped into five categories: an overview of the questionnaire is provided in Table 4.

Table 4: Semi-Structured Interview Questions Used to Garner Stakeholder Perceptions Relating to Rating Agencies

Theme	Question
Status quo – helpfulness of ratings and absence of binding guidelines with reference to ratings	Are ratings helpful in principle? What would you do in case neither public nor binding guidelines for the assessment of credit-risk for financial instruments exist?
Challenging the terminology and methodology of rating agencies and alternative ways of risk assessment	As I am sure you well know, the terminology of rating agencies is very obscure. Could it be made more uniform? Something that the man in the street could easily understand? The methodology of rating agencies too is to convoluted and unintelligible. Look at the sub-prime methodology and you will understand me. Could this be made simpler? Something at the same simplicity as the Dow Jones stock index? What other ways are there to assess the quality of financial instruments in a more transparent way?
Hypothetical situation in which rules to comply with minimum ratings were rendered inoperative	Supposed the mandatory guidelines in accordance with current ratings would be suspended. In this case the European Central Bank (ECB) would and should not stick on ratings when it concerns securities eligible for refinancing facilities granted to financial institutions. Would this restrict the relevance of rating agencies? Or would rating agencies even become meaningless? In case the mandatory guidelines of operation in accordance with the current ratings would be cancelled, how would this affect your investment recommendations and decisions?

Theme	Question
Liability of rating agencies	The basic logic of the market system is that those who make mistakes must pay for their errors. How can this be made applicable to the rating agencies too? In many professions there exists insurance against malpractice. The professional himself pays the insurance premiums for his malpractice policy. Can we not ask the rating agencies to do it similarly?
Alternatives to rating agencies in general, as well as their integration in a governmental setting	Everybody thinks that the Central bank has to be a government institution (same for the Financial Service Authority). On the same reasoning, shouldn't the rating agencies to become an autonomous government institution? There is increasingly vociferous demand for a counter pole to the 'Big Three'. Do you believe that more competition would be helpful? Would it not be a good idea to set up a rating agency with a powerful background to close up as quickly as possible to the 'Big Three'? A subsidiary of a national- or supranational institution, i.e. an EU or OECD agency, could have a powerful background. Could their ratings be quite different from the ratings of the 'Big Three'?

Source: Author.

9. Empirical Research: Results

The presentation of the results is divided into the following five topics:

(1) The helpfulness of credit ratings and the absence of binding guidelines with reference to ratings;
(2) Challenging the terminology and methodology of ratings, and alternative ways of assessing credit risk;
(3) Removing reference to credit ratings;
(4) Liability of rating agencies;
(5) Alternatives to rating agencies in general and their embedding in the governmental setting.

These topics describe different aspects of market participants' perceptions after the financial crisis of 2007–2008. It should be noted that the interview quotes presented in this chapter are transcribed verbatim and that any grammatical or language errors come directly from the comments made by the interviewees. The first topic reflects how they view the helpfulness of rating agencies' credit ratings post-crisis, and the environment in which they operate, given that the control of financial risk is largely affected on the basis of directives or with reference to guidelines for action (Jeon and Lovo, 2013). The second topic explores how they characterize the intelligibility of rating agencies' terminology and methodology, and how alternatives to existing credit risk assessment could be shaped. The third topic covers how removing mandatory references to credit ratings would affect rating agencies from the participants' perspective. The fourth topic considers how survey respondents assess the possibility of holding rating agencies liable for their actions. Finally, the fifth topic describes whether the interviewees believe rating agencies should become a governmental agency and whether competitor at a national or supranational levels might contribute to the production of alternative and more transparent credit ratings by providing structure and competition to the market.

9.1 Topic 1: Helpfulnes of Credit Ratingss and the Absence of Binding Guidelines

Credit ratings enable investors to save time and effort in analyzing the financial strengths of a financial instrument (Darbellay, 2013). The recent crisis has shaken market participants' confidence in ratings (Utzig, 2010). Nevertheless, whatever the 'Big Three' rating agencies' performance may have been, investors remain heavily dependent on these agencies and their ratings are still used in capital adequacy and portfolio guidelines (Levine, 2012). The pre-crisis overreliance on ratings with questionable accuracy (Kenyon and Green, 2012) led to questions relating to how helpful rating agencies' ratings in debt pricing would be viewed in the post-crisis period. Given that controlling financial risk is largely based on legal, client and internal investment-guiding principles, what could be done in the absence of public or binding policies relating to credit ratings?

When asked, the majority of participants considered that ratings, while not infallible, still provide an important determinant for evaluating companies and simple bonds. When it comes to assessing the risk inherent in structured products, the interviewees further suggested that the ratings of the three major rating agencies should be seen as one 'piece' of an investment decision, and that investors should not rely solely on rating agencies' ratings. This is illustrated by the following responses:

> *I think for a type of product we are investing (in) as well [...]: let's stick to vanilla products; it is quite helpful if we trust rating agencies. Now, for some asset-backed securities, this will be a different attitude reaching an opinion. (P14)*

> *I think so, because it is associated with the legal framework. Using a rating provides protection insofar that in case of any dissonance between bank and client, we [the bank] express a general market opinion, which is important in a possible legal situation [...]. I consider it important to have creditworthiness assessment by rating agencies for the bond market. However, large investors should do their own [risk] assessment and not rely solely on rating agencies. (P10)*

> *Additional research has to be carried out [...] one cannot place undue reliance on rating agencies. (P20)*

> *The credit rating is important for us depending on the mandate [...]. There are limits as to what you can purchase, and some mandates say only in investment grade or not more than 10% below investment grade. (P12)*

In addition, the following statement relating to the helpfulness of ratings addressed topics that are dealt with in the following topics:

> *Basically yes, but I wonder how does one establish a rating. How is it calculated? Is it transparent? Is it good? Can one understand it? (P6)*

Many institutional investors, financial institutions, and banks have investment guidelines that limit their holdings to financial instruments that carry investment-grade ratings assigned by recognized rating agencies (Levine, 2012). Rating downgrades would thus force those investors to dispose of downgraded securities, thereby having a significant impact on investment decisions, a consequence that is noted by Choudhry (2010) and reinforced by the findings of this research. Only a small portion of those questioned stated that they have no legally binding guidelines. In addition, it was evident that most contracts with clients indicate that bonds or securities must have at least investment grade ratings. Given that there are contractual arrangements, the absence of guidelines – in the form of a credit rating – would impact their investment strategy. Although two participants stated that ratings are not relevant for them, the only reason why ratings are assigned relevance is that there are clients in a regulated environment, as well as private investors, who require a minimum rating. Without such provisions, ratings would effectively become irrelevant.

The predominant view expressed by the participants was that banks, financial institutions, and individuals should take more responsibility for their actions:

> *Without such guidelines investors would have to decide themselves how to measure risk. (P3)*

> *It would facilitate our business, insofar as an insignificant regulation or an indicator would be omitted, and following the withdrawal be disregarded by investors and [our] clients. I think people would commence to act in a more reasonable manner. (P7)*

> *The individual responsibility would be in the foreground […]. I believe this would be more direct and would work better than what we have currently in place. (P17)*

The absence of binding guidelines for investment decisions would require a more active process of analysis and risk assessment, something that might better conform to policy-makers' expectations of how investors should use ratings. Taking into consideration that US bank regulation under the Dodd-Frank Act (2010) strives to abandon reliance on rating agencies in several rules (Krainer, 2012) and the European Supervisory Authorities intend to decrease the reliance on ratings (EBA, 2013).

9.2 Topic 2: Intelligibility of Rating Agencies' Terminology and Methodology – Alternative Ways to Assess Credit Risk

Terminology. According to the rating agencies, their ratings represent a uniform measure of credit quality across all types of asset classes, whether a corporate, sovereign, or structured finance rating (Cornaggia, Cornaggia, and Hund, 2013). Their ratings are ranked on a scale, divided into segments representing investment-grade and below investment-grade ratings. To the untrained eye, the scales look very similar, and, according to Langohr and Langohr, "identical symbols have different meanings for different CRAs" and one cannot derive from this that "a

Moody's C is the same as an S&P C" (2008, p. 49). As Everling (1991) observes, this makes it difficult to determine the differences in the various ratings. This gives rise to question of whether this could be made more uniform, and understandable for the 'man in the street'. Participants from the survey made a number of statements, suggestions, and proposals on this topic:

First, there were recurring comments that, in the opinion of the participants, existing rating agencies' terminology is appropriate, sufficiently clear and accessible for those who have to deal with it. Two participants expressed the fear that, if the terminology was 'standardized', a standardized terminology could lead to standardized rating procedures and, in consequence, that *"all ratings [would] look the same". (P15)*

However, the foremost view was that the terminology could be improved. The predominant view was that more uniform rating terminology would be easier to understand:

> *They should use the same. I think that could be reasonable to have them unify their codes so that it is [...] much easier to understand what Moody's and Fitch and S&P are saying on the same time. (P6)*

> *This would be a good reform to make. (P12)*

> *I would very much welcome a simplified and more uniform terminology. (P1)*

> *Certainly it would make sense to introduce a more uniform terminology. (P8)*

> *One could implement a uniform framework for all rating agencies to display different risks positions [...]. A scale considered as being directly comparable among rating agencies. And not somewhat like 'our AA is different from the AA of the others'. (P11)*

> *It could be unified, so that all rating agencies use the same terminology with the same symbols.[...] it should be possible to adopt a uniform terminology, also for the purpose to provide greater clarity. (P16)*

> *To have the same scale for all rating agencies would be good, but, we have to make sure to maintain their different approaches. I really don't like to see a regulation to force them to use the same approach, that wouldn't be useful. (P14)*

In order to achieve simpler and more uniform terminology for expressing different degrees of credit risk, one might, according to the participants, use a numerical scale ranging from 1–10 or 1–15 points. Another option raised is that of adopting a grading system ranking from 1–6 (with graduations) like the school grading system used in Germany (where one is the highest grade possible and six a failing grade) or Switzerland (where it is opposite). From the views of the participants noted below, it can be concluded that there was a general consensus that a more uniform rating terminology for every agency would be advantageous and easier.

One could use a distribution system similar to a school grading system, [...] either with a point-grading scale ranking form 1–15, or with a grading system ranking from 1–6, whereby 6 determines a credit default. (P1)

One should classify ratings in terms of school grades; then everyone would know for a good quality stands number 1, and 6 would thus classify the lowest grade and is thus insufficient. (P17)

On a scale of 1–10 [points]. (P7)

If we would use a scale ranging from 1–10, or any other simpler scale, then it would be easier to understand. (P3)

The easiest would be to ensure uniform interpretation of the nomenclature [...] and one defines a standard set of maybe 5–10 basic parameters. (P9)

I would say ... it is quite simple, one agrees on a range from very bad to the highest quality, with graduations, say 10 [...] comparable to a school grading system. (P18)

One could define an equal framework for all [CRA], where we say we have different [school] marks [...] this is directly comparable. (P11)

Table 5 illustrates how a more uniform rating terminology might look.

Table 5: Proposal for a New Grade-System

Description	Points	"School-Marks"	
		Scale Range	Ranking System
Investment grade (prime/ extremely strong) High Grade	15	1+	1
	14	1	
	13	1-	
Upper medium grade	12	2+	2
	11	2	
	10	2-	
Lower medium grade	9	3+	3
	8	3	
	7	3-	

Description	Points	"School-Marks"	
		Scale Range	Ranking System
Non-investment grade (speculative)	6	4+	4
Highly speculative	5	4	
	4	4-	
Substantial risk	3	5+	5
Very highly speculative	2	5	
Default imminent	1	5-	
In default	0	6	6

Source: Author.

Although a simpler and more uniform terminology could be easier to understand by the 'man in the street', the majority of participants expressed the following view:

> *The man on the street? I think for him it is fairly irrelevant if bonds are rated or not [...]. Private investors have no vested interest in that. That is something that counts for institutional investors. (P3)*

> *I think [the terminology] is appropriate for the public that are getting them [the ratings], and ratings are not really for the man on the street; it's for investors, not only specialized investors, but for everybody who has a bit of interest in it. (P14)*

> *The valuation of corporates is not easy, this counts even more for structured products [...]. I think that cannot be presented that easily that the man on the street then says: yes, I understand how these asset-backed securities have been assessed. (P21)*

The findings indicate that there is a broad consensus that a simpler and more uniform terminology could be feasible, and that it would be desirable. Adopting a new rating terminology would, however, require an agreement on international classification standards. Furthermore, not only is there no requirement that existing ratings terminology be understood by the 'man in the street', there is also no guarantee that any new system would be more accessible to the average person.

Methodology. The use of a methodology should describe how rating agencies assess the risk of financial instruments and relate them to a specific rating (Duff and Einig, 2007). Following the subprime debacle, rating agencies' methodologies have been subject to scrutiny by a range of stakeholders, including policymakers, regulatory authorities, and academics. Nevertheless, as Bondarouk notes, "nobody still knows what methodologies the rating agencies use. In fact nobody can really monitor their calculations" (2010). Rating agencies underestimated the default probabilities of securities backed by risky subprime mortgages in their models (Utzig, 2010). In addition, rating agencies are required to disclose their rating policies and methodologies under the current regulatory framework. However, as Miglionico notes, "the usefulness of such general disclosure is likely to be limited" given that it "could be written in a way that would allow a significant amount of deviation in the use of information" (2012, p. 62). The result would be that the question arises as to whether the methodology employed could be made simpler. Although a minority of participants agreed that a simpler methodology could be quite helpful, the following comments reflect the prevailing opinion:

> *I find it difficult ... to say 'let's create systems that are very transparent, very open', which implies to me objective and quantitative [criteria]. (P12)*

> *Rating agencies statements (on the probability of default) are very complex, I believe it is thus difficult to present it in a way to improve understanding for non-experts. (P2).*

> *I am certainly for more transparency, but not necessarily for simplicity. The rating methodology must not necessarily be simple, it must be transparent, and the 'transparency' must be accessible. That means that investors have access by simple means how the rating is derived. (P15)*

In response to the question of whether a simpler methodology could be similarly simple to the Dow Jones index, some of those questioned thought that it could provide a feasible proposal; however, the predominant view amongst the participants is illustrated by the following quotes:

> *Calculating a rating systematically like the Dow Jones would not meet the case, because it would miss facts that need to be considered. (P3)*

> *I think simply applying transparency in form of quantitative [evaluations of risks] is not going to be the solution [...]. I think the judgment aspect becomes very important. So there is no easy way to simplify. (P12)*

> *Important is transparency and comprehensibility of the methods, and supervision that the methods applied are 1:1 in accordance to the published ones, but I do not believe that it could be as simple as the Dow Jones. (P1)*

Participants were largely of the opinion that more transparency and better supervision would be required instead of a simpler methodology:

> *In the area of corporate bonds and sovereign [bonds] I do not see an excessive deficit; in the area of structured products ratings [...] which are difficult to fully understand, agencies should focus on explaining the functioning of structures and procedures. (P10)*

Definitely more transparency, ... since we do not know how they finally arrive at a rating. [...] but the question would be if this can be done in the current system. They have no incentive to disclose this information. Then one arrives at the point where one says there is a need for a government agency to deal with it. (P16)

If we would have more transparency and the process details and how they arrive at a judgment becomes more apparent, it would provide far more information about the quality of their opinions [...]. This means the traceability of rating agencies' methods through transparency. (P15)

There are different attitudes if something is good or bad [...]. A diversification of views seems justified. (P19)

Increased transparency should not, however, lead to a single approach to risk assessment, as this would entail disadvantages from the participants' point of view:

Their models are perhaps not easy to understand and not transparent. They should state how they arrive at a rating opinion;[...] however, it's their professional secrecy. (P21)

The methodology behind their predictions is very complex; [...] if there should be transparent decision-making, they would have to disclose their procedures, and this would not be reasonable. (P2)

Rating agencies are private companies; forcing them to disclose their methods would, in free markets, evoke market disadvantages if rival agencies could assess the methods. (P2)

I think regulation forcing rating agencies to show what they do, the way they do their analysis, the way they look at members [other rating agencies], can effort them to look only at members, and all do the same thing. So if there would be something new created on the market, they won't look at it because they (would) have guidelines already on how to do things, and so they will miss new innovation in the market. I think just control [...] control (supervision) instead of regulation because markets move fast, faster than regulation. (P14)

In summary, the participants indicated that they would not prefer having a simpler methodology due to the complexity of the transactions, specifically in the structured finance sector. The majority of the participants consider increased transparency of the valuation methods to be important. However, this transparency should not lead to a 'standardized' valuation method where all rating agencies arrive at the same result. In a free market and under the current business structure, full disclosure of rating methodologies could lead to several disadvantages for the market and ultimately a loss of innovation.

Alternative ways to assess credit risk. Policymakers and governments in the United States and European Union strive to reduce reliance on credit ratings and replace ratings with alternative standards of risk assessment. It is, however, according to the Financial Stability Board Report of August 2013, a "challenge to identify credible alternative standards of creditworthiness" (FSB, 2013, p.1).

The participants of the survey delivered several proposals, which fall into three categories as outlined below:

Market based measures:

I would analyze the strength of the company, the balance sheet, the management, leverage, business and positioning [...] doing underlying analyses of the company. (P13)

It is very important [to compare balance sheets], it is very important [to do one's own analyses]. Most large asset managers and most investment assistants in large investment firms already do [their] own assessment; we do our own assessment. (P12)

When the market tends towards 'selling', there are financial indicators, if the volatility is very high it is interesting to look at how it deviates from rating agencies ratings. For us it is another indicator to be considered in the overall analysis. (P15)

Analysis is based on equity, but I leverage the research available from the equity-analysts and what is available from Bloomberg and information systems. (P12)

The first (possibility) would be CDS, the simplest way. The other way would be through market prices. (P4)

From my point of view CDS spreads – the insurance premiums one pays for CDS. (P8)

Fundamental analysis of credit issuers and issues. The traditional approach to credit analysis work carried out by the 'buyer' of debt is also seen as an alternative. This alternative, however, would require the bank, financial institution, or private investors to do their own homework.

The market is the quickest path to information; the other [way] would be fundamental analysis. (P4)

There are large amounts of detailed data which are available to the public to a great extent [...]. If we consider for example the US, they have the largest capital market and probably the greatest level of transparency. If one looks at the EDGAR filings, [...] they are provided online making the same information available to everybody at the same time. (P17)

Another way would be fundamental analysis. (P8)

The path is simple: one does one's own analyses, especially because of the availability of special expertise of banks, and in many cases it is done this way. (P16)

Third-party assessment. Another alternative to risk assessment is the use of a third party. The majority of comments reflecting on third-party assessment are illustrated with the following quotes:

There are other institutions like Bloomberg and Thompson Reuters. They have the data, they could offer such [alternative] service. (P7)

You have different research houses[44] *that offer market research related to credit risks for different financial instruments. (P13)*

What we do as well is to get other brokers […], we ask some other firms, we can go across the different banks [for their] opinions. (P14)

Besides the so-called independent rating agencies, there are other experts or sources of information, which could provide the service. These could be other banks or large investor groups. (P15)

Alternatives to credit ratings fall into the categories of market based measures, fundamental analysis and third-party service providers. These measures have the advantage of being objective and forward looking, and they allow market participants such as financial institutions, pension funds, banks, and private investors, to define specific risk weightings to be assigned for a given asset class.

9.3 Topic 3: Removal of References to Credit Ratings

The questionnaire item focused on the removal of references to ratings. In the United States and in the European Union, new rules requiring the removal of references to ratings where appropriate have been introduced or are underway (Carbone, 2010; Manaigo-Vekil, 2012). However, ratings are still used as a benchmark in much legislation and by financial and other regulators. The item addressed whether the removal of any reference to ratings would minimize or restrict the relevance of rating agencies:

If a rating wouldn't be any more significant for the investment decision, [e.g. for an investment fund] it would surely restrict their relevance […] but they do not become absolutely insignificant. (P17)

Definitely, it would restrict their relevance, but they would not become meaningless. (P1)

Yes, but their business model wouldn't be totally called into question. Probably this would be the case if several central banks would say: […] we have the manpower, we can do the analysis. (P11)

If one would remove reference to ratings, one must find alternatives to credit ratings, […] whether introduced by the ECB or by others to define a 'safe' security. (P3)

One cannot force market participants to move away from the use of ratings, but it would be good for the market if investors would make their own assessment and not depend 'that' much on rating agencies. (P10)

44 Independent subscriber-paid firms.

The following quotes reflect the participants' views on the issue of whether the removal would have any impact on participants' investment decisions:

> *It would surely influence the decision – what would be the advantage of a rating agencies rated security if the ECB wouldn't recommend it? (P11)*

> *Among some colleagues, and above all in wealth management, this would have an impact as an automatism would disappear. (15)*

> *It would have an impact; it would be likely that one would adopt a more defensive approach. (P16)*

The removal of a mandatory reference to credit ratings would affect or restrict the reliance on rating agencies' ratings. Removing references to credit ratings would require alternatives. However, as long as the market calls for rating agencies and their ratings, they will be used (Litan, 2008).

9.4 Topic 4: Liability of Rating Agencies

Numerous market participants suffered enormous losses during the crisis, and in turn "many investors sued various CRAs in the wake of the financial crisis for violations of the Securities Act of 1933 (Securities Act) and the Securities Exchange Act of 1934 (Exchange Act), fraud, negligent misinterpretation, breach of fiduciary duty, and abuse of control" (Harper, 2011, p. 1927). However, in most cases, ratings agencies have been able to successfully defend themselves from being held liable for their actions based on various exemptions and defense measures and possibilities (Harper, 2011). Regulatory authorities in the United States and the European Union have either taken, or plan to take, steps to improve rating agencies' civil liability (Haar, 2013). Little has been achieved in terms of actual measures (UN 2013). The questionnaire items of topic 4 focused on how liability for rating agencies could be made feasible. Although a large proportion of those questioned would welcome liability, it seems more difficult to put in practice. Participants opined:

> *Rating agencies should be held actually liable in cases of evidently caused gross negligence. (P10)*

> *It is certainly desirable, but I have some doubts about it. If rating agencies could be held liable for their rating, how meaningful it would be? (P1)*

> *I think it would be very good having the possibility to demand liability, but in practice, if they would be held liable, they would be bankrupt. (P13)*

From a legal point of view, we should be in a position to hold them liable when one can prove that they deliberately wrongly informed the market or steered the market in the wrong direction; then it should be possible to bring legal actions against them. However, I think it is very difficult to prove. (P17)

Furthering such views, one participant suggested establishing a special pool to which all rating agencies would contribute to any rating change or by adding x-notches in favor of a change within a certain period. However, this would also lead to a kind of 'collateral damage' for the rating:

There is than a threshold, and once this threshold is exceeded rating agencies would have to pay – with the result that no rating change will occur. (P11)

Accordingly, the participants' dominant view was that the following difficulties for implementation remained:

This is difficult, because there is no thing that defines malpractice for rating agencies; ratings are just an opinion. (P14)

From the economic point of view, it would be impossible for rating agencies to operate in a market faced with such liability [...]. They would reduce the scope and areas they cover, and innovation would get lost. (P17)

Due to the magnitude of losses in question it would be impossible for rating agencies to cover such losses. (P16)

Moreover, as one participant commented, the ways in which rating agencies would be held liable must also be taken into consideration. In many professions, it is possible to insure oneself against liability by taking out malpractice insurance. The next item questioned whether insurance against malpractice for rating agencies could be taken into consideration to establish a form of professional insurance. This concept was appreciated by the majority of the participants, as indicated in the quotes below. As one participant explained, it should be possible for insurers to offer such insurance to financial professionals.

If they are doing something clearly illegal or wrong, clearly than they should be punished. But if you are saying they have been incompetent [and] we need to punish them; that would be different [...]. Everybody makes mistakes. (P12)

As investor I would appreciate it, as, in the end, everybody else in the market has insurance. (P9)

For insurance companies it should be possible to design [an insurance model]. There must be on one side the willingness to pay premiums, on the other, willingness to insure such events. This could be done by bond insurers which expand their business to ratings. (P7)

Although the idea was appreciated by many respondents, participants identified a number of obstacles that stand in the way of achieving this concept:

That rating agencies finance liability with premiums and are liable for errors in judgment? […] I cannot imagine how this could function in practice, given the volume of possible potential obligations. No privately-run company will pay such premiums; they will decline such a commitment. […] and someone would have to pay a premium, but solely due to the sheer amount of possible losses, I don't think that someone will find an insurance company willing to do so. (P16)

There is a tremendous leverage, billions and billions, such insurance would be impossible to pay. (P4)

For insurance it is always a question of how high is the insurable risk. For a profitable rating agency where business is running well, there will be a high risk level … this risk cannot be insured against. (P18)

The question will be if the insurer, my counterpart, remains solvent in case of event. And who is going to pay if the insurer is defaulting on its obligations? (P7)

In short, the respondents were largely in agreement that they would generally welcome greater liability for rating agencies. The same applies for the concept of malpractice insurance. However, according to prevailing opinion, introducing such an insurance scheme seems like it would be difficult. The reasons for this include the amount of compensation in question, the disproportionate level of the insurance premium, and managing to find an insurance company willing to provide the insurance. Moreover, the reduced informative value of ratings and reduced scope of coverage would inevitably counteract the benefits of the insurance – to the detriment of investors.

9.5 Topic 5: Alternatives to Rating Agencies in General and their Embedding in a Governmental Setting

Governmental Institution. Rating agencies act as gatekeepers in financial markets (Langner, 2012). Their prominent position, uncritical acceptance, and high level of market penetration are further fostered by the regulatory embedding of these agencies by regulatory authorities (Kerwer, 2005). Given that rating agencies are government-sanctioned or government-protected institutions with quasi-governmental power, the question arises as to whether rating agencies should be run by the government itself:

When asked, one out of 21 respondents polled saw it as a possibility:

This is not necessarily bad, […] important would be that this is truly independent, and then it could be an alternative model. (P9)

Although it might theoretically be a possibility, such 'agencies' would not be seen as autonomous:

> *Theoretically achievable, but the problem would be whether it would be truly autonomously, but, yes; ... even the ECB is not truly autonomous. I think it is virtually impossible. (P4)*

Indeed, establishing rating agencies as government institutions was largely seen in a critical light:

> *A governmental institution? I see it in a critical light. Could this autonomous agency be free from conflicts of interest? I am afraid that that would not be the case [...]. A foundation model [as under discussion for a European rating agency] may offer the best solution – if the organization supporting facility should be supranational can be discussed. (P1)*

> *I don't think that if a credit rating agency is run by government the risk of not acting properly would be eliminated [...]. I think more transparency should be the right solution. (P6)*

The majority of respondents in the sample reported that they would not consider rating agencies to be independent if they were in fact 'governmental' institutions:

> *A governmental institution would only make sense if it would be truly independent and not politically influenced [...]. I would like to see more competition in the rating market. (P2)*

> *No, because we do not trust government in this type of things. (P16)*

> *A governmental institution would not be independent, imagine a European Agency, how much pressure this agency would be exposed to. (P10)*

> *Independence is important [...]. There would not be valid investors if this agency would get instructions from government of how to rate. (P13)*

> *Not a priori [governmental], nowadays we have business models which are not governmental, but nonetheless 'institutional' in nature and not commercial. In today's context, it would be both, the credibility point of view and de-politicization, [and] for a possible operational work more appropriate if this would be a supranational institution. (P19)*

> *I think it is the wrong focus that they should be governmental. I think for the risk assessment, the legal form is not the question, it is more the way how we regulate rating agencies to ensure that [they] don't act as in the past. (P3)*

In addition, the majority of participants did not see any benefits from rating agencies being run by government. They consider increased transparency and improved regulation for rating agencies to be a better solution – an opinion that is in line with the dominant view in the existing literature, as noted by the de Larosière report (2009). A majority of participants would also like to see more competition:

I would appreciate more competition, particularly as it would provide a counterpart to the Anglo-Saxon agencies.[45] *(P1)*

Competition would be helpful, if there would be 2 more ratings opinions offered to the market – either from Europe, or even an Asian ratings opinion. (P2)

I would like to see minimum two on European level [...] some distance to the Anglo-Saxon institutions[46] *– and an Asian counterpart. (P15)*

More rating agencies would be probably helpful, but there is a high barrier to entry. (P9)

I think there is room [...] it's a very difficult market, it cost a lot of money [...] they have to gain credibility, that could took years. (P6)

A really independent agency would have the advantage of not being dependent on issuers or investor's wishes. If it would be possible to establish something really acting independent from political issues, however, such an agency must start from scratch, they must gain reputation and rating volume, this would be a counter-argument. (P9)

Although a large proportion of participants expressed a desire to see more competition within the sector, they also believed that due to high costs, barriers to entry, and acceptance by market participants, it would be difficult to establish additional agencies, as explained by the following quotes:

Absolutely, it definitely should have strong resources and significant manpower to be able to [perform] a quality job, otherwise people do not trust it. [...] this is very, very important. Otherwise it would fail from the start if it is not resourced properly. (P13)

I think under the present circumstances that wouldn't be bad. I think if one creates something new like this, it must be powerful. And this would justify an institutional form. (P19)

To install something that is really independent, I think the European Commission is not supranational enough [...]. This [business]) is too particular, they would have conflicts of interest. To ensure independency it should be a subsidiary of the IMF or OECD. (P14)

However, when questioned whether ratings from such a 'new' agency should be different in scope from those presently advanced by existing agencies, only a minority of the respondents was in agreement:

If we would have an additional institution [to the rating agencies], perhaps we would have a different rating. (P19)

---

45 Upon further enquiry, the respondent clarified that the agencies they were referring to are S&P, Moody's and Fitch – all of which are American.

46 Ibid.

The predominant view was that ratings would not be very different:

> *No, I don't think so [that they would be different]. I don't think so because it is the type of 'reading' [the way of interpretation], common and understood by the whole market participants [...]. It is generally accepted and so I think they would come up with something very similar. (P6)*

> *I don't think that they would be very different, if they would be different, then because it is politically influenced. (P11)*

Thus, the responses received demonstrate that the majority of participants did not support the idea of having rating agencies be a kind of 'governmental institution,' and that any such move would compromise the independence and autonomy ratings agencies currently have. Additionally, the majority of participants believed that a better way forward would be to encourage greater transparency and more competition within the sector. However, it was felt that more competition would be difficult to establish, given that there are several obstacles, including the costs required to establish a rating agency, barriers to entry in the market, and market acceptance in general. Against this background it followed from the participants' comments that a rating agency with a strong background could overcome these obstacles. However, such an agency should carry out its role independently. A national or supranational agency model might be the best approach, and it would have more credibility as a governmental institution. Nevertheless, it was noted that the ratings assigned by such an agency would probably not be very different from those that already exist within the current system.

9.6 Summary

This section presents an overview of the findings of the interview questionnaire as discussed earlier in this chapter. The key findings to emerge from the survey are organized in accordance with the topics researched.

Topic 1
The participants still consider ratings to be important for investment decisions. However, ratings should generally be used as 'just one input' to arrive at investment decisions. The absence of binding policies with reference to ratings would require a more active approach to evaluating financial instruments.

Topic 2
It would be valuable to introduce more uniform and simpler ratings' terminology, where all rating agencies were to use the same symbols. Table 5 illustrated how such a new terminology might look from the participants' perspective. It

was suggested that a uniform terminology should not lead to a 'standardized' terminology, as this would not be desirable for market participants, particularly investors, who benefit from a diversity of experiences and perspectives. Simplifying rating agencies' methods therefore does not seem to be appropriate. Moreover, it is unlikely that the rating methodology could be as simple as the Dow Jones index. Such a simplified methodology would not be able to address or reflect the complexity of the products rated. A diversity of views and methodologies, with appropriate transparency, comprehensibility of the methods, and an ongoing supervisory process would, be preferable.

Alternative ways to assess the risk of financial instruments fall into one of three primary categories. The first category is market-based measures, as illustrated by Table 6:

Table 6: Market-Based Measures

Evaluating issuers creditworthiness from simple and publicly available market data (e.g. balance sheets, company strengths, business, positioning, leverage, cash flow, and stock price volatility)			
Leverage	**Cash Flow**	**Stock Price Volatility**	**Credit Default Swap (CDS) Spreads**
$\frac{\text{Equity + Liabilities}}{\text{Liabilities}}$	$\frac{\text{EBITDA}}{\text{Equity + Liabilities}}$	Standard deviation of stock prices	Whether a security is subject to a particular amount of credit risk based on the spread

Source: Author.

The advantage of each of the market-based measures is that they are objective and forward looking, and allow specific risk weightings to be assigned to each given asset.

The second category is a fundamental analysis of credit issuers and issues. A fundamental analysis, as Fabozzi, Jones, and Johnson (2002) note, focuses on company-specific facts and expectations of its future prospects, along with economic and industry-based factors. It includes reading and analyzing balance sheets and financial statements in order to garner an understanding of a specific company's advantages or benefits enjoyed by its particular sector. The analysis allows a fuller understanding as to whether a stock price is overvalued or undervalued at the current market price.

The third category is risk assessment by third-party service providers to achieve an appropriate and accurate risk assessment. Such service providers may include brokers, research houses, other financial institutions, or banks. A further option would be that financial data providers like Bloomberg or Thomson Reuters could offer a range of broader services to facilitate risk assessment for financial instruments.

Topic 3
Removing reference to ratings in regulations and legislation would definitely diminish the relevance of rating agencies in the market, but they would not become meaningless. As long as the market calls for rating agencies and their research, they do deserve to exist. Abolishing regulatory reference to ratings would have an impact on investment decision-making and would require credible alternatives to be made available.

Topic 4
Although it was generally appreciated, liability for rating agencies is viewed with criticism. There is a broad consensus that from an economic point of view, the disproportionate nature of amounts in question in relation to rating agencies' revenues from rating activities would it make difficult to hold them responsible. The same opinion is also held with regard to insurance against malpractice; the sheer volume of what would have to be insured makes such an insurance scheme virtually impossible to implement.

Topic 5
The idea of rating agencies becoming government institutions is not supported. Such government-run agencies would be seen as neither autonomous nor independent. Participants believed the preferable solution would be to provide greater accountability through better regulation and higher levels of transparency. Nevertheless, increased competition in the rating industry would be welcomed, but any such competitor would need a strong background to be accepted in the market. A rating agency at national or supranational level would be regarded as largely independent and would therefore have more credibility. However, their ratings were seen as unlikely to be very different.

Having outlined the view of questionnaire participants in this chapter, Chapter 10 discusses each topic in a critical manner with reference to existing theory. The following chapter builds upon the primary data presented in this chapter and discusses relevant issues relating to rating agencies and the events that have shaped the global financial markets since the events of 2007–2008.

10. Discussion, Further Research, Limitations, and Conclusion

In this final chapter, the main findings to emerge from the survey are critically discussed, with reference to existing theory and in light of what has happened in financial markets since the collapse of 2007–2008. In addition, suggestions for further research are proffered and a range of conclusions are drawn.

10.1 Discussion

Rating agencies exert a strong influence on financial markets given that "they influence investor behavior and regulate issuers' access to financial market and thus, act as markets' gatekeepers" (Jain and Sharma, 2008, p. 89–90). However, their role as gatekeepers is difficult to define: even though they "clearly belong within the broad classification of financial gatekeepers", they "differ from other gatekeepers in several important ways" (Partnoy, 2006, p. 59–60). As Partnoy notes, rating agencies face "conflicts of interest that are potentially more serious than those of other gatekeepers" (2006, p. 60). Although they have been comprehensively criticized, they have also benefited from the oligopolistic market structure, "reinforced by regulations that depend exclusively on credit ratings issued by Nationally Recognized Statistical Rating Organizations" (Partnoy, 2006, p. 60). In addition, with respect to structured finance instruments further argues, they have "become more 'gate openers' than gatekeepers" (Partnoy, 2006, p. 60). When conflicts of interest undermine the independence of rating decisions, their credibility can be seriously shaken (IOSCO, 2013a). The ambiguous role of rating agencies as privately run companies and their intermediary function as gatekeepers makes it quite difficult to "introduce some kind of gatekeeper liability" (Haar, 2013, p. 6). Thus, following the recent crisis, their role as gatekeepers has been questioned, as well as their quasi-regulatory role. This has led to a number of issues being addressed, as outlined in the theoretical and empirical parts of the research.

The survey addressed, among other subjects shown below, the importance of credit ratings for decision making in the investment process. The findings are compared to Duff and Einig's study (2007) in which the authors looked at the views of market participants before the crisis and provided insight into to the characteristics of ratings' quality. The authors found that 43% of their respondents thought that ratings provide useful information about a company's financial situation, 27% used it as a control function, 24% as a means of pre-selection, and 54% responded that it "is just one input of many" (Duff and Einig, 2007, p. 72). The results of the present survey assessing market participants' post-crisis views show that ratings still provide valuable information when it comes to evaluating companies or simple bonds. However, for structured finance products, ratings should just be seen as providing preliminary information. Nearly all of the participants indicated that ratings should only be used as a means of pre-selection and as a contributory element rather than standalone. In addition, the survey shows that market participants lost their individual and collective trust in rating agencies (their integrity and credibility), and that one should not rely solely on rating agencies when making investment decisions. In direct contrast, this was amongst the most highly rated items by stakeholders in Duff and Einig's study (2007). In summary, it can be ascertained that there has been a move away from the pre-crisis overreliance on rating agencies and their ratings in favor of making investment decisions supplemented by complementary risk assessment.

The survey also addressed the absence of binding guidelines for financial investments. The control of financial risk is largely based on public, contractual, or internal investment guidelines. Moreover, "investors can tie asset managers contractually to buy only those debt securities that have been rated to be of a certain quality (investment grading)" (Amtenbrink and Heine, 2013, p. 3). Such guidelines provide legal protection in disputes where contractual arrangements have been made with customers, given that a credit rating is a generally accepted opinion about default risks. As Amtenbrink and Heine argue, this is "economically meaningful only if credit ratings truly measure and reveal all risks attached to debt securities" (2013, p. 3). The authors further contend that although it is "reasonable to oblige asset managers to act in a prudent way" it would not be useful to have "a rating-based automated buying and selling of debt securities" (Amtenbrink and Heine, 2013, p. 8). Accordingly, the authors suggest that abandoning such requirements would not only foster competition between rating agencies, placing greater responsibility with investment managers, but "will make them more aware of the actual risk" inherent to a debt security (Amtenbrink and Heine 2013, p.8). The authors' views are reinforced by the findings of this survey, which argues that the absence of binding guidelines would require asset managers at banks, financial institutions and other investment firms, as well as individual investors, to take more responsibility for their actions. In addition, removing ratings from guidelines would require suitable alternatives. This might conform to policy-makers expectations of how ratings should be used by investors (Cound and Fisher, 2012).

In view of the general economic uncertainty that has arisen from the global financial crisis, a "fresh need for new regulatory requirements was felt", leading to numerous measurements being introduced in the United States and Europe relating to regulatory frameworks for rating agencies (Nijhawan and Nijhawan, 2013, p. 62). One of these measures was the removal of references to ratings in regulatory rules and guidelines (Ellis, Fairchild, and D'Souza, 2012). In 2010, the Financial Stability Board (FSB) "endorsed principles to reduce overreliance of authorities and financial institutions on credit ratings" (Bayar, 2014, p. 54; EC, 2013b, p. 3). "The Basel Committee on Banking Supervision has also proposed to reduce overreliance on CRAs' ratings in the regulatory capital framework" (EC, 2013b, p. 3). Based on these efforts, this survey (which was carried out in 2011), obtained stakeholder perspectives on the issue. The survey findings are further discussed below in light of events that have shaped financial markets since 2007–2008.

In 2012, the FSB "adopted a roadmap to accelerate the implementation of the principles" aimed at removing reference to ratings wherever possible; in the United States, the Dodd-Frank Act (2010) "requires federal agencies to review how existing regulations rely on ratings" (European Commission, 2013, p. 3). In December 2013, the Securities and Exchange Commission (SEC) "announced that it has adopted amendments to eliminate references in certain of its rules and forms to credit ratings by nationally recognized statistical ratings organizations (NRSROs)" (SEC. 2013b, para. 1). "These regulatory reforms will [...] reduce CRA oligopolistic and artificial demand for their ratings", as Ekins and Calabria contend (2012, p. 1). The purpose of the survey item in relation to these efforts was to determine how it would affect rating agencies' power if they lost their government protection. In the marketplace, as Gravas notes, if a rating agency crosses a "threshold of unreliability, it will lose customers and eventually fail" (2012, p. 35). However, the author argues that if rating agencies are part of the regulatory framework, their mistakes may have "severe implications" but they are less likely to fail "as long as they are part of the regulatory framework" (Gravas, 2012, p. 35). Given that it is the regulator's intention around the world to remove reliance and reference to ratings in their frameworks wherever appropriate, the survey questioned whether this would actually restrict rating agencies' relevance and whether they might become meaningless. In addressing this issue, this research makes a unique contribution to furthering existing academic knowledge. The survey results show that participants were of the prevailing opinion that such reforms would undoubtedly have an impact on rating agencies' relevance to the market, but that it would not mean that they would become meaningless.

The findings show that removing references to ratings would have an impact on investment decisions, as automatism would disappear, automatism in form of provisions governing financial markets. Investing in securities without relying on ratings would require alternatives to be available so that investors could maximize their confidence in the investment process they are involved in. Furthermore, the findings indicate that one cannot force market participants not to use ratings. Demand for ratings is highly dependent on market conditions (Fons, 2010). Although references to ratings will be removed in the rules and guidelines, there will be continued demand from issuers and investors, and "as long as the market calls for them, they 'deserve' to exist" (Litan, 2008, p. 14). Removing references to ratings and replacing them with alternative standards is what regulatory authorities aimed to achieve with their 2010 efforts; however, it is still an environment with a high demand, but a low supply of feasible alternatives. This issue is discussed below.

Removing references to ratings requires the introduction of a "substitute [that possesses][…] a standard of creditworthiness as the [Federal] agency shall determine as appropriate" (SEC, 2014, para. 3). However, as Clarke notes, "regulators have struggled to come [up] with an alternative" (2011, para. 2). The European Securities and Markets Authority (ESMA, 2012) clarified its position on how a management company – with respect to its money market fund classification – should assess the credit quality of financial instruments rated by rating agencies. According to ESMA, they "should ensure that they have proper procedures and processes in place to enable them to assess the credit quality of an instrument without relying solely on credit ratings produced by credit rating agencies" (2012, p. 9). A key element of their decision-making should always be conducting internal assessments on the credit quality of specific investment instruments. The SEC's (2013a) final rule (introduced in February 2014 and entered into force in August 2014) relates to the elimination of reference in rules for funds and broker-dealers. The new definition for credit quality standards the SEC adopted "requires an issuer to have an 'exceptionally strong' capacity to meet its financial obligations on the collateral securities" (SEC, 2013a, p. 12). Funds are also permitted to "consider alternative approaches to presenting credit quality that accurately and effectively describes the credit quality of the fund's portfolio" (SEC, 2013a, p. 21). In accordance with the Credit Rating Agencies Regulation III (CAR3) (in force since June 2013), the European Banking Authority (EBA), the European Securities and Markets Authority (ESMA), and the European Insurance and Occupational Pensions Authority (EIOPA) have, "reviewed all their existing guidelines and recommendations" to identify "references to external credit ratings that could trigger sole or mechanistic reliance on ratings" (EBA, 2014, para. 1). The final report from the EBA, EIOPA, and ESMA from February 2014 notes that the FSB "is undertaking a thematic peer review, whose main objective is to help national authorities to fulfill their commitment under the roadmap", published in 2012 by the FSB. The FSB aims to "end the mechanistic reliance on ratings by banks, institutional investors and other market participants" as set out in its principles endorsed 2010 (EBA, EIOPA and ESMA, 2014, p. 19). The report from February 2014, however, stated that it was inappropriate to "repeal or amend the [EBA] guidelines to remove references to external ratings" as proposed in the Basel II capital adequacy accord (requiring a standardized approach). The report found that further work is needed "especially in the international context [...] to find alternatives for mapping to external ratings in the standardized approach" (EBA, EIOPA and ESMA, 2014, p. 14–16). Moreover, the report proposed amendments for money market fund guidelines (MMF Guidelines). Thus, financial managers should "undertake a new assessment of the credit quality of the money market instrument to ensure it continues to be of high quality" when "there is a downgrade below the two highest ratings by any agency registered and supervised by ESMA" (EBA, EIOPA and ESMA, 2014, p. 17). The report describes this as a more principle-based approach, avoiding mechanistic reliance on ratings. The reference to ratings remains, but there would not be any "automatic exclusion of any rated money market instruments from the range of instruments of good quality based on a minimum rating provided by credit ratings agencies" (EBA, EIOPA and ESMA, 2014, p. 18). Accordingly, managers are required to perform their own assessments of creditworthiness in case of a downgrade of a money market instrument below a certain threshold (EBA, EIOPA and ESMA, 2014). All the measures and initiatives outlined above show that it is still not clear how to replace references to ratings in rules and guidelines.

What are some possible alternatives to credit ratings? What other methods could be used to assess the quality of financial instruments? The findings of this survey show that proposed alternatives fall within three categories: (1) market-based measures; (2) fundamental analysis; and (3) risk assessment by third parties. Market-based measures fall into several categories. One market-based approach to risk is based on market-based information and publicly available accounting information, using the data from the individual issuer's balance sheet, annual reports, equity prices, and equity volatilities (Löffler, 2004). Components of these measures focus on analyzing cash flow, leverage, and stock price volatility. Cantor and Mann (2003) demonstrate that these market-based measures are better tools for predicting short-term default. Yet another market-based measure for credit risk assessment is comparing the size of bond spreads, such as CDS spreads, which are a contemporary measure and more informative than ratings (Rachidy, 2012). The value of CDS is derived from the value of the referenced asset (Mengle, 2007).

Flannery, Houston, and Partnoy (2010) evaluated the viability of CDS spreads as a substitution for credit ratings, and their findings revealed "that CDS spreads reflect information more quickly and accurately than credit ratings" (2010, p. 2114). Specifically, the authors found that CDS spreads reflected information about financial institutions' exposure to risky subprime mortgages disclosed during 2007–2008, "whereas credit ratings remained relatively unchanged", and thus they argued that "if regulators and investors had looked to CDS spreads to assess the riskiness of financial instruments during this period, they would have found as early as April 2007 that such risk [was] significant and increasing" (Flannery, Houston, and Partnoy, 2010, p. 2114). In contrast, rating agencies' ratings reflected only very limited or no information about these risks (Flannery, Houston, and Partnoy, 2010). In their research on spreads, Chava, Ganduri, and Ornthanalai (2012) found evidence that the CDS market can serve as a viable alternative to ratings from rating agencies. This is confirmed by Lee, Naranjo, and Sirmans, whose findings support the view of recent research that CDS spreads are a useful alternative to credit ratings, assessing credit quality in a "more timely and informative manner" (2013, p. 7). Comparing the findings of the survey with the findings of recent studies suggests that CDS spreads could be a suitable alternative to credit rating agencies. The advantage of all market-based measures is that they are transparent, easy to observe, frequently updated, and build on both "expectations and actual transactions of all relevant market participants" (Schüler, 2008, p. 45).

Fundamental analysis focuses on a broader area of analysis than technical analysis, studying the overall state of investment products. Fundamental analysis is much more far reaching and also takes macroeconomic factors into account, such as the overall economy and industry conditions including the strength of a company, its management advantages, and the company's positioning in the market, as well as its competitors and its competitive commercial advantages. In contrast to credit ratings, fundamental analysis is performed on historical *and* present data to determine the financial health of an issuer. Fundamental analysis seeks to make forecasts based on a present company's stock valuation to make predictions for its future performance. Specifically, as Fabozzi, Jones, and Johnson note, investors "can use fundamental analysis to identify stocks that are candidates for purchase or sale" (2002, p. 104). This traditional approach requires investors to do their own homework instead of relying on credit ratings. However, this approach is tedious and time-consuming, which might be considered a drawback (Bhat, 2009).

In addition to the aforementioned alternatives, there are independent research houses in the market performing their own analysis. These research houses play a useful role in the market system "by providing third party analysis of financial products" (ASIC, 2008, p. 23). The advantage of independent and properly explained research house ratings is that investors have the ability to "make better-informed investment decisions" when assessing and comparing financial products (ASIC, 2008, p. 23). Research houses can come from various sectors of the industry, may be embedded in investment banks or stockbrokers, or even combined with an asset management company (ASIC, 2008). In its Document 63107 of October 2010, the US Department of the Treasury questioned the proposed rules for the advantages and disadvantages of alternative standards to risk assessment, including whether it should be permitted to "rely on investment quality or credit quality determination made by other financial institutions or another third party that is independent from the seller or counterpart" (US Treasury, 2010, p. 4). In addition to the general requirement of the regulators to use alternative standards to assess creditworthiness, the findings of the survey propose fundamental analysis, in-house, and third party analysis to be suitable alternatives.

In light of internationally required regulatory changes, and the need to address identified shortcomings, the International Organization of Securities Commissions (IOSCO) revised its code of conduct for rating agencies. This was done, as the Chairman of the Committee, Michael Prada explained, "to improve investor protection, improve the fairness, efficiency and transparency of securities markets and to reduce systematic risk" (IOSCO, 2008c, para. 2). In order to revise the code, the IOSCO "engaged in a frank and constructive dialogue with CRA industry, issuers and investors, taking their views into account in finalizing required changes to the code", (IOSCOb, 2008c, para. 2). As noted by Prada, the IOSCO believed "that these changes to the Code of Conduct will help to address a number of issues [that have] arisen [...] regarding how the credit ratings for structured finance are developed by the credit rating agencies and relied upon by issuers and investors" (2008c, para. 4). The IOSCO (2008a) report further took into consideration comments regarding the distinction between different bond/securities structures. Using a separate symbol system has been suggested for traditional bonds and structured finance products due to the differences in available historical data for these two asset types. The report emphasizes that in theory, the use of different symbols might make it easier for investors to recognize that "structured products may be more volatile and less liquid under stress conditions than more traditional debt instruments might be" (IOSCO, 2008a, p. 10). It further emphasizes that "separate symbols may also put investors on notice" and that for rating this type of product, rating agencies might have to "assess to different types of information" and use "different types of methodologies than they might for a 'plain vanilla' corporate bond" (IOSCO, 2008a, p. 10). Nevertheless, the report observed that this system could confuse investors and other market participants given that "theoretically default risk for structured products are not different than they are for other types of debt" (IOSCO, 2008a, p. 10). The report thus recommended conducting a study on the desirability of such an approach. Rating agencies have, meanwhile, supplemented their existing symbols with the "SF" modifier, even though it does not address any difference in risk (e.g. Fitch, 2011b).

Another approach to regulatory reform concerns the rating agencies' terminology. Section 939(h) of the Dodd-Frank Act (2010) required the SEC "to undertake a study on whether the standardization of credit rating agencies terminology [...] would be feasible and desirable" (ASF, 2011, p. 2). That regulatory authorities mandate uniform rating symbols as an effective means for reducing the risk of market confusion must also be considered in light of the fact that rating agencies "are required to publicly disclose the definitions of their credit ratings categories" (SEC, 2012a, p. 15). The SEC study also focused on issues relating to ratings methodology, i.e. "standardizing credit rating terminology, so that all credit rating agencies issue credit ratings using identical terms" and "standardizing credit rating terminology across asset classes, so that named ratings correspond to a standard range of default probabilities and expected losses independent of asset class and issuing entity" (SEC staff report, 2012a, p. 2). The SEC study aimed to address the differences in the meanings of the rating agencies, given that the current terminology "can represent [the] probability of default, expected loss or distance-to-default depending on to the rating agencies in question" (Weston, 2013, p. 22). The difference is that, for instance, Standard and Poor's (S&P) rating represents the pure probability of default, whereas Moody's notches each issued rating in order to reflect the loss-given default (Weston, 2013). These variations in approach "reflect the reality that users of credit ratings are not homogenous and may have different views as to which rating approach is most useful for them", as Moody's emphasizes (Zarin, 2011, p. 2–3). This is one argument against standardization. The American Securitization Forum (ASF) claims that standardizing the rating agencies' terminology would not be feasible or desirable, as they believe that "different ratings terminology appropriately reflects the differences among CARs" (ASF, 2011, p. 3). The ASF further stated that standardized symbols may imply to investors that there is a "uniformity of underlying ratings criteria that both does not exist and is not desired by investors and other users", which may have a negative impact on the interpretation of ratings assigned to structured finance products (ASF, 2011, p. 3). Moody's, in its comment letter on the issue, argued that standardizing the terminology would "likely motivate CRAs to reach the same or similar opinions" leading to significantly increased risk "of wide disruption, since there will be a greater likelihood that different CRAs will move in lockstep" (Zarin, 2011, p. 4). This, as Zarin further posits, will in turn make it more likely that "market participants that use different CRAs' ratings, either for regulatory purposes or in portfolio or investment guidelines, could be motivated to respond in a similar fashion as the different CRAs' ratings move at the same time in the same direction" (2011, p. 4). Further, the staff report argues that standardizing the terminology would not be feasible "given the number and uniqueness of rating scales and differences in credit rating methodologies" (SEC, 2012a, p. 3). Requiring such standardization may, "reduce incentives for credit rating agencies to improve their credit ratings" (SEC, 2012a, p. 3). The SEC (2012a) findings are largely based on comment letters on the matter. The 2012 report, citing these comments, recommends that the SEC should not take any further action at this time to standardize ratings terminology (SEC, 2012).

EU Regulations no.1060/2009 and 513/2011 seek to achieve a harmonization of rules relating to rating agencies. These regulations are aimed at improving the quality of ratings and following amendments introduced by the proposal the ESMA "will be able to interfere in the way of supervising agency operations through the imposition of standardized rating scale definitions and methodologies" (Host, Cvečić, and Zaninović, 2012, p. 650). Similar to the SEC staff report, commenters on the ESMAS proposal expressed their concern that the standardization of rating scales and definitions would lead to a standardized rating methodology and, thereafter, to a "reduced range of diverse ratings" (CBI, 2012, p. 3). The ESMA discussion paper of July 2013 on Credit Rating Agency Regulation (CRA3) implementation is also concerned with rating agencies' terminology (ESMA, 2013). However, it takes a different approach insofar as it focuses on mapping the ratings' scales. Keogh, Managing Director, Policy, of the Dominion Bond Rating Service (DBRS), responded to the discussion paper, arguing that "a comparison of CRA ratings and information would also benefit from ensuring that data received from each CRA is provided at the same organizational or structural level" (2013, p. 5). The new approach is far from standardizing rating scales and it seems that the proposal of a standardized terminology has had to be shelved for the time being by both the ESMA and the SEC.

The findings of the survey are in line with the findings of the SEC's staff report (2012a) and that of the ESMA (2013). The results show that the survey participants share the view that standardizing ratings' terminology would ultimately be to the detriment of market participants because all rating agencies would essentially provide the same opinions. Further, standardizing the terminology could lead to a uniform approach to risk assessment, reduced scope of coverage, and would provide disincentives for innovation. However, the semi-structured interview approach used in this research enabled participants to expand upon their answers beyond their initially expressed opinions and 'fears', which revealed that it is not standardization but a 'more uniform' ratings terminology that would be both, feasible and desirable. That a more uniform terminology could be useful was also been expressed by some commentators in their comment letters to the SEC. Citing one comment, for example, the report notes that a "[a] basic set of rating systems would provide a useful simplification and we advocate this" (SEC, 2012a, p. 5). This approach was not pursued, though, given that the majority expressed their concern about standardization, although it remains to be seen whether this result was an issue of semantic interpretation. However, the results presented in this research show that a more simplified and more uniform terminology could make ratings more readily comparable and easier to understand. How such a uniform and simpler terminology could look is outlined in Table (6)[47]. The idea of requiring universal rating symbols is backed by a "Request for Re-Proposal" letter published on March 3, 2014, by Hauptman and Roper from the Consumer Federation of America (CFA) (2014, p. 1) to the SEC, who argued that the "do-nothing approach suggested by the [Commissions] staff is not acceptable", as the "Commission has the clear authority to hold NRSROs accountable for producing comparable ratings across asset classes (2014, p. 28).

The European and US regulatory authorities have also focused on rating agencies' methodologies. The Committee of European Securities Regulators (CESR) was requested by the European Union in September 2007 to review the role of rating agencies with respect to their compliance with the IOSCO Code. In February 2008, the CESR published its consultation paper with the aim of seeking comments on their conclusions drawn from their market survey and evidence gathered from the major rating agencies. In addition to other areas,

47 See page 199.

the consultation paper covered the transparency of rating agencies' methodologies, with a particular focus on "the ease of investor access to information on key limitations and assumptions in complex structured finance methodologies" (CESR, 2008, p. 2). Proposals requiring rating agencies to further educate investors about their methods and regulatory reform efforts were welcomed by commenters in both the United States and in Europe (Schacht and Rittenhouse, 2008). The CESR report found that respondents advocated "the use of different analytical models for various types of transactions" (2008, p. 13). However, the comments also highlighted a need to improve modeling, given that the quantitative and qualitative assumptions can differ very significantly between the different rating agencies. Moreover, there are limits to standardizing the approach due to the complexity and differences in the transactions, especially with regard to structured finance products (CESR, 2008b). Comments made on the issue, such as the joint response of the British Bankers Association (BBA) and the London Investment Bankers Association (LIBA) by Barret and Hilleard show that "there is no simple way for investors in the secondary market to know which methodology has been used for a ratings given transaction" (2008, p. 4). However, rating agencies should make their methods more transparent in order to enable investors to better understand the risk inherent within structured finance products (Barret and Hilleard, 2008).

The IOSCO's (2008a) final report on rating agencies' methodology concluded that when it comes to transparency and market perceptions relating to rating agencies methodology, "these methodologies are transparent enough" for financial institutions and investors that have "the analytical capability to understand and evaluate them" (IOSC, 2008a, p. 9). However, there have been complaints that rating agencies "do not publish verifiable and easily comparable historical performance data regarding their ratings" (IOSCO, 2008a, p. 9). Rating agencies commented on the issue, noting that "coming up with a common metric to evaluate the performance of ratings is not practical or desirable given the differing methodologies they employ" (IOSCO, 2008a, p. 9). Nonetheless, the IOSCO report (2008a) found that rating agencies should make the rating performance more transparent and comparable.

The SEC staff report (2012a) noted that the diversity of the methodologies used by the different rating agencies offered a depth of analysis of risk in financial instruments that would be lost if rating methodologies were harmonized. Such harmonization of rating agencies methodology "could create disincentives for credit rating agencies to improve their methodologies" (SEC, 2012a, p. 23). Commenting to the SEC staff report, Moody's argued that their ratings "cannot be reduced to an output from formulaic methodology or model" (Zarin, 2012, p. 2). Moreover, requesting harmonization or standardization would likely "interfere with the independence of the rating process by regulating the substance of rating opinions and methodologies" (Zarin, 2012, p. 6). However, as Miglionico (2012) notes, it is important that ratings agencies ensure transparency, disclose information, and monitor the integrity of their methods. The quality of the rating agencies' rating process should be geared toward the perspective of the investor (Miglionico, 2012). The SEC staff report concluded that given the difficulties identified by commentators regarding the implementation of standardization subjects of the study, "it would be more efficient to focus on rulemaking initiatives designed to promote transparency with respect to the performance of credit ratings and the methodologies used to determine credit ratings" (SEC, 2012a, p. 44).

With further reference to measures enacted in relation to rating agencies, the Dodd Frank Act requires rating agencies to publicly disclose certain material (Bayar, 2014). In 2012, the SEC proposed new rules for the implementation of certain provisions relating to rating agencies; one of these proposals entailed "publishing a standard form with each credit rating disclosing, among other things, the assumptions underlying the methodology used to determine the credit rating" (SEC, 2012b, p. 2). Furthermore, the SEC "has taken steps to enhance this disclosure requirement to make disclosure more comparable across NRSROs" (SEC, 2012a, p. 38). The SEC also proposed a paragraph requiring rating agencies to publish promptly:

> "on an easily accessible portion of its website material changes to the procedures and methodologies, the reason for the changes, and the likelihood the changes will result in changes to any current ratings and significant errors identified in a procedure or methodology that may result in a change in current credit ratings; and that it discloses the version of a credit rating procedure or methodology, used with respect to a particular rating." (2012a, p.42)

Similar to that which has been proposed and implemented in the United States, EU regulations for rating agencies require the disclosure of rating agencies' methodologies, models, and rating assumptions (OECD 2010). As noted by Miglionico, (2012), it could be the case that such disclosure would allow market participants, including competitive rating agencies, to evaluate a rating agency's procedures and methods, thereby enabling them to draw reasonable conclusions about the accuracy and credibility of a rating agency's rating. The transparency of such disclosure "would allow third parties to detect, issue, and challenge any inaccuracy" (Miglionico, 2012, p. 59). Full disclosure can thus contribute to a better understanding of the value of ratings (de Haan and Amtenbrink, 2011).

The findings of the survey are primarily in line with those of the reports outlined above. The majority of the survey participants thought that although *prima facie* it might have advantages, the sophistication of financial instruments does not allow for a simplification of rating agencies' methodologies. The findings also showed that there is demand for greater transparency relating to rating agencies' methodologies and the need for better supervision. However, the survey findings show that full disclosure would also lead to disadvantages for the market. The survey participants did not support disclosure of rating agencies' methodologies, given that the exact rating process and techniques applied are their trade secrets. Disclosure would lead to competitive disadvantages and a loss of innovation in the financial market. A view shared only by a handful of academics, including de Haan and Amtenbrink, is that full disclosure "could have strong disincentives to use the best available methodologies and to invest in better rating methodologies, i.e., to innovate, since the outcome could be immediately copied by competing CRAs" (2011 p. 23).

Greater transparency for structured finance products could, as expressed by Miller in Reuters'[48] response to the CESR Consultation Paper (2008a) be achieved by "[m]ore sources of ratings" and would furthermore "reduce information asymmetry for investors" (Miller, 2008, p. 2). Reuters argues that "while the need for greater transparency around structured products has been recognized by many commentators, the issue is often viewed as solely related to methodologies" (Miller, 2008 p. 2). Reuters submitted that transparency for them is a broader issue and "relates to the structured products themselves, as well as CRAs" (Miller, 2008, p. 2). More sources of ratings could be provided if there were alternative business models or more rating providers. In their report, Fennel and Medvedev (2011) provided a brief overview of possible alternative business models to the issuer-pays regime, among which was the idea of a public-run agency. Lynch defined the basic characteristics of such a public run model as one that could "be funded by the tax paying public" (Lynch, 2010, p. 38). The concept of a taxpayer-funded agency was also put forward by Deb and Murphy (2009). In expanding their view, the authors argue that this agency would not inflate ratings given that it would not be driven by commercial interests. According to Lynch, "[i]n order to minimize political bias it would be imperative that this public agency [is] independent and shielded as much as possible from political

48 The foreign news services Reuters.

pressure" (Lynch, 2010, p. 38). Moreover, such a public agency would be committed to work with the greatest possible transparency (Lynch, 2010). The survey garnered market participants' views on different alternatives to rating agencies' models and the findings of the survey with regard to this topic are discussed in the following sections.

The European Central Bank, along with other national central banks, was called upon by European lawmakers in 2011 "to issue credit ratings as an alternative to private credit rating agencies" (Central Banking Newsdesk, 2011). The ECB expressed that "while the Eurosystem supported efforts to reduce the reliance of financial markets on credit rating agencies' ratings it "'should not issue public ratings to be used for regulatory purposes"' (Central Banking Newsdesk, 2011, para. 2.). Given that the privately run major rating agencies perform a quasi-regulatory role, the survey addressed whether the respondents believed that agencies should be run by the government. Lynch emphasized that a public agency would be free from conflicts of interest and that this independence "would not be surprising, given the fact that this agency will operate from the influential platform of a government agency with a voice of presumed authority" (2010, p. 39). Gravas argues that one solution could be to bring "one or more of the private credit rating agencies" under public control, or replacing the agencies "by a new public agency" (2012, p. 36). The advantage would be that such an agency would "follow a transparent and approved rating methodology" (Gavras, 2012. p. 36). The business focus of this agency would be to provide accurate rating information, and it would just be paid to cover its costs, and not focus on profit maximization (Gavras, 2012). Contrary to these assumptions, the findings of the survey show that market participants would not have confidence in ratings issued by a government-run institution, even if the ECB were to carry out this function. Such a government agency would not truly be free from political interference (a factor that should form an essential prerequisite, according to Lynch [2010]). However, the results of this survey show that competition in the form of providing competing analysis would be welcome in the ratings marketplace. The ECB also rejected proposals "for a new, independent, but private sector funded European credit rating agency" (Central Banking Newsdesk, 2011, para. 2). The Central Bank "questioned the agency's ability to remain independent" and argued further that "it would take time to acquire the relevant data, models and experienced staff for it to function" (Central Banking Newsdesk, 2011, para. 3). Moreover, it would be unclear "how long it would take until the agency could credibly issue ratings" (Central Banking Newsdesk, 2011, para. 3). In addition to the natural barriers to entry due to the fact that the market is an oligopoly of three rating agencies who hold 95% of the market share (Deb and Murphy, 2009), there is, as the survey participants observed, yet another obstacle: the high costs of establishing a new agency of this kind. In addition, as Fennel and Medvedev note, this would involve a "high fixed cost, large economics of scale and network externalities" (2011, p. 4). The survey findings show that an agency with a strong background could overcome these obstacles and could have the capacity and the power to challenge the major rating agencies, but a prerequisite would be its independence.

Fennel and Medvedev emphasize that a public rating agency, "where [it] takes the form of a non-profit, national or international CRA" would be able to offer the advantage of freely available ratings, but there would be "the danger that political pressures could compromise ratings" (2011, p. 4). Could a national or supranational agency make ratings more credible? For the sovereign bond market, the idea of setting up a supranational agency "financed with multilateral funds like an UN agency" which does not rate corporate bonds has been suggested, and would be "above government" (Shari, 2012, p. 4). The solution to "set up a supranational state-backed rating agency" is not embraced, but although "this idea still has support and passing mention" in EU legislation "it looks very unlikely to happen and has zero support across the Atlantic" (Mindful Money, 2013, section 6). .One reason for this might be that the rating industry is dominated by American-centered firms, which is particularly evident when it comes to sovereign ratings, and one of the reasons why politicians are calling for changes (Ryan, 2012). According to Fuchs and Gehring, it is evident that ratings for agencies' home countries are "on average almost one point higher than what would be justified" (2014, p. 27). This is what the authors call "the home bias in sovereign ratings" (Fuchs and Gehring, 2014, p. 1). There is consensus globally among many scholars and policymakers that rating agencies issue biased ratings influenced by other factors than those justified by an assessment of purely economic and political fundamentals for sovereign debt (Fuchs and Gehring, 2014). This is one of the reasons why a "specialised European rating agency is demanded or at least some form of regulation and control of the incumbent agencies" (Tichy, 2011, p. 232).

Flassbeck argues that a fundamental reform relating to rating agencies is "an indispensable step towards increasing transparency of the whole financial system", yet, "there is no private solution to this matter anymore" (2008, p. 13). The author further claims that "what is needed is the establishment of a public regulatory agency that takes over the role of credit rating agencies" (Flassbeck, 2008, p. 13). The advantage of this agency would be that "such a non-partisan agency would certify that an AAA asset has indeed minimal probability of default and can be used by risk-adverse investors like pension funds" (Flassbeck, 2008, p. 13). If it were an agency on a national basis, the question arises as to how "such an agency would deal with political sensibility linked to rating sovereign bonds" (Flassbeck, 2008, p. 13). The findings of the survey indicate that creating a supranational agency could be a solution for an independent rating agency. It would, as the survey shows, have more credibility and be seen as less vulnerable to political influence. Moreover, such an agency could be capable of transcending national interests and would have the competence to provide unbiased ratings. This agency would, therefore, conduct independent risk analysis based on objective models. However, contrary to Flassbeck's view (2008), the results show that the ratings from such an agency would probably not be very different from the ratings issued by the major three rating agencies.

Reforming rating agencies, and holding rating agencies legally liable, is also on the agenda of the regulatory authorities. In the United States, the Dodd Frank Act (2010) has offered a regulatory response to a number of issues relating to rating agencies, but reform in the United States has generally not been comprehensive; the European regulatory framework is the most vigorous and far reaching (Hill, 2011). Tackling "obstacles to plaintiffs bringing suits against rating agencies" the Dodd Frank Act (2010) subjects "rating agencies to 'expert liability' for misleading statements (Haar, 2013, p. 8). However, implementing "this newly created liability turned out to be difficult […] and does not have the previous hoped effect as a regulatory behavior control" (Haar, 2013, p. 8). Although the idea behind this innovation was to provide increased protection to investors, possible consequences for the financial market had not been taken into account. When this rule became law in July 2010, it required that rating agencies be subject to expert liability when assigning ratings to asset-backed securities. The new rule thus "opened the agencies to lawsuits from investors" (Morgenson, 2011, para. 4). In response, rating agencies refused "to allow their ratings to be disclosed in asset-backed securities deals. As a result, the market for these instruments froze" (Morgenson, 2011, para. 4). The SEC then backpedaled by issuing a 'non-action' letter, stating that it would not take any legal action against issuers that did not disclose ratings in the prospectus. This was an action that removed the 'expert liability' for rating agencies (Morgenson, 2011). That far-reaching liability can have severe consequences has been demonstrated by its chilling effect on financial markets (Haar, 2013). The non-action letter was intended to last for six months only, yet the SEC "extended the disclosure exemption indefinitely" in order to avoid a further market freeze or "shutdown of the securitization market" (Tempkin, 2011, para. 6), which somehow means "reversing rating agencies' liability advances" (Tempkin, 2011, para 1 and in the process, leaving the question as to how it will move forward on the matter unanswered.

In 2009, European legislators adopted regulation No. 1060/2009 to enhance the transparency, integrity, reliability, and responsibility of rating agencies (as discussed above). This was followed by the amending regulation No. 513/2011 (Oster, 2012). In the next phase, the CRA3 proposal addressed, *inter alia*, civil liability. Among the regulations focusing on rating agencies' liabilities is Regulation (EC) No. 4662/2103, containing a new Article 35a, which allows for civil claims to be made against rating agencies (Norton Rose Fulbright, 2014). However, as Haar argues, Art. 35a of the draft proposal contained "the most controversial changes" to introduce mandatory liability (Haar, 2013, p. 2). More recently, in June 2013, CRA3 came into force, amending the regulatory framework (ESMA, 2013). Under the provision, an issuer or investors may claim damages in the following cases:

> An issuer in case "it or its financial instruments are covered by that credit rating and the infringement was not caused by misleading and inaccurate information provided by the issuer" (Norton Rose Fulbright, 2014, p. 18).
>
> An investor in case it can establish "that it has reasonably relied [...] on a credit rating" for investment decisions (Norton Rose Fulbright, 2014, p. 18).

The new regulatory requirement is intended to provide financial incentives for rating agencies to ensure high quality ratings (The Geneva Association, 2011). Furthermore, the new directive intends to make quite clear from the outset that issuers and investors may seek redress for damages without contractual arrangements. In the United States, there are two House bills that remove rating agencies' exemption from fair disclosure[49]. Both bills define the responsibility and liability of rating agencies for knowingly engaging in reckless behavior and seek to incentivize rating agencies for doing their work correctly (Altman et. al., 2010). Many international bodies like the Group of 20 (G20), the Financial Services Authority (FSA), the Financial Stability Board, and the European Commission (EU), strongly encouraged implementing measurements of regulatory oversight "to encourage good governance" (Altman et al, 2010, p. 458). With recent developments pertaining rating agencies' liability, "while there may be some who welcome these changes" it is argued that "the new provisions will be of concern to CRAs" (Craske et al., 2013, section 13). The strict regulatory regime for holding rating agencies' civil liabilities is accompanied by the fear that this may

49 On September 29, 2010 the SEC issued the final rule release.

have negative implications for financial markets. As shown empirically in this research, this concern is now reflected in the statements given by commentators and academics that have furthered opposing arguments.

Those opposing the imposition of increased liability for rating agencies argue that the measures proposed and/or implemented increase the cost for monitoring and recordkeeping by the agencies, which, "of course, will be passed on to the issuers leading to an increased cost of ratings" (Ellis, Fairchild, and D'Souza, 2012, p. 216). Imposing mandatory liability on rating agencies would lead to reduced rating quality, while adjusting the rules for the burden of proof, which as the CBI expressed "would lead to more prudent ratings or potentially no rating at all for issuers or instruments deemed too risky to rate such as new business or products" (2012, p. 2). If one accepts this argument, then it can also be argued that rating agencies would delay the issuance of ratings, as they would be obliged to spend considerable amounts of time preparing ratings to avoid potential liability (Ellis, Fairchild, and D'Souza, 2012). Moreover, the proposed liability regime would have a counterproductive effect in terms of competition; new competitors would be reluctant to enter the market because of the fact that they will be faced with significantly increased costs arising from these high liability risks (CBI, 2012). As the EBIC concludes, it will "deter new entrants [...], as, with less experience, they are more likely to make errors (2012, p. 3).

A problem related to the proposed undertaking of liability measures for rating agencies is the difficulty in determining the causality of the infringement and the amount of losses incurred (The Geneva Association, 2011). Imposing rating agencies with stringent and wide-reaching liability through damages constitutes a significant problem "because a credit rating agency has no control over who relies on its ratings or to what extent", and it would expose rating agencies to "potentially unlimited and unquantifiable liability" (FSA, HM Treasury, and BoE, 2010, p. 19). As the United Kingdom authorities noted in their joint response to the European Commission, "[t]his is something they could not easily insure against" (FAS, HM Treasury, and BoE, p. 19). The latter argument was also brought forward by one survey participant who opined that:

> *For insurance it is always a question of how high is the insurable risk. For a profitable rating agency where business is running well, there will be a high risk level; ... this risk cannot be insured against (P18).*

Although the survey findings showed that liability for rating agencies is generally supported, the arguments put forward by those opposing liability were underpinned by the findings of this empirical survey. The survey participants outlined that, from an economic point of view it would not be possible to impose such liability on rating agencies, and neither would it be easy to insure against infringements. Given the amounts of money at stake, such risks are not justifiable economically, and could easily bankrupt rating agencies. As Harper summarizes, "CRAs have rated trillions of dollars' worth of debt, yet they have earned only a fraction of that amount in fees" (2011, p. 1970). Thus, as Harper argues, liability has to be "limited to a fraction" or at most to a "multiple of the fees CRAs earn" (2011, p. 1970). If a rating agency "is simply negligent, liability should be limited to some percentage of the fees earned, not to exceed the total fee" (Harper, 2011, p. 1970). What they should be liable for should also be taken into account was also an opinion voiced by an interview participant, who noted:

> *If they are doing something clearly illegal or wrong, than they should be punished. But if one says they have been incompetent and we have to punish them; that would be different. Everybody makes mistakes. (P12)*

In addition to the large amounts of money at stake, "there is a risk that investors may consider they are more likely to recoup their losses where an issuer defaults if they can demonstrate they relied on a CRA's rating rather than on their own analysis" (EBIC, 2012, p. 3). With regard to competition issues, the European Banking Industry Committee (EBIC), in its comment letter from June 2012 on the regulation of rating agencies, supported the idea of the "deletion of the civil liability provisions" as proposed under amendments 347 to 349 (EBIC, 2012, p. 3). These developments show that there will now be no easy solutions for holding rating agencies liable. Indeed, the findings of this survey indicate that there is more than one area that deserves further action, and that fresh thinking on the role of rating agencies as intermediaries in financial markets, and the desired goals of further regulations in the rating industry are required.

10.2 Further Research

This research is focused on issues relating to rating agencies after the crisis of 2007–2008 and was motivated by the desire to gain an understanding of market participants' perceptions of a range of issues concerning rating agencies. The research is exploratory in nature, given that there is limited empirical research on the quality of rating agencies as service providers, as well as pertaining to questions of liability, and their embedding in the regulatory environment. The following section addresses the paths and approaches future research on this topic could follow:

First, further research could consider what economic effects the removal of references to ratings in rules, guidelines, and regulations would have on rating agencies. This research has solicited the views from market participants in Germany, Switzerland and the United Kingdom on the removal of ratings with respect to their investment decisions, but has not considered the direct effects on rating agencies' business. Accordingly, further research could focus on the impact of such removal on rating agencies' revenues. The geographical focus could also be expanded to include additional national or regional perspectives.

Second, further research could consider what would be the best and most practical model for a more uniform ratings' terminology, along with the specific benefits that such a change would bring to the financial markets. This research translated market participants' views and developed a model on the form of possible solutions that could provide the basis for comparable ratings across asset classes. Future research could build upon this work by taking the proposals made and the simplifications presented in the model as starting point for further research.

Third, the present research focused on market participants' views of a potential legal liability for rating agencies. This survey revealed that although there is consensus that rating agencies should be held liable in cases where they intentionally or negligently mislead market participants, there are a number of drawbacks to be taken in consideration. Further research could examine the extent to which a reasonable and financially justifiable liability might be imposed on rating agencies.

Fourth, further research could look at how the landscape of competition in the rating industry could be changed. The present survey has shown that a supranational agency could possess some advantages over other business models. This survey also revealed a number of arguments supporting initiatives of this nature. Such observations could serve as a basis for future research, which could seek to explore how a fully operational agency model of this nature could be achieved.

In addition to making a distinctive and unique contribution to existing academic knowledge, this research has also revealed additional issues that deserve to be pursued and unveiled new targets for further research that would build upon the findings contained herein.

10.3 Limitations

Most research, including this study, is influenced by various limiting factors. In the chosen methodology – the qualitative research approach – these limiting factors are the research participants and the form of data analyses utilized. Qualitative research applying grounded theory, however, has its limitations. The amount of data collected through a qualitative approach can be substantial, and the task of reducing the data depends heavily on the individual judgment and interpretation of the researcher. Another limitation is that the proper analysis of text is time consuming and involves data collection, transcription, coding, and interpretation. A further limitation of qualitative research is the lack of ability to generalize the results. These limitations have previously been acknowledged (see Chapter 8). Through semi-structured interviews, which allowed for more detailed information to be gathered, this research was able to obtain rich, valuable data that could be analyzed in accordance with existing academic literature to satisfactorily answer the research questions and identify possible remedies to the present problems regarding issues of terminology, competition and liability, and alternatives to credit risk assessment for rating agencies.

Conclusion

Although there is substantial consensus among politicians, governments, regulatory authorities, academics, and other interested parties on the need for the fundamental reform of rating agencies, much remains to be done. Recent developments, in both the financial markets and the regulatory landscape, demonstrate that some measures and proposals are not going far enough, whilst others have 'overstepped the mark' in terms of what is needed. Many initiatives have already been undertaken to remove references to ratings, and it is also apparent that they must be replaced with appropriate alternatives. However, as this research has shown, it is not clear what form these will eventually take. Furthermore, even when references to ratings are removed, this will not, as Litan notes, lead to the disappearance of ratings, given that there will be "continued to be a demand by both investors and securities issuers for some kind of rating" (2008, p. 14). The findings from this research reveal that there are feasible alternatives to risk assessment that could replace credit ratings. As for the question of what the most viable alternative would be, a realistic solution might be a more pluralistic approach that takes into account rating agencies' views *and* market-based measures (or a combination of the three alternatives found in the survey). These are issues, however, that fall beyond the scope of this research, which reinforces the need to carry out further research using this research as a basis.

Rating agency terminology gained critical attention following the structured finance product debacle, and regulatory authorities consequently engaged in studies of standardized rating terminology. It seems that following the SEC report (2012a) and the ESMA report (2013), the issue has been shelved for the time being by both American and European regulators. Although there is consensus that some form of standardized approach would lead to disadvantages (uniformity of views, reduced scope of coverage, a uniform approach for risk assessment, uniform methodologies, and competitive disadvantages), using more uniform terminology could be a simplification that would make ratings more readily comparable and easier to understand. Viewed from this perspective, regulators should consider a more uniform terminology and re-invigorate and include this in their rating agencies' reform agenda. With regard to the rating agencies' methodologies that have been under discussion, this research has shown that simplification, standardization, or harmonization, and the disclosure of methodologies, would have a range of negative impacts on financial markets. Such concerns are justified. Requiring greater disclosure would lead to a loss of innovation, since competing agencies could immediately copy the methodologies used by others. Moreover, the existing diversity of methodologies offers a depth of analysis that would also disappear. Breaking up the oligopolistic market structure, however, could lead to better ratings' quality; a prerequisite for the development of such a scenario would, as Gavras notes, be independence from conflicts of interest and political influence (2012). An agency model at the supranational level could offer the necessary degree of independence to provide proper quality ratings and a fair approach; however, as study participants admitted, the ratings from such an agency would probably not differ greatly from those presently advanced by the Big Three.

The developments in the financial markets after the 2007–2008 global crisis are evidence of a move away from initial calls for more stringent liability for rating agencies towards a more economically appropriate regime. Liability standards, as required from academics, regulators, governments, and other interested parties following the 2007–2008 crisis, and the measures actually undertaken not only interfere with rating agencies' business affairs, but could also lead to wider disadvantages for the financial markets. Indeed, as was noted in Chapter 3, such measures could cause ratings to disappear from the public domain, which would be a problem because they offer easy and cost-effective access to risk assessment. Innovation in the financial markets would be lost. Finally, as demonstrated by the survey findings, it is unrealistic to impose such high liability standards on rating agencies, for as Haar notes, "civil liability for rating[s] has to strike a balance between over-deterrence and overly lax behavior" (2013, p. 1). While there is a clear need for a practicable and fair solution to the issue of rating agencies' liability, this research concludes that the unresolved challenge still facing regulators and politicians is that financial markets need more reliable risk assessment opinions based on transparently disclosed methodologies, in conjunction with a reduced dependency on the major rating agencies, without weakening the independence of those agencies. In this way, the likelihood of a repetition of the devastation caused by the global financial crisis would be diminished, and the concept of a responsible and relatively autonomous market could be restored.

References

Adams, M., Mullins, T. and Thornton, B. (2011). Pedagogical strategies for incorporating behavioral finance concepts in investment courses. *Journal of College Teaching & Learning* (TLC), 4(3), 21–32.

Acerbi, C. and Scandolo, G. (2008). Liquidity risk theory and coherent measures of risk. *Quantitative Finance*, 8(7), 681–692.

Acharya, V. V. and Richardson, M. (2009). Causes of the financial crisis. *Critical Review*, 21(2–3), 195–210.

Acharya, V. V. et al. (2009). The financial crisis of 2007–2009: Causes and remedies. *Financial markets, institutions & instruments*, 18(2), 89–137.

Acharya, V. V. and Schnabl, P. (2010). Do global banks spread global imbalances? Asset-backed commercial paper during the financial crisis of 2007–09. *IMF Economic Review*, 58(1), 37–73.

Acharya, V. V. and Merrouche, O. (2013). Precautionary hoarding of liquidity and interbank markets: evidence from the subprime crisis. *Review of Finance*, 17(1), 107–160.

Ackerman, F. (2002). Still dead after all these years: interpreting the failure of general equilibrium. *Journal of Economic Methodology*, 9(2), 119–139.

Adair, A. and Hutchison, N. (2005). The reporting of risk in real estate appraisal property risk scoring. *Journal of Property Investment & Finance*, 23(3), 254–268.

Adrian, T., Covitz, D. and Liang, N. (2013). Financial stabilitiy monitoring. *Federal Reserve Bank of New York Staff Reports*, Staff Report No. 601.

Aikins, S. K. (2009). Global financial crisis and government intervention: a case for effective governance. *International Public Management Reviews*, 10(2), 23–43.

Akerlof, G. (1970). The market for 'lemons': Quality uncertainty and the market mechanism. *Quarterly Journal of Economics* (The MIT Press), 84(3), 488–500.

Alcubilla, R. G. and Pozo, J. R. del (2012). *Credit rating agencies on the watch list: Analysis of European Regulation*. Oxford, UK: Oxford University Press.

Allen, F. (2008). Design of contracts and securities. In Thakor, A. V. and Boot, A. W. A. (Ed.), *Handbook of financial intermediation and banking*. Amsterdam (North-Holland): Elsevier, 1–61.

Altman, E. I. (1998). The importance and subtlety of credit rating migration. *Journal of Banking & Finance*, 22, 1231–1247.

Altman, E. I., Öncü, T. S., Richardson, M., Schmeits, A., and White, L.J. (2011). Regulation of rating agencies. In Acharya, V. V., Cooley, T. F., Richardson, M., Walters, I. (Eds.), *Regulating Wall Street: The Dodd-Frank Act and the New Architecture of Global Finance. Hoboken, NJ: John Wiley & Sons*, 443–468.

Amato, J. D. and Gyntelberg, J. (2005). CDS index tranches and the pricing of credit risk correlations. *Bank for International Settlements (BIS) Quarterly Review*, March, 73–87.

Amenc, N. and Le Sourd, V. (2007). Rating the ratings: A critical analysis of fund rating systems. *EDHEC* Working Paper.

AMF (2009). AMF 2009 Report on rating agencies *(Autorité des marchés financiers (AMF)*.

Amtenbrink, F. and Heine. K. (2013). Regulating credit rating agencies in the European Union. Lessons from behavioral science. *The Dovenschmidt Quarterly*, 1 (Forthcoming).

Anastasoaie, M. V. (2012). Valuing the unique: the economics of singularities, by Karpik, L. *Social Anthropology*, 20(1), 107–108.

Anderson, C. (2010). Presenting and evaluating qualitative research. *American journal of pharmaceutical education*, 74(8), Article 141, 1–7.

Andreff, W. (2013). Crisis as unexpected transition … to a greed-based economic system. In Zarembka, P. (Ed.), *Contradictions: Finance, Greed, and Labor Unequally Paid*, Research in Political Economy, 28, Bingley (UK): Emerald Group Publishing, 1–48.

Andrew, B. (2008). What the hell happened? The financial crisis of 2007 -???. *Updated presentation to the Juniata College Community* October 2008. URL: http://services.juniata.edu/jcpress/voices/pdf/2009/What%20The%20Hell%20Happened%20-%20Brad%20Andrew%20-%20Juniata%20Voices.pdf (Retrieved August 6, 2012).

Angelini, P., Nobili, A. and Picillo, C. (2011). The interbank market after August 2007: what has changed, and why? *Journal of Money, Credit and Banking*, 43(5), 923–958.

Anonymous, The Economist (2009). AIG, Fannie Mae and Freddie Mac – the toxic trio. *The Economist*, August 13, 2009.

ASF, American Securitization Forum, (2011). *Comment letter Re: Release No. 34-63573; File No. 4-622. Credit Rating Standardization Study Required by Section 939(h) of the Dodd-Frank Wall Street Reform and Consumer Protection Act of 2010*. Letter to the Securities and Exchange Commission, attn. Elizabeth M. Murphy, Secretaryy, February 4, 2011.

Ashcraft, A. B. and Schuermann, T. (2008). Understanding the securitization of subprime mortgage credit. *Foundations and Trends in Finance*, 2(3), 191–309.

Ashcraft, A. B., Goldsmith-Pinkham, P. and Vickery, J. (2010). MBS ratings and the mortgage credit boom. *Federal Reserve Bank of New York*, Staff Reports No. 449, 1–54.

Asian Development Bank (2008). Emerging Asian regionalism: A partnership for shared prosperity. *Asian Development Bank*, Mandaluyong City, Philippines, 1–304

ASIC, Australian Securities and Investment Commission (2008). Review of credit ratings agencies and research houses. *A joint report by the Treasury and The Australian Securities and Investment Commission.* Report 143.

ASIC (2011a). Repot 268: Response to submissions on CP 160 Credit rating agencies: ISOCO Code Annual Compliance Report. In Australian Securities & Investment Commission (Ed.), *Report 268, 1–15.*

ASIC (2011b). 11–111MR ASIC proposals for credit rating agencies' compliance reporting. URL: http://www.asic.gov.au/asic/asic.nsf/byheadline/11-111MR+ASIC+proposal+for+credit+rating+agencies+compliance+reporting?openDocument (Retrieved February 15, 2013).

Aspers, P. (2005). Status markets and standard markets in the global garment industry. *MPIfG Discussion Pape*r 05/10, Max Plank Institute for the Study of Societies, Cologne.

Aspers, P. (2009). Knowledge and valuation in markets. *Theory and Society*, 38(2), 111–131.

Aspers, P. and Beckert, J. (2011). Value in markets. In Beckert, J. and Aspers, P. (Eds.). *The worth of goods: valuation and pricing in the economy*. Oxford: Oxford University Press, 3–38.

Australian Bureau of Statistics (2009). *1301.0 – Year Book Australia, 2009–10. Feature Article: The Global Financial Crisis and its Impact on Australia*. URL: http://www.abs.gov.au/AUSSTATS/abs@.nsf/Lookup/1301.0Chapter27092009%E2% (Retrieved March 8, 2013).

Avetisyan, E. and Gond, J. P. (2012). Institutional dynamics of corporate social responsibility standardization: A multilevel perspective on the ESG rating field. *EGOS 2012*, Helsinki.

Awrey, D. (2012). Complexity, innovation and the regulation of modern financial markets. *Harvard Business Law Review*, 2, 235–294.

Babbie, E. R. (2008). *The basics of social research.* Belmont, CA: Wadsworth Publishing Company.

Bai, L. (2010). On regulating conflicts of interest in the credit rating industry. *New York University Journal of Legislation and Public Policy*, 13, 253–313.

Baker, D. (2008). The housing bubble and the financial crisis. *Real-world economics review*, 46, 73–81.

Baker H. K., Mansi, S.A. (2002). Assessing credit agencies by bond issuers and institutional investors. *Journal of Business Finance & Accounting*, 29(9–10), 1367–1398.

Bakos, Y. (1998). The emerging role of electronic marketplaces on the Internet. *Communications of the ACM*, 41(8), 35–42. URL: http://citeseerx.ist.psu.edu/viewdoc/download?doi=10.1.1.83.180&rep=rep1&type=pdf (Retrieved April 24, 2013).

Baldwin, R. (2009). The great trade collapse: What caused it and what does it mean? In Baldwin, R. (Ed.), *The great trade collapse: Causes, consequences and prospects*. Geneva: VoxEU. Org Publication, 1–14.

Ball, R. (2009). The global financial crisis and the efficient market hypothesis: What have we learned? *Journal of Applied Corporate Finance*, 21(4), 8–16.

Banerjee, A. (2001). Contracting constraints, credit markets and economic development. *Working Paper* No. 02-17, Massachusetts Institute of Technology (MIT) – Dept. of Economics. URL: http://ssrn.com/abstract=306990 (Retrieved November 25, 2012).

Bannier, C. E. and Müsch, S. (2008). Die Auswirkungen der Subprime-Krise auf den deutschen LBO-Markt für Small- und MidCaps. Frankfurt School of Finance & Management, *Working Paper Series*, August 2008 (No. 103).

Bannier, C. E. and Hirsch, C. W. (2010). The economic function of credit rating agencies–What does the watchlist tell us? *Journal of Banking & Finance*, 34(12), 3037–3049.

Banton, A. and Theodorou, D. (2013). Holding ratings agencies to account: court issues landmark decision. *Piper Alderman*. URL: http://www.lexology.com/library/detail.aspx?g=fff922a1-dde2-49b8-a63f-13067f0498d0 (Retrieved November 20, 2013).

Bapir, M. A. (2012). Validity and reliability in qualitative research. *Working Paper*, The University of Warwick.

Baresa, S., Bogdan, S. and Ivanovic, S. (2012). Role, interests and critics of credit rating agencies. *UTMS Journal of economics*, 3(1), 71–82.

Barker, C., Pistrang, N., and Elliott, R. (2005). *Research methods in clinical psychology: An introduction for students and practitioners*. Chichester: John Wiley & Sons.

Barth, J., Caprio, G. and Levine, R. (2001). Financial regulation and performance: cross-country evidence. In Hernández L. and Schmidt-Hebbel, K., *Banking, Financial Integration, and International Crises*. Santiago, Chile: Central Bank of Chile, 113–141.

Barth, J. (2009). *The rise and fall of the US mortgage and credit markets: A comprehensive analysis of the market meltdown*. Hoboken, NJ: Wiley & Sons.

Barret, R. and Hilleard, D. (2008). *Joint Response to CESR Consultation Paper on the Role of Credit Rating Agencies in Structured Finance*. URL: http://www.esma.europa.eu%2Fsystem%2Ffiles%2FBBA___LIBA___Joint_Response_to_CESR_cp__CRAs_and_SF_.pdf&ei=bVde4fEOYjvswbx5oGoDw&usg=AFQjCNFj033e5wvQhT4a5EbC5U39j6kXdg&sig2=gchvv5ODocWKY9w1NB19gg (Retrieved 7, March 2014).

Barry, C. B. and Brown, S. J. (1986). Limited information as a source of risk. *The Journal of Portfolio Management*, 12(2), 66–72.

Bashir, M., Afzal, M. T., and Azeem, M. (2008). Reliability and validity of qualitative and operational research paradigm. Pakistan *Journal of Statistics and Operation Research*, 4(1), 35–45.

Batchvarov, A., Collins, J., and Davies, W. (2004). Mechanics of securitisation. In Fabozzi, F. and Choudhry, M. (Ed.).*The Handbook of European Structured Financial Products*. Hoboken, NJ: John Wiley & Sons, 19–56.

Bauer, M.W. and Gaskell, G, (2000). *Qualitative researching with text, image and sound: A practical handbook for social research*. Thousand Oaks, CA: SAGE Publications.

Bayar, Y. (2014). Recent financial crises and regulation on the credit rating Agencies. *Research in World Economy*, 5(1), 49–58.

Beachy, B. (2011) A financial crisis manual: causes, consequences, and lessons of the financial crisis. Global Development and Environment Institute. Tufts University, *Working Paper* No, 12–6, 1–91.

Beaver, W. H., Shakespeare, C. and Soliman, M. T. (2006). Differential properties in the ratings of certified versus non-certified bond-rating agencies. *Journal of Accounting and Economics*, 42(3), 303–334.

Becker, B. and Milbourn, T. (2011), How did increased competition affect credit ratings? *Journal of Financial Economics*, 101(3), 493–514.

Beckert, J. (2007). The social order of markets. *MPIfG Discussion Paper* 07/15. Cologne: Max-Planck-Institute for the Study of Societies.

Beckert, J. (2011). Where do prices come from? Sociological approaches to price formation. *Socio-Economic Review*, 9(4), 757–786.

Beckert, J. (2012). Capitalism as a system of contingent expectations, toward a sociological mircofoundation of political economy. *MPIfG Discussion Paper* 12/4, Cologne: Max-Planck-Institute for the Study of Societies.

Benmelech, E. and Dlugosz, J. (2010). The credit rating crisis. *NBER Macroeconomics Annual 2009*, 24, 161–207.

Berg, C. (2011). The financial crisis and the great recession: causes, effects, measures and consequences for the economic analysis and policy. *Workshop*

Monetary Policy, Macroprudential Policy and Fiscal Policy. Center for Central Banking Studies, Bank of England, May 17–19, 2011.

Bernanke, B. S. (2007). The recent financial turmoil and its economic and policy consequences. *Speech on October 15, 2007*. URL: http://www.bis.org/review/r071019a.pdf (Retrieved September 15, 2012).

Berry, L. L. and Yadav, M. S. (1996). Capture and communicate value in the pricing of service. *Sloan Management Review*, 37(4), 41–51.

Berrospide, J. (2012). Liquidity hoarding and the financial crisis: an empirical evaluation. Manuscript, Federal Reserve Board, *Finance and Economic Discussion Series*: 2013–03, Washington, DC. URL: http://www.bis.org/bcbs/events/bhbibe/berrospide.pdf (Retrieved April 22, 2013).

Besley, T., Coate, S. and Loury, G. (1994). Rotating savings and credit associations, credit markets and efficiency. *The Review of Economic Studies*, 61(4), 701–719.

Best, J. (2010). The limits of financial risk management: or what we didn't learn from the Asian crisis. *New Political Economy*, 15(1), 29–49.

Bethel, J. and Ferrell, A. (2006). Policy issues raised by structured products. *Discussion Paper* No. 560, 10/2006, MA 02138. Cambridge: Harvard Law School.

Bharath, S .T., Pasquariello, P. and Wu, G. (2009). Does asymmetric information drive capital structure decisions? *Review of Financial Studies*, 22(8), 3211–3243.

Bhat, S. (2009). *Security analysis & portfolio management*. New Delhi: Excel Books India.

Bhushan, H. (2012). Credit rating agencies in India: have we done enough?' *DLSU Business & Economics Review*, 22(2), 37–53

Biais, B., Bossaerts, P. and Spatt, C. (2010). Equilibrium asset pricing and portfolio choice under asymmetric information. *Review of Financial Studies*, 23(4), 1503–1543.

Bianco, K. M. (2008). *The subprime lending crisis: causes and effects of the mortgage meltdown*. CCH, Wolters Kluwer Law & Business.

BIS, Bank of International Settelements (2012). *Report to G20 leaders in Basel III implementation, June, 2012*. URL: http://www.bis.org/publ/bcbs220.htm (Retrieved February, 8, 2014).

BIS-Working-Group (2005). *The role of ratings in structured finance: issues and implications*. Bank for International Settlements (Ed). Committee on the Global Financial System. URL: www.bis.org (Retrieved August 22, 2012).

Bisin, A. and Gottardi, P. (1999). Competitive equilibria with asymmetric information. *Journal of Economic Theory*, 87(1), 1–48.

Blaikie, N. (2007). *Approaches to social enquiry: advancing knowledge, 2nd edition*. Cambridge: Cambridge Polity Press.

Blaurock, U. (2007). Control and responsibility of credit rating agencies. *Electronic Journal of Comparative law*, 11(3), 1–37.

Bloise, G. (2005). A remark on the fiscal theory of price determination. *Journal of Mathematical Economics*, 41(8), 1037–1052.

Blumenthal, R. (2008). The Honorable Christopher Cox, Chairman, U.S. Securities and Exchange Commission – letter re: Credit Rating Agency Reform. *Blumenthal, R., Attorney General, State of Connecticut, May 31, 2008*. URL: http://www.ct.gov/ag/lib/ag/antitrust/coxcreditratingagencreform.pdf (Retrieved April 25, 2012).

Böcking, D. (2011). Fear or junk status: Europe seeks to free itself from rating agencies' grip. *Spiegel Online International*, July 6, 2011. URL: http://www.spiegel.de/international/business/fear-of-junk-status-europe-seeks-to-free-itself-from-rating-agencies-grip-a-772733.html (Retrieved March 6, 2013).

Bolton, P., Freixas, X., and Shapiro, J.D. (2012). The credit ratings game. The *Journal of Finance*, 67(1), 85–111.

Bondarouk, E.V. (2010). The taming of the shrew, regulating the credit rating agencies in the European Union, in Dr. habil. Shawn Donnelly 18/5/2010 s0145815. Prepared for the courses *"Current Topics in Regulation & European Regulatory Governance,"* Thaught by Ph.D.Dr. habil. Shawn Donnelly (Ed.), University of Twente.

Booth, J. R. and Smith, R.L. (1986). Capital raising, underwriting and the certification hypothesis. *Journal of Financial Economics*, 15(1), 261–281.

Boot, A. W. A., Milbourn, T.T. and Schmeits, A. (2006). Credit ratings as coordination mechanisms. *Review of Financial Studies*, 19(1), 81–118.

Borio, C. and Zhu, H. (2011). Capital regulation, risk-taking and monetary policy: a missing link in the transmission mechanism? *Journal of Financial Stability*, 8(4), 236–251.

Brabänder, B. (2008). Subprime-Krise – Die Rolle der Rating-Agenturen. *Die Bank – Zeitschrift für Bankpolitik und Praxis*, Nr. 8/2008, URL: http://www.die-bank.de/index.php?id=107&tx_ttnews%5Btt_news%5D=15663&cHash=6b8bba49a4343f13715d4af4e5f71ae9 (Retrieved April 23, 2013).

Brennan, G. and Buchanan, J.M. (1988). Is public choice immoral? The case for the 'Nobel' lie. *Virginia Law Review*, 74, 179–190.

Brewer, M. K., Gough, O. and Shah, N. S. (2010). *Reconsidering disclosure and liability in the transatlantic capital markets*. URL: http://works.bepress.com/mark_brewer/1 (Retrieved January 28, 2013).

Brown, C.A. and Davis, K. (2010). Australia's experiance in the global financial crisis. In Kolb R.W. (Ed.), *Lessons from the financial crisis, causes, consequences, and our economic future*. Hoboken, NJ: John Wiley & Sons, 537–44.

Brown, C.D. (2011*). FitchRatings Re: solicitation of comment to assist study on assigned credit ratings release No. 34-64456; file 4-629.* Letter to Secretary Ms. Elizabeth M. Murphy, U.S. Securitites and Exchange Commission, Washington D.C.

Brunner, A., Pieter, J. and Weber, M. (2000). Information production in credit relationship: on the role of internal ratings in commercial banking. *CFS Working Paper Series* 2000/10. URL: http://www.econstor.eu/bitstream/10419/25371/1/326511040.PDF (Retrieved April 24. 2014).

Brunnermeier, M. K. (2008). Deciphering the liquidity and credit crunch 2007–08. *NBER Working Paper* No. w14612. The National Bureau of Economic Research.

Brunnermeier, M. et al. (2009).The Fundamental Principles of Financial Regulation. In International Center for Monetary and Baking Studies (Ed.), *Geneva Reports on the world economic 11.* Geneva London 2009: ICMN International Center for Monetary And Banking Studies.

Brunsden, J. (2012), Credit rating firms in EU to face sovereign-debt limits. *Bloomberg,* November 28, 2012. URL: http://www.bloomberg.com/news/2012-11-27/credit-rating-companies-to-face-sovereign-debt-curbs-in-eu-plan.html (Retrieved July 23, 2013).

Bryant, A. and Charmaz, K. (2007). *The Sage handbook of grounded theory*. London: SAGE Publications.

Bryman, A. and Bell, E. (2011). *Business research methods, 3rd ed.* Oxford: Oxford University Press.

Bubb, R. and Kaufman, A. (2009). Securitization and moral hazard: evidence from a lender cutoff rule. *Federal Reserve Bank of Boston, public policy, Discussion Paper* No. 09-5.

Buckberg, E. et al. (2010). Subprime and synthetic CDOs: structure, risk, and valuation. *NERA Economic Consulting,* 1–37. URL: http://www.nera.com/nera-files/PUB_CDOs_Structure_Risk_Valuation_0713.pdf (Retrieved April 23, 2014).

Bunjeva, T.A. (2009). Credit rating agencies: a regulatory challenge for Australia. *Melbourne University Law Review*, 33, 39–67.

Bloise, G. (2005). A remark on the fiscal theory of price determination. *Journal of Mathematical Economics*, 41, 1037–1052.

Buiter, W.H. (2007). Lessons from the 2007 financial crisis. *CEPR Policy inside* (No. 18). URL: http://www.cepr.org/pubs/policyinsights/CEPR_Policy_Insight_018.asp (Retrieved April 25, 2012).

Burnie, D.A. and Langsam, S.A. (2004). How SOX affects investing through credit rating agencies. *Journal of Corporate Accounting & Finance*, 15(6), 49–56.

Business Standard, (2012). Avoid litigation with credit rating agencies. *Business Standard*, October 18. URL: http://www.business-standard.com/article/markets/-avoid-litigation-with-credit-rating-agencies-112101800011_1.html (Retrieved February 2, 2013).

Caijing (2012). *Three sponsors from China, U.S. and Russia establish joint venture credit rating agency*. October 24. URL: http://english.caijing.com.cn/2012-10-24/112222628.html (Retrieved January 15, 2013).

Callon, M. (1998). Introduction: The embeddedness of economic markets in economics. In Callon, M. (Ed.). *The laws of the market*. Oxford: Blackwell Publishers, 1–57.

Camanho, N., Deb, P. and Liu, Z. (2012). *Credit rating and competition*. London School of Economics and Political Science: Financial Markets Group.

Cannata, F. and Quagliariello, M. (2009). The Role of Basel II in the Subprime Financial Crisis: Guilty or Not Guilty? *CAREFIN Research Paper* No. 3/09. URL: http://papers.ssrn.com/sol3/papers.cfm?abstract_id=1330417 (Retrieved April 27, 2013).

Cantor, R. and Packer, F. (1994). The credit rating industry. *Federal Reserve Bank of New York Quarterly Review*, 19(2), 1–26.

Cantor, R. and Mann, C. (2003). Measuring the performance of corporate bond ratings. *Special Comment, Moody's Investors Service*. URL: http://ssrn.com/abstract=996025 (Retrieved April 28, 2013).

Cantor, R. (2009). *Testimony of Richard Cantor, Chief Credit Officer, Moody's Investors Service, before the United States House of Representatives Committee on Financial Services, Subcommitee on Oversight and Government Reform*. URL: http://www.financialservices.house.gov (Retrieved June, 27, 2012).

Canuto, O., dos Santos, P. F. P., and de Sá Porto, P. (2007). Macroeconomics and sovereign risk ratings. *Working Paper*, 1–36.

Canuto, O., dos Santos, P. F. P., and de Sá Porto, P. (2012). Macroeconomics and sovereign risk ratings. *Journal of International Commerce, Economics and Policy (JICEP)*, 3(02). 1250011-1-1250011-25.

Capital Markets Devision (2009). *Report of the Committee on comprehensive regulation for credit Rating agencies*. Ministry of Finance, India, 2009-2010/1191.

Carapeto, M. et al. (2010). Distress resolution strategies in the banking sector – Implications for global financial crisis. In Suk-Joong, K. and McKenzie, M. (Eds.), *International banking in the new era: post-crisis challenges and opportunities. International Finance Review* Vol. 11, Part IV. Bingley (UK): Emerald Group Publishing, 335–360.

Carbone, D. (2010). The impact of the Dodd-Frank Act's credit rating agency reform on public companies. *The Corporate & Securities Law Advisor*, 24, 1–7.

Carneiro, P. E. (2009). Ten years' analysis of sovereign risk: noise-rater risk, panels, and errors. *Journal of Risk Finance*, 19(2), 107–130.

Carron, A., Dhrymes, P. J., and Beloreshki, T. N. (2003). Credit ratings for structured products. *National Economic Research Associates, NERA Economic Consulting report* 65.

Carson, J. (2011). Self-regulation in securities markets. *Working Paper* (5542), World Bank Policy Research.

Carter, J. and Watson, R. (2006). The rating process for structured finance instruments. In Watson R., Carter, J. (Ed.), *Asset securitization and synthetic structures: innovations in the European credit markets*. London: Euromoney Institutional Investor Plc, 88–96.

Castle, M. N. (2009). *Approaches to improving credit rating agency regulation*. Subcommittee on Capital Markets, Insurance, and Government Sponsored Enterprises of the Committee on Financial Services U.S. House of Representatives, (111th Congress), First Session, May 19, 2009, Serial No. 111–33, 1–141.

CBI, Confederation of British Industry (2012). Credit rating agency reform (CRA III), *CBI position paper*.

C.D. Howe Institute, (2012). Better regulation needed for credit rating agencies: *C.D. Howe Institue. Canada Free Press Online*, July 26, 2012. RL: http://www.canadafreepress.com/index.php/article/48356 (Retrieved August 1, 2013).

Cecchetti, S. G. (1999). Future of financial intermediation and regulation: an overview. *Current Issues in Economics and Finance*, 5(8), 1–6.

Central Banking Newsdesk (2011). *ECB rejects public credit rating agencies role*. URL: http://www.centralbanking.com/central-banking/news/2028474/ecb-rejects-public-credit-rating-agency-role (Retrived April 8, 2014).

Ceresney, A. J., Eng, G. and Nuttall, S. R. (2009). Regulatory Investigations And The Credit Crisis: The Search For Villains. *American Criminal Law Review*, 46(2), 225–274.

Cerny, P. G. (1994). The dynamics of financial globalization: Technology, market structure, and policy response. *Policy Sciences*, 27(4), 319–342.

CESR, (2006). *CESR's report to the European Commission on the compliance of credit rating agencies with the IOSCO Code*, December 2006. URL: http://www.esma.europa.eu/ga/system/files/06_545.pdf (Retrieved May 28, 2013).

CESR, The Committee of European Securities Regulators (2008). The role of credit rating agencies in structured finance. *Consultation Paper*.

CGFS, Committee on the Global Financial System (2008). Rating in structured finance: what went wrong and what can be done to adress shortcomings?, *CGFS Papers*. Basel: Bank for International Settlements (BIS).

CGFS, Committee on the Global Financial System (2010). The role of margin requirements and haircuts in procyclicality. *CGFS Papers*, No. 36.

Chambers, D. R. et al. (2011). CDO squareds: the case of subprime mortgages. *The Journal of Structured Finance*, 17(2), 96–113.

Chance, D. M. and Brooks, R. (2009). *An introduction to derivatives and risk management*. Mason, OH: South-Western Cengage Learning.

Chang, Winston W. (2011). Financial crisis of 2007–2010. *Working Paper Series*, June 30, 2011. State University of New York and Buffalo: Department of Economics.

Changxin (2013). Credit ratings JV to be launched in Hong Kong, *China Daily Online*, August 5, 2013. URL: http://www.chinadaily.com.cn/business/2013-05/08/content_16484470.html (Retrieved May 8, 2013).

Chant, J. (2009). *The ABCP Crisis in Canada: The implications for the regulation of financial markets* (Expert Panel on Securities Regulation). URL: http://www.google.de/url?sa=t&rct=j&q=&esrc=s&frm=1&source=web&cd=1&ved=0CCwQFjAA&url=http%3A%2F%2Fwww.investisseurautonome.info%2FPDF-Downloads%2FCOMMENT-INVESTIR-RENDEMENT-INDEX%2Fdoc.1495-%2520Chant%25202009%2520ABCP%2520report%2520.pdf&ei=4fVTU_HkOcmw7Abc24DIAg&usg=AFQjCNE0NhCFPr0LI5AwxgP2cRiXMjqVpA&sig2=85NOGSJUJYGeNKQym_O_nA&bvm=bv.65058239,d.bGE (Retrieved January 6, 2013).

Charmaz, K. (2006). *Constructing grounded theory: a practical guide through qualitative analysis*. London/Thousand Oaks: SAGE Publications.

Chava, S., Ganduri, R., and Ornthanalai, C. (2012). Are credit ratings still relevant? *Working Paper*, Georgia Tech and University of Toronto.

Cheng, M. and Neamtiu, M. (2009). An empirical analysis of changes in credit rating properties: timeliness, accuracy and volatility. *Journal of Accounting and Economics*, 47(1), 108–130.

Christopoulos, A. G., Mylonakis, J., and Diktapandis, P. (2011). Could Lehman Brothers' collapse be anticipated? An examination using CAMELS Rating System. *International Business Research*, 4(2), 11–19.

Choudhry, M. (2010). *Structured credit products: credit derivatives and synthetic securitisation*.Wiley Finance, Book 579, Hoboken, NJ: John Wiley & Sons.

Cifuentes, A. (2010). *Testimony of Arturo Cifuentes, Ph.D. – Department of Industrial Engineering, University of Chile, Santiago, Chile*. U.S. Senate, Washington, D.C.

Cinquegrana, P. (2009). The reform of the credit rating agencies: a Comparative perspective. *ECMI Policy Brief* No. 12.

Cisneros, D., Lizarzaburu, E. R. and Salguero, J. Q. (2012). Credit information in emerging markets: the rating agencies and credit risk reports, Peruvian experience. *International Journal of Business and Management*, 7(24), 35–43.

Claessens, S. and Embrechts, G. (2003). Basel II, sovereign ratings and transfer risk external versus internal ratings. *Working Papers Series*, SSRN 386480.

Claessens, S. et al. (2010). Cross-country experiences and policy implications from the global financial crisis. *Economic Policy*, 25(62), 267–293.

Clarke, D. (2011). Regulators propose credit rating alternatives. *Reuters Edition US*, URL: http://www.reuters.com/article/2011/12/07/us-financial-regulation-fdic-idUSTRE7B61IG20111207 (Retrieved November 30, 2012).

Clark, A. (2012). The case for the ratings agencies' defence…just read it yourself. *The Times Online*, October 15, sec. Banking and Finance. URL: http://www.thetimes.co.uk/tto/business/industries/banking/article3568045.ece (Retrieved June 5, 2013)

Clarkson, B. (2010). *Testimony of Brian Clarkson – Before the Financial Crisis Inquiry Commissioin, creditbility of credit ratings, the investment decision made based on those rating, and the financial crisis*. FCIC at SLS, The Report, Resource Library. URL: http://fcic-static.law.stanford.edu/cdn_media/fcic-testimony/2010-0602-Clarkson.pdf (Retrieved April 23, 2104).

Clerides, S., Nearchou, P., and Pashardes, P. (2008). Intermediaries as quality assessors: tour operators in the travel industry. *International Journal of Industrial Organization*, 26(1), 372–392.

Coates, J. C. (2007). The goals and promise of the Sarbanes-Oxley Act. *The Journal of Economic Perspectives*, 21(1), 91–116.

Cochrane, J. H. (2009). Lessons from the financial crisis. *Regulation, 32(4)*, 34–37.

Coffee, J. C. (2010). Ratings reform: the good, the bad, and the ugly. *Columbia Law and Economics Working Paper* No. 379, 1–58. URL: http://ssrn.com/abstract=1650802 (Retrieved June 10, 2012).

Cohen, G. (2014). On the impact of bond's rating changes on the firm's stock price. *International Journal of Financial Research*, 5(1), 64–70.

Cohen, J. P., Coughlin, C. C., and Lopez, D. A. (2012). The boom and bust of US housing prices from various geographic perspectives. *Federal Reserve Bank of St. Louis Review*, 94(5), 341–367.

Colander, D. et al. (2009). The financial crisis and the systemic failure of the economics profession. *Critical Review*, 21(2–3), 249–267.

Collins, W. (2008). Developments in banking and financial law: 2007–2008: IV. valuing opaque assets in an illiquid market. *Review of Banking & Financial Law* 27, 285–405.

Combris, P., Lecocq, S., and Visser, M. (2003). Estimation of a hedonic price equation for Bordeaux wine: does quality matter? *The Economic Journal*, 107(441), 390–402.

Congress, (2006). *S. 3850 (109th): Credit Rating Agencies Reform Act of 2006.* GovTrack.us (Database of Federal Legigislation). URL: https://www.govtrack.us/congress/bills/109/s3850 (Retrieved June 10, 2012).

Congress, 111th (2010). *One Hundered Eleventh Congress of the United States of America, at the Second Session. January.* URL: https://www.uscg.mil/hq/cg5/cg544/docs/CG%20Authorization%20Act.pdf (Retrieved June 15, 2012).

Congleton, R. (2009). On the political economy of the financial crisis and bailout of 2008–2009. (Editorial commentary). *Public Choice*, 40(3–4), 287–317.

Conway, P. (2010). *The IMF and the international financial crisis, Egon Sohmen Memorial Conference "The Political Economy of International Financial Institutions,"* Tübingen, June, 10–13, 2010.

Cornaggia, J., Cornaggia, K. J., and Hund, J. (2013). Credit ratings across asset classes. *Indiana University and Rice University working paper.*

Coskun, D. (2008). Credit rating agencies in a post-Enron world: Congress revisits the NRSRO concept. *Journal of Banking Regulation*, 9(4), 264–283.

Cound, J. and Fisher, S. (2012). Reform of credit rating agency regulation in Europe: an end-investor perspective. *TMI (treasury management international). Special Report, International Cash Management 2012*, 13–16.

Coval, J. D., Jurek, J. W., and Stafford, E. (2008). Re-examining the role of rating agencies: lessons from structured finance. *Unpublished manuscript.*

Coval, J. D., Jurek, J. W., and Stafford, E. (2009). The economics of structured finance, *Journal of Economics Perspectives* 23(1), 3–25.

Craske, M. et al. (2013). *United States: CRA3 – new requirements affect issuers, originators and sponsors.* Cadwalder, Wickersham & Taft LLP. URL: http://www.mondaq.com/unitedstates/x/255402/securitization+structured+finance/CRA3+New+Requirements+Affect+Issuers+Originators+And+Sponsors (Retrieved March 12, 2014).

Creswell, J. W. (2002). Educational research: planning, conducting, and evaluating quantitative. *Course Syllabus, MCT 690 – Research Methodology.* URL: http://scholar.google.ch/scholar?hl=de&q=creswell+Educational+research%3A+Planning%2C+conducting%2C+and+evaluating+quantitative..+&btnG=&lr= (Retrieved July 28, 2013).

Creswell, J. W. (2009). *Research design: qualitative, quantitative, and mixed methods approaches, 4th ed.* Thousand Oaks, CA: SAGE Publications.

Creswell, J. and Bajaj V. (2007). $3.2 Billion move by Bear Stearns to rescue fund. *The New York Times*, June 23, 2007. URL: http://www.nytimes.com/2007/06/23/business/23bond.html?pagewanted=all (Retrieved August 6, 2012).

Crotty, J. and Epstein, G. (2008). Proposals for effectively regulating the US financial system to avoid yet another meltdown. *Working Paper*, University of Massachusetts, Department of Economics, No. 2008–15, 1–15.

Crotty, J. (2009). Structural causes of the global financial crisis: a critical assessment of the 'new financial architecture'. *Cambridge Journal of Economics*, 33(4), 563–580.

Crotty, J. (2011). The realism of assumptions does matter: why Keynes-Minsky theory must replace efficient market theory as the guide to financial regulation policy. *Working paper*, University of Massachusetts – Amherst.

Crouhy, M. G. (2010). Risk management failures during the financial crisis. In Kolb, R. W. (Ed.), *Lessons from the financial crisis: causes, consequences and our economic future*. Hoboken, NJ: John Wiley & Sons, 283–292.

Crouhy, M. G., Jarrow, R.A., and Turnbull, S.M. (2008). The subprime credit crisis of 07. *Journal of Derivatives*, 16(4), 81–110.

CSA, Canadian Securities Administrators (2008). *Securities regulatory proposals stemming from the 2007–2008 credit market turmoil and its effects on the ABCP market in Canada*,. URL: https://www.bcsc.bc.ca/Securities_Law/Policies/Policy1/PDF/11_405_CSA/ (Retrieved March 8, 2013).

Culp, C. L. (2011). *Structured finance and insurance: the ART of managing capital and risk*, (Vol. 339). Hoboken, NJ: John Wiley & Sons.

Dale, R. and Thomas, S. (2000). *The role of credit ratings in the Basel capital adequacy proposals* (European Capital Markets Inst.).

Damgaard, T., Freytag, P. V., and Darmer, P. (2001). *Qualitative methods in business studies*, (Vol. 9), Bingley (UK): Emerald Group Publishing, 143–186.

Danielsson, J. et al. (2001). An academic response to Basel II. *Special Paper Series* No. 130, LSE Financial Markets Group, ESRC Research Centre.

Darbellay, A. (2013). *Regulating credit rating agencies*. Cheltenham, UK: Edward Elgar Publishing Limited.

Darcy, D. (2009). Credit rating agencies and the credit crisis: how the Issuer pays conflict contributed and what regulators might do about it. *Columbia Business Law Review*, 2, 605–668.

Daul, J. (2009). Solving the economic crisis: the role of the EU. *European View*, 8(1), 21–27.

Davis, M. H. A., Panas, V. G., and Zariphopoulu, T. (1993). European option pricing with transaction costs. *SIAM Journal on Control and Optimization*, 31(2), 470–493.

Davis, K. (2011). *Regulatory reform post the global financial crisis: an overview.* Melborne APEC Finance Centre, Australian APEC Study Center at RMIT Uni versity. URL: http://www.apec.org.au/docs/11_CON_GFC/Regulatory%20Reform%20Post%20GFC-%20Overview%20Paper.pdf (Retrieved April 24, 2014).

Deats, C. (2010). Talk that isn't cheap: does the first amendment protect credit fating agencies' faulty methodologies from regulation? *Columbia Law Review*, 110(7), 1818–1864.

Deb, P. and Murphy, G. (2009). Credit rating agencies: an alternative model. *Working paper*, London School of Economics.

Deb, P. et al. (2011). Whither the credit ratings industry? *Bank of England Financial Stability Paper*, (9).

de Haan, J. and Amtenbrink, F. (2011). Credit rating agencies. *De Nederlandsche Bank (DNB) Working Paper* No. 278.

De Larosière, Jacques (2009). *The high-level group on financial supervision in the EU: Report* (European Commission).

DeMarzo, P. (2005). The pooling and tranching of securities: a model of informed intermediation. *The Rewiev of Financial Studies* 18(1).

Demerjian, P. (2010). Financial covenants, credit risk, and the resolution of uncertainty. *Working paper series*, University of Washington, February 25, 2010, 1–42.

Demirgüç-Kunt, A. and Servén, L. (2010). Are all the sacred cows dead? Implications of the financial crisis for macro-and financial policies. *The World Bank Research Observer*, 25 (1), 91–124.

Dennis, K. (2009). The rating game: explaining rating agency failures in the buildup to the financial crisis. *University of Miami Law Review*, 63, 1111–1150.

Dillard, J., Brown, D., and Marshall, R. S. (2005). An environmentally enlightened accounting. *Accounting Forum*, 29(1), 77–101.

Dionne, G. (2009). Structured finance, risk management, and the recent financial crisis. *Ivey Business Journal*, 1–4.

Duarte, J. et al. (2008). Information asymmetry, information dissemination and the effect of regulation FD on the cost of capital. *Journal of Financial Economics*, 87(1), 24–44.

Duff. A. and Einig, S. (2007). *Credit rating agencies: meeting the need of the markets?* Edinburgh: Institute of Chartered Accountants of Scotland, 1–127.

Duff, A. and Einig, S. (2009a). Understanding credit ratings quality: evidence from UK debt market participants. *The British Accounting Review*, 41(2), 107–119.

Duff, A. and Einig, S. (2009b). Credit ratings quality: The perceptions of market participants and other interested parties. *The British Accounting Review*, 41(3), 141–153.

Duffie, D. (2008). Innovations in credit risk transfer: implications for financial stability. *Working Papers* No. 255, Bank for International Settlements (BIS).

Dodd, R. (2002). The economic rational for financial market regulation. Derivatives Study Center, Financial Policy Forum (Ed.), *Special Policy Report* No. 12.

Dodd, R. (2012). Markets: exchange or over-the-counter. *Finance & Development*, URL: http://www.imf.org/external/pubs/ft/fandd/basics/markets.htm (Retrieved January 10, 2013).

Dooley, M. (2010). Central Bank responses during the financial crisis. *BIS Working Papers* 51, 2010.

Dwyer, G.P. (2010). *The financial system after the crisis: structured finance and credit rating agencies.* CenFIS Center for Financial Innovation and Stability, URL: https://www.frbatlanta.org/cenfis/pubscf/vn_financial_system_after_crisis.cfm (Retrieved January 5, 2013).

Eaglesham, J. Neumann, J. and Perez, E. (2013). U.S. sues S&P over ratings – Justice Department says endorsements of risky mortgage bonds fueled crisis. *The Wall Street Journal*, February 5. URL: http://online.wsj.com/news/articles/SB10001424127887324445904578284064003795142 (Retrieved February 5, 2013).

Eales, B. and Choudhry, M. (2003). *Derivative instruments: a guide to theory and practice* (Vol. 1). Oxford: Butterworth-Heinemann Elsevier Ltd.

Earl-Slater, A. (2004). *Lay involvement in health and other research.* Oxon, UK: Radcliffe Publishing.

EBA, European Banking Authority, (n.d.). *Implementing Basel II in Europe: CRD IV package.* URL: http://www.eba.europa.eu/regulation-and-policy/implementing-basel-iii-europe (Retrieved February 8, 2014).

EBA, European Banking Authority (2013). *EBA, EIOPA and ESMA joint consultation paper on mechanistic reference to credit ratings in ESAs' guidelines and recommendations (JC-CP-2013-02).* URL: http://www.eba.europa.eu/-/eba-esma-and-eiopa-publish-final-report-on-mechanistic-references-to-credit-ratings-in-the-esas-guidelines-and-recommendations (Retrieved March 7, 2014).

EBA (2014). *EBA, ESMA and EIOPA publish final report on mechanistic reference to credit ratings in the ESAs' guidelines and recommendations.* February 1, 2014. URL: http://www.eba.europa.eu/-/eba-esma-and-eiopa-publish-final-report-on-mechanistic-references-to-credit-ratings-in-the-esas-guidelines-and-recommendations (Retrieved March 7, 2014).

EBA, EIOPA and ESMA (2014). *Final report on Mechanistic references to credit ratings in the ESAs' guidelines and recommendations (JC 2014 004)*. URL: https://www.eba.europa.eu/documents/10180/534414/JC+2014+004+%28Final+Report+Mechanistic+References+to+Credit+Ratings%29.pdf (Retrieved 7, March 2014).

EBIC, European Banking Industry Committee (2012). *Re: The current review of the regulation on credit rating agencies. Letter to the EU, 6. June 2012*. URL: http://www.ebf-fbe.eu/uploads/D1101A-2012-EBIC%20letter%20on%20the%20current%20Review%20of%20the%20Regulation%20on%20Credit%20Rating%20Agencies.pdf (Retrieved March 5, 2014).

EC, European Commission, (2008). *Proposal for a regulation of the european parliament and of the Council on Credit Rating Agencies*, Brussels: European Commission. COM (2008) 704 final, 2008/0217 (COD).

EC, European Commission (2009). *Regulation (EC) No. 1060/2009 of the European Parliament and the Council*. URL: http://www.esma.europa.eu/system/files/L_302_1.pdf (Retrieved February 8, 2012).

EC, European Commission, (2010). *Public Consultation on Credit Rating Agencies. European Commission, Financial Services Policy and Financial Markets*. Securities Markets. 05.11.2010. URL: http://ec.europa.eu/finance/consultations/2010/cra/docs/cpaper_en.pdf (Retrieved November 13, 2012).

EC, European Commission (2011). *Proposal for a regulation of the European Parliament and the Council amending Regulation (EC) No. 1060/2009 on credit rating agencies*. COM(2011) 747 final, 2011/0361 (COD). URL: https://www.google.be/#q=european+commission+adopted+CRA+regulation+on+december+7+2010+may+2011+ESMA (Retrieved May 6, 2013).

EC, European Commission, (2012). *Commision implementing decision of 5 October 2012*. The European Commission (Ed.) (2012/627/EU).

EC, European Commission, (2013a). *Statement by Commissioner Michel Barnier following the vote in the European Parliament on new European rules to regulate credit rating agencies*. URL: http://ec.europa.eu/internal_market/securities/agencies/index_en.htm (Retrieved February 3, 2012).

EC, European Commission (2013b). *Memo "New rules on credit rating agencies (CRAs) enter into force – frequently asked questions*. June 18, 2013. URL: http://europa.eu/rapid/press-release_MEMO-13-571_en.htm (Retrieved May 18, 2014).

ECOFIN (2008). *Implementation of the roadmap on financial stability: financial transparency and credit rating agencies*. Economic and Financial Affairs, Council of the European Union of July 8, 2008.

EFSF, European Financial Stability Facility (n.d.). *About EFSF.* URL: http://www.efsf.europa.eu/about/index.htm (Retrieved March 5, 2013).

Eggert, K. (2009). The great collapse: how securitization caused the subprime meltdown. *Conneticut Law Review*, 41(4), 1257–1312.

Ekins, E. McClintock and Calabria, M. (2012). Regulation, market structure, and role of the credit rating agencies. *Policy Analysis*, 704, 1–36.

Elamin, M. (2011). Believe only what you see: credit rating agencies, structured finance, and bonds. *FRB of Cleveland Working Paper* No. 122–22.

Elkhoury, M. (2008). Credit rating agencies and their potential impact on developing countries. *United Nations Conference on Trade and Development. Discussion Paper* No. 186, 1–27. URL: http://unctad.org/en/docs/osgdp20081_en.pdf (Retrieved April 23, 2013).

Ellis, D.M. (1998). Different sides of the same story: investors' and issuers' view of rating agencies. *The Journal of Fixed Income*, 7(4), 35–45.

Ellis, N. S., Fairchild, L. M., and D'Souza, F. (2012). Is imposing liability on credit rating agencies a good Idea? Credit agency reform in the aftermath of the global financial crisis. *Stanford Journal of Law, Business & Finance*, 17, 175–222.

ESMA, European Securities and Markets Authority (2012). *Questions and Answers, a Common Definition of European Money Market Funds.* ESMA/2012/113. URL: http://www.esma.europa.eu%2Fsystem%2Ffiles%2F2012-113.pdf&ei=2sVDU4izEYGa4wSHj4HwCw&usg=AFQjCNGruQuWSc_c8GgpLSPEU7soXZQDMg&sig2=DTiqVYNAu2rKRFC8tdo0xg (Retrieved March 3, 2014).

ESMA, European Securities and Market Authority (2013). *Discussion paper on CRA3 implementation.* 10/07/2013 to 10/10/2013. URL: https://www.esma.europa.eu/consultation/Discussion-Paper-CRA3-Implementation (Retrieved March 6, 2014).

EU C59/2 (2006). Communication from the Commission on Credit Rating Agencies (2006/C 59/02). *Official Journal for the European Union*, C59/2.

EU, European Union (2009). *Regulations. Regulation (EC) No. 1060/2009 of the European Parliament and the Council of 16 September 2009 on credit rating agencies.* URL: http://www.esma.europa.eu/system/files/L_302_1.pdf (Retrieved February, 8, 2012).

European Parliament (2009). *Credit rating agencies: partially responsible for the current financial crisis say MEPs.* URL: http://www.europarl.europa.eu/sides/getDoc.do?language=en&type=IM-PRESS&reference=20090422IPR54187 (Retrieved, May 4, 2012).

European Parliament (2013). *Review of the new European System of Financial Supervision (ESFS), Part 1: The work of the European Supervisory Authorities* (EBA, EIOPA and ESMA). URL: www.europarl.europa.eu%2FRegData%2Fetudes%

2Fetudes%2Fjoin%2F2013%2F507446%2FIPOL-ECON_ET(2013)507446_EN.pdf&ei=6_doU5WDPLKe7AaxiYDICw&usg=AFQjCNE4uM2f6YzQgj9ETcReNjXVrkgXgQ&sig2=QAxNmzxJElIhXLOet8AC_Q (Retrieved May 6, 2014).

Erkens, D. H., Hung, M., and Matos, P. (2012). Corporate governance in the 2007–2008 financial crisis: evidence from financial institutions worldwide. *Journal of Corporate Finance*, 18(2), 389–411.

Everling, O. (2008). Ratings and the efficient market hypothesis. Dr. Oliver Everling, *Den Nutzen von Ratgins erschliessen*. URL: http://www.everling.de/?p=150 (Retrieved November 22, 2011).

Fabozzi, F. J., Davis, H. A., and Choudhry, M. (2006). *Introduction to structured finance*. Hoboken, NJ: John Wiley & Sons.

Fabozzi, F. J. and Goodman, L. S. (2001). *Investing in collateralized debt obligations*, (Vol. 81), Hoboken, NJ: Wiley Finance.

Fabozzi, F. J, Jones, F. J. and Johnson, R. R. (2002). Common stock. In Fabozzi F. J. (Ed.), *The handbook of financial instruments*. Hoboken, NJ: John Wiley & Sons Inc., 67–118.

Fama, E. F. (1970). Efficient capital markets: a review of theory and empirical work. *The Journal of Finance*, 25(2), 383–417.

Farber, S. C., Constanza, R., and Wilson, M. A. (2002). Economic and ecological concepts for valuing ecostem services. *Ecological Economics* (Elsevier), 41, 375–392.

Frankfurter Allgemeine Zeitung (FAZ) (2007). Agenturen sehen sich zu Unrecht in der Kritik. *Frankfurter Allgemeine Zeitung*, September 5, 2007.

FCIC (Financial Crisis Inquiry Commision) (2010). *Preliminary staff report – credit ratings and the financial crisis.* June 2, 2010, URL: https://fcic-static.law.stanford.edu/cdn_media/fcic-reports/2010-0602-Credit-Ratings.pdf (Retrieved November 22, 2012)

Federal-Reserve (2011). *Report to the Congress on credit ratings.* Board of Governors of the Federal Reserve System, July 2011. URL: http://www.federalreserve.gov/publications/other-reports/files/credit-ratings-report-201107.pdf (Retrieved January 16, 2013).

Feldstein, M. (2009). The global impact of America's housing crisis. *Project Syndicate*. URL: http://www.nber.org/feldstein/projectsyndicate082009.pdf (Retrieved April 22, 2014).

Fender, I. and Kiff, J. (2005). CDO rating methodology: some thoughts on model risk and its implications. *Journal of Credit Risk*, 1, 3. Also available as *BIS Working Paper* No. 163, November 2004, 1–25.

Fender, I. and Mitchell, J. (2005). Structured finance: complexity, risk and the use of rating. *BIS Quarterly Review*, June, 2005, 67–79.

Fender, I. and Mitchell, J. (2009). Incentives and tranche retention in securitisation: a screening model. *Working Paper* No. 289, Bank for International Settlements.

Fender, I., Tarashev, N., and Zhu, H. (2008). Credit fundamentals, ratings and value-at-risk: CDOs versus corporate exposures. *BIS Quarterly Review*, March 2008, 87–101.

Fennel, D. and Medvedev, A. (2011). An economic analysis of credit rating agency business modles and ratings accuracy. *Financial Service Authority (FAS) Occasional Paper Series*, 41.

Ferguson, C. et al. (2011). *Inside job*. production notes, Sony Pictures Home Entertainment.

Finanzlexikon (n.d). *Verlust, unerwarteter*. URL: http://www.finanz-lexikon.de/verlust,%20unerwarteter_3711.html (Retrieved June 15, 2012).

Fischel, D. R. (1978). Efficient capital market theory, the market for corporate control, and the regulation of cash tender offers. *Texas Law Review*, 57, 1–46.

Fischer, S. (2003). Financial crises and reform of the international financial system. *Review of World Economics*, 139(1), 1–37.

Fishman, St. (2008). Burning down his house: is Lehman CEO Dick Fuld the true villain in the collapse of Wall Street, or is he being sacrificed for the sins of his peers? *New York Magazine*, December 8, 2008.

Fitch Ratings (2011a). Managing and developing criteria and models. *Credit Policy*. September 30, 2011. URL: http://www.fitchratings.com/web_content/nrsro/nav/NRSRO_Exhibit-2.pdf (Retrieved August 9, 2013).

Fitch Ratings (2011b). Understanding the structured finance rating Pprocess. *Special Report*. October 4, 2011. URL: http://www.fitchratings.com/web_content/nrsro/nav/NRSRO_Exhibit-2.pdf (Retrieved August 9, 2013).

Fitch Ratings (2011c). The ratings process. *Special Report, Credit Policy*. December 2, 2011. URL: http://www.fitchratings.com/web_content/nrsro/nav/NRSRO_Exhibit-2.pdf (Retrieved August 9, 2013).

Fitch Ratings (2013). *Definitions of ratings and other forms of opinion – July 2013*. Online Resource, URL: http://www.fitchratings.com/web_content/ratings/fitch_ratings_definitions_and_scales.pdf (Retrieved August 4, 2013).

Financial Times (2008). A history of Freddie Mac and Fannie Mae. *Financial Times Online*, September 8, 2008. URL: http://www.ft.com/intl/cms/s/0/e3e1d654-5288-11dd-9ba7-000077b07658.html#axzz2bCLgkUGs (Retrieved August 6, 2012).

Fishman, S. (2008). Burning down his house: is Lehman CEO Dick Fuld the true villain in the collapse of Wall Street, or is he being sacrificed for the sins of his peers? *New York Times Magazine*, November 30, 2008. URL: http://nymag.com/news/business/52603/ (Retrieved May 24, 2012).

Flannery, M. J., Houston, J. F., and Partnoy, F. (2010). Credit default swap spreads as viable substitutes for credit ratings. *University of Pennsylvania Law Review*, 2085–2123.

Flassbeck, H. (2008). They should be taken over by a public regulatory agency. *The International Economy*, Fall 2008.

Fons, J. (2010). The future of the ratings markets. In Konczal, M. (Ed.), *Will it work? How will we know?* New York: Roosevelt Institute, 69–73.

Forti, D. W. and Iaconelli, B. B. (2001). *Commercial mortgage backed securites and the rating process.* URL: http://www.dechert.com/files/Publication/9c4602af-8e26-40e5-8f2a-009804952770/Presentation/PublicationAttachment/adf5c8b2-ae2c-4044-86af-01b5ab7cb208/Commercial%20Mortgage%20Backed%20Securities-Forti%20D%205-02.PDF (Retrieved August 22. 2012).

Fox, J. (2011). *The myth of the rational market: a history of risk, reward, and delusions on Wall Street.* Hampshire (UK): Harriman House Limited.

Fons, J. (2010). The future of the ratings markets, In Konczal, M. (Ed.), *Roosevelt Institute project on global finance conference report.* New York: Roosevelt Institute Organization, 69–73.

Foster, J. B. (2008). The financialization of capital and the crisis. *Monthly Review-New York*, 59(11), 1–12.

Franke, G. and Krahnen, J. P. (2007). Default risk sharing between banks and markets: the contribution of collateralized debt obligations. In Carey M. and Stulz R. M. (Ed.), *The risks of financial institutions.* Boston: National Bureau of Economic Research, 603–634.

Frankel, T. (2006). *Trust and honesty: America's business culture at a crossroad.* Oxford: Oxford University Press. URL: http://web4.uwindsor.ca/units/law/CARC/main.nsf/0/e096c2495caf982b852570fb00737f6a/$FILE/Frankel.pdf (Retrieved Apeil 28, 2014).

Freeman, L. (2008). Who's guarding the gate-credit-rating agency liability as control person in the subprime credit crisis. *Vermont Law Review*, 33, 585–619.

French, S., Leyshon, A., and Thrift, N. (2009). A very geographical crisis: the making and breaking of the 2007–2008 financial crisis. *Cambridge Journal of Regions, Economy and Society*, 2(2), 287–302.

Friedman, D.D. (1990). *Price theory: an intermediate text.* Cincinnati: South-Western Publishing Co.

Frisby, D. (Ed.) (2004). *The philosophy of money, Georg Simmel.* London: Routledge.

Frost, C. A. (2006). Credit Rating Agencies in Capital Markets: A Review of Research Evidence on Selected Criticisms of the Agencies. *Working paper series*, URL: http://ssrn.com/abstract=904077 (Retrieved, April 22, 2014).

FSA, Financial Service Authority (2009). *The Turner Review: a regulatory response to the global banking crisis*. Online Resource. URL: http://www.fsa.gov.uk/pubs/other/turner_review.pdf (Retrieved January 15, 2013).

FSA, HM Trasury and BoE (2010). *The United Kingdom authorities response to the European Commission internal market and services consultation document on credit rating agencies*. URL: https://www.google.be/#q=the+united+kingdiom+authorities+response+to+the+european+commissiion (Retrieved April 14, 2014).

FSB, Financial Stability Board (2010). *Principles for reducing reliance on CRA ratings*. URL: http://www.financialstabilityboard.org/publications/r_101027.pdf (Retrieved January 27, 2013).

FSB, Financial Stability Board (2013). *Credit rating agencies, reducing reliance and strengthening oversight, progress report to the St Petersburg G20 summit*. URL: http://www.financialstabilityboard.org/publications/r_130829d.pdf (Retrieved December 19, 2013).

FSF, Financial Stability Forum (2008). *Report of the Financial Stability Forum on enhancing market and institutional resilience*. URL: http://www.financialstabilityboard.org/publications/r_0804.pdf (Retrieved January 15, 2013).

FT-Editorial (Financial Times-Editorial) (2011). Berating agencies. *Financial Times, editorial comment*, July 26, 2011.

Fuchs, A. and Gehring K.(2013). Does the home country of credit-rating agencies affect sovereign ratings? *University of Heidelberg Department of Economics Discussion Paper Series* No. 552.

G20, Group of Twenty (2008). *Declaration of the Summit on financial markets and the world economy*. URL: http://www.g20.utoronto.ca/2008/2008declaration1115.html (Retrieved, January 15, 2013).

GAO (United States Government Accountability Office) (2011). *Financial markets and institutions: Securities fraud liability of secondary actors*. GAO-11-664.

Gavras, P. (2012). Ratings. *Finance & Development*, 49 (1), 34–37.

Ghauri, P. (2004). Designing and conducting case studies in international business research. In Piekkari, R. and Welch, C., *Handbook of qualitative research methods for international business*, Cheltenham, UK: Edward Elgar Publishing, 109–124.

Gennaioli, N., Shleifer, A., and Vishny, R. (2012). Neglected risks, financial innovation, and financial fragility. *Journal of Financial Economics*, 104(3), 452–468.

Gibbs, G. R. (2008). *Analyzing qualitative data*. Thousand Oaks, CA: SAGE Publications.

Gibson, M. (2004). Understanding the risk of synthetic CDOs. *FEDS Working Paper* No. 2004-36. URL: http://www.curacao-law.com/wp-content/uploads/2008/10/federal-reserve-cdo-analysis-2004.pdf (Retrieved April 23, 2013).

Gill, I. S.; Raiser, M. (2013). Country benchmarks. (Vol. 3) *Golden growth: restoring the luster of the European economic model*. Washington DC: World Bank. URL: http://documents.worldbank.org/curated/en/2013/01/18515860/golden-growth-restoring-lustre-european-economic-model-vol-3-3 (Retrieved March 8, 2013).

Gill, P. et al. (2008). Methods of data collection in qualitative research: interviews and focus groups. *British dental journal*, 204(6), 291–295.

Glaser, B. G. and Strauss, A. (1998). *Grounded Theory. Strategien qualitativer Forschung*. Bern: Huber.

Goldsmith-Pinkham, P. and Yorulmazer, T. (2010). Liquidity, bank runs, and bailouts: spillover effects during the Northern Rock episode. *Journal of Financial Services Research*, 37(2–3), 83–98.

Goldstein, M. (2008). Bear Stearns' big bailout. *Bloomberg BusinessWeek* March 14, 2008. URL: http://www.businessweek.com/stories/2008-03-14/bear-stearns-big-bailoutbusinessweek-business-news-stock-market-and-financial-advice (Retrieved August 6, 2012).

Goodhart, C. et al. (1998). *Financial regulation: why, how and where now?* Oxon, UK: Routledge.

Goodhart, C. A. (2008). The background to the 2007 financial crisis. *International Economics and Economic Policy*, 4(4), 331–346.

Gopalan, R., Song, F., and Yerramilli, V. (2009). Do credit rating agencies underestimate liquidity risk? *Working paper*, SSRN eLibrary 2009, Washington University, 1–35. URL: http://ssrn.com/abstract=1495849 (Retrieved April 23, 2013).

Gordon, R.A. (1948). Short-period price determination in theory and practice. *The American Economic Review*, 38(3), 265–288.

Gotham, K. F. (2009). Creating liquidity out of spatial fixity: the secondary circuit of capital and the subprime mortgage crisis. *International Journal of Urban and Regional Research*, 33(2), 355–371.

Govtrack.us (Database of Federal Legislation) (n. d.). S3850 (109th): *Credit Rating Agencies Reform Act of 2006*. URL: https://www.govtrack.us/congress/bills/109/s3850 (Retrieved June 10, 2012).

Gras, I. (2003). The Power to Rate. Eine Untersuchung zur Rolle der Ratingagenturen auf den internationalen Finanzmärkten. Research Group on Equity Market Regulation (Ed.), *REGEM Analysis* No. 6, May 2003, Trier University.

Gray, D. F. (2009). Modeling financial crises and sovereign risks. *Annual Review of Financial Economics*, 1(1), 117–144.

Gregory, J. (2010). *Counterparty credit risk: the new challenge for global financial markets*. Chichester: John Wiley & Sons.

Greenspan, A. (2004). Risk and uncertainty in monetary policy. *The American Economic Review*, 94(2), 33–40.

Grewal, R. (2012). Canadian regulators adopt new requirements for credit rating agencies. *Canadian Securities Law*, Stikeman Elliott, April 18, 2012, URL: http://www.canadiansecuritieslaw.com/2012/04/articles/securities-law-compliance/canadian-regulators-adopt-new-requirements-for-credit-rating-agencies/print.html (Retrieved February 20, 2013).

Griffin, J. M., Nickerson, J., and Tang, D.Y. (2013). Rating shopping or catering? An examination of the response to competitive pressure for CDO credit ratings. *Review of Financial Studies*, 26(9), 2270–2310.

Guegan, D. and Houdain, J. (2005). *Collateralized debt obligations pricing and actor models: a new methodology using normal inverse Gaussian distributions*. URL: http://papers.ssrn.com/sol3/papers.cfm?abstract_id=900543 (Retrieved April 5, 2012).

Güttler, A., and Wahrenburg, M. (2007). The adjustment of credit ratings in advance of defaults. *Journal of Banking & Finance*, 31(3), 751–767.

Gupta, V., Mittal, R. K., and Bhalla, V. K. (2010). Role of the credit rating agencies in the fiancial market crisis. *Journal of Development and Agricultural Economics*, 2(7), 268–276.

Haar, B. (2013). Civil liability of credit rating agencies after CRA 3- regulatory all-or-nothing approaches between immunity and over-deterrence. *University of Oslo Faculty of Law Research Paper*, (2013–02).

Hall, R. E. (1988). The relation between price and marginal cost in U.S. industry, *Journal of Political Economy*, 96(5), 921–947.

Han, S. H. et al., (2009). Market segmentation effects in corporate credit rating changes: the case of emerging markets. *Journal of Financial Services Research*, 35(2), 141–166.

Harper, S. (2011). Credit rating agencies deserve credit for the 2007–2008 financial crisis: an analysis of CRA liability following the enhancement of the Dodd-Frank Act. *Washington and Lee Law Review*, 68(4), 1925–1972.

Harris, L. (1988). The dangers of regulatory overreaction to the October 1987 crash. *Cornell Law Review*, 74, 927–942.

Harris, L. (2002). *Trading and exchanges: market microstructure for practitioners*. Oxford: Oxford University Press.

Harris, J. M. and Spivey, M. F. (1990). Systematic pricing during the stock crash: assessing market efficiency. *Journal of Business Research*, 21(1), 59–68.

Hassairi, S.A. and Kahn, H. (2011). Herd behaviour and market Stress: the case of four European countries. *Journal of International Buisiness Research*, 4(3), 53–67.

Hassan, M. and Kalhoefer, C. (2011). Regulation of credit rating agencies – evidence from recent crisis. *Working Paper* No. 26, German University in Cairo, Faculty of Management Technology, 1–13. URL: http://mgt.guc.edu.eg/wpapers/026hassan_kalhoefer2011.pdf (Retrieved May 18, 2013).

Hau, H., Langfield, S. and Marques-Ibanez, D. (2012). Bank ratings: what determines their quality? *Working Paper Series* No. 1484, European Central Bank.

Hauptman, M. and Roper, B. (2014). *Re: File Number S7-18-11, Request for re-proposal to Nationally Recognized Statistical Rating Organizations.* To: Elisabeth M. Murphy, Secretary, Securities and Exchange Commission, March 3, 2014.

Håverstad, B. (2010). *Unsecured money market risk premium and the financial crisis: An econometric study of influential factors.* Master thesis, University of Oslo (UiO) 2008–2010.

Hay, C. (2010). The political economy of price and status formation in the Bordeaux en primeur market: the role of wine critics as rating agencies. *Socio-Economic Review*, 8(4), 685–707.

Hayek, F. V. (1940). Socialist calculation: the competitive solution. *Economica, New Series*, 7(26), 125–149.

Healy, P. M. and Palepu, K. G. (2001). Information asymmetry, corporate disclosure, and the capital markets: a review of the empirical disclosure literature. *Journal of Accounting and Economics*, 31(1–3), 405–440.

He, J., Qian, J. and Strahan, P. E. (2012). Are all ratings dreated equal? The impact of issuer size on the pricing of mortgage-backed securities. *Journal of Finance*, 67(6), 2097–2137.

Heinke, V. G. and Steiner, M. (2007). Rating aus Sicht der modernen Finanzierungs-theorie. In Büschgen, H. E. and Everling, O. (Eds.): *Handbuch Rating* (2nd edition). Wiesbaden: Gabler Verlag, 655–708.

Helleiner, E. (1995). Explaining the globalization of financial markets: bringing states back in. *Review of International Political Economy*, 2(2), 315–341.

Helleiner, E. (2009). Die Finanzkrise und ihre Reaktionen–was bisher geschah. Fünf Ansätze auf der Suche nach einem Ergebnis. *Internationale Politikanalyse*. Berlin: Friedrich Ebert Stiftung.

Helleiner, E. (2011). Understanding the 2007–2008 global financial crisis: lessons for scholars of international political economy. *Annual Review of Political Science*, 14, 67–87.

Hendershott, T. J., Namvar, E., and Phillips, B. (2011). The intended and collateral effects of short-sale bans as a regulatory tool. *Journal of Investment Management*, 11(3), 5–13.

Herring, R. J. and Kane, E. J. (2009). Financial economists roundtable statement on reforming the role of the rating 'agencies' in the securitization process. *Journal of Applied Corporate Finance*, 21(1), 28–33.

Hess, A. C. and Frost, P. A. (2012). Tests for price effects of new issues of seasoned securities. *The Journal of Finance*, 37(1), 11–25.

Hicks, J. R. (1946). *Utility and preference. Value and capital* (2nd ed.). Oxford: The Clarendon Press.

Hill, St. (2011). Happy 2011: Europe's year of reining in the banks. *Social Europe Journal*. URL: http://www.social-europe.eu/2011/01/happy-2011-europes-year-of-reining-in-the-banks/ (Retrieved April 12, 2014).

Hiss, S. and Rona-Tas, A. (2010). Preis Werte Gesellschaft: Ratingagenturen als Marktmacher. In Soeffner. H.-G. (Ed.) *Transnationale Vergesellschaftungen. Verhandlungen des 35. Kongress der Deutschen Gewellschaft für Soziologie in Frankfurt am Main 2010*. Wiesbaden: Springer VS, CD-ROM.

Hiss, S. and Rona-Tas, A. (2011). Wie entstehen Preise? Zur Lösung des Bewertungsproblems auf dem Markt für Ratingurteile strukturierter Finanzprodukte. *Berliner Journal für Soziologie*, 21, 469–494.

HLCCFM, High Level Coordination Committee on Financial Markets (2009), *Report of the Committee on comprehensive regulation for credit rating agencies.*

Hochberg, M. (2010). *How regulatory arbitrage contributed to the financial crisis of 2007–2009; and how we can prevent regulatory avoidance in the financial services sector going forward.* (Doctoral dissertation, University of Toronto).

Holmquist, J. (2007). *Implementation of Basel II: challenges and opportunities*, [Speech]. Institute of International Bankers, March 5, 2007.

Holthausen, R. W. and Leftwich, R. W. (1986). The effect of bond rating changes on common stock prices. *Journal of Financial Economics*, 17(1), 57–89.

Holtmann, C. and Neumann, D. (2003). Market and firm–two sides of a coin. In Lechner, U. (Ed.) *Proceedings of the Tenth Research Symposium on Emerging Electronic Markets* (RSEEM 2003). A Research Agenda for Emerging Electronic Markets, Bremen, 79–91.

Hooper, V., Hume, T., and Kim, S.-J. (2008). Sovereign rating changes – do they provide new information for stock markets? *Economic Systems*, 32(2), 142–166.

Host, A., Cvečić, I., and Zaninović, V. (2012). Credit rating agencies and their impact on spreading the financial crisis on the Eurozone. *Ekonomska misao i praksa: časopis Sveučilista u Dubrovniku.* XXI (2012), 2, 639–657.

House of Lords (2009). *The future of EU financial regulation and supervision.* The European Union Committee of the House of Lords, 14th Report of Session 2008–09, Volume I: Report.

Hu, J. (2007). Assessing the credit risk of CDOs backed by structured finance securities: rating analysts' challenges and solutions. *Working Papers*, Moody's Investors' Service. URL: http://www.ssrn.com/abstract=1011184 (Retrieved March 18, 2012).

Hu, J. C. (2011). *Asset securitization: theory and practice*, No. 679. Singapore: John Wiley & Sons.

Huber, E., Rueschemeyer, D., and Stephens, J. D. (1999). The paradoxes of contemporary democracy: formal, participatory, and social dimensions. In Anderson, L. (Ed.) *Transitions to democracy*, New York/Chichester: Columbia University Press, 168–192.

Hume, Tim (2013). Hong Kong-based credit rating agency launched to challenge the 'Big Three". *CNN Online*, June 25. URL: http://edition.cnn.com/2013/06/25/business/universal-credit-rating-group/index.html (Retrieved July 28, 2013).

Hunt, J. P. (2009). Credit rating agencies and the 'worldwide credit crisis': The limits of reputation, the insufficiency of reform, and a proposal for improvement. *Columbia Business Law Review*, 1, 109–209.

IMF International Monetary Fund (2010). The uses and abuses of sovereign credit ratings. In IMF (Ed.), *Global financial stability report, sovereigns, funding, and systemic liquidity*, October 2010, Chapter 3. Washington, D.C.: IMF, 85–122.

IMF International Monetary Fund (2008). Containing systemic risks and restoring financial soundness. *Global financial stability report*, Washington D.C., April 2008.

Immergluck, D. (2009). *Foreclosed: High-risk lending, deregulation, and the undermining of America's mortgage market.* Ithaca, NY: Cornell University Press.

IOSCO, International Organization of Securities Commissions (2008a). *The role of rating agencies in structured finance markets. Final report.* Technical Committee of the International Organization of Securities Commissions, May 2008.

IOSCO, International Organization of Securities Commissions (2008b). *Code of Conduct Fundamentals for credit Rating Agencies, revised May 2008.* The Technical Committee (Ed.), Madrid: IOSCO.

IOSCO, International Organization of Securities Commissions (2008c). *IOSCO to implement changes to Code of Conduct for Credit Rating Agencies*. Media Release IOSCO/MR/006/2008, May 28, 2008.

IOSCO (2013a). *The role of credit rating agencies in structured finance markets, final report*. Technical Committee of the International Organization of Securities Commissions. May 2008.

IOSCO, (2013b). *IOSCO to implement changes to Code of Conduct for Credit Rating Agencies*, Media Release, IOSCO/MR/006/2008, Paris, May 28, 2008.

Issing-Committee (IMF) (2008). New Financial Order: Recommendations by the Issing Commitee, Part 1 (October 2008) Preparing G 20 – Washington D.C., November 15, 2008, *White Paper No. 1*.

Ivashina, V. and Scharfstein, D. (2010). Bank lending during the financial crisis of 2008. *Journal of Financial Economics*, 97(3), 319–338.

Jain, T. and Sharma, R. (2008). Credit rating agencies in India: a case of authority without responsibility. *Company Law Journal*, 3, 89–109.

Jareño, F. and Tolentino, M. (2012). A brief review of the US financial crisis origin. *American Journal of Scientific Research*, (74), 51–57.

Jarobe, K. P. and Ellis, I. (2010). Intangible assets: innovative financing for innovation. *Issues in Science and Technology*, 26(2), 75–80.

Jarrow, R. A. (2012). The Role of ABS, CDS, and CDOs in the credit crisis and the economy. Russell Sage Foundation, *Conference on the economic lessons from the finanical crisis on April 13, 2012, Session Two: Rethinking Financial Innovation*. (The Princeton Club, New York), 1–29. URL: http://www.russellsage.org/sites/all/files/Rethinking-Finance/Jarrow%20ABS%20CDS%20CDO%202.pdf (Retrieved May 23, 2013).

Jensen, M.C. (1978). Some anoumalous evidence regarding market efficiency. *Journal of Financial Economics*, 6(2–3), 95–101.

Jeon, B. N. and Chiang, T. C. (1991). A system of stock prices in world stock exchanges: common stochastic trends for 1975–1990. *Journal of Economics and Business*, 43(4), 329–338.

Jeon, D. S. and Lovo, S. (2013). Credit rating industry: a helicopter tour of stylized facts and recent theories. *Working Papers*, No. IDEI-762. Toulouse School of Economics.

Jianzhong, G. (2011). *The aurora of international credit rating systems reform – commemorating the First Anniversary of President Hu's Statement on International Rating System Reform*. URL: http://en.dagongcredit.com/content/details20_5002.html (Retrieved September 9, 2012).

Jickling, M. (2009). *Causes of the financial crisis. CRS Report for* Congress, Congressional Research Service, 7–5700, January 1, 2009.

Jones, C. I. (2009). *The global financial crisis: overview. A supplement to macroeconomics.* (W. W. Norton, 2008) May 22, 2009, URL: http://www2.econ.iastate.edu/classes/econ502/tesfatsion/globalfinancialcrisisoverview.2009.cjones.pdf (Retrieved July 15, 2012).

Jorge, J. (2012). Endogenous Credit Ratings. URL: http://cefup.fep.up.pt/uploads/wip%20seminars/2012/Paper_Jose%20Jorge_13.04.2012.pdf (Retrieved October 3, 2013).

Jorion, P. (2009). Risk management lessons from the credit crisis. *European Financial Management*, 15(5), 923–933.

Joynt, S. (2009a). *Statement of Stephen W. Joynt (President and Chief Executive Officer Fitch Ratings) before the hearing of the United States Senate, Committee on Banking, Housing, and Urban Affairs on examining proposals to enhance the regulation of credit rating Agencies*, August 5, 2009.

Joynt, S. (2009b). *Prepared Statement of Stephen W. Joynt (President and Chief Executive Officer Fitch, Inc.) before a hearing of the Subcommittee on Capital Markets, Insurance, and Government Sponsored Enterprises, Committee on Financial Services, United States House of Repesentatives on "Reforming Credit Rating Agencies"* September 30, 2009.

Kabahar, A. and Gambel, R. (2005). *FitchRatings – CDOpinions. A bi-weekly market update from Fitch's Global CDO Group.*

Kadish, S. H. (1963). Some observations on the use of criminal sanctions in enforcing economic regulations. *The University of Chicago Law Review*, 30(3), 423–449.

Kahn, G.A. (1984). Theories of price determination. *Economic Review*. Federal Reserve Bank of Kansas City, April 1984, 16–27.

Kamin, S. B. and DeMarco, L. P. (2012). How did a domestic housing slump turn into a global financial crisis? *Journal of International Money and Finance*, 31(1), 10–41.

Kambil, A. and Van Heck, E. (1998), Reengineering the Dutch flower auctions: a framework for analyzing exchange organizations. *Information Systems Research*, 9 (1), 1–19.

Kanef, M. (2007). *Testimony of Michael Kanef, Group Managing Director Moody's Investors Service, before the United States Senate Committee on Banking, Housing and Urban Affairs*, September 26, 2007.

Karpik, L. (1999). *French lawyers: a study in collective action, 1274 to 1994.* Oxford: Oxford University Press.

Karpik, L. (2000). Le Guide rouge Michelin. *Sociologie du travail*, 42(3), 369–389.

Karpik, L. (2010). *Valuing the unique: the economics of singularities.* Princeton, NJ: Princeton University Press.

Katz, J., Salinas, E. and Stephanou, C. (2009). Credit rating agencies, no easy regulatory solution. *Crisis response*. Washington, D.C.: The World Bank.

Kemmer, M. (2011). Do we really need a European credit rating agency? *defacto*, Association of German Banks, April, 1–4.

Keogh, M. (2013). *Re. Discussion paper on CRA3 implementation. Letter to the ESMA, submitted online: www.esma.europe.eu. October 9, 2013*. URL: http://www.esma.europa.eu%2Fsystem%2Ffiles%2Fdbrs_response_to_esma_discussion_paper_-_october_9_2013_1.pdf&ei=JrVXU-i-EueS7Qaf_4H4Cg&usg=AFQjCNGkXwGtlGDLjM2kL136MMNLT8d3LA&sig2=OoaZfzYkwNrpyd8e37ACxw (Retrieved April 7, 2014).

Kerwer, D. (2001). Standardizing as governance: the case of credit rating agencies. *Reprints aus der Max-Planck-Projektgruppe Recht der Gemeinschaftsgüter*, Nr. 2001/3.

Kerwer, D. (2005). Holding global regulators accountable: the case of credit rating agencies. *Governance*, 18(3), 453–475.

Kettering, K.C. (2008). Securitization and its discontents: the dynamics of financial product development. *Cardozo Law Review*, 29, 1553–1728.

Key, R. and Key, A.R. (2005), *TND Design Rating Standards. Version 2.2.* http://www.google.de/url?sa=t&rct=j&q=&esrc=s&frm=1&source=web&cd=1&ved=0CCwQFjAA&url=http%3A%2F%2Fwww.epa.gov%2Fdced%2Fscorecards%2FTND_Design_Rating_Standards_2.2.pdf&ei=ODtvU9_ZNrGv7Aa0-oDwDA&usg=AFQjCNGnWuvvq4j8T197NFFaK23Nb4PtBQ&sig2=cMo2ibyqk_aRMHMVENkOYQ&bvm=bv.66330100,d.bGE (Retrieved November 26, 2012).

Khadem, V. and Parisi, F. (2007). Residential mortgage-backed securities. In De Servigny, A. and Jobst, N. (Ed.), *The handbook of structured finance*. New York: McGraw-Hill, 543–592.

Kim, S. (2012). Structured finance deals: a review of the rating process and recent evidence thereof. *Working Paper Series*, Santa Clara University. URL: http://papers.ssrn.com/sol3/papers.cfm?abstract_id=2142061 (RetrievedNovember05, 2012).

Kirshner, J. (2013), The Indian anomaly: rethinking credit rating agency regulation from the economic perspective of Hyman Minsky. *CRP Working Paper Series*, No. 9.

Klenke, K. (2008). *Qualitative research in the study of leadership*. Bingley (UK): Emerald Group Publishing.

Knight, F. H. (2006). *Risk, uncertainty and profit*. Mineola, NY: Dover publications.

Knight, M. (1998). Developing countries and the globalization of financial markets. *World Development*, 26(7), 1185–1200.

Kolchinsky, E. (2010). *Statement and Testimony by Eric Kolchinsky – Before the Financial Crisis Inquiry Commission, June 2, 2010.*

Kopecki, D. (2010) 'Fannie, Freddie 'insolvent' after losses, Poole says' (Update 1). *Bloomberg News*, July 10, 2010. URL: http://www.bloomberg.com/apps/news?pid=newsarchive&sid=as4DEc5UFopA (Retrieved August 5, 2012).

Kortian, T. (1995). Modern approaches to asset price formation: a survey of recent theoretical literature. *Research Discussion Paper*, Reserve Bank of Australia, WP 9501. URL: http://citeseerx.ist.psu.edu/viewdoc/download?doi=10.1.1.201.416&rep=rep1&type=pdf (Retrieved April 26, 2013).

Kotecha, M., Ryan, S., and Weinberger, R. (2010). The future of structured finance ratings after the financial crisis. *Journal of Structured Finance*, 15(4), 67–74.

Kovanis, M. and Kvalem A.T. (2010). Basel III: A global regulatory framework for more resilient banks and banking systems. *University of Gothenburg Working Paper*, November, 19, 2010.

Krahnen, J. P. and Wilde, C. (2008). Risk transfer with CDOs and systemic risk in banking. *CEPR Discussion Paper Series*, No. 5618.

Kräussl, R. (2003). Do changes in sovereign credit ratings contribute to financial contagion in emerging market crises? Center for Financial Studies, *Working Paper*. No. 22. URL: http://papers.ssrn.com/sol3/papers.cfm?abstract_id=473262 (Retrieved January 30, 2012).

Kräussl, R. (2005). Do credit rating agencies add to the dynamics of emerging market crises? *Journal of Financial Stability*, 1(3), 355–385.

Krebs, J. D. (2009). The rating agencies: where we have been and where do we go from here? *The Journal of Business Entrepreneurship & the Law*, 3(1), 133–164.

Krebsz, M. (2011). *Securitization and structured finance post credit crunch: a best practice deal lifecycle guide*. Chichester: John Wiley & Sons.

Krainer, R. E. (2012). Regulating Wall Street: the Dodd–Frank Act and the new architecture of global finance, a review. *Journal of Financial Stability*, 8(2), 121–133.

Lander, G. H. et al. (2009). Subprime mortgage tremors: an international issue. *International Advances in Economic Research*, 15(1), 1–16.

Lange, O. (1936). On the economic theory of socialism: part one. *The Review of Economic Studies*, 4(1), 53–71.

Langley, P. (2009). *The everyday life of global finance. Saving and borrowing in Anglo-America*. Oxford: Oxford University Press.

Langley, P. (2008). *Financializaton and the consumer credit boom*. Draft paper, Newcastle-upon-Tyne, Northumbria University.

Langohr, H. and Langohr, P. (2008). *The rating agencies and their credit ratings: what they are, how hey work, and why they are relevant*. Wiley Finance Series 661. Chishester: John Wiley & Sons.

Lapanan, N. and Anchev, S. (2011). *Wealth effects from asset securitization: (the case of Australia)*. Umeå University. URL: http://www.essays.se/essay/84cbb8ea05/ (Retrieved February, 19, 2012).

Lastra, R. M. (2003). The governance structure for financial regulation and supervision in Europe. *Columbia Journal of European Law*, 10, 49–68.

Laux, C. and Leuz, C. (2009). The crisis of fair value accounting: making sense of the recent debate. *Working Paper* No. 33, Chicago Booth. The Initiative on Global Markets.

Lee, H. Y., Mande, V., and Son, M. (2009). The effect of the Private Securities Litigation Reform Act of 1995 on the cost of equity capital. *Quarterly Journal of Finance and Accounting*, 48(2), 85–106.

Lee, J., Naranjo, A. and Sirmans, S. (forthcoming). The exodus from sovereign risk: Sovereign ceiling violations in credit default swap markets. *Journal of Finance forthcoming*. (Working paper version, (2013)), URL: http://papers.ssrn.com/sol3/papers.cfm?abstract_id=2237913 (Retrieved, March 6, 2014).

LeRoy, S. F. (1976). Efficient capital markets: comment. *Journal of Finance*, 31(1), 139–141.

Leuthold, R. M. (1972). Random walk and price trends: the live cattle futures market. *The Journal of Finance*, 27(4), 879–889.

Levich, R. M., Majnoni, G., and Reinhart, C. M. (2002). *Ratings, rating agencies and the global financial system*. Berlin: Springer.

Levy, H., Levy, M., and Solomon, S. (2000). *Microscopic simulation of financial markets: from investor behavior to market phenomena*. San Diego: Academic Press.

Levine Coburn Report (2011). *Wall Street and the financial crisis: anatomy of a financial collapse*. Majority and Minority Staff Report. Permanent Subcommittee on Investigations, United States Senate.

Levine, R. (2012). The governance of financial regulation: reform lessons from the recent crisis. *International Review of Finance*, 12(1), 39–56.

Lillo, F., Farmer, J. D., and Mantegna, R. N. (2003). Econophysics: master curve for price-impact function. *Nature*, 421(6919), 129–130.

Lincoln, Y. S. and Guba, E. G. (1985). *Naturalistic inquiry*. Newbury Park, CA: SAGE Publications.

Linsmeier, T. J. et al. (2002). The effect of mandated market risk disclosures on trading volume sensitivity to interest rate, exchange rate, and commodity price movements. *The Accounting Review*, 77(2), 343–377.

Lipszyc, D. (2009). *Credit Rating Agencies and conflicts of interest: comparative study of the post-crisis regulatory reforms.* Thesis. Université Paris 1 – Panthéon-Sor bonne, 1–54.

Lipton, A. and Rennie, A. (2013). *The Oxford handbook of credit derivatives.* Oxford: Oxford University Press.

Litan, R. E. (2008). Only if they become less opaque. In: Do the credit rating agencies deserve to exist? *The International Economy*, fall 2008, Washington, D.C.: The Magazine of International Economy Policy, 14.

Llewellyn, D. T. (2009). The Northern Rock crisis: a multidimensional problem waiting to happen. In Bliss, R.R. and Kaufman, G.G. (Eds.) *Financial institutions and markets: 2007–2008 – the year of crisis.* New York: Palgrave MacMillan, 101–130.

Lo, A. W. (2004). The adaptive markets hypothesis: market efficiency from an evolutionary perspective. *Journal of Portfolio Management*, 30th Anniversary, 30(5), 15–29.

Löffler, G. (2004). Ratings versus market-based measures of default risk in portfolio governance. *Journal of Banking and Finance*, 28, 2715–2754.

Longstaff, F. A. (2010). The subprime credit crisis and contagion in financial markets. *Journal of Financial Economics*, 97(3), 436–450.

Lugo, S. (2013). The grasshopper and the grasshopper: credit rating agencies incentives: regulatory use of ratings and the subprime crisis'. Financial Globalization and Sustainable Finance: *Implications for Policy and Practice, Conference & Special Edition of the Journal of Banking and Finance*, South Africa, May 29–31, 2013.

Lupica, L. R. (2009). Credit rating agencies, structured securities, and the way out of the abyss. *Review Banking & Finance Law*, 28, 639–674.

Lütz, S. (2002). *Der Staat und die Globalisierung von Finanzmärkten.* Frankfurt am Main: Campus-Verlag.

Lynch, T. E. (2010). Deeply and persistently conflicted: credit rating agencies in the current regulatory environment. *Indiana Legal Studies Research Paper* No. 133. URL: http://dx.doi.org/10.2139/ssrn.1374907 (Retrieved April 22, 2013).

MacKenzie, D. (2011). The credit crisis as a problem in the sociology of knowledge, *American Journal of Sociology*, 116(6), 1778–1841.

MacKenzie, D., Muniesa, F. and Siu, L. (2007). *Do economists make markets? On the performativity of economics.* Princeton: Princeton University Press.

MacKenzie, D. and Millo, Y. (2003). Constructing a market, performing theory: the historical sociology of a financial derivatives exchange. *American Journal of Sociology*, 109(1), 107–145.

Malkiel, B. G. (2003). The efficient market hypothesis and its critics. *The Journal of Economic Perspectives*, 17(1), 59–82.

Manaigo-Vekil, A. (2012). The regulation of credit rating agencies in Europe and ESMA's supvervisiory power. *The Columbia Journal of European Law Online*, 18, 33–45. URL: http://www.cjel.net/online/the-regulation-of-credit-rating-agencies-in-europe-and-esma%E2%80%99s-supervisory-power/ (Retrieved August 3, 2013).

Manicas, P. T. (2007). Endogenous growth theroy: the most recent "revolution" in economics?. *Postautistic economic review*, 41, 39–53.

Marshall, J. (2009). The financial crisis in the US: key events, causes and responses. *House of Commons Library Research paper* 09/34, April 22, 2009.

Martin, R. (2011). The local geographies of the financial crisis: from the housing bubble to economic recession and beyond. *Journal of Economic Geography*, 11(4), 587–618.

Martins, J. T. and Nunes, M. B. (2011). A critical discussion on the selection of a data collection technique for an interpretivist grounded theory study: in-depth interviews vs. focus groups. In Ashwin, M (Ed.) *The Proceedings of the 10th European Conference on Research Methodology for Business and Management Studies*. Reading (UK): Academic Conferences Limited, 339–347.

Masciandaro, D. and Pansini, R.V. (2011). Economic crisis: did financial supervision matter? *IMF Working Paper*, International Monetary Fund, WP/11/261.

Masera, R. (2010). Reforming financial systems after the crisis: a comparison of EU and USA. *PSL Quarterly Review*, 63(255), 297–360.

Mason, J. (2004). Semistructured interview. In Lewis-Beck, M., Bryman, A., and Liao, T. (Eds.), *Encyclopedia of social science research methods*. Thousand Oaks, CA: SAGE Publications, 1021–1022.

Masters, B. (2012). Credit rating agencies face new scrutiny. *Financial Times*, July 6, 2012. URL: http://www.ft.com/cms/s/0/3a81d80c-c791-11e1-a850-00144feab49a.html#axzz2K9Ehxgbe (Retrieved January 25, 2013).

Mathis, J., McAndrews, J., and Rochet, J. C. (2009). Rating the raters: are reputation concerns powerful enough to discipline rating agencies? *Journal of Monetary Economics*, 56(5), 657–674.

Matz, L. and Neu, P. (2006). *Liquidity risk measurement and management: a practitioner's guide to global best practices*. Singapore: John Wiley & Sons.

Mayntz, R. (2012). Institutional change in the regulation of financial markets: questions and answers. In Mayntz, R. (Ed.), *Crisis and control.* Frankfurt a.M., Campus: Institutional Change in Financial Market Regulation, 7–27.

McCleskey, S. (2010). *When free markets fail: saving the market when it can't save itself.* Hoboken, NJ: John Wiley & Sons.

McCallum, Bennett T (2001), Indeterminacy, bubbles, and the fiscal theory of price level determination. *Journal of Monetary Economics*, 47(1), 19–30.

McDaniel, R. (2009). *Testimony of Raymond W. McDaniel (CEO and President, Moody's Investors Service) before the United States Securities and Exchange Commission.* Roundtable on Credit Rating Agencies, April 15, 2009.

McDaniel, R. (2010). *Testimony of Raymond W. McDaniel (Chairman and Chief Executive Officer of Moody's Corporation) before the Financial Crisis Inquiry Commission. June 2*, 1–11. URL: http://fcic-static.law.stanford.edu/cdn_media/fcic-testimony/2010-0602-McDaniel.pdf (Retrieved April 23, 2012).

Mengle, D. (2007). Credit derivatives: an overview. *Economic Review*, Q4, 1–24.

Merriam, S. (1995). What can you tell from an N of 1? Issues of validity and reliability in qualitative research. *PAACE Journal of Lifelong Learning*, 4, 50–60.

Micu, M., Remolona, E. M. and Wooldridge, P. D. (2006). The price impact of rating announcements: which announcements matter? *BIS Working Papers*, No. 207.

Miglionico, A. (2012). *Enhancing the regulation of credit rating agencies, in search of a method.* Monograph, July 2012.

Miller, N. (2008). *Reuters response to CESR 'consultation paper on the role of credit rating agencies in structured finance'* (Ref: CESR/08-036). URL: http://www.esma.europa.eu%2Fsystem%2Ffiles%2FMicrosoft_Word___RTRS_to_CESR_re_Credit_Ratings_080331.pdf&ei=GFleU-TpMsiqtAbl84CgBA&usg=AFQjCNGhzzEaydy_0zGjFTvWETyts0v3qw&sig2=KAFnIrAa14TdTOuis1W27Q&bvm=bv.65397613,d.Yms (Retrieved April 7, 2014).

Miller, S. S. (1985). Self-regulation of the securities markets: a Critical Examination. *Washington and Lee Law Review*, 42(3), 853–887.

Min, L. (2012). *Financial regulatory reform: an evolving rebalancing process.* China Banking Regulatory Commission, Shanghai Office, April 18, 2012.

MindfulMoney (2013). *EU completely misses the target on rating agency reform – a Mindful Money view.* January 17, 2013. URL: http://www.mindfulmoney.co.uk/investment-insight/investing-strategy/test14995/ (Retrieved July 24, 2013).

Mitchell, J. (2005). Financial intermediation theory and implications for the sources of value in structured finance markets. *NBB Working Paper* No. 71, National Bank of Belgium.

Mizen, P. (2008). *The credit crunch of 2007–2008: a discussion of the background, market reactions, and policy responses*. Federal Reserve Bank of St. Louis Review, 90(5), 531–567.

Moody's (2005). *Moody's modeling approach to rating structured finance cash flow CDO transactions*. Moody's Investors Service. URL: http://fcic-static.law.stanford.edu/cdn_media/fcic-testimony/2010-0602-exhibit-moody-model.pdf (Retrieved April 28, 2012).

Moody's, (2012a). *Rating symbols and definitions*. URL: https://www.moodys.com/researchdocumentcontentpage.aspx?docid=PBC_79004 (Retrieved, September 18, 2012).

Moody's, (2012b). *Moody's approch to rating asset-backed commercial paper*. Moody's Investors Service. URL: http://www.moodys.com (Retrieved January 14, 2013).

Morgenson, G. (2011). Hey, S.E.C., that escape hatch is still open. *The New York Times*, March 5, 2011. URL: http://www.nytimes.com/2011/03/06/business/06gret.html?_r=0 (Retrieved March 6, 2014).

Morkötter, S. and Westerfeld, S. (2008). Die Geschäftsmodelle von Ratingagenturen im Spannungsfeld einer Principal-Agent-Betrachtung. *Zeitschrift für das gesamte Kreditwesen*, 9, 23–26.

Morse, M. et al. (2008). Verification strategies for establishing reliability and validity in qualitative research. *International journal of qualitative methods*, 1(2), 13–22.

Moshirian, F. (2011). The global financial crisis and the evolution of markets, institutions and regulation. *Journal of Banking & Finance*, 35(3), 502–511.

Mostowfi, M. (2011). Mobilizing structured finance for development – potential welfare benefits and challenges of securitization in large emerging markets', In Köhn, D. (Ed.), *Mobilizing capital for emerging markets*. Chapter 5. Berlin/Heidelberg: Springer, 51–62.

Mu, C. (2013). A different rating. *Global Times*. URL: http://www.globaltimes.cn/content/779927.shtml (Retrieved July 23, 2013).

Mühl, T. (2010). *Haftung für fehlerhafte Ratings*. Berlin: Erich Schmidt.

Mukherjee, S. (2005). *Modern economic theory*. New Delhi: New Age International.

Mullard, M. (2011). Explanations of the financial meltdown and the present recession. *The Political Quarterly*, 82(2), 204–221.

Mullard, M. (2012). The credit rating agencies and their contribution to the financial crisis. *The Political Quarterly*, 83(1), 77–95.

Müller, P., Sauga, M., and Schult, Ch. (2011). Breaking the power of the 'Big Three': German firm wants to set up new rating agency. *Spiegel Online International.* URL: http://www.spiegel.de/international/europe/breaking-the-power-of-the-big-three-german-firm-wants-to-set-up-new-rating-agency-a-773549.html (Retrieved July 28, 2013).

Mulligan, C.B. (2008). Fundamental origins of the housing boom and bust. *CATO Unbound, Response Essay,* December 5, 2008. URL: http://www.cato-unbound.org/2008/12/05/casey-b-mulligan/fundamental-origins-housing-boom-bust (Retrieved April 22, 2013).

Murad, A. (1958). Das Problem der Geldeinheit. *Zeitschrift für die gesamte Staatswissenschaft*, 709–813.

Nagy, T. (2009). Credit rating agencies and the First Amendment: applying Constitutional Journalistic Protections to Subprime Mortgage Litigation. *Minnesota Law Review*, 94, 140–167.

Nayak, S. (2013). *The global financial crisis, genesis, policy response and road ahead.* New Delhi: Springer.

Neisser, H. (1968). Competitive equilibrium: existence and approach. *Journal of Political Economy,* 76(6), 1199–1208.

Nichita, R.-A. (2009). AIG – The strenght to be there… in the middle of the crisis. The story before and after the bailout. *Theoretical and Applied Economics*, 12(541) (supplement), 436–442.

Nijhawan, D. P. and Nijhawan, St.P. (2013). A tale of transition – evolution of credit rating agency industry amidst a decade of crisis. *Journal of Indian Research*, 1(4), 60–65.

Norton Rose Fulbright (2014). Civil liability of credit rating agencies. *Banking and finance disputes review*. March 2014, 18–20.

Noyer, Ch., (2009). The future of financial regulation. *Financial Stability Review* No. 13, 1–7, URL: http://www.banque-france.fr/fileadmin/user_upload/banque_de_france/publications/Revue_de_la_stabilite_financiere/etude00_rsf_0909.pdf (Retrieved July 31, 2013).

Nyborg, K. (2000). Homo economicus and homo politicus: interpretation and aggregation of environmental values. *Journal of Economic Behavior & Organization*, 42(3), 305–322.

O'Brien, J. (2010). The future of financial regulation, enhancing integrity through design. *Sydney Law Review*, 32, 63–85.

OCC, Office of the Comptroller of the Currency (1990). *Investment securities: Comptroller's handbook*, Section 203. Comptroller of the Currency. URL: http://www.occ.gov/publications/publications-by-type/comptrollers-hand book/investsecurities1.pdf (Retrieved January 15, 2013).

O'Donnell, J. (2012) 'EU agrees to new controls for credit rating agencies.' *Reuters*, November 27, 2012.: http://fcic-static.law.stanford.edu/cdn_media/fcic-testimony/2010-0602-McDaniel.pdf URL: http://uk.reuters.com/article/2012/11/27/uk-eu-ratings-idUKBRE8AQ18E20121127 (Retrieved January 25, 2013).

OECD (2010). *Hearings competition and credit rating agencies 2010*. URL: http://www.oecd.org%2Fcompetition%2Fsectors%2F46825342.pdf&ei=YlheU6XoBoSWtAbi9YHwBA&usg=AFQjCNElL1TvgUu4m7r6C3dhmaCgHihz1A&sig2=bZsHlP4BWgPqOR4Aje1OAg (Retrieved April 7, 2014).

OECD (2012). Financial contagion in the era of globalised banking? *OECD Economics Department Policy Notes*, No. 14, June 2012.

Omarova, S. T. (2011). From Gramm-Leach-Bliley to Dodd-Frank: the unfulfilled promise of Section 23A of the Federal Reserve Act. *North Carolina Law Review*, 89, 1683–1776.

Orb, A., Eisenhauer, L., and Wynaden, D. (2001). Ethics in qualitative research. *Journal of Nursing Scholarship*, 33(1), 93–96.

Orlowski, L. (2008). Stages of the 2007/2008 Global financial crisis is there a wandering asset-price bubble? *Economics Discussion Paper* No. 2008–43. Cacred Heart University, Halle Institue for Economic Research.

Ory, J. N. and Raimbourg, P. (2008). *Credit rating agencies' function on bond markets: price stability vs. information transmission*. URL: http://www.finance-innovation.org/risk09/work/8292433.pdf (Retrieved April 24, 2012).

Oster, J. (2012). The Commission Proposal to amend the Regulation on Credit Rating Agencies. In: Recent Legal Developments. *Maastricht Journal of European and Comparative Law*, 19(1), 206–211.

Osugi, K. (2007). What is converging-rules on hostile takeovers in Japan and the convergence debate. *APLPJ*, 9, 143.

Owusu-Ansah, Y. (2012). What went wrong? Examining Moody's rated CDO data. *Working Paper Series*, Columbia University, November 12, 2012.

Pacces, A. M. (2010). Uncertainty and the financial crisis. *Journal of Financial Transformation*, 29, 79–93.

Pagano, M. and Volpin, P. (2010). Credit ratings failures and policy options. *Economic Policy*, 25(62), 401–431.

Pagliari, S. (2012). Who governs finance? The shifting public-private divide in the regulation of derivatives, rating agencies and hedge funds. *European Law Journal*, 18(1), 44–61.

Partnoy, F. (1999). The Siskel and Ebert of financial markets: two thumbs down for the credit rating agencies. *Washington University Law Quarterly*, 77(3), 619–712.

Partnoy, F. (2006). How and why credit rating agencies are not like other gatekeepers. *University of San Diego Legal Studies Research Paper Series*. Research Paper No. 07–46, May 2006, 59–102.

Partnoy, F. (2009a). Historical perspectives on the financial crisis: Ivar Krueger, the credit-rating agencies, and two theories about the function, and dysfunction, of markets. *Yale Journal on Regulation*, 26, 431–443.

Partnoy, F. (2009b). Overdependence on credit ratings was a primary cause of the crisis. *Nota di Lavoro* 27.2009, Institutions and Markets Series, Fausto Panunzi (Ed.), 1–25.

Partnoy, F. (2009c). *Rethinking regulation of credit rating agencies: an institutional investor perspective*. Council of Institutional Investors, April 2009.

Patton, M.Q. (2002). *Qualitative evaluation and research methods*. Thousand Oaks, CA: SAGE Publications.

Pattanaik, S. (2009). The global financial stability architecture fails again: subprime crisis lessons for policymakers. *Asian-Pacific Economic Literature*, 23(1), 21–47.

Paul, St. (2012). Banken-, Wirtschafts-, Politikkrise – Wie konnte es wo weit kommen? Hintergründe zur Entstehung von "Bad Banks". In Bolder, M. and Wargers, M. (Eds.), *Modell Bad Bank: Hintergrund-Konzept-Erfahrungen: Ein Praxisbericht zur Arbeit der ersten Abwicklungsanstalt*. Heidelberg: Gabler, 15–32.

Pederzoli, C. and Torricelli, C. (2005). Capital requirements and business cycle regimes: forward-looking modelling of default probabilities. *Journal of Banking & Finance*, 29(12), 3121–3140.

Pezzuto, I. (2012). Miraculous financial engineering or toxic finance? The genesis of the US subprime mortgage loans crisis and its consequences on the global financial markets and real economy. *Journal of Governance and Regulation*, 1(3), 114–125.

Philipose, Mobis (2013). 'Regulators should give less importance to rating agencies', *lievemint & The Wall Street Journal*, April 15, 2013. URL: http://www.livemint.com/Money/NrZTbnMosGthpZnqVFhUoM/Regulators-should-give-less-importance-to-rating-agencies.html (Retrieved July 30, 2013).

Picone, D. (2002). *Collaterelised debt obligations*. City University Business School, London & Royal Bank of Scotland. URL: http://scholar.google.ch/scholar?hl=de&q=picone+collateralized+debt+obligations&btnG=&lr= (Retrieved, July 4, 2012).

Pinches, G. E. and Singleton, J. C. (2012). The adjustment of stock prices to bond rating changes. *Journal of Finance*, 33(1), 29–44.

Pinto, A. R. (2006). Control and responsibility of credit rating agencies in the United States. *American Journal of Comparative Law*, 54, 341–356.

Poole, W. (2010). Causes and consequences of the financial crisis of 2007–2009. *Harvard Journal of Law & Public Policy*, 33, 421–442.

Poon, W. P. H. (2003). Are unsolicited credit ratings biased downward? *Journal of Banking & Finance*, 27(4), 593–614.

Poon, W. P. H. and Firth, M. (2005). Are unsolicited credit ratings lower? International evidence from bank ratings. *Journal of Business Finance & Accounting*, 32 (9–10), 1741–1771.

Poon, W. P. H. and Evans, D. A. (2011). Regulation fair disclosure's effect on the information content of bond fating changes. *European Financial Management*, 19(4), 775–800.

Poon, W. P. H., Chan, K. C., and Firth, M. A. (2013). Does having a credit rating leave less money on the table when raising capital? A study of credit ratings and seasoned equity offerings in China. *Pacific-Basin Finance Journal*, 22, 88–106.

Portes, R. (2008). Ratings agency reform. In Reinhart, C. M. and Felton, A. (Eds.), *The first global financial crisis of the 21st century*. GeCentre for Economic Policy Research, Geneva: VoxEu.org, 145–149.

Pottier, S. W. and Sommer, D. W. (1999). Property-liability insurer financial strength ratings: differences across rating agencies. *Journal of Risk and Insurance*, 621–642.

Preda, A. (2006). Socio-technical agency in financial markets the case of the stock ticker. *Social Studies of Science*, 36(5), 753–782.

Prince, J. T. (2005). Is one rating enough? *The Journal of Structured Finance*, 11(2), 40–43.

PSLRA (1995). *Private Securities Litigation Reform Act of 1995*. URL: http://www.gpo.gov/fdsys/pkg/PLAW-104publ67/html/PLAW-104publ67.htm (Retrieved January 15, 2013).

Quillin, B. (2008). *International financial co-operation: political economics of compliance with the 1988 Basel Accord*. Abingdon: Routledge.

Rachidy, F. (2012). Measuring credit risk within corporate bond index construction. *Financial Times online*, August 10, 2012. URL: http://discussions.ft.com/alchemy/forums/edhec-risk-forum/measuring-credit-risk-within-corporate-bond-index-construction (Retrieved April 5, 2014).

Raynes, S. and Rutledge, A. (2003). *The analysis of structured securities, precise risk measurement and capital allocation*. Oxford: Oxford University Press.

Reckers, H. (2008). Bankenaufsicht und die Rolle von Ratingagenturen. *Die Politische Meinung*, 462, 31–34.

Reinhart, C. M., & Rogoff, K. S. (2010). From financial crash to debt crisis. *National Bureau of Economic Research*, No. 15795.

Reiss, D. J. (2006). Subprime standardization: how rating agencies allow predatory lending to flourish in the secondary mortgage market. *Florida State University Law Review*, 33, 985–1065.

Reiss, D. (2009) Rating agencies and reputational risk. *Journal of Business & Technology Law*, 4(2), 295–299.

Ribstein, L. E. (2003). Bubble laws. *Houston Law Review*, 40, 77–98.

Richardson, M. and White, L. J. (2009). The rating agencies: is regulation the answer? In Acharya, R. and Richardson, M. (Eds.), *Restoring financial stability: how to repair a failed system*. Hoboken, NJ: John Wiley & Sons, 101–116.

RMI, (2010). *A new regulatory framework for credit rating agencies*. URL Online Resource. URL: http://rmi.nus.edu.sg/gcr/files/02%20GCR%20vol%201.pdf (Retrieved January 15, 2013).

RMI, (2011). A New Regulatory Framework for for Credit Rating Agencies. In NUS Risk Management Institue (Ed.) *Global Credit Review*. Singapore: National University of Singapore, 15–31.

Rom, M. C. (2009). The credit rating agencies and the subprime mess: greedy, ignorant, and stressed? *Public Administration Review*, 69(4), 640–650.

Rona-Tas, A. and Hiss, S. (2010). The role of ratings in the subprime mortgage crisis. The art of corporate and the sience of consumer credit rating. In Hirsch, P.M. and Lounsbury, M. (Eds.), *Markets on the trial: the economic sociology of the U.S. financial crisis: part A. Research in the sociology of organizations*, Vol. 30. Bingley (UK): Emerald Group Publishing, 115–155.

Rona-Tas, A. and Hiss, S. (2011). Forecasting as valuation: the role of ratings and predictions in the subprime mortgage crisis in the United States. In Beckert, J. and Aspers, P. (Eds.), *The worth of goods*. Oxford and New York: Oxford University Press, 223–246.

Rosenbaltt, J. and Golvin (2009). Moody's, S&P losse free-speech bid to end fraud suit (Update5). September 3. *Bloomberg*. URL: http://www.bloomberg.com/apps/news?pid=newsarchive&sid=aiyfkkqoy.A8 (Retrieved June 6, 2012).

Rössel, J. and Beckert, J. (2012). Quality classification in competition: price formation in the German wine market. *MPIfG Discussion Paper* 12/3. Cologne: Max-Planck-Institute for the Study of Societies.

Rousseau, S. (2009). Regulating credit rating agencies after the financial crisis: The long and winding road toward accountability. *Capital Markets Institute Research Paper*.

Rousseau, S. (2012). A question of credibility: enhancing the accountability and effectiveness of credit rating agencies. *Institute C.D. Howe Commentary*, No. 356. URL: http://www.cdhowe.org/a-question-of-credibility-enhancing-the-accountability-and-effectiveness-of-credit-rating-agencies/18439 (Retrieved March 7, 2013).

Rowan, M. (2011). *Testimony of Michael Rowan (Managing Director Moody's Investors Service) before the United States House of Representatives, Committee on Financial Services, Subcommittee on Oversight and Investigations, July 27, 2011.*

Royce, E. R. (2009). Approaches to improving rating agency regulation. *Subcommittee on Capital Markets, Insurance, and Governement Sponsored Enterprises of the Committee on Financial Services U.S. House of Representatives,* (111th Ed.), Serial No. 111–33, 1–141.

Roxana, H., Oana, M., and Alexandru, C. (2010). The development and implications of the subprime crisis. *Annals of the University of Oradea, Faculty of Economics*, 1(2), 742–747.

Rajya Sabha (2009). *Global economic crisis and its impact on India*. In Rajya Sabha Secretariat (Ed.). New Delhi: Rajya Sabha.

Ruan, V. (2012). Ratings agencies from China, Russia, and US to take on big three. *South China Morning Post*, October 25, 2012. URL: http://www.scmp.com/business/banking-finance/article/1068900/ratings-agencies-china-russia-and-us-take-big-three (Retrieved, January 30, 2013).

Rudolph, B. (2004). Analyse hybrider Finanzinstrumente: Mezzanine-Kapital. *Zeitschrift für das Gesamte Kreditwesen*, 57(1), 14–18.

Rumelt, R. P. (2003). Towards a strategic theory of the firm. In Foss, N. J. (Ed.), *Resources firms and strategies, a reader in the resource-based perspective*. Oxford: Oxford University Press, 131–145.

Russel, P. S. and Torbey, V. M. (2002). The efficient market hypohesis on trial: a survey. *Business Quest Journal, Section Research*, 1–19. URL: http://www.westga.edu/~bquest/2002/earket.htm (Retrieved December 8, 2010).

Rutledge, A. and Raynes, S. (2010). *The elements of structured finance*. Oxford: Oxford University Press.

Ryan, S. G. (2008). Accounting in and for the subprime crisis. *The Accounting Review*, 83(6), 1605–1638.

Ryan, J. (2012). The negative impact of credit rating agencies and proposals for better regulation. *Stiftung Wissenschaft und Politk (SWP), Working Paper* 1. Research Division EU Integration, German Institute for International and Security Affairs. URL: http://www.swp-berlin.org/fileadmin/contents/products/arbeitspapiere/The_Negative_Impact_of_Credit_Rating_Agencies_KS.pdf (Retrieved January 15, 2013).

Salmon, F. (2011). The difference between S&P and Moody's. *Reuters*, August 9, 2011. URL: http://blogs.reuters.com/felix-salmon/2011/08/09/the-difference-between-sp-and-moodys/ (Retrieved August 30, 2012).

Samolyk, K. (2004). The future of banking in America – the evolving role of commercial banks in US credit markets. *FDIC Banking Review Series*, 16(2), 29–65.

Sandoval, L. and Franca, I. D. P. (2012). Correlation of financial markets in times of crisis. *Physica A: Statistical Mechanics and its Applications*, 391(1–2), 187–208.

Sangiorgi, F., Sokobin, J., and Spatt, C. (2009). Credit-rating shopping, selection and the equilibrium structure of ratings. *NBER Working Paper Series.*

Sangiorgi, F. and Spatt, C. (2011). Opacity, credit rating shopping, and bias. *Working Paper*, Carnegie Mellon Unitersity.

Sato, T., (2009). Global financial crisis – Japan's experience and policy response. *Federal Reserve Bank of San Francisco Proceedings*, 285–289.

Schüler, M. (2008). Measuring risk. *The markit magazine*, Winter 2008. London: Markit Group, 44–48.

Scharfenstein, D. S. and Stein, J. C. (1990). Herd Behaviour and Investment. American Economic Review, 80(3), 465–479.

Schacht, K. N. and Rittenhouse, L. (2008). *Re: Proposed rules for Nationally Recognized Rating Organizations – File No. S7-13-08.* Letter to Nancy M. Morris. Secretary U.S. Securities and Exchange Commission, July 25, 2008. CFA Institute: Center for Financial Market Integrity.

Schätzle, D. (2011). Ratingagenturen in der neoklassischen Finanzierungstheorie – Eine Auswertung empirischer Studien zum Informationsgehalt. *IfG Arbeitspapier*, No. 110.

Schneiberg, M. and Berk, G. (2010). From categorical imperative to learning by categories: cost accounting and new categorical practices in American manufoctoring, 1900–1930. In Hsu, G., Negro, G., and Kocak, Ö. (Eds.), *Categories in markets, origins and evolution. Research in the sociology of organizations, 31*: Bingley (UK): Emeral Group Publishing, 255–292.

Schneider, S., Gräf, B. and Peter, M. (2010). *Homo economicus – or more like Homer Simpson?* Frankfurt am Main: Deutsche Bank Research.

Schwarcz, S. L. (2002). Private ordering of public markets: the rating agency paradox, *University of Illinois Law Review*, 1, 1–27.

Schwarcz, S. L. (2011). Regulating shadow banking. *Review of Banking and Financial Law*, 31(1), 619–642.

Schwartz, A. J. (2009). Origins of the financial market crisis of 2008. *Cato Journal*, 29(1), 19–24.

Schweimayer, G. (2010). Valuation of synthetic and cash CDO in practice and related issues. *Working Paper*. URL: http://www.schweimayer.de/research/BasketCds.pdf (Retrieved April 24, 2014).

SEBI (1999). *Credit Rating Agencies Regulations, 1999*. Securities and Exchange Board of India. URL: http://www.sebi.gov.in/acts/CreditRatingAgencies.pdf (Retrieved February 2, 2013).

SEBI (2010). *Circular: guidelines for credit rating agencies*. Securities and Exchange Board of India. URL: http://www.sebi.gov.in/circulars/2010/cirmirsd06.pdf (Retrieved February 2, 2013).

SEBI (2012). *Name and registered address of credit rating agencies*. Securities and Exchange Board of India. URL: http://www.sebi.gov.in/investor/addcra.html (Retrieved February 2, 2013).

Segal, D. (2009). Debt raters avoid overhaul after crisis. The New York Times De cember 8, 2009. URL: http://www.nytimes.com/2009/12/08/business/08ratings.html&pagewanted=3?_r=0 (Retrieved July 18, 2012).

Seibt, C. H. and Schwarz, S. (2011). European financial market regulation in the wake of the financial crisis: a functional approach. *China EU Law Journal*, 1, 95–118.

SEC (2008a). *SEC approves measures to strengthen oversight of credit rating agencies*. SEC Press Release. URL: http://www.sec.gov/news/press/2008/2008-284.htm (Retrieved June 10, 2012).

SEC (2008b). *Press Release 2008–135. SEC examinations find shortcomings in credit rating agencies practices and disclosure to investors*. Washington, July 8, 2008. URL: http://www.sec.gov/news/press/2008/2008-135.htm (Retrieved June 10, 2012).

SEC (2008c). Summary Report of Issues Idenified in the Commission Staff's Examinations of Selected Credit Rating Agencies by the Staff of the Office of Compliance Inspections and Examinations Devision of Trading and Markets and Office of Economic Analysis. United States Securities And Exchange Commission, July 2008.

SEC (2009). *Credit rating agencies disclosure. Release No.s.33-9070; 34-60797; IC-28942; File No. S7-24-09*. URL: http://www.sec.gov/rules/proposed/2009/33-9070.pdf (Retrieved May 24, 2013).

SEC (2010). Removal from Regulation FD of the exemption for credit rating Agencies. In *SEC Issues Final Rule Release*. Securities and Exchange Commission (Ed.), 17 CFR Part 243, Release Nos. 33–9146; 34–63003; IC-29448; File No. S7-23-10.

SEC (2011a). *2011 Summary Report of Commissions Staff's examinations of each Nationally Recognized Statistical Rating Organization. As Required by Section 15E(p)(3)(C) of the Securities Exchange Act of 1934.*

SEC (2011b). *Regulation of investment advisers by the U.S. Securities and Exchange Commission.* US Securities and Exchange Commission.

SEC (2011c). *17 CFR, Final Rule.* URL: http://www.sec.gov/rules/final/2011/33-9245.pdf (Retrieved January 15, 2013).

SEC (2012a). Report to Congress credit rating standardization study. September 2012. URL: http://www.sec.gov/reportspubs/special-studies/939h_credit_rating_standardization.pdf (Retrieved July 25, 2013).

SEC (2012b). 2012 Summary Report of Commission Staff's Examinations of each Nationally Recognized Statistical Rating Organization. URL: https://www.sec.gov/news/studies/2012/nrsro-summary-report-2012.pdf (Retrieved July 25, 2013).

SEC (2013a). *Securities and Exchange Commission 17 CFR Parts 239, 270 and 274. Release Nos. 33-9506; IC-30847; File No. S7-711.* URL: http://www.sec.gov%2Frules%2Ffinal%2F2013%2F33-9506.pdf&ei=c3pFU-ijJaKN7QbY-oHgBg&usg=AFQjCNHLWeZc7afIQ0oz7Fc0-prOX-6Xkw&sig2=Sc5IyF1pLb5t1zLRv8-mAw (Retrieved March 6, 2014).

SEC (2013b). *SEC removes references to NRSRO ratings in certain rules and forms.* Press Release 2013–274. URL: http://www.sec.gov/News/PressRelease/Detail/PressRelease/1370540564425 (Retrieved 6, March 2014).

SEC (2014). *Credit Rating Agencies.* U.S. Securities and Exchange Commission. URL: https://www.sec.gov/spotlight/dodd-frank/creditratingagencies.shtml (Retrieved March 5, 2014).

Serfling, K. (2007). Möglichkeiten und Grenzen des Credit Ratings. In Büschgen, H. und Everling, O. (Eds.), *Handbuch Rating,* 2nd ed. Deutschland: Gabler, 709–746.

Sève, M. (2009). II–6.8: Credit rating agencies: post-crisis regulatory measures adopted by the European Union regulation of 16 September 2009. *The Journal of Regulation, Regulatory Lawreview* Web Site. URL: http://www.regulatorylawreview.com/II-6-4-Credit-Rating-Agencies-Post.html (Retrieved December 13, 2013).

Sharma, D. (2011a). *Testimony of Deven Sharma, President, Standard & Poor's Before The United States House of Representatives Committee on Financial Services, Subcommittee on Oversight and Investigations.* URL: http://financialservices.house.gov/uploadedfiles/072711sharma.pdf (Retrieved April 23, 2012).

Sharma, D. (2011b). *Credit rating standardization study, Securities Exchange Act of 1934 – Rel. No. 34–63573; File No. 4–622* (December 17, 2010). Letter to

Secretary U.S. Securities and Exchange Commisson Ms. Elizabeth Murphy. Washington, D.C.: SEC.

Sharma, D. (2011c). Policymakers must reduce reliance on credit ratings. *Financial Times*, July 25, 2011.

Shahzad, K. (2013). *Credit rating agencies, financial regulations and the capital markets.* (No. EPS-2013-283-F&A). Erasmus Research Institute of Management (ERIM).

Shari, M. (2012). Politics and the sovereign rating. *Global finance, rating the ratings agencies*, April 2012, 1–6.

Shelby, D. H., and Morgan, R. M. (1996). The resource-advantage theory of competition: dynamics, path dependencies, and evolutionary dimensions. *Journal of Marketing*, 60(4), 107–114.

Sherry, N. (2008). *Improved Australian controls for credit rating agencies and research houses.* Media Release of 13/11/2008 No.077. URL: http://ministers.treasury.gov.au/DisplayDocs.aspx?doc=pressreleases/2008/077.htm&pageID=003&min=njs&Year=&DocType= (Retrieved March 8, 2013).

Shiller, R. J. (2009). *Irrational exuberance.* Princeton, NJ: Princeton University Press.

Shleifer, A. and Vishny, R. B. (2010). Unstable banking. *Journal of Financial Economics*, 97, 306–318.

Siddaiah, T. (2011). *Financial services.* New Delhi: Pearson Education India.

SIFMA (Securities Industry and Financial Makres Association) (2008). *Recommendations of the Securities Industry and Financial Markets Association Credit Rating Agency Task Force.* New York: SIFMA.

SIFMA (2013). *Credit Rating Agencies Resource Center.* URL: https://www.sifma.org/issues/regulatory-reform/credit-rating-agencies/overview/ (Retrieved December 13, 2013).

Sinclair, T.J. (1994). Between state and market: hegemony and institutions of collective action under conditions of international capital mobility. *Policy Sciences*, 27(4), 447–466.

Sinclair, T. J. (2001). The Infrastructure of global governance: quasi-regulatory mechanisms and the new global finance. *Global Governance*, 7(4), 41–551.

Sinclair, T. J. (2005). *The new masters of capital: American bond rating agencies and the politics of creditworthiness.* Ithaca, NY: Cornell University Press.

Sinclair, T. (2011). Im Inneren der Weltfinanzkrise: Eine kritische Analyse zum Problem des Interessenkonflikts. In Kessler, O. (Ed.). *Die Internationale Politische Ökonomie der Weltfinanzkrise.* Deutschland: VS Verlag für Sozialwissenschaften, 183–197.

Sinkovics, R. R , Penz, E., and Ghauri, P. N. (2008). Enhancing the trustworthiness of qualitative research in international business. *Management International Review*, 48(6), 689–714.

Skreta, V. and Veldkamp, L. (2009). Ratings shopping and asset complexity: a theory of ratings inflation. *Journal of Monetary Economics*, 56(5), 678–695.

Skreta, V. and Veldkamp, L. (2010). Did asset complexity trigger ratings fias? In Kolb, R. (Ed.), *Lessons from the financial crisis: causes, consequences, and our economic future*. Hoboken, NJ: John Wiley & Sons.

Smith, E. B. (2008). 'Race to bottom' at Moody's, S&P secured subprime's boom, Bust. *Bloomberg*, URL: http://www.bloomberg.com/apps/news?pid=newsarchive&sid=ax3vfya_Vtdo (Retrieved June 12, 2012).

Smith, N. (1979). Toward a theory of gentrification a back to the city movement by capital, not people. *Journal of the American Planning Association*, 45(4), 538–548.

Smith, V. L., Suchanek, G. L., and Williams, A. W. (1988). Bubbles, crashes, and endogenous expectations in experimental spot asset markets. *Econometrica, Journal of the Econometric Society*, 56(5), 1119–1151.

Snower, Dennis (2011). Snower: a European Rating Agency would not resolve the rating agency problem, in Kiel Institute for the World Economic (ed.) *Press Release:* Kiel. URL: http://www.ifw-kiel.de/media/press-releases/2011/snower-a-european-rating-agency-would-not-resolve-the-rating-agency-problem/view?set_language=en (Retrieved July 28, 2013).

Solomon, D. (2012). The rise of a giant: securitization and the global financial drisis. *American Business Law Journal*, 49(4), 859–890.

Sorkin, A. R. and Thomas Jr., L. (2008). JPMorgan acts to buy ailing Bear Stearns at huge discount. *The New York Times*, March 16, 2008. URL: http://www.nytimes.com/2008/03/16/business/16cnd-bear.html (Retrieved July 15, 2012).

Spence, A. M. (2009). The financial and economic crisis and the developing world. *Journal of Policy Modeling*, 31, 502–508.

Standard & Poor's (1999). *Structured finance. Global CBO/CLO criteria*. URL: http://www.stern.nyu.edu%2F~igiddy%2FABS%2Fglobalcboclo.pdf&ei=eKpnU5tLybDsBqehgMAN&usg=AFQjCNHrtyiALy_LkuyC2-GTZpqT_DWZ4w&sig2=l_0PKXQGh4wuJEtArhKW-Q&bvm=bv.65788261,d.bGE (Retrieved June 17, 2013).

Standard & Poor's (2007). *Structured finance commentary. The fundamentals of structured finance ratings*. URL: http://www.standardandpoors.com (Retrieved December 23, 2012).

Standard & Poor's (2012a). *Process for rating structured finance instruments – key differences highlighted.* URL: http://www.standardandpoors.com/aboutcreditratings/ (Retrieved August 20, 2012).

Standard & Poor's (2012b). *Criteria / structured finance / general: global methodoly for rating repackaged securities.* URL: http://www.standardandpoors.com (Retrieved October 17, 2012).

Standard & Poor's. (2012c). *About credit ratings.* URL: http://www.standardandpoors.com/aboutcreditratings/RatingsManual_PrintGuide.html (Retrieved November 5, 2012).

Standard & Poor's (2012d). *The role of credit ratings in the financial system.* URL: http://www.standardandpoors.com/ratings/articles/en/us/?articleType=HTML&assetID=1245333793833 (Retrieved November 12, 2012).

Standard & Poor's (2012e). *General description on the credit rating process.* URL: Online Resource. Accessed January 15, 2013 from: http://www.standardandpoors.com/servlet/BlobServer?blobheadername3=MDT-Type&blobcol=urldata&blobtable=MungoBlobs&blobheadervalue2=inline%3B+filename%3DEX2-1.July2012.pdf&blobheadername2=Content- (Retrieved January 15, 2013)

Standard & Poor's (2013). *Standard & Poor's ratings definition, June 17, 2013.* Online Resources. URL: ttps://www.globalcreditportal.com/ratingsdirect/renderArticle.do?articleId=1019442&SctArtId=147045&from=CM&nsl_code=LIME (Retrieved July 25, 2013).

Standard & Poor's (2014). *Form NRSRO.* URL: www.standardandpoors.com/aboutcreditratings/ (Retrieved May 12, 2014).

Starr, M. A. (2012). Qualitative and mixed-methods research in economics: surprising growth, promising future. *Journal of Economic Surveys*, 28(2), 238–264.

Stempel, J. (2012). NY Judge won't dismiss lawsuits vs Moody's, S&P. *Reuters.* URL: http://www.reuters.com/article/2012/05/07/ratingagencies-rulings-idUSL1E8G7PKB20120507 (Retrieved July 5, 2012).

Stiglitz, J. E. (1993). *The role of the state in financial markets.* Institute of Economics, Academia Sinica.

Stiglitz, J. E. (2009). The financial crisis of 2007–2008 and its macroeconomic consequences. *Initiative for Policy Dialogue Working Paper Series*, Board of Columbia University, April 2009.

Stiglitz, J. E. and Walsh, C. (2005). *Economics.* 4th edition. New York: W. W. Norton & Company Inc.

Stiglitz, J. E. and Weiss, A. (1992). Asymmetric information in credit markets and its implications for macro-economics. *Oxford Economic Papers*, 44(4), 694–724.

Strobl, G. and Xia, H. (2012). *The issuer-pays rating model and ratings inflation: evidence from corporate credit ratings*. Frankfurt School of Economics. URL: www.frankfurt-school.de/clicnetclm/fileDownload.do?goid=000000401336AB4 (Retrieved May 5, 2013).

Strulik, T. (2002). Paradoxes of governance. In Heritier, A. (Ed.): *Common goods: reinventing european and international governance*. Lanham: Rowman & Littlefield Publishers, 317–336.

Stuwe, A., Weiß, M. and Philipper, J. (2012). *Rating agencies: are they necessary, superfluous, a necessary evil or harmful?* Permanent Working Group 'Financial Policy, Taxation, Budgets and Financial Markets' of FES Managerkreis. Friedrich Ebert Stiftung, November 2012.

Sun, J. H. (2009). *Basel II Implementation in the Chinese banking system*. Simon Fraser University. Thesis.

Swedberg, R. (2007). *Principles of economic sociology*. Princeton: Princeton University Press.

Sy, A. N. R. (2009). The systemic regulation of credit rating agencies and rated markets. *IMF Working Paper*, WP/09/129.

Sykes, W. (1990). Validity and reliability in qualitative market research: a review of the literature. *Journal of the Market Research Society*, 32(3), 289–328.

Tabellini, G. (2008). Why did bank supervision fail? In Felton, C. and Reinhart, A. (Eds.), *The first global financial crisis of the 21st dentury*. London: CEPR, 45–47.

Taleb, N. N. and Martin, G. A. (2012). How to prevent other financial crisis. *SAIS Review of International Affairs*, 17(1), 49–60.

Tatom, J. (2008). The Fed's new front in the financial crisis. *Research Buzz*, 4(8), 1–6.

Taylor, J. B. (2009). The financial crisis and the policy responses: an empirical analysis of what went wrong. *NBER Working Paper* 14631.

Tempkin, A. (2011). IFR-ABS; Bill reversing rating agency liability advances. *Reuters* July 20. URL: http://www.reuters.com/article/2011/07/20/abs-ratin gagencies-idUSN1E76J17U20110720 (Retrieved April 14, 2014).

Telpner, J. (2003). A securitization primer for first time issuers. Global Securitisation and Structured Finance, Atlanta: Greenberg Traurig LLP.

The Geneva Association (2011). Études et Dossiers. Extract Études et Dossiers No. 377, 13th Meeting of the Geneva Association's Amsterdam Circle of Chief Economics, February 17–18, 2011, Amsterdam & the 75th International Liability Regimes Conference of The Geneva Association, June 17, 2011, Beijing.

The Hindu, (2013). SEBI mulls checks on 'conflicts of interest' at rating agencies' *The Hindu Businiess Line Online*. April 14, 2013. URL: http://www.thehindu businessline.com/markets/stock-markets/sebi-mulls-checks-on-conflict-of-interest-at-rating-agencies/article4617002.ece (Retrieved June 29, 2013).

Theurl, T. and Schaetzle, D. (2011). Ratingagenturen in der Kritik: eine Analyse der Reformforderungen und -vorschläge. *Working Paper Series*, Arbeitspapier des Instituts für Genossenschaftswesen der Westfälischen Wilhelms-Universität Münster (116). URL: http://www.wiwi.uni-muenster.de/06/aktuelles/material/ap116_schaetzle.pdf (Retrieved April 22, 2013).

Thomas, C. (1998). *Multimarket contact and ímperfect information*. Washington D.C.: Federal Trade Commission.

Tichy, G. (2011). Credit rating agencies: part of the solution or part of the problem? *Intereconomics*, 5(5), 232–262.

Tillman, V. A. (2006). *Testimony of Vickie A. Tillman (Executive Vice President Standard & Poor's Credit Market Services) before the Committee on Banking, Housing, and Urban Affairs, United States Senate. March 7, 2006.*

Tillman, V.A. (2007a). Don't blame the rating agencies. *The Wall Street Journal*, August 31, 2007.

Tillman, V. A. (2007b). The role and impact of credit aating Agencies on the subprime credit markets. *Hearing before the Committee on Banking, Housing, and Urban Affairs, United States Senate. First Session, September 26, 2007.*

TNN, The Times of India (2012). Don't sue rating agencies: SEBI. *The Times of India*, October 18, 2012. URL: http://articles.timesofindia.indiatimes.com/2012-10-18/india-business/34554202_1_india-ratings-fitch-ratings-srei-infrastructure-finance (Retrieved February 2, 2013).

Tobin, J. (1978). A proposal for international monetary reform. *Eastern Economic Journal*, 4(3–4), 153–159.

Treasury (2010). Alternatives to the Use of External Credit Ratings in the Regulations of the OTC. Federal Register/Vol. 75, No. 198/Thursday, October 14, 2010/Proposed Rules. Department of the Treasury, Office of Thrift Supervisions, Doc. 63107.

Turhan, I. M. (2010). Beyond the global financial crisis: central banking in a new global financial system. *MPRA Paper*, MRPA. Munich: Personal RePEc Archive.

Tweksbury, R. (2009). Qualitative versus quantitative methods: understanding why qualitative methods are superior for criminology and criminal justice. *Journal of Philosophical and Theoretical Criminology* 1(1), 38–58.

Ubide, A. (2008). *Anatomy of a modern credit crisis*. Bretton Woods Conference in Madrid, April 17–18, 2008. URL: http://www. rbwf. org/2008/madrid/Ubide.pps (Retrieved July 13, 2013).

UN, United Nations (2013). The Role of Credit Rating Agencies on the International Financial System. Thematic Debate, 67th Session of the General Assembly, September 10, 2013. URL: http://www.un.org/en/ga/president/67/issues/pdf/Credit%20Rating%20Agencies%20thematic%20debate%20CONCEPT%20PAPER_Final.pdf (Retrieved March 6, 2014).

US-Congress (2010). *Dodd-Frank Wall Street Reform and Consumer Protection Act. Public Law 111–203 [HR 4173], 2010.* URL: http://www.sec.gov/about/laws/wallstreetreform-cpa.pdf (Retrieved January 15, 2013).

Utzig, S. (2010). The financial crisis and the regulation of credit rating agencies: a European banking perspective. *ADBI Working Paper* 188. Tokyo: Asian Development Bank Institute. URL: http://www.adbi.org/working-paper/2010/01/26/3446.credit.rating.agencies.european.banking/ (Retrieved April 22, 2013).

Van Roy, P. (2006). Is there a difference between solicited and unsolicited ratings and, if so, why? *Journal of Financial Services Research*, 44(1), 53–86.

Velben, T. (1899). The preconceptions of economic science. *The Quaterly Journal of Economic Science*, 13, 121–150.

Velthuis, O. (2005). *Talking prices: symbolic meaings of prices on the market for contemporary art*. Princeton: Princeton University Press.

Vink, D. and Thibeault, A. (2008). ABS, MBS and CDO comparisons – an empirical analysis. *Journal of Structured Finance*, 14(2), 27–45.

Violi, R. (2010). Credit ratings in structured finance: some lessons from the current credit crisis and beyond. *Journal of Structured Finance*, 16(3), 65–87.

Vittas, D. (1991). The impact of regulation on financial intermediation. *Working paper series* 746, Country Economics Department, World Bank.

Yoizey, G. (2006). The treausres guid to investing corporate cash. Sherington: *WWCP, WorldWideCountryProfiles*, Milton Keynes.

Wainwright, T. (2009). Laying the foundations for a crisis: mapping the historico-geographical construction of residential mortgage backed securitization in the UK. *International Journal of Urban and Regional Research*, 33(2), 372–388.

Wallison, P. J. (2009). The true origins of this financial crisis. *The American Spectator*, 42(1), 22–27.

Watkins, A.L., Hillison, W., and Morcroft, S.W. (2004). Audit quality: a synthesis of theory and empirical evidence. *Journal of Accounting Review*, 7(1), 1–15.

Watkins, M. et al. (2012). Copycat litigation threat for rating agencies. *Financial Times*, November 5, 2012.

Weber, T. A. (2012). Price theory in economics. In Özer, Ö. and Phillips, R. (Eds.): *Oxford handbook on pricing management*. Oxford University Press.

Weill, N. (2010). *Testimony of Nicolas Weill (Group Managing Director Moody's Investors Service) before the Financial Crisis Inquiriy Commission*. URL: http://fcic-static.law.stanford.edu/cdn_media/fcic-testimony/2010-0602-Weill.pdf (Retrieved April 23, 2014).

Welfens, P. J. J. (2010). Transatlantic banking crisis: analysis, rating, policy issues. *International Economics and Economic Policy*, 7(1), 3–48

Welfens, P. J. J. (2011). The transatlantic banking crisis: lessons, EU reforms, and G20 issues. In Welfens, P. J. J. and Ryan, C. (Eds.), *Financial market integration and growth*. Berlin: Springer, 49–125.

Wessendorf, E. M. (2008). Regulating the credit rating agencies. *Entrepreneurial Business Law Journal*, 3, 155–175.

Westerhoff, F. (2003). Speculative markets and the effectiveness of price limits. *Journal of Economic Dynamics and Control*, 28(3), 493–508.

Weston, J. (2013). An improved regulatory framework for credit rating agencies. In: NUS, RMI, World Scientific (Eds.), *Global credit review, Volume 2*. Singapur: World Scientific Publishing co. Plc. Ltd., 11–38.

Weßel, C. (2010). Semi-strukturierte Interviews im Software-Engineering: Indikationsstellung, Vorbereitung, Durchführung und Auswertung – Ein Fallbasiertes Tutorium. In *GI Jahrestagung* (2), 927–937.

White, L. J. (2009a). *The credit rating agencies: understanding their role in the subprime debacle of 2008–2008*. Stern School of Business New York University. URL: http://papers.ssrn.com/sol3/papers.cfm?abstract_id=1434483 (Retrieved June 10, 2012).

White, L. J. (2009b). The credit rating agencies and the subprime debacle. *Critical Review*, 21(2–3), 389–399.

White, L. J. (2010). Credit-rating agencies and the financial crisis: less regulation of CRAs is a better response. *Journal of International Banking Law*, 25(4), 170–195.

Wildmoser, G., Schiffer, K. J., and Langoth, B. (2009). Haftung von Ratingagenturen gegenüber Anlegern? *Recht der Internationalen Wirtschaft* 2009, 10, 657–668.

Wishart, I. (2013). MEPs seek tougher rules for rating agencies' *EuropeanVoice.com*, January 15, 2013. URL: http://www.europeanvoice.com/article/2013/january/meps-seek-tougher-rules-for-ratings-agencies/76156.aspx (Retrieved August 8, 2013).

Witt, G. (2010). Statement of Gary Witt, Former Managing Director, Moody's Investors Service, submitted by request to the Financial Crisis Inquiry Commission, February 6, 2012. In *Senate Subcommittee on Investigations, Wall Street and the Financial Crisis: anatomy of a financial collapse*. USA: Cosimo Reports. URL:

http://www.hsgac.senate.gov//imo/media/doc/Financial_Crisis/FinancialCrisisReport.pdf?attempt=2 (Retrieved November 22, 2012)

Wolfson, J. and Crawford, C. (2010). Lessons from the current crisis: should credit rating agencies be re-structured? *Journal of Business & Economics Research*, 8(7), 85–92.

Woodford, M. (1994). Monetary policy and price level determinacy in a cash-in-advance economy. *Economic theory*, 4(3), 345–380.

Wong, B. K. and Selvi, Y. (1998). Neural network applications in finance: a review and analysis of literature (1990–1996). *Information & Management*, 34 (3), 129–139.

Wray, L. R. (2009). Minsky, the global financial crisis, and the prospects before us. *Development*, 52(3), 302–307.

Wu, H.-K. (1968). An economist looks at Section 16 of the Securities Exchange Act of 1934. *Columbia Law Review*, 68(2), 260–269.

Wurgler, J. (2000). Financial markets and the allocation of capital. *Journal of Financial Economics*, 58(1–2), 187–214.

Wyszomierski, T. (2007). Moody's credit ratings are never compromised. *Wall Street Journal*, September 4, 2007, A15.

Xudong, An (2011). CMBS subordination and securitiy design: credit quality, learning and demand Feeding. *World Finance & Banking Symposium – 'Asian Finance & Banking'. World Finance Conference*, Shanghai, China.

Xudong, An, Yongheng, Deng and Sanders, A. B. (2008). Subordination levels in structured financing. In Thakor, A. V. and Boot, A.W. (Eds.). *Handbook of finance intermediation and banking.* Amsterdam: Elsevier Sience, 41–60.

Yamaguchi, A. (2013). Evolving international discussions on credit rating agencies and Japanese registration system for agencies: can Japan's experience be any lesson to Asia? Institute for International Monetary Affairs. *Newsletter* No. 15, April 12, 2013. URL: http://www.iima.or.jp%2FDocs%2Fnewsletter%2F2013%2FNLNo_15_e.pdf&ei=n1JiU5W_G47n7AbWtoCQDw&usg=AFQjCNG5DtHcuxxz46IK4Rnkk73bf3FJxQ&sig2=5uJ5H-Uh4hxUyruBEkGxRQ (Retrieved February 15, 2013).

Yang, J. et al. (2008). Fighting global food price rises in the developing world: the response of China and its effect on domestic and world markets. *Agricultural Economics*, 39(s1), 453–464.

Yeates, C. (2009). Agenices pulled into ASIC net. *The Sydney Morning Herald*, November 13. URL: http://www.smh.com.au/business/agencies-pulled-into-asic-net-20091112-icdg.html (Retrieved March 8, 2013).

Yeh, C.-H. and Yang, C.-Y. (2010). Examining the effectiveness of price limits in an artificial stock market. *Journal of Economic Dynamics and Control*, 34(10), 2089–2108.

Yongding, Y. (2010). The impact of the global financial crisis on the Chinese economy and China's policy responses. *TWN Global Economy Series* 25. Penang, Malaysia: Third World Network.

Yoshioka, K. (2012). China firm to set up alternative credit rating agency with Russia, US partners. *The Asahi Shimbun* online resource, October 25, 2012. URL: http://ajw.asahi.com/article/economy/business/AJ201210250067 (Retrieved January 30, 2013).

Zhang, X. (2010). Global forces and corporate reforms in South Korea, *International Political Science Review*, 31(1), 59–76.

Zappia, C. (1999). The economics of information, market socialism and Hayek's legacy. *History of Economic Ideas*, 7(1/2), 105–138.

Zarin, F. (2013). *Re: Release No. 34–69433; File 4–661*. Letter to Secretary Ms. Elizabeth M. Murphy, U.S. Securitites and Exchange Commission (Ed.), New York: Securities and Exchange Commission.

Zhou, B. and Kumar, P. (2012). Economic Considerations in Litigation Against the Credit Rating Agencies. *Discussion Paper*, The Brattle Group, 1–17. URL: http://www.brattle.com/system/publications/pdfs/000/004/664/original/Economic_Considerations_in_Litigation_Against_Credit_Rating_Agencies_Apr_2012.pdf?1379103033 (Retrieved April 28, 2013).

Ziebart, D. A. and Reiter, S. A. (2010). Bond ratings, bond yields and financial information. *Contemporary Accounting Research*, 9(1), 252–282.

www.ingramcontent.com/pod-product-compliance
Ingram Content Group UK Ltd.
Pitfield, Milton Keynes, MK11 3LW, UK
UKHW021831100926
8556IPUK00004B/276

9 783631 676219